EMPOWERING EARLY CHILDHOOD EDUCATORS

International Pedagogies as Provocation

Edited by Naomi McLeod and Patricia Giardiello

Routledge
Taylor & Francis Group
LONDON AND NEW YORK

First published 2019
by Routledge
2 Park Square, Milton Park, Abingdon, Oxon OX14 4RN

and by Routledge
52 Vanderbilt Avenue, New York, NY 10017

Routledge is an imprint of the Taylor & Francis Group, an informa business

British Library Cataloguing in Publication Data
A catalogue record for this book is available from the British Library

Library of Congress Cataloging-in-Publication Data
Names: McLeod, Naomi, editor. | Giardiello, Patricia, editor.
Title: Empowering early childhood educators : international pedagogies as provocation / Edited by Naomi McLeod and Patricia Giardiello.
Description: Abingdon, Oxon ; New York, NY : Routledge, 2019. | Includes bibliographical references and index.
Identifiers: LCCN 2019006149| ISBN 9781138309647 (hb. : alk. paper) | ISBN 9781138309678 (pbk. : alk. paper) | ISBN 9781315143729 (ebook)
Subjects: LCSH: Early childhood education--Cross-cultural studies. | Early childhood educators--Cross-cultural studies. | Critical pedagogy--Cross-cultural studies | Motivation in education--Cross-cultural studies.
Classification: LCC LB1139.23 .E586 2019 | DDC 372.21--dc23
LC record available at https://lccn.loc.gov/2019006149

ISBN: 978-1-138-30964-7 (hbk)
ISBN: 978-1-138-30967-8 (pbk)
ISBN: 978-1-315-14372-9 (ebk)

Typeset in Bembo
by Taylor & Francis Books

EMPOWERING EARLY CHILDHOOD EDUCATORS

This forward-thinking text challenges educators to think about and question the purpose of education and explores international understandings of the role played by early years professionals in promoting participatory, ethical and reflexive practice which benefits children as independent decision-makers.

By exploring the different perspectives, concepts and practices adopted in early childhood settings in Denmark, Finland, Aotearoa, New Zealand and Sweden, *Empowering Early Childhood Educators* demonstrates the potential of participatory and democratic approaches in day-to-day practice. Illustrating how pedagogical approaches such as Te Whāriki, Reggio Emilia and the Montessori method may be understood and interpreted to maximise children's engagement in their socio-cultural context, chapters empower educators to question their professional experience, knowledge and initiative to find a balance between directives and ethical practice. A rich combination of case studies, commentaries, interviews and conversations, the text offers critical insight into the daily practices and challenges of early years educators around the world and inspires critical reflection on practices which empower them.

A powerful revaluation of the purposes and value of early childhood education, *Empowering Early Childhood Educators* will be of interest to early years practitioners, students and researchers.

Naomi McLeod leads the MA in International Approaches to Early Childhood Education and teaches across Early Childhood and Education Studies at Liverpool John Moores University, UK.

Patricia Giardiello is Award Lead for the MA in Early Childhood Studies and Leadership in Early Years. She is also a researcher in the Education and Social Research Institute at Manchester Metropolitan University, UK.

CONTENTS

FIGURES

TABLES

ACKNOWLEDGEMENTS

Special thanks to Professor Peter Moss who provoked the initial thoughts for this book through his gentle questioning around what matters. Thanks also to the inspirational ECE leaders and educators we met when we visited different settings in Sweden, Finland, Denmark, Aotearoa, New Zealand and England, which in turn inspired open discussions and confirmed our commitment to ethical and participatory practice with young children.

Further thanks to those who provided rich case studies and conversations, namely: Jane Williams-Siegfredsen, Ulkika Sjöberg, Johan Laigaard, Fern Brooks, Julie Allen, Mikaela Nugent-Jones, Ellen Morgan, Julie Butterfield, Susanna Nopanen and Helen Lowry.

CONTRIBUTORS

Editors:

Naomi McLeod started her career as an early years and Key Stage 1 teacher in the North West of England. For many years she led Early Childhood Studies and the Undergraduate and Postgraduate Early Years Teacher Education programme at Liverpool Hope University, UK. Most recently Naomi is at Liverpool John Moores University, UK teaching across Early Childhood and Education Studies and leads the MA in International Approaches to Early Childhood Education. Her doctorate focused on developing pedagogical participation for young children, and critical reflection as a tool for Continued Professional Development for early childhood educators across the sector. This focus on valuing children as agents of change, and on the need for reflexivity, continues to be a research interest evident in her published work and in the working partnerships she has developed with educators and creative professionals in the field of early years, creativity and participation.

Patricia Giardiello has been involved in the field of Early Childhood Education during the last four decades as a teacher, school inspector, consultant, lecturer, researcher, author, parent and grandparent. Patricia's interest in early years pedagogy led her to pursue a doctorate at the University of Sheffield, UK. Her doctoral research into the bedrock principles of early childhood education and the work of the pioneers has resulted in various publications. She has presented lectures and papers at national and international conferences across the world, including most notably Bulgaria, where she was involved in government policy formation around safeguarding and children's rights. Patricia is the Award Lead for the MA Early Childhood Studies and MA Leadership in Early Years at Manchester Metropolitan University, and is also an Associate Member of the Education and Social Research

Institute. Her current research interests include principled pedagogical approaches in early childhood education, children's voice, and intergenerational learning.

Contributors:

Annette Hargreaves was an early years practitioner and now works at Manchester Metropolitan University, UK as a lecturer for early years and primary education. Annette is an ambassador for the Wave Trust. Annette's research interests are children and family mental health and wellbeing in the community, for which she was awarded the Winston Churchill Memorial Fund fellowship and travelled to New Zealand, Australia and America to research good practice in this field. From this experience, she has developed her professional and personal perspective by researching an issue that she cares about, and has delivered findings to local policymakers and post-graduate students. Annette is currently studying for a doctorate in education with regard to resilience in early childhood education.

Ulla Härkönen's career in early childhood education science spans 49 years. She has worked as a kindergarten teacher, a lecturer, and as a professor at the University of Eastern Finland, where she continues as an emeritas professor. Her research focuses on pedagogy, work education and gender, meanings of various concepts of early childhood education, and systems theories. She contributed to the UNESCO project "Reorienting Teacher Education towards Sustainability", the JTEFS/BBCC consortium, and the Journal of Teacher Education for Sustainability. She acted as President of the conference in 2012. She has reviewed international journals of education and sustainability. Ulla Härkönen is an Honorary Member of Daugavpils University and continues to write her Pedagogical Systems Theory, which she first introduced in 2009.

Tarja Karlsson Häikiö is Professor in Visual and Material Culture, Academy of Design and Crafts at the University of Gothenburg, Sweden. Her PhD is in Art History and Visual Studies and she works with teachers within the School of Pre-School Teacher Education as well as Research Education. Her research areas are visual art education, child and youth culture, aesthetic learning, art pedagogy, documentation and assessment, as well as different kinds of artistic practices related to teaching and learning. She has published articles and has co-authored several anthologies in the field of early childhood and visual art education in preschool and compulsory school, where she has written about children's use of visual tools for mapping their surroundings and spaces, and about spaces for learning.

Geraldine Leydon's interest in early years education began when she was as a practitioner and senior manager in primary schools in the North West of England. She studied for a Master's Degree in Education as a vehicle to explore the many quandaries she faced in her own teaching practice. Now working in Initial Teacher Education at Manchester Metropolitan University, UK, she continues to observe and problematise the continuing complexity of the schoolification of young children. To this end, she was awarded a Winston Churchill Travelling Fellowship and as part of this project visited New Zealand where she observed first-hand the implementation of the Te Whāriki Curriculum. These experiences have deepened Geraldine's commitment to a professional and academic understanding and subsequent implementation of best practice in educational settings. These drivers continue into her doctoral studies today.

Liisa Lohilahti is a kindergarten teacher and Head of Taikatahti preschool and primary school in the city of Oulu in northern Finland. Her work is influenced and inspired by the Reggio Emilia Approach as a collaborative endeavour. This is reflected in her progressive developmental work. Liisa is also engaged in collaborative work with researchers at the University of Oulu, Finland where she is a lecturer and a co-partner to the university in the professionalisation practice of becoming preschool teachers. Liisa is continually assigned as a consultant in the early childhood education for the city of Oulu, for example using her workplans as an inspiration in the writing of the national curriculum for primary education.

Pernilla Mårtensson is a former compulsory school teacher who specialised in early and primary education and the language development of children. Mårtensson previously worked as a Junior Lecturer with specialisation in pre-primary and primary reading and writing at the Institution of Education, Communication and Learning at the University of Gothenburg, Sweden. She is today active as Junior Lecturer at the Academy of Music and Drama at the University of Gothenburg, working with pre-school teachers in Teacher Education. She is a pioneer in working with the Reggio Emilia philosophy in Sweden and a representative for the Reggio Emilia Institute in Stockholm. Mårtensson, together with Karlsson Häikiö, is responsible for the ongoing professionalisation education at the University of Gothenburg for pedagogistas, and pedagogical supervisors.

Kerstin Signert is a lecturer at the Department of Education at University of Gothenburg, Sweden. She has a background as a primary school teacher and has a Montessori teacher's degree for ages 2.5-12 at St. Nicholas in London, and has experiences as a Montessori teacher both in local primary schools and private schools. Since 1995, Kerstin has been responsible for Montessori teacher training at the University of Gothenburg. She completed her PhD in November 2012, her thesis entitled "Variation and invariance in Maria Montessori's sensorial material", in which she compared the Variation theory with the Montessori method. Kerstin has from the start attended the network M.E.R. (Montessori Education and Research) and is a keen promoter. She is also part of a network for principals in Montessori schools. Kerstin's research interests now focus on children's play and Montesssori's thoughts about it, and internet and technology in the Montessori environment.

FOREWORD

Professor Peter Moss

Early childhood education, indeed all education, is today under sustained assault from a particular way of thinking about the world, a powerful blend of positivism and neoliberalism that has created a potent story about education and the powerful 'human technologies' to enact that story in nurseries, schools, colleges and universities. The story is instrumental in rationality, technical in practice and economistic in concept, and is about how the application of standardised methods and outcomes by autonomous educational institutions compete in the marketplace to produce high returns on investment, in particular through the successful realisation and application of 'human capital',[1] a vital ingredient for success in an ever more competitive global economy. As David Laberee says:

> In the twenty-first century, we have seen the educational policy discourse converge on a single overarching goal for education. From the global education reform movement to its policy apparatus in the OECD [Organisation for Economic Cooperation and development] and its policy police in the PISA testing program, we have seen one goal trump the others. Nowadays, the uniform message is human capital *uber alles*. The convergence of purpose is strong, consistent and pithy.
>
> *(2017, p.281)*

The story is heard as much today in early childhood education as any other sector, indeed more so since eminent economists assure policy-makers that early childhood is the best age to invest in to maximise later returns of human capital.

This story, which elsewhere I have termed for early childhood 'the story of quality and high returns' (Moss, 2014), emerges originally from the Anglophone world, and has since spread, through the pervasive influence of the English language and international organisations, around the world. It has crossed borders and gained international credibility in a process of hegemonic globalisation, 'the successful globalisation of a particular local and culturally-specific discourse to the point that it makes universal truth claims and "localises" all rival discourses' (Santos, 2004, p.149). It is today so loud that it threatens to drown out the rich diversity of other stories, past and present, that offer different perspectives on education – its purposes, its values, its practices.

I say 'threatens' because this loud story has not yet managed to overwhelm and suppress all others. There is, in fact, a vibrant resistance movement, contesting the dominant story and listening to and telling other stories. This book is part of that burgeoning resistance movement. A central theme is the importance of questioning, self-awareness and reflection, of the need for critical thinking that challenges the taken-for-granted, for example the assumptions of the dominant story, and which, in the vivid words of Nikolas Rose, is

> a matter of introducing a critical attitude towards those things that are given to our present experience as if they were timeless, natural, unquestionable: to stand against the maxims of one's time, against the spirit of one's age, against the current of received wisdom. It is a matter of introducing a kind of awkwardness into the fabric of one's experience, of interrupting the fluency of the narratives that encode that experience and making them stutter. (Rose, 1999, p.20)

To develop that critical attitude, that capacity for questioning, that ability for making dominant narratives or stories stutter is necessary if educators (of whatever type or for whatever age of learners) are to join the resistance movement and so to participate in what is so urgently needed: a genuinely democratic and participatory politics of education, in which politics, not technology, is first practice and different perspectives are recognised, valued and discussed.

Such an education is one that starts with political questions and political choices, fundamental questions to which there are alternative and often conflicting answers (as opposed to technical questions to which there is one right answer, which can be supplied by experts). Political questions such as: What is our diagnosis of the times? What is our image of the child? Of the educator? Of the school? What is the purpose of education? What is knowledge? What pedagogy? What are the fundamental values of education? What ethics should we work with? What do we want for our children, here and now and in the future? This understanding of education, as a fundamentally political practice, was central to the thinking of the great Italian educator, Loris Malaguzzi, who insisted that '[pedagogy is] always a political discourse whether we know it or not . . . it clearly means working with political choices' (Cagliari et al., 2016, p.267).

This book not only calls for critical thinking, or critical reflexivity, which is 'key to the process of seeing and appreciating different perspectives'. It also raises political questions, in particular about the purposes of education and its values, and the pedagogies that are commensurate with such purposes and values. It also offers some alternative stories, which take the form of different early childhood pedagogies, drawing on experiences from Denmark, Finland, New Zealand and Sweden. Telling such alternative stories is an important complement to critical thinking or reflexivity. We must be critical, questioning and contesting that which is dominant, but we also need to put forward alternatives and demonstrate not only their desirability but also their feasibility, being able to show different pedagogies being put to work in practice. But not, as the editors of this book recognise, to treat these alternatives as blueprints that can be exported and copied in a sort of global franchising exercise. Each pedagogy can be seen as a local project, evolving in its distinctive way within its own particular socio-cultural context, even if and when it draws on an internationally recognised pedagogical experience, such as Montessori or Reggio Emilia.

Such examples, such local stories are important for giving us hope, for showing that another world is possible; for asserting the potential of local democratic creativity and experimentation; and for provoking thought by confronting us with difference. At a time when the dominant discourse is offering an 'uncritical appropriation and generalisation of global solutions imposed by data and evidence on "what works" and "where the best results are" . . . [an] approach based on the false idea of consensus on the aims of education and the paths to achieving them' (Nóvoa, 2018, p.4), the alternative pedagogies in this book contribute to what the distinguished comparative educationalist António Nóvoa calls 'a science of difference'; this is a science that rather than seeking 'a "solution" that tends to homogenise educational directions throughout the world' (ibid., p.5), seeks to contribute to illuminating and stimulating different perspectives and possibilities.

For me, comparative work, seeking an understanding of different perspectives, concepts and practices, of different political choices and educational stories, has been a great source of satisfaction, serendipity and stimulation – constant encounters with difference that have made me question my assumptions, and helped generate new thinking and so see things in a different light. It is, quite simply, a great stimulus to critical reflection. But it has also been a source of new friendships and invigorating conversations, a convivial experience that has enriched both my personal and professional life. The pleasure of new relationships made with colleagues from different countries and the personal and professional benefits that have followed runs through this book; for though our contexts and experiences may be very different, through comparative work we also discover shared interests, values and desires that cut across borders and transcend national identities.

The editors of this book express the hope that 'the reader will develop new insights and ways of seeing and appreciating otherness, so a deep personal philosophy of ECE will be nurtured that empowers practitioners to create the conditions and apply new participatory and ethical perspectives that are appropriate in a globally changing world'. I share that hope and believe this book will make an important contribution to empowering early childhood educators and, more generally, to the growing resistance movement that is contesting dominant stories in early childhood and beyond.

Professor Peter Moss

Note

1 'Human capital, as defined by OECD is the knowledge, skills, competences, and other attributes embodied in individuals that are relevant to econ activity. . . The term coalesces around the concepts of the use of skills in an economy and the need for investment to develop these and that this investment, like capital itself, should bring returns . . . Human capital has now become a core plank of neoliberal ideology' (Holborow, 2014).

OUR REASONS FOR WRITING THIS BOOK

Reflections from the editors

Naomi:

My early days as a researcher focused mainly on exploring creative ways of encouraging young children's talk. Sadly, due to top-down priorities and pressures associated with data collection, targets and outcomes, I observed very few opportunities for exploratory talk. The more I came to understand what quality in early childhood education looked like and involved, the more I grew to appreciate a need for supporting and working with educators in developing self-awareness and questioning. Only then is it possible to stand back, see and appreciate potential new ways of being. For me, this has involved an ongoing journey of deep self-awareness and becoming conscious of entangled personal views, understandings and associated assumptions – which I have come to understand as reflexivity. I now appreciate just how crucial questioning taken for granted views are as a first step in valuing democratic, socially just and ethical approaches to learning with children. This new way of reconfiguring seeing and being, to appreciate other lenses, continues to inform my research and professional practice.

Patricia:

My increasing interest in early years pedagogy led me to research into the bedrock principles of early childhood education. Adopting an historical stance, I began by exploring and reflecting upon the early philosophers and pioneers, whose ideas, values and beliefs were influential in shaping current thinking about effective early childhood education. In part as a reaction to the changing socio-cultural and political landscape in relation to children, childhood and early childhood provision in the twenty-first century, my desire to de-familiarise that which is already known in order to reflect upon and identify new ways of understanding has provided myriad opportunities for me to observe, ask questions, reflect on practice and above all – always learning, always empowered.

A major strength of this book is the variety of contributions from different countries which enhances and authenticates the reliability of how each international approach is interpreted as a provocation. As part of the writing process it was important to engage in regular, open and frank conversations, to check our interpretation and ensure there was an accurate convergence of meaning so that a reliable and useful resource could be shared. The book is the culmination of the countries we have visited, the lengthy conversations we have had with like-minded colleagues and our reflections which we hope will inspire and empower other early childhood educators in valuing participatory learning with young children.

References

Cagliari, P., Castegnetti, M., Giudici, C., Rinaldi, C., Vecchi, V. and Moss, P. (2016) *Loris Malaguzzi and the schools of Reggio Emilia: A selection of his writings and speeches 1945–1993*, London: Routledge.

Holborow, M. (2012) 'Neoliberalism, human capital and the skills agenda in higher education – An Irish case', *Journal for Critical Education Policy Studies*, 10(1), p.93–111.

Labaree, D. (2017) 'Futures of the field of education', in: G. Whitty and J. Furlong (ed.) *Knowledge and the study of knowledge: An international exploration*, Oxford: Symposium Books, p.277–283.

Moss, P. (2014) *Transformative change and real utopias in early childhood education: A story of democracy, experimentation and potentiality*, London: Routledge.

Nóvoa, A. (2018) 'Comparing Southern Europe: The difference, the public, and the common,' *Comparative Education*, 54(4), p.548–561. DOI: doi:10.1080/03050068.2018.1528781.

Rose, N. (1999) *Powers of freedom: reframing political thought*, Cambridge: Cambridge University Press.

Santos, B. de S. (2004) 'Interview with Boaventura de Sousa Santos', *Globalisation, Societies and Education*, 2(2), p.147–160.

INTRODUCTION

Naomi McLeod and Patricia Giardiello

The purpose of this book is to empower early childhood educators and provide a sense of ownership, by disrupting and challenging thinking around the purpose of education to promote socially just, participatory and democratic practice often associated with international pedagogies in early childhood education (ECE). More than ever before, current pressures of accountability have resulted in standardisation of learning and teaching with a focus on data collection and a prescriptive measuring of outcomes (DfE, 2017; Moss, 2018; Urban, 2017), for example, the school readiness agenda which has resulted in a narrowing of the curriculum that focuses on literacy and mathematics. Tensions between early childhood education and compulsory education (Preschool PISA) (OECD, 2018) are evident in the Two-year-old Integrated Review (NCB, 2015), a progress checklist to assess children's development between the ages of 24 to 36 months, and the Reception Baseline Assessment (DfE, 2015), which indicates how getting children ready for formal education is prioritised. Furthermore, a prime concern, which is open for debate and contestation, is the OECD's International Early Learning Study (IELS), a cross-national assessment of early learning outcomes involving the testing of 5-year-old children in participating countries (OECD, 2015, 2018; Moss et al., 2016). The programme assesses four early learning domains (emerging literacy, emerging numeracy, self-regulation, empathy and trust), each noted as taking approximately 15 minutes to assess using a tablet-based test (Urban, 2017). This standardised, positivistic approach to testing involving two artificial caricatures called 'Mia and Tom' shows a total disregard for the complexity of ECE and the value of 'locally embedded approaches to early childhood education and care' based on holistic rights of children (Urban and Swadener, 2016, p.7,8). This has consequences for urgently building an awareness of the need to question dominant discourses, so participatory and democratic practice based on children's individual needs and interests can be promoted rather than a top-down, one-size-fits-all approach where the curriculum is controlled and educators are not trusted in making a professional judgement. Urban (2017) talks of the need for resistance amongst professionals and policy-makers, so we are ready, as Peter Moss notes, to challenge the crisis in early childhood education (2017).

Wasmuth and Nitecki (2017) draw our attention to a global predicament described as Global Education Reform Movement (GERM) which Sahlberg (2011, 2016) refers to as an unofficial educational agenda that is rooted in an over focus on accountability, testing, standardisation, prescriptive and outcome-driven practice that prioritises literacy and numeracy. Urban (2017) draws our attention to the fact that so far there has been little resistance from educators to this economic and political manipulation of early childhood education, which has resulted in a marketisation of quality often leading to negative consequences on children's well-being. GERM perceives early childhood education as a commodity that can be 'purchased as a means to high returns . . . or as the object of market transactions between parent consumers and provider businesses' (Moss, 2014, p. 67). GERM and its root in neo-liberalism and marketisation is discussed further in Chapter 1.

As the title of this book indicates, the focus is on '*pedagogies*' as provocation to encourage questioning not only around 'what' is associated with early childhood curriculum, but 'how' it is taught and 'why' it is relevant and 'right' in the current political, economic and socio-cultural climate. It is concerned with the 'how' of adult-child interactions, recognising and valuing learning as a respectful process rather than just a product. In acknowledging the importance of questioning, '*why*' different approaches are appropriate, a democratic and participatory approach to learning and teaching is advocated. This is important as it requires a readiness to question personal views, beliefs and assumptions so we are able to make entangled connections and reconfigure new ways of seeing, and appreciate other lenses, such as the child's viewpoint. It is the first step to improving quality of practice. We refer to this process of internal questioning and self-awareness as critical reflection or reflexivity, which is about working out how our physical and social positions, our experiences, subjectivity and our view of the world influence our knowledge, perceptions and actions (Bolton, 2014; Fook and Gardner, 2007). It is about making sense of our existence through engaging in a process of continuous ongoing rhizomatic interactions and configuration (Barad, 2007). We look at this process in more detail in Chapter 2.

Constructing our own self-awareness and making sense of different understandings can be challenging and uncomfortable, but it can also be empowering and can provide a sense of ownership and instil confidence, rather than a feeling of being manipulated as part of a political top-down data and outcome-driven model of education. Becoming critically reflective/reflexive is key to the process of seeing and appreciating different perspectives, and in doing so as part of this book we explore different critically reflective frameworks. For example, we look at McLeod's Framework (2015) as a tool for engaging professionals in becoming open to different viewpoints, developing new insights and appreciating otherness.

Our aim ultimately, is to empower educators by developing and sustaining a critically reflective (reflexive) approach to contest and tackle the pressures of outcome-driven curricula and a low-risk approach. Closely linked to this is the relationship between perceptions of children and pedagogy (informed by different socio-cultures, traditions, beliefs and values) that inform personal pedagogical practice: for example, children being viewed as in need and vulnerable compared to capable and independent. If children are considered as needy, the learning experiences presented to them will be restrictive with few opportunities for independent thinking or making individual choices. In contrast, children who are perceived as capable are likely to be presented with opportunities where they can take risks and be encouraged to be independent in making decisions. Both in England and international contexts, consequently, there is a need to understand *why* alongside *how*, so educators are empowered and children can be agents of change and independent decision-makers.

In an attempt to empower educators and challenge some of the diverse issues and pressures in our globally changing world, this book identifies and examines the relevance of participatory and democratic practice, promoting respectful learning that acts consciously as part of socially just and ethical practice. A combination of case studies is included to demonstrate the distinctive nature of pedagogical approaches (Reggio Emilia, Montessori and Te Whāriki), from Sweden, Finland, Denmark and New Zealand, which are as a result of relationships we have developed through visits made to settings and rich conversations between ourselves and educators around personal pedagogical values and associated pressures. Narratives and conversations are used to provide authentic insights into each approach from a variety of perspectives as well as provoking further reflection in relation to key concepts, debates and current issues in early childhood education.

As a hallmark of democratic, ethical practice and humanising education, we recognise the importance of young children's participation as a universal entitlement reaffirmed by the United Nations Convention on the Rights of the Child (UNCRC, 1989) as previous studies and reviews also do, for example, Clark (2005, 2017); Dahlberg and Moss (2005); Pascal and Bertram (2009); Rinaldi (2006); Nutbrown (1996); and Davies and Artaraz (2009). Consequently, there is a desire to build respectful, democratic and participatory communities as part of everyday routines with young children. Persuasive arguments in favour of early childhood education and demand is expanding rapidly around the world, reflecting its significance in both the developed and developing countries.

A critical lens is used to evaluate, rather than seeing different approaches as a blueprint that can be exported and copied. In this way, international pedagogical practice is used as a provocation for stimulating critical discussions around the relevance to 'local ECE projects' and the necessary conditions for promoting sustainable socially just practice. Here McLeod's framework (2015) is offered and presented as a tool for engaging professionals in developing new ways of seeing. Taken for granted assumptions around dominant political and socio-cultural discourses and interpretations about the purpose of knowledge are deconstructed along with associated issues and future implications for sustainable participatory and democratic practice.

Essentially, the reader will be engaged in a process of questioning and de-familiarising of personal underpinning influences around the purpose of education within a globally changing world. A participatory and democratic lens is used to examine the inter-relationship between ethics, epistemology, ontology and the various socio-cultural, political and historical influences so that a sense of ownership and empowerment can be developed. The hope is that the reader will develop new insights and ways of seeing and appreciating otherness, so a deep personal philosophy of ECE will be nurtured that empowers practitioners to create the conditions and apply new participatory and ethical perspectives that are appropriate in a globally changing world.

Structure of the book

In order to achieve these aims and empower professionals in developing an ownership of knowledge, this book pulls together several inter-related themes and processes, such as questioning dominant discourses within ECE, examining the purpose of knowledge, different perceptions of children and the impact on practice. At the heart of these processes the reader will develop new insights into the value of reflexivity. Each chapter presents a particular focus, relevant to international pedagogies as a provocation and outlines the associated political, socio-cultural and ethical ECE challenges. Based on research, sound theoretical frameworks and policy critiques, the authors use case studies to illustrate links between theory, research, policy and practice in order to support the process of understanding and embedding democratic practice in ECE. Each chapter concludes with reflective questions that prompt educators to question their own practice and deal with personal and professional challenges.

The following offers an insight into each of the chapters included in this book.

Part 1

Chapter 1: The Purpose of Education (which is quite heavily theorised) offers the opportunity for early childhood educators to de-construct and question different views around the purpose of knowledge in relation to education, in particular Early Childhood Education (ECE) and personal experiences and values. We examine different economic and political pressures on education, specifically the impact of neo-liberalism and marketisation in relation to the requirements of a socially just, ethical approach to pedagogy. Here, the relationship between power dynamics, perceptions of children and the influence on the type of pedagogy offered is explored in terms of future implications. The chapter begins by considering different historical and socio-cultural influences and perspectives on the purpose and value of education (McLeod, 2015; Moss, 2006; Kingdon, Gourd and Gasper, 2017). The legacy of Aristotle is used to explore how education is viewed, how this influences the purpose it serves and the distinction between education as a process or a product. In particular, educational practices are examined where there is an over-focus on norms, expected ways of developing, a narrowing curriculum and test-based accountability for educators. We look at how this has resulted in an obsession with data and measuring outcomes (Murris, 2013; PISA, 2018) in comparison to a democratic approach to learning and the paradigm of children as agents in their own lives so they are viewed as rich in their potential and capable of voicing their opinions and participating in meaningful ways (Dahlberg and Moss, 2005; Rinaldi, 2006). The chapter concludes by identifying the need for a questioning of personal assumptions in relation to dominant discourses of education for an ownership of knowledge. A commitment to human well-being and what is right is promoted.

Chapter 2: The Reflexive Educator explores how questioning is the first step to disrupting thinking and self-awareness of biases and assumptions so new ways of seeing can be enabled. Through developing a reflexive approach, the chapter explores how educators are better positioned to take responsibility, make informed decisions about everyday developmental and outcome-driven models of practice, and understand why different approaches are more effective. for enhancing participation with young children (Dahlberg and Moss, 2005; McLeod, 2011, 2015; McLeod, 2017). As different theories and ideas pertinent to reflexivity are presented in this chapter, links are made with McLeod's Reflexivity Framework (2015) as a practical set of principles for applying critical reflection in a sustainable way. Collectively this is offered as an alternative approach to the mechanistic product-driven view of teaching often associated with Western practice (Moss, 2013). The chapter concludes with prompts for reflection.

Chapter 3: Democracy and Participation in Early Childhood Education starts by defining what is understood by listening, consultation and participation in the context of early education as a democratic and social construction. In particular Articles 12 and 13 of the United Nations Convention on the Rights of the Child (UNCRC) (1989) are used as a benchmark for children's voice and participation. Different models of participation are explored including Hart's (1992) Ladder of Participation and Shier's (2001) *Pathways to Participation* model in the context of international approaches and quality early education. Examples of what participation looks like in practice and reflexive prompts are provided. Finally, barriers to participatory practice are considered and the importance of the right conditions involving a safe, trusting pedagogical environment so educators feel they are able to ask questions, and make mistakes as they begin to value democratic learning for young children.

Part 2

Chapter 4: Maria Montessori (with Perspectives from Sweden), Chapter 5: Reggio Emilia (with Perspectives from Sweden), Chapter 6: A Finnish Perspective, Chapter 7: Te Whāriki and Chapter 8: Danish Outdoor Nature Pedagogy

Part 2 builds on Chapters 1–3 and looks in detail at five different international approaches to ECE from Sweden, Italy, Finland, Denmark and New Zealand, namely the Reggio-inspired approach, the Maria Montessori method, Finnish ECE, Te Whāriki pedagogy and Danish outdoor nature pedagogy using a critical lens. We evaluate the distinctive philosophical, theoretical and practical interpretations of each looking at the contextual historical, socio-cultural and current political influences, using case studies and narratives to illustrate links between theory, research, policy and practice. In doing so we look how different democratic and ethical approaches can be integrated within one's own culture and ECE provision, and what can be learned.

Part 3

Chapter 9: Wider Issues Affecting Early Childhood Education in the twenty-first century (in particular, in England, Finland and Sweden) focuses on four key aspects of wider contemporary issues that have impacted on global childhoods (as identified by UNICEF, 2016). These are: children's health and well-being, child poverty, English as an Additional Language (EAL) and inclusion of migrants and intercultural perspectives. Case studies are used to provide different insights and lenses. In doing so the reader will be invited to consider new ways of seeing and consider alternative possibilities within an ethical framework.

Chapter 10: Hope for the Future: New Possibilities for Sustaining a Reflexive Approach offers hope for the future of ethical and participatory early childhood education practice. Within the current political climate and the emphasis on outcomes, we emphasise the need for a shrewder awareness about power (politics) and an increased focus on values (ethics) as part of practice with reflexivity (phronesis) and action (praxis) embedded at the heart of professional inquiry. We concur with Pascal and Bertram's (2018, 2012) idea of 'praxeology' which fundamentally challenges the top-down approach associated with government policy and training and is about questioning 'how' and 'why' in relation to local and real world situations. In doing so we look at the significance of facilitating the right conditions (such as a collaborative, open and trusting safe environment so that uncertainty and willingness to take personal risks can be embraced (by both educators and children). Next, mentoring, coaching and the use of journal-keeping are explored with case study examples to support discussion related to reflexivity. The chapter concludes with a series of reflective questions that relate to current global challenges and debates in ECE.

Finally, we end the book by considering a way forward for sustaining an ethical and participatory pedagogical approach to early childhood education.

References

Barad, K. (2007) *Meeting the universe halfway: Quantum physics and the entanglement of matter and meaning*, Durham – London: Duke University Press.

Bolton, G. (2014) Reflective practice : Writing and professional development. 4th edn. London: SAGE Publications Ltd.

Barad, K. (2007) *Meeting the universe halfway: Quantum physics and the entanglement of matter and meaning*, Durham – London: Duke University Press.

Clark, A. (2017) *Listening to young children, expanded: A guide to understanding and using the Mosaic Approach* (3rd edn.), London: Kingsley Publishers.

Clark, A. (2005) 'Listening to and involving young children: A review of research and practice', *Early Child Development & Care*, 175(6), p.489–505. DOI: doi:10.1080/03004430500131288.

Dahlberg, G. and Moss, P. (2005) *Ethics and politics in early childhood education*, Abingdon: Routledge Falmer.

Davies, S. and Artaraz, K. (2009) 'Towards an understanding of factors influencing early years professionals' practice of consultation with young people', *Children and Society*, 23(1), p.57–69. DOI: doi:10.1111/j.1099–0860.2008.00142.x.

Department for Education (DfE) (2017) *Statutory framework for the early years foundation stage: Setting the standards for learning, development and care for children from birth to five*, Crown copyright.

Department for Education (DfE) (2015) *Reception baseline research: Views of teachers, school leaders, parents and carers research report*, National Foundation for Educational Research, July 2015, Lynch, L., Bamforth, H. and Sims, D.

Fook, J. and Gardner, F. (2007) Practising Critical Reflection : A Resource Handbook. Maidenhead: Open University Press.

Hart, R. (1992) 'Children's participation: From tokenism to citizenship', UNICEF Innocenti Essays, Florence, Italy: UNICEF.

Kingdon, Z., Gourd, J. and Gasper, M. (2017) *Flourishing in the early years: Contexts, practices and futures*, Oxon: Routledge.

National Children's Bureau (NCB) (2015) *The integrated review bringing together health and early education reviews at age two to two-and-a-half: Supporting materials for practitioners working with young children*. Published online by the NCB Early Childhood Unit. Available from: www.foundationyears.org.uk/files/2015/03/IR_Supporting_Material.pdf.

McLeod, N. (2015) 'Reflecting on reflection: Improving teacher's readiness to facilitate participatory learning with young children', *Professional Development in Education*, 41(2), p.254–272.

McLeod, N. (2011) 'Exploring early years educators' ownership of language and communication knowledge and skills: A review of key policy and initial reflections on Every Child a Talker and its implementation', *Education 3–13 International Journal of Primary, Elementary and Early Years Education*, 39(4), p.429–445. DOI: doi:10.1080/03004271003776850.

Moss, P. (2018) *Alternative narratives in early childhood: An introduction for students and practitioners*, London: Routledge.

Moss, P. (2014) *Transformative change and real utopias in early childhood education: A story of democracy, experimentation, and potentiality*, New York: Routledge.

Moss, P. (2010) 'We cannot continue as we are: The educator in an education for survival', *Contemporary Issues in Early Childhood*, 11(1), p.8–19.

Moss, P. (2006) 'Early childhood institutions as loci of ethical and political practice', *International Journal of Educational Policy, Research and Practice: Reconceptualising Childhood Studies*, 7, p.127–136.

Moss, P., Dahlberg, G., Grieshaber, S., Mantovani, S., May, H., Pence, A., . . . Vandenbroeck, M. (2016) 'The Organisation for Economic Co-operation and Development's International Early Learning Study: Opening for debate and contestation', *Contemporary Issues in Early Childhood, 17*(3), p.343–351. DOI: doi:10.1177/1463949116661126.

Murris, K. (2013) 'The epistemic challenge of hearing a child's voice', *Studies in the Philosophy of Education*, 32, p.245–259.

Nutbrown, C. (ed.). (1996) *Respectful educators – Capable learners: Children's rights and early education*, London, England: Paul Chapman.

Organization for Economic Co-operation and Development (OECD) (2018) *Programme for International Student Assessment (PISA)*. Retrieved 14 March 2018 from: www.oecd.org/pisa/.

Organization for Economic Co-operation and Development (OECD) (2015) 'Call for tenders: International early learning study'. Retrieved from: www.oecd.org/callsfortenders/CfT100001420 International Early Learning Study.pdf.

Pascal, C. and Bertram, T. (2018) 'Effective early learning: A praxeological and participatory approach to evaluating and improving quality in early childhood education', Research Gate, *Revista da FAEEBA – Educação e Contemporaneide, Salvador*, 27(51), p.105–120. DOI: doi:10.21879/faeeba2358–0194.2018.v27.n51.p105–120.

Pascal, C. and Bertram, T. (2012) 'Praxis, ethics and power: Developing praxeology as a participatory paradigm for early childhood research', *European Early Childhood Education Research Journal*, 20(4), p.477–492. DOI: doi:10.1080/1350293X.2012.737236.

Pascal, C. and Bertram, T. (2009) 'Listening to young citizens: The struggle to make real a participatory paradigm in research with young children', *European Early Childhood Education Research Journal*, 17(2), p.249–262.

Rinaldi, C. (2006). *In dialogue with Reggio Emilia: Listening, researching and learning*, London: Routledge.

Sahlberg, P. (2016) 'Professional autonomy, trust and collaboration in educators' work', Philosophy of Education Society of Great Britain. Annual Conference New College, Oxford1–3 April 2016. Retrieved on 26 May 2017 from: www.philosophy-of-education.org/dotAsset/bc4f09b5-a27f-4306-9966-3aa1fa2cf12c.pdf.

Sahlberg, P. (2011). *Finnish lessons: What can the world learn from educational change in Finland*, New York: Teachers College, Columbia University.

Schön, D. A. (1987) *Educating the reflective practitioner toward a new design for teaching*, San Francisco, CA: Jossey-Bass.

Shier, H. (2001) 'Pathways to participation: Openings, opportunities and obligations', *Children and Society*, 15(2), p.107–117. DOI: doi:10.1002/CHI.617.

UNICEF (2016) *The state of the world's children 2016: A fair chance for every child*. Retrieved 9 January 2019 from: www.unicef.org/publications/index_91711.htm.

United Nations (1989) *Convention on the rights of the child*, New York: United Nations.

Urban, M. (2017) 'We need meaningful, systematic evaluation, not a preschool PISA', *Global Education Review*, 4(2), p.18–24.

Urban, M. and Swadener, B. B. (2016). 'Democratic accountability and contextualised systemic evaluation. A comment on the OECD initiative to launch an International Early Learning Study (IELS)', *International Critical Childhood Policy Studies*, 5(1), p.6–18.

Wasmuth, H. and Nitecki, E. (2017) 'Global early childhood policies: The impact of the global education reform movement and possibilities for reconceptualization', *Global Education Review*, 4(2), p.1–17.

PART 1
The foundations

Chapters 1 to 3 establish the foundations for Parts 2 and 3 of the book. More than ever before, with current pressures of accountability and an obsession with data collection, the need to question not only 'what' is taught but 'how' and 'why' is emphasised. Constructing our own self-awareness and making sense of different understandings can be challenging and uncomfortable, but it can also be empowering and can provide a sense of liberation and ownership, rather than a feeling of being manipulated as part of a political top-down data and outcome-driven model of education. In doing so, Part 1 disrupts and challenges thinking around political questions such as the purpose of early childhood education. The importance of reflexivity is presented as the key to appreciating different perspectives and new ways of thinking. In the spirit of the book, to empower educators and challenge some of the diverse issues and pressures in early years education, Part 1 identifies and examines the relevance of participatory and democratic practice (often associated with international approaches) for promoting respectful learning that acts consciously as part of socially just and ethical practice.

1

THE PURPOSE OF EDUCATION TODAY

Naomi McLeod and Patricia Giardiello

This chapter offers the opportunity for early childhood educators to deconstruct and question different views around the purpose of knowledge in relation to education, in particular, Early Childhood Education (ECE) and personal experiences and values. We examine different historical, cultural, economic and political pressures on education, looking specifically at the impact of neo-liberalism and marketisation in relation to the requirements of a socially just, ethical approach to pedagogy. Here, the relationship between power dynamics, perceptions of children and the influence on the type of pedagogy offered is explored in terms of future implications.

The chapter begins by considering different historical and socio-cultural influences and perspectives on the purpose and value of education (Moss, 2006; Kingdon, Gourd and Gasper, 2017; McLeod, 2016). The legacy of Aristotle is used to explore how education is viewed and how this influences the purpose it serves. The distinction between education as a process or a product is examined as a starting point, in particular educational practices in which there is a focus on norms, expected ways of developing and measuring outcomes (Murris, 2013), in comparison to a democratic approach to learning and the paradigm of children as agents in their own lives where children are viewed as rich in their potential (Rinaldi, 2006; Dahlberg and Moss, 2005) and capable of voicing their opinions and participating in meaningful ways. As such, questioning skills and the need for practical wisdom to inform ethical judgments as a source of moral action is required by the educator (Carr and Kemmis, 1986; Kemmis, 2010). We conclude this chapter by recognising that becoming wise requires open questioning so that a critically reflective (reflexive) approach by the adult, educator or facilitator can be nurtured and developed (McLeod, 2011, 2015). Only then can a democratic approach to learning and teaching as a process of phronesis-praxis (action that is consciously committed to human well-being) be embedded.

It is our intention that this chapter will act as a provocation for the reader to reflect on the purpose of education in relation to personal values. We show how this self-awareness is the first step in valuing a socially just, ethical and democratic approach to pedagogy so that it can be considered on a personal level and inform practice.

A historical overview of the purpose of education: The legacy of Aristotle and knowledge as a process or product

In considering the purpose of education it is essential to look back as far as the Ancient Greeks and the legacy of Aristotle (384–322 BCE). Aristotle, very much a Platonist, shared Plato's ideas regarding the importance of early childhood education but went further in arguing that children possessed differing talents and skills that should be nurtured and enhanced (Giardiello, 2014).

Aristotle was concerned with the philosophical understandings of epistemology (what knowledge is, how we develop knowledge and understanding ethics and the notion that actions should be good and moral) (Aristotle, 1925; original work published circa 334 BCE). Almost all of Aristotle's work was concerned with what constitutes happiness, the 'good life' and seeking better ways of living (Noddings, 2003). He was concerned with the ethics of virtue and questioning aspects of everyday life. As Kristjansson (2013) suggests, for Aristotle developing one's own virtues is not possible without at the same time benefitting others. As such his ideas are relevant to this book and ethical education.

The distinction between the technical (i.e., productive and product / outcome-related) and practical (process / questioning / knowing why) is important as a starting point in determining the function of education. Here the legacy of Aristotle and his classification of knowledge is drawn on as a way of showing how knowledge can be viewed and how this influences the purpose it serves (Barnes, 1976). If the purpose of knowledge is the pursuit of making action, its function is the attainment of knowledge to make or produce something. According to Aristotle, this kind of knowledge and enquiry is involved in productive disciplines. Aristotle associated this form of thinking and doing with the work of craftspeople or artisans. Making action is dependent upon the exercising of skill (what the Greeks called *techne*), which always results from the idea, image or pattern of what the artisan wants to make. In other words, a person has a guiding plan or idea. This way of thinking is dominated by the plan, and actions are directed towards the given end product (Grundy, 1987). Here a parallel can be drawn with the outcome-driven model of education dominant today in England, but also in Nordic countries (Åsén and Moberg, 2015; and Perry, 2009; Nygård, 2017; Sahlberg, 2010, 2016; Urban, 2017).

In contrast, the *practical* (process of knowing why), according to Aristotle (Barnes, 1976), deals with an awareness of ethical and political life; the intention is on developing practical wisdom and knowledge involving the making of moral judgments and human interaction (Carr and Kemmis, 1986). By reflecting on collective and individual action and its consequences, Kemmis (2010) argues that this is 'how we learn *wisdom* and how we develop what Aristotle called *phronesis-praxis* or the "knowing-why"', the source of moral action. Likewise, Winch (2015) considers the importance of 'know how' for professionalism, but acknowledges knowing 'why' for excellence in performance. In this respect the activity form of Aristotle's phronesis-praxis is the key to understanding how knowledge is learnt. In the *Nicomachean Ethics* (NE), Aristotle suggests that knowledge should be learnt in the same way as the knowledge unfolds itself:

> We learn an art or craft by doing the things that we have to do when we have learnt it. For instance, men become builders by building houses, harpers by playing on the harp. Similarly we become just by doing just acts, temperate by doing temperate acts, brave by doing brave acts.
>
> *(NE19; 2.2. 103b1)*

Phronesis-praxis

Praxis is an open form of reasoning or an intentional and committed action with moral intent that involves behaving 'for the good of humankind in acts consciously and *collectively* performed to contribute to the good' (Kemmis, 2010, p.419). Praxis involves a continual interplay between ends and means so that action is informed with a moral intent. Echeverria and Hannam (2016, p.4) describe educational praxis as

> an intervention that intentionally opens up the conditions for change, and the deliberate change intended is to enable children and young people to exist in the world as an integral part of a well-informed democratic citizenry.

Freire (1972) considered 'praxis' as action supported by reflection (examining one's own experiences and views) but requiring theory to illuminate it (Barnes, 1976). This process or *phronesis*, results in a doing-action or *praxis*, and is therefore process-centred. The 'idea' in the interaction is personal, subjective and never fully formed, rather it is constantly being formed and influenced by the situation in a very organic way (Grundy, 1987). This process is held together by a way of 'saying, doing and relating, so that each informs the other' (Kemmis, 2010, p.419).

For Aristotle, *phronesis-praxis* was guided by a moral disposition to act truly and rightly, a concern to further human well-being and the good life. This process of *phronesis-praxis* begins with a question or situation, which then leads to thinking about a situation in the light of personal understandings of what is good, ethical or what makes for human flourishing (Kemmis, 2010). Such a process is influenced by the identity of an individual as a result of their experiences, beliefs, values and understandings of education as a whole (Reed and Canning, 2010). The difficulty here, as Hassan (2005) acknowledges, lies in the fact that everything we do is based on a lifetime of values, beliefs and biases which influences consideration of what is desired, and might alter the way something is achieved or done. This is also advocated by Kernick's comment that honesty is the best way forward in relation to practitioner research and positionality for informing professional practice (1998). Rokeach (1973), in his conceptualisation of values, notes the added complication of 'good and bad' values which include both moral values (what a person feels is the 'right' thing to do) and competency values (what an individual believes is the most effective way to go about doing something). He also identifies 'terminal values', which relate to what the educator wants to achieve for themselves (personal values) and how they wish society to function. Schwartz and Bilsky (1987) developed these concepts further and defined values as '(a) concepts or beliefs, (b) about desirable end states or behaviours, (c) that transcend specific situations, (d) guide selection or evaluation of behaviour and events, and (e) are ordered by relative importance' (p.551). The virtue of this definition is that it distinguishes values from attitudes by pointing at their generalised nature, whereas attitudes are people's beliefs about specific objects or situations (Roe and Ester, 1999). With this intermingling of belief systems, achieving a system of shared values and approaching controversial issues constructively can best be done through an attitude of critical affirmation. As Ashton and Watson (1998, p.191) point out 'critical affirmation has something in common with the idea of the "impartial sympathetic observer" as developed by Dewey (1932)'. As Dewey and Tufts contend:

> To put ourselves in the place of another, to see things from the standpoint of his [or her] aims and values, to humble our estimate of our own pretensions to the level they assume in the eyes of an impartial observer, is the surest way to appreciate what justice demands.
>
> *(Dewey and Tufts, 1932, p.275)*

There is a close connection between values and education with a high degree of super imposing mutuality between the two. This includes political and educational values and beliefs as Stenhouse discusses in his seminal texts (1975, 1983). Stenhouse argues that being an 'extended professional' involved three main elements: 'the commitment to systematic questioning of one's own teaching as a basis for development the commitment and skills to study one's own teaching, and the concern to question and to test theory in practice' (Stenhouse, 1975, p.143). An understanding of education as a process in this sense involves personal and professional attributes that merge as one and ownership of why different approaches are taken as part of practice / teaching. During this process, the relationship between theory (the thinking process) and practice (the action as a result) fuse and the educator develops a personal responsibility for the outcomes experienced by the learner.

Current educational pressures: The influence of neo-liberalism and marketisation

The field of early childhood education is increasingly dominated by a strongly positivistic (outcome-driven) and regulatory discourse (over assessment, testing and

Ofsted), so the focus is on assessing performance of predetermined outcomes where there is often no room for creativity and experimentation (Moss, 2017). This is recognised most recently in the expectations around testing, accountability and competition manifested in the Programme for International Student Assessment (PISA), and the launch of the International Early Learning and Child Well-being Study (IELS), which focus very narrowly on emerging literacy and numeracy, self-regulation, empathy and trust (Urban, 2017) using a baseline assessment test of children in Reception (Bold Beginnings, Ofsted, 2017). Moss (2017) puts this down to 'the story of markets and neo-liberalism', of 'quality and high returns' (p.11) in which 'businesses compete for the custom of parent-consumers' (p.14) and in doing so focus on the best value for money. As a result of this free market or liberalisation in the private sector rather than quality being the priority, this has gone by the wayside in return for high returns. Neo-liberalism is concerned with the extensive economic policies of the twentieth and twenty-first centuries relating to privatisation, deregulation, free trade and reductions in government spending in the public sector in society. While it could be argued that neoliberalism shares many attributes with democracy and the associated classical philosophy of liberalism, the major defining characteristic of the term neo-liberalism today tends to refer to the promotion of a market economy and profit-making and greed where decisions regarding investment and production are based on the interplay of supply and demand which determines the prices of goods and services. Investment decisions, or the allocation of services, are primarily made through capital and financial markets in contrast to production decisions that are embodied as part of an integrated system established by the government.

As Moss (2010) identifies, 'neo-liberalism has a deep suspicion of democratic politics and anything public, and a strong preference for private business and property, with governance through markets, managers and technical experts' (p.12).

The current focus on economic competition, profit-making and global consumer markets of neo-liberalism has had negative connotations in terms of preparing children for the twenty-first century workplace, resulting in a culture of performance and accountability. Within the context of early childhood education settings in England, such as schools, preschools and private day nurseries, this has resulted in an outcome-driven system of measurement and accountability (Headington, 2000). This data-driven, narrowing curriculum and test-based accountability for educators is in direct contrast to the promotion of quality early childhood education based on positive dispositions to learning and imaginative play incorporating participatory approaches.

As a result of a free market or liberalisation in the private sector, rather than quality being the focus, high returns are the priority. Neo-liberalism has resulted in educators being 'reconstituted as technicians' (Moss, 2010, p.12; 2017). The task of the educator-as-technician is to apply prescribed human technologies of proven effectiveness ('what works') without any opportunities to question and explore and to produce predetermined outcomes (Moss, 2010, p.12). This dominates and exercises 'power over our thoughts and actions' (Moss, 2012) so only one way or 'truth' is seen. In this way EC educators have become 'hard of hearing (and) totally deaf to other voices' (Moss, 2017, p.12) or alternative ways of being. This dominant approach acts as a barrier to democratic and socially just pedagogies. Instead, evidenced-based testing and a deficit model of education based on a constructivist stage theory developmental approach has become the norm and children have become institutionalised (Moss, 2006). According to Ellyatt (2011) this narrow focus on standardisation and conformity is responsible for a generation of children who are disengaged from the joy of indulging in critical enquiry, exploring personal interests and being curious. Furthermore, such mechanistic, technical, outcome-driven approaches to teaching are detrimental to children flourishing (Kingdon et al., 2017).

This 'story' of marketisation (of quality and high returns) has been normalised further by international organisations such as the OECD, World Bank, UNESCO and Government think tanks, and the costly research they have engaged in to set out repetitious recommendations that 'advance the story of quality and high returns' (Moss, 2017, p.17). The reality is that most of the studies carried out are from the United States (van Huizen and Plantenga, 2015); for example, the study that looked at 'universal child care and children's outcomes' which involved in the main (two-thirds) America or Canada with very little involvement from European countries. Moss questions whether such studies are reliable, particularly given the US has such a poor reputation of inequality and bias in EC, as represented in the lack of willingness and engagement in international comparisons it engages in to do with health and well-being of its youngest children (Moss, 2014). If we are to understand why education in one country outperforms others, Alexander (2012) warns of the dangers of stripping 'a country of the complexities of culture, values social structure politics and demography' (p.2) which are needed for an accurate and meaningful understanding. In contrast to the creation of 'universal actions', which according to Alexander are artificial and lack any depth, the only way to fully appreciate educational policy is to examine the 'inherited ideas and values, habits and customs, institutions and world views that make a country unique from another' (ibid.). A technical fix is far simpler and cheaper to introduce as a way of evidencing a short-term outcome rather than tackling deep-seated social and economic issues that prevent socially just democratic practice.

According to Moss (2010) and Nussbaum (2010), as a result of neo-liberalism and marketisation, there is a crisis across the world in education (including early childhood education) referred to as the Global Education Reform Movement (GERM) (Wasmuth and Nitecki, 2017), which is an unofficial neo-liberal educational agenda that reinforces a particular set of assumptions regarding the purpose of early childhood education, namely an over focus on accountability, testing, standardisation, prescriptive outcome-driven practice with a focus on literacy and numeracy where there is a distrust of professional educators. As Alexander (2014) warns, GERM reduces the performance of entire education systems to a single questionable measure at a particular moment in time and in a relatively narrow spectrum of their learning (p.159).

Educators can feel restricted by the outcome-driven curriculum and targets imposed by government as part of a top-down approach (Dockett and Perry, 2009; Sahlberg, 2010, 2016; Urban, 2017). As a result there is the tendency to 'play it safe' and follow rules (such as the data-driven focus in English educational settings) without questioning (Wilkins, 2011). For an effective response to the challenges of neo-liberalism, for Moss (2010) democracy is fundamental. Foucault (1980) focused on how the power / knowledge relationship operated within what he called institutional apparatuses, such as the school and its technologies (techniques). The discourse of the classroom, its architectural plan, regulations and administrative measures, is filled with controlling techniques of power / knowledge (Millei, 2005). Being aware of these power relations promotes a consciousness of reality so that educators are more able to make informed decisions and take ownership of their practice (Freire, 1994; MacNaughton, 2005).

In contrast to the outcome-driven model of education dominant today, Orlandi (2014) emphasises the importance of nurturing positive dispositions to learning in early childhood education through open, participatory and democratic, child-led, experiential, creative approaches to learning. In doing so, she emphasises qualities such as self-discovery, intuition, curiosity and confidence. Engagement in this sense is a sign of quality (Norling, Sandberg and Almqvist (2015)) with an emphasis on 'process' making opportunities for young children to engage at a deeper level in enjoyable and meaningful experiences. The intention of making an end product can be a significant part of the engagement process but how children get there and the decisions they make along the way are what give education as a process the ability to engage at a deeper level, with opportunities for expanding thoughts and possibilities (Beetlestone, 1998; Craft, 2002; Jeffrey and Woods, 2009). This requires addressing the power balance so a more creative, democratic, open process of working in collaboration with children is taken by educators. In this way the educator is viewed as an artist and engages in critically reflective practice (Schön, 1983, 1987).

In the context of educator – child interactions, and education as a process – Gilroy (1993) emphasises the value of questioning personal values, interpretations and giving reasons for actions. Such skills are the underpinning of developing a critically reflective / reflexive approach, necessary for questioning the product-driven dominant discourse often associated within education today in England. (This is looked at in more detail as part of Chapter 2 along with tools for promoting a critically reflective / reflexive approach).

Clough and Nutbrown (2007) suggest there is a need for educators to find 'new ways of listening and interpreting' and to develop an awareness of ethical problems as part of interpretation. They emphasise the importance of 'faithful interpretation of what is heard, arising from radical listening' (2007, p.95), which is to do with honesty, authenticity and values. This operational aspect of conscience has been at the heart of this chapter and the need to question the purpose of education and develop an awareness of the influences. There are consequential interconnected implications for pedagogical approaches adopted by early childhood educators, as will be discussed later.

Social constructs of childhood: Changing mindsets

As we have seen, the mindset perpetuated by educators about the value of education is influenced by the purpose it serves. This in turn is / can be affected by neo-liberalism, a focus on outcomes, performance and an association with a developmental deficit model based on norms of the 'Universal Child' (Smith, 2010) as discussed later. Consequently, there is a diversion from personal, core values and the holistic nature of education which focuses on a 'becomings model' (incomplete – in preparation for the next stage), rather than children as 'beings' (competent in the here and now) (Murris, 2013, p.254). Instead of valuing the individual child within education and prioritising opportunities for creative thinking so children can explore, be curious and follow their interests as part of a meaningful process (Kingdon et al., 2017), set developmental norms have become the dominant (deficit) discourse for guiding early childhood curricula and learning in England.

In contrast to the biological maturation view of childhood regulated by developmental norms that informs and dictates achievement, an alternative view is the social construction of childhood, which according to May (2011) is about analysing how a particular way of seeing or defining something came about and the underpinning reasons. Gergen and Gergen (2003, p.2) define social constructivism as 'an unfolding dialogue among participants who vary considerably in their logics, values and visions'. Social construction is concerned with acknowledging the processes and relationships that generate the lived reality at different levels of society (i.e. micro, meso and macro levels) across different cultures and how this has changed over time and place. It is therefore a more natural approach than the biological model and offers a more contextual and inter-related lens that can help early childhood educators understand the complexities and challenges associated with children and childhood at any one time and place. In doing so we present a historical overview of different lenses constructed of children and childhood through time and place.

Post Aristotle and the purpose of education: Alternative perspectives on childhood

This section draws attention to key thinkers that have influenced and continue to influence contemporary childhood theory and the field of early childhood education.

Plato (circa 428–347 BCE), who first debated issues of socialisation and morality, wrote that from birth onwards the welfare of the child was the responsibility of the entire community. He demonstrated through his Socratic dialogues that education and the love of learning should begin early because of the impressions on the formation of a child's character (Giardiello, 2014). Unlike Socrates, his mentor and teacher, who viewed education as transforming childhood into what it ought to be, Plato believed the opposite and set out to make education childlike (Kohan, 2013).

Plato's opposing stance is motivated by the concern that Athenians suffer the political consequences of a bad education. He sees the *polis* (city state) as unfair to its citizens because it has not had the knowledge to educate children in the right way and, consequently, has not provided its childhood with the knowledge necessary to transform it. The implication is that the sole means to save the *polis* is to educate children with true knowledge (ibid.).

In contrast, **Phillippe Aries (1962)** believed that in medieval society the idea of childhood did not exist. Rather than being a social category of 'childhood', children were viewed as under-developed adults. They were viewed as young members of the human species but were not distinctive to adults. As depicted by artists, they wore the same clothes and did the same activities as adults. There was no concept of right and wrong and no clear boundaries, so children were exposed to all aspects of human and adult life. Morality was not yet established. According to Aries, the concept of childhood was not apparent until well after the Middle Ages.

However, Aries' understanding and view of children and childhood is restricted by the sources he used, which consisted of analysis of diaries found in literate aristocratic homes, from which he made sweeping generalisations about childhood (Shahar, 1990). Postman (1983) challenges Aries' ideas that the construct of childhood began around the seventeenth century and suggests that while past societies may not have had the modern concept of childhood, differences did exist between children and adults.

Thomas Hobbes (1558–1679), considered to be a founding father of political philosophy, observed children as being innately evil, born evil, by which only thinking about themselves and their own possessions was the first thing that they cared about, and consequently needed civilising. Hobbes believed that it was society, including but not necessarily solely the parents, that 'uncleans' them (Marshall, 2017).

By contrast **John Locke**'s **(1632–1704)** view was that at the time of birth a child's mind was a *tabula rasa* (a blank slate) that could be moulded and shaped by their experiences and environment. Capturing and maintaining individual children's attention was central to Locke's philosophy, however he also believed that children should conform to culture rather than the view Rousseau held that culture should conform to children's nature (Giardiello, 2014).

Jean-Jacques Rousseau (1712–1778) as a Romantic naturalist saw children as innocent and naturally good beings, with childhood being socially constructed as a time of flourishing and innocence. He rejected the Christian notion of 'original sin' and instead promoted human goodness and freedom. Rousseau believed children would learn and develop if they were guided by nature rather than society (Barrow and Woods, 2006). Without the corrupt influence of society, children could allow their inherent goodness to unfold naturally (Carr, 2003). Rousseau's ideas of seeing the child as naturally good led to his understanding that play was natural for children and that they should have the freedom to play (Grieshaber and McCardle, 2010). He outlined his underpinning beliefs and concepts about early childhood education in his writings about a fictional character called '*Emile*'. This contained details of what Rousseau believed a young boy should experience as part of being educated. For example, Rousseau wrote, '*Let them (children) eat, run and play as much as they want*' (Rousseau, 1762 / 2007 / 2003) (cited in Grieshaber and McCardle, 2010, p.3). His child-centred approach rooted in nature and freedom is the foundation of many early childhood educators' play-based and child-centred philosophy today (Wood and Atfield, 2005).

Johan Pestalozzi (1746–1827) was greatly influenced by Rousseau's theories and set about putting them into practice. Thus began a new era in education when the ideas of earlier reformers were actually tried out and tested. Pestalozzi observed that each child learnt in his or her own way drawing on direct experience through reflections fostered by the teacher and through discussions and reconstructions and problem-based learning based on children's developing interests (Adelmann, 2000; Giardiello, 2014). These ideas inspired future early childhood educators and remain current to notions of effective early years pedagogy.

The enormous contribution to early childhood education by **Friedrich Froebel (1782–1852)** was influenced by what he had learnt whilst visiting Pestalozzi's school at Yverdon, Switzerland. The creating of self through play and the 'self-activity' of the child, first termed by Pestalozzi, was central to Froebel's philosophy. However, whereas Pestalozzi was instinctive and inspirational, Froebel was philosophical and investigative and in the formulation of his own educational ideas he eventually took a different path (Giardiello, 2014). For example, whilst building on Pestalozzi's ideas on experiential learning and the use of first-hand activities, Froebel developed specifically designed didactic materials that he referred to as *gifts* and *occupations* (Taylor Allen, 1988). Froebel also linked his concept of self-activity to self-fulfilment and brought young children into contact with nature as advocated by Rousseau. Searching for a word that best reflected his environment for young children which he compared to a nursery where a gardener tended his young plants, Froebel chose the name *Kindergarten* literally meaning a child's garden. *Kindergarten* soon came to represent a particular form of early childhood education far removed from the traditional schools at the time with their emphasis on fostering early academic skills and traditional rote learning. Froebel's kindergarten was not just a philosophy but a call to action which would eventually be taken up by McMillan, Montessori and Isaacs (Giardiello, 2014).

Margaret McMillan (1860–1893) turned to the Froebelian movement for inspiration on how to go about establishing her own design of early childhood practice and provision. However, despite drawing on Froebel's influences, her open air nursery garden school was very different, being less philosophical and orientated purely and simply to education. Conscious that childhood was a time of change and transformation, McMillan planned her nursery garden school to promote all aspects of the child's development alongside the promotion of good health, happiness and respect for others (Giardiello, 2014).

Maria Montessori (1870–1952) argued for the liberty of the child, not one of pure abandonment, as advocated by Rousseau but a freedom that should 'permit development of the individual, spontaneous manifestations of the child's nature' (Montessori, 1965, p.2). Seeing education as a process in setting children free, Montessori demonstrated that within a carefully structured environment children could be free to teach themselves, first through the senses and then through the intellect (Duckworth, 2006). Although critically disposed to Froebel's gifts and occupations, she found inspiration for her didactic equipment in the theories of Jean Itard (1775–1838) and Eduard Seguin (1812–1880) who believed in educating children through their senses. In depth analysis of Montessori contribution to early childhood education can be found in Chapter 4.

Susan Isaacs (1885–1948), greatly influenced by Dewey, felt a strong connection to Montessori's idea of the child having the freedom to choose but disagree with Montessori's marginalisation of children's fantasy and imaginative play (Giardiello, 2014). It is Isaacs' observations of children, left free to occupy themselves as they wished, that provided a greater understanding of the vital role of spontaneous imaginative play in early childhood education in promoting children's competencies. Isaacs grasped, as Dewey did, that the work of schools to be effective in building intellectual growth must be based on and proceed form children's natural tendencies. Isaacs, building on the work of her contemporaries and predecessors, contributed to current effective pedagogical understanding that helping children to be reasonable and effective in their surroundings would have long-term social and moral benefits.

Table 1.1 summarises key perceptions of childhood and concepts of early childhood education as outlined by each of these philosophers. It also identifies the pedagogical approach required by educators.

Perceptions of children and childhood

'What children are like, or what we think they should be like, influences our constructions of the ideal adult role' (Kalliala, 2011, p.238). As identified, concepts of competence are a key feature that influence how children are viewed and the pedagogical approach adopted by early childhood educators (Clark and Moss, 2001, 2005; Clark, McQuail and Moss, 2003).

In relation to contemporary discourses of childhood, different ideas and discussions have arisen over what it is to be a child. In terms of law and policy about what constitutes childhood, the boundaries vary substantially even between relatively developed countries and the dividing line between childhood and adulthood and characteristics and responsibility (Muncie and Goldson, 2006). The most readily available and most widely accepted framework is offered by the United Nations on the Convention of the Rights of the Child (UNCRC) (1995) which provides an agreed age-based definition of childhood (of between birth and 18) that is recognised internationally.

Despite various adult lenses that problematise childhood, the UNCRC's (1989) definition of childhood is useful as a starting point for examining different social and environmental contexts and perceptions of children and childhood particularly

TABLE 1.1 Perceptions of childhood, concepts of ECE and associated pedagogy

Philosopher	*Key concept of ECE*	*Pedagogical approach required*
Plato (c. 428–347 BCE)	Education and the love of learning should begin early because of the importance of initial impressions on the formation of a child's character	To encourage young children's learning as a form of play which he viewed as a proactive socialisation. He emphasised purposeful play as the link to learning through effective pedagogical approaches
Aristotle (384–322 BCE)	There should be no demands for formal study until the age of 7. Before then emphasis should be placed on play and physical exercise	To appreciate the importance of early learning experiences in the recognising of skills, talents and abilities of young children. Understand the importance of nurturing good moral social values which Aristotle viewed as essential for later lifelong learning
Hobbes (1588–1679)	In contrast to earlier thinking ECE owes little to Hobbes' philosophy which considered children as being in a 'state of nature'. In their 'natural' condition human beings lack self-government, consequently the prime factors of early development were control and discipline	He viewed children from birth as incapable of developing cognitively unless directed by adults – i.e. their parents. Children therefore should be grateful to their parents for the benefit of their education. The trustworthiness of a parent would render that parent worthy of 'filial' or respectful obedience, and the benefits conferred on the child merit gratitude. Children possessed no rights and were subservient to their parents
Locke (1632–1704)	Driving belief that a child's mind is a *tabula rasa* upon which experiences make their mark. Placed emphasis on learning through the senses and first-hand experiences as opposed to rote learning	Placed importance on the child's environment which facilitated freely chosen activities. Disagreed with physical punishment, preferring the use of intrinsic rewards such as verbal praise or stern looks
Rousseau (1712–1778)	As children are born innocent with natural goodness, education should take its cues from nature and allows time for children to develop and learn through self-discovery and natural unfolding of their abilities	Advocated a child-centric approach to education in which the educator should allow children to be shaped through their own senses and inner voice. Play should be a central component in children's lives
Pestalozzi (1746–1827)	Endeavoured to keep children's hands, heart and head in equilibrium. No undue pressures or influences should warp the development intended by nature and thereby preventing the child from growing to fulfil their inherent potential	Encouraged reflective learning in children through innovative pedagogic means such the promotion of self-driven activity through apperception, i.e. building on previously assimilated ideas; simultaneous teaching through unhurried group discussion; peer tutoring and the object lesson. He was the first educator to promote the value of reflexive practice

Philosopher	*Key concept of ECE*	*Pedagogical approach required*
Froebel (1782–1852)	Early childhood education should be provided within a specially created environment named a *Kindergarten*, described as a place where children could grow and develop in harmony with their natural surroundings	Introduced the concept of structured guided play through the specially devised Gifts and Occupations which were seen as key to the children's intellectual development. Songs, games and stories to be incorporated in to the *Kindergarten*'s daily routine
Montessori (1870–1952)	ECE should be a liberating and socialising force. Within a carefully structured environment children could be free to teach themselves, first through the senses and then through the Emphasis on Practical Life Exercises and didactic materials as tools for the child's self- construction	The environment should be meticulously prepared before the children arrive with careful use of space and separate work areas. Stressed importance of intervening only when necessary or asked to by the child. 'Teacher as director': to demonstrate procedures and show the correct use of the self- correcting didactic materials. Emphasis on observing and keeping records of the children's activities recognising children's growth at crucial developmental moments
McMillan (1860–1893)	Developed the provision of nurseries with gardens. Understood the value of outdoor play in enabling the children to make scientific and environmental discoveries whilst developing their language skills	Placed importance of providing and planning for a provocative outdoor environment. Organised in to different sections in order for children to follow own interests. There should be ample space for children to move around freely. Encouraged parents to participate with the activities and develop skills alongside their children
Isaacs (1885–1948)	Advocated free play that should be truly open-ended, unpredictable and controlled and directed by the children	Supported children's freely chosen activities in such a way as not to dampen their natural curiosity. Stressed importance of observing everything that children do and say in order to build up an accurate picture of the children's learning

(table adapted from Giardiello, 2014)

either as 'becoming' or 'beings' (Murris, 2013). By this we mean, immature, dependent, incomplete and vulnerable or rich in potential (Dahlberg and Moss, 2005; Rinaldi, 2006) and capable decision-makers (Clark, 2005; Murris, 2013; Prout, 2005). For too long, protection and safety are seen as priorities in early childhood education rather than consultation and decision-making. As a result, children are not presented with opportunities to make decisions, take responsibility and be independent (Christensen, 2004; Clark, Moss and Kjorholt, 2005). This has resulted in a concern with measurable physical characteristics and educational targets associated with developmental models of curriculum that prioritise ability with ages such a Piaget's Constructivist staged theory (1952, 1954, 1965). While Piaget believed that learning started from within, to understand the nature of knowledge, it is important to explore the process rather than just examining the end product (Kamii and Ewing, 1996). Even though Piaget explained the nature of human knowledge by studying children (Bringuier, 1980), he viewed the construction of knowledge (intelligence) in relation to biological development. In this way Piaget's construction of learning is very scientific, based on clinical outcomes or stages and expectations, which has led to the practice of identifying inappropriate gaps in children's learning rather than the competencies of the child, and what they can do and enjoy. As Wadsworth (1996) identifies, such expectations do not support children with specific learning needs and tend to be very adult-led and highly structured. These approaches are at odds with notions of autonomy, decision-making and being independent. Such developmental, output-driven forms of education are therefore referred to as deficit models of education. In doing so the output (the '*what*') becomes the focus rather than Vygotsky's consideration of the '*how*' and the social influences (Wadsworth, 1996). While Kamii and Ewing (1996) acknowledge the 'gaps' in Piaget's theory (p.261), this developmental approach to learning is still very prominent in many ECE settings and is evident in readiness expectations, particularly in relation to starting school (McDowall-Clark, 2017).

If children are always viewed as being in preparation for the next developmental stage of life, any one moment or phase in its own right is devalued. For example, by using the term 'pre-school', the implication is that children are being prepared. In this way, the next developmental stage is perceived as more important than the moment in time. Early childhood in this way is seen as getting 'ready' (McDowall-Clark, 2017) for formal schooling. We would argue that children are not 'pre-anything' and that children and childhood as a whole should be valued and regarded as meaningful in its own right. Still the Nordic countries, written about in this book, use this term. However, it is interpreted in a more holistic way.

Sadly, in practice the image of children and childhood as passive in receiving knowledge has been a dominant construct in early childhood education throughout history (Branscombe, et al., 2000; Woodrow, 1999). This construct views children as 'being done to' and incapable, powerless and in need of adult protection. Consequently, children are viewed as needing to receive knowledge and experiences chosen and provided for them by adult educators as part of a developmental approach such as Piaget's staged theory. More recently, though, in response to recognising new demands of our changing world, the dominant discourses of developmental deficit models are being challenged. Yelland and Kilderry (2005) and Smith (2010) identified the need for a rethinking of pedagogy and practice so children can think for themselves and make informed decisions. As identified already, an alternative view is the social construction of childhood, which is concerned with the processes (of *how*) and relationships that generate the lived reality at different levels of society across different cultures and how this has changed over time and place (May, 2011; Gergen and Gergen, 2003). It begins with and involves an awareness of underpinning views and values (questioning *why*) and is therefore a more natural approach than the biological model. Here there is a need for more positive perceptions of children such as rich in potential, capable, empowered, independent decision-makers through which the notion of agency has developed as part of democratic and participatory early childhood pedagogy (Dahlberg and Moss, 2005; Moss, 2013, 2014; Woodrow and Brennan, 2001) (cited in Arthur et al., 2005). This however is inextricably and intimately linked to how education is viewed.

Sorin and Cook (2005) present different constructs of childhood that are useful as a means of identifying personal concepts of children and childhood, as well as supporting a process of challenging educators to reconceptualise how children and childhood are viewed. Their overview provides insight into dominant images of the child that perpetuate an imbalance of power between the educator and child rather than a reciprocal respectful relationship. For example, when children are viewed as evil, this gives rise to the need to punish and control behaviour so they become submissive (Sorin and Cook, 2005). This was particularly evident in seventeenth century England during the Reformation and the Puritan movement when children were seen as being beset by Original Sin and viewed as inherently evil. The view that they needed to be saved from their natural wickedness resulted in harsh treatments to beat the Devil out of them and use discipline as a way of making them obedient. Still today, this power imbalance is evident particularly where there is an expectation for children to respect adults or where adults feel the need to control children. In comparison to the 'evil' child, Sorin and Cook's 'snowballing' child (2005) is seen as having control or being spoiled in the way they have their wishes or desires pampered to. This uneven imbalance of power can result in adults bribing children in an attempt to regain power (for example by using rewards or stickers for acceptable behaviour). Roald Dahl's character of Veruca Salt in his renowned children's book *Charlie and the Chocolate Factory* (Dahl, 1964) demonstrates, through characterisation, how the power dynamic here positions the child as in control and the adult attempting to regain control either through bribery or acquiescing to the demands. While the snowballing child could be seen as manageable, the child who is viewed as 'out-of-control' or 'aggressive' leaves adults feeling 'helpless' (Sorin and Cook, 2005, p.15) and can result in inappropriate behaviour by adults in order to get children to conform. Here we would suggest there has been a failure to develop secure, healthy attachments that are productive with loving caregivers in the early years (Bowlby, 1953). Smith (2010) suggests the need to look at the influence of wider social relationships and relook at adults' expectations of children, which can often be very unrealistic given children's negative early experiences of life and relationships.

Disappearing childhood: A new crisis of exploitation and abandonment

The disappearance of childhood still resonates today in the representation of children as 'miniature adults' (Buckingham, 2000; Smith, 2010; Sorin and Cook, 2005) which can occur when children are viewed as a commodity and dressed in 'cute' or sometimes sexually explicit outfits and encouraged to compete in competitions and performance. This is reinforced by Palmer's view that 'selling adult fashion trends to children inevitably leads to the premature sexualisation of little girls' . . . (2007, p.235) More recently, in contemporary society, Slater and Tiggemann (2016) raise concerns over very young girls in a grown-up world, the exposure of a sexualised media and the impact on body image and career aspirations. In addition, the impact of social media on young girls' mental health is a real concern raised by McDade-Montez, Wallander and Cameron (2017).

The disappearance of childhood is particularly obvious for children who are victims of war, terror, famine and poverty and have no voice in their plight: for example, refugee and asylum-seeking children from different parts of the world. Of recent concern are the orphaned children of Isis fighters which, as a result of children being abandoned or 'not wanted' by the Syrian authorities, could lead to a new crisis of radicalisation. Scorned and stateless, the children of Isis fighters face an uncertain future (Chulov, 2017) and traumatised by war they are targeted for recrimination. To add insult to injury (both physical and psychological), these children are not recognised by aid agencies or state welfare systems and are being stripped of their childhood (Chulov, 2017).

For children in non-Western parts of the world, Kuyinia and Alhassanb (2016) highlight how notions of a universalised childhood are pressurising Indian children to conform to Western-dominated ideas of childhood. At the same time, Indian childhood is also subject to internal forces of a colonial desire for education of upper-caste and upper-class childhood. Similarly, in African societies Kuyinia, and Alhassanb (2016) highlight the plight of young children experiencing severe poverty, their exposure to living on the streets in Tamale, Ghana, caring for blind parents and the devastating, detrimental impact on their well-being and education.

As Smith (2010, p.39) highlights, 'the world is changing and so is the child's place and role within the family', which provides opportunities for agency and children's rights as part of the restructuring of social life. The agentic child actively participates and flourishes within their education and lives in an environment of reciprocal relationships based on a pedagogy of listening. This involves a positive view of children in society, as rich in potential, competent and active in their co-creation of knowledge, as associated with the Reggio Emilia Approach (Dahlberg and Moss, 2005; Kingdon, et al., 2017; Moss, 2010; Rinaldi, 2006). In Part 2, as part of different international approaches to early childhood education, we return to the agentic child in the context of democratic and socially just practice.

Each of these different perceptions of children involves and indicates a power relationship which often involves an imbalance that can be present in early childhood education. An awareness of such power dynamics continues to be controversial (Catling, 2004) and provides the basis on which pedagogy is built. When a power differential is present, there is a lack of reciprocal trust and respect between educators and children. In doing so there is a need for educators to recognise the historical, political and social nature (Cannella, 2005) of these constructs; to identify events where they may be present in their practice; and to question whether these constructs create power imbalances between children and adult educators (Yelland and Kilderry, 2005). Building on Vygotsky's and Bruner's (Smidt, 2009, 2011) social constructivism, and used productively by Rogoff (2003), we would advocate an active socio-cultural lens of childhood (Mayall, 2002), where children are seen not as passive objects in society in general but as social actors (Qvortrup et al., 1994, p.2) with an emphasis on viewing children as able and competent and valuing their interests, and concerns (Christensen and James, 2002).

Children's views of childhood

While some of the research presented here includes children's experiences of childhood, we are conscious that research carried out by adults can often offer a skewed and partial understanding if children's personal views and concerns are not directly included. Without consideration of how children themselves construct and make sense of childhood, the account is incomplete and inaccurate. This book is based on a democratic approach that is respectful of children's opinions in line with the UNCRC (1989) and Article 12. Evaldsson and Sparrman (2009) acknowledge the long absence of studies 'about what children themselves do with the material culture that is part of their lives' (p.108). Children's first-hand personal experiences of different socio-cultural structures are therefore respected as 'a source of insight into the meanings and dynamics of childhood itself' (Smith, 2010, p.161).

Lowe's (2012) research is relevant here as it involved consulting directly with children aged between 3 years to 4 years as 'experts in the field' (p.269). The purpose was to explore children's understanding about the nature of childhood. Four categories were identified: the 'Playful Child', the 'Unknowing Child', the 'Needful Child' and the 'Unauthorised Child'. For the 'Playful Child', play was found to be a key feature of childhood, but excluded the adult as the children perceived adults as not understanding their 'tending' (pretend) play. The play is therefore controlled by children. The 'Unknowing Child' demonstrates how children perceive their lack of knowledge or understanding about a range of situations in comparison to adults who were perceived as 'knowing'. There are some similarities here with the 'Romantic Child' as identified by Hendrick (1990), and the idea of the child being an empty vessel needing nurturing, and the child as innocent and unknowing. The 'Needful Child' demonstrates children's dependency or trust for adults to 'make it better' (Lowe, 2012, p.276) by providing physical care, solving problems and protecting. This represents the dominant discourse in contemporary Western society of the child as innocent, in need of adult protection from danger. Finally, the 'Unauthorised Child' presents the child's unwilling acceptance of adults' rules and control and having to accept a less dominant role. These perspectives highlight contrasting positions of power and control and children's own views of themselves as 'becoming' adults rather than 'being' individuals in their own right.

As we progress through the book, children's voice is central through the case studies and conversations provided as part of different chapters. In our final chapter we look at appropriate Continuing Professional Development (CPD) that advocates sustainable participatory and creative approaches using different frameworks associated with nurturing a critically reflective approach.

Perceptions on power relationships within childhood

For too long, children's competency has faced numerous challenges in relation to their struggle for voice and participation (Pascal and Bertram, 2009). Despite Article 12 of the UNCRC (1989) clearly identifying that children have the right to express their views about matters that are important to them and participate in meaningful learning opportunities, children are generally expected to express their voices through adult-initiated platforms. This in turn can result in a tokenistic representation of facilitating children's voice (Burke, 2007; Pascal and Bertram, 2009) and is a cause for concern (Clark 2004, 2005; Murray, 2015). As identified by Whitty and Wisby (2007), one of the main hurdles that inhibits the facilitation of young children's participation is the fear that giving children responsibility for making decisions encroaches on educator's conventional professionalism and the power imbalance. The apprehension experienced by educators when relinquishing sole responsibility of a task by allowing children to have ownership results in a feeling of losing control (Bragg, 2007; Cox and Robinson-Pant, 2008; Flutter, 2007). The idea of consulting 'with' children for some practitioners is interpreted as giving children the opportunity to make unrealistic requests which in turn relinquishes fears that children could possibly undermine their authority (Bragg, 2007; Cox and Robinson-Pant, 2008; Lundy, 2007). This can result in a need to control and resume an unequal power imbalance (Flutter and Ruddock, 2004). In contrast, children's agency is supported by democratic, respectful practice where educators are aware of power dynamics between themselves and the child and children are viewed positively as rich in potential, capable, independent decision-makers (Dahlberg and Moss, 2005; Moss, 2013, 2014; MacNaughton, 2005). This will be looked at in detail in Chapter 3 when we consider participatory approaches in early childhood education.

Respectful power relationships as a necessary future pedagogy

As a way forward, in contrast to a deficit model of education (comprising a narrowing curriculum, test-based accountability for educators), which has resulted in a low risk, outcomes-based approach (Dockett and Perry, 2009; Dockett and Perry, 2010, 2016; Urban, 2017;), we advocate an open form of praxis as an intentional and committed democratic action with a moral intent (Kemmis, 2010). This involves a pedagogy that draws on more participatory and collaborative approaches where children are viewed as competent learners and encouraged to take responsibility and make decisions about things that are important to them. In doing so, a philosophical approach, committed to phronesis (critical reflection) is promoted where children interpret for themselves, make connections, question and make sense of situations.

By examining and comparing different democratic international approaches later in this book, we present the opportunity to not only investigate *how* learning occurs (Rinaldi, 2006), but also to examine *why* such methods or processes are effective, in relation to our personal philosophy of education, so that early education educators can be empowered to make appropriate changes to personal learning and teaching relationships. As Alexander (2014) notes, a heightened awareness of politics and questioning top-down government-imposed approaches in early childhood is the first step in being GERM resistant. In Chapter 2, we therefore explore Dewey's attitudes, competencies and lenses for critical reflection alongside Schön's 'new epistemology' (1987) for praxis and Brookfield's lenses (1995, 2017). McLeod's Reflexivity Framework (2015) is presented as a practical tool for becoming critically reflective. Collectively, these processes offer an alternative approach to the mechanistic product driven view of teaching often associated with Western practice (Moss, 2008).

POINTS FOR REFLECTION

- Aristotle considered questioning about everyday life as core to living well.
- Seeing children as 'becomings' does not support children as capable decision-makers with views that are valued.
- How would you describe your own philosophy of early childhood education and why?

References

Alexander, R. (2014) 'The best that has been thought and said', *Forum*, 56(1), p.157–169.

Alexander, R. (2012) 'Moral panic, miracle cures and education policy: What can we really learn from international comparisons?' *Scottish Education Review*, 44(1), p.4–21.

Adelmann, C. (2000) 'Over two years what did Froebel say to Pestalozzi', *History of Education*, (29), p.102–114. DOI: doi:10.1080/004676000284391.

Aries, P. (1962) *Centuries of childhood*, London: Pimlico.

Aristotle (1925) *The Nicomacheon ethics*, Oxford: Oxford University Press.

Aristotle (1908) *Nicomachean ethics* (W.D. Ross Trans.), Oxford: Clarendon. Available at www. ilt.columbia.edu/publications/aristotle.html

Ashton, E. and Watson, B. (1998) 'Values education: A fresh look at procedural neutrality', *Educational Studies*, 24(2), p.183–193. DOI: doi:10.1080/0305569980240204.

Arthur, L., Beecher, B., Death, E., Dockett, S. and Farmer, S. (2005) *Programming and planning in early childhood settings* (3rd ed.), Southbank, Victoria: Thomson.

Åsén, G. and Moberg, E. (2015) 'Den statliga synen på och styrningen av utvärdering i förskolan [The state view on assessment in early childhood education]', in: I.G. Åsén (Red.), *Utvärdering & pedagogisk bedömning i förskolan* [*Assessment in preschool*], Stockholm: Liber,p.18–37.

Beetlestone, F. (1998). *Creative children, imaginative teaching*, Buckingham: Open University Press.

Barrow, R. and Woods, R. (2006) *An introduction to philosophy of education.* Abingdon: Routledge.

Barnes, J. (1976). *Introduction to Aristotle: The Nicomachean ethics ('Ethics'),* Harmondsworth: Penguin.

Bowlby, J. (1953) *Child care and the growth of love*, Harmondsworth: Penguin.

Bragg, S. (2007) *Consulting young people: A literature review*, London: Creative Partnerships/ Arts Council England.

Branscombe, N.A., Castle, K., Dorsey, A.G., Surbeck, E., and Taylor, J.B. (2000) *Early childhood education: A constructivist approach*, Boston: Houghton Mifflin Company.

Bringuier, J.C. (1980) *Conversations with Jean Piaget* (B.M. Gulati, Trans.), Chicago: University of Chicago Press. (Original work published 1977).

Brookfield, S.D. (1995) *Becoming a critically reflective teacher*, San Francisco: Jossey-Bass A Wiley Company.

Buckingham, D. (2000) *After the death of childhood*, Cambridge: Polity.

Burke, C. (2007) 'The view of the child: Releasing "visual voices" in the design of learning environments ', *Discourse: Studies in the Cultural Politics of Education*, 28(3), p.359–372. DOI: doi:10.1080/01596300701458947.

Cannella, G.S. (2005) 'Reconceptualizing the field (of early childhood care and education): If "Western" child development is a problem, then what do we do?' in: N. Yelland (Ed.) *Critical issues in early childhood education*, New York: Open University Press, p.17–39.

Carr, D. (2003) *Making sense of education: An introduction to the philosophy and theory of education and teaching*, Abingdon: Routledge.

Carr, W. and Kemmis, S. (1986) *Becoming critical. Education, knowledge and action research*, Lewes: Falmer Press.

Catling, S. (2014) 'Giving younger children voice in primary geography: Empowering pedagogy – A personal perspective', *International Research in Geographical and Environmental Education*, 23(4), p.350–372. DOI: doi:10.1080/10382046.2014.946321.

Craft, A. (2002). *Creativity and early years education: A lifewide foundation*, London: Bloomsbury.

Clark, A. (2005) 'Listening to and involving young children: A review of research and practice', *Early Child Development & Care*, 175(6), p.489–505. DOI: doi:10.1080/03004430500131288.

Clark, A. (2004) *Listening as a way of life: Why and how we listen to young children*, London: National Children's Bureau for Department for Education & Science.

Clark, A. and Moss, P. (2005) *Spaces to play, more listening to young children using the Mosaic approach*, London: National Children's Bureau.

Clark, A., and Moss, P. (2001) *Listening to young children: The Mosaic Approach*, London: National Children's Bureau for the Joseph Rowntree Foundation.

Clark, A., Moss, P. and Kjorholt, A. (2005) *Beyond listening: Children's perspectives on early childhood services*, Bristol: Policy Press.

Clark, A., McQuail, S. and Moss, P. (2003) *Exploring the field of listening to and consulting with young children*, Research Report 445, Nottingham: Department for Education & Skills.

Clough, P. and Nutbrown, C. (2007) *A student's guide to methodology*, London: SAGE.

Christensen, P. (2004) 'Children's participation in ethnographic research: Issues of power and representation', *Children and Society*, 18(2), p.165–176.

Christensen, P. and James, A. (2002). 'Research with children: Perspectives and practices', *The International Journal of Children's Rights*, 10(3), p.291–294. DOI: doi:10.1163/157181802761586725.

Christensen, P. and James, A. (Eds.) (2000) *Research with children*, London: Falmer Press.

Chulov, M. (2017) 'Scorned and stateless: Children of Isis fighters face an uncertain future', *The Observer*, Saturday 7 October 2017.

Cox, S. and Robinson-Pant, A. (2008) 'Power, participation and decision making in the primary classroom: Children as action researchers', *Educational Action Research*, 16(4), p.457–468. DOI: doi:10.1080/09650790802445643.
Craft, A. (2002) *Creativity and early years education: A lifewide foundation*, London: Continuum.
Dahl, R. (1964). *Charlie and the chocolate factory*, London: Penguin Books.
Dahlberg, G. and Moss, P. (2005) *Ethics and politics in early childhood education*, Abingdon: Routledge Falmer.
Dewey, J. (1933) *How we think: A restatement of the relation of reflective thinking to the educative process*, New York: Heath and Company.
Dewey, J. and Tufts, J.H. (1932) *Ethics*, (revised edition) in: *The Later Works*, vol. 7 (entire volume).
Dockett, S. and Perry, B. (2009) 'Readiness for school: A relational construct', *Australian Journal of Early Childhood*, 34(1), p.20–26.
Duckworth, C. (2006) 'Teaching peace: A dialogue on the Montessori method', *Journal of Peace Education*, 3, p.39–53. DOI: doi:10.1080/17400200500532128.
Echeverria, E. and Hannam, P. (2017) 'The community of philosophical inquiry (P4C): A pedagogical proposal for advancing democracy', in: M.R. Gregory, J. Haynes and K. Murris (Eds.) *The Routledge international handbook on philosophy for children*, Abingdon: Routledge.
Ellyatt, W. (2011) 'The Democratisation of Learning', in: House, R. (Ed.) *Too much too soon? Early learning and the erosion of childhood*, Stroud: Hawthorn Press.
Evaldsson, A.C. and Sparrman, A. (2009) 'Barns kamratkulturer & Barns visuella kulturer = Sant. Två analyser av barns samtal om reklam [Children's peer cultures & Children's visual cultures = True],' in: A. Sparrman, J. Cromdal, A.-C. Evaldsson and V. Adelsvärd (Eds.) *Den väsentliga vardagen; Några diskursanalytiska perspektiv på TAL, TEXT och BILD* [*The importance of the every-day life; Some discourse-analytical perspectives on speech, text and images*], Stockholm: Carlssons förlag.
Flutter, J. (2007) 'Teacher development and pupil voice', *The Curriculum Journal*, 18(3), p.343–354. DOI: doi:10.1080/09585170701589983.
Flutter, J. and Rudduck, J. (2004) *Consulting pupils: What's in it for schools?*London: Routledge Falmer.
Freire, P. (1994) *Pedagogy of hope*, New York: Continuum.
Freire, P. (1972) *Pedagogy of the oppressed*, Harmondsworth, England: Penguin.
Freire, P. (1970) *Cultural action for freedom* (M. Bergman Trans.), Middlesex: Penguin.
Foucault, M. (1980) *Power/knowledge: Selected interviews and other writings, 1972–1977*, Brighton: Harvester Press.
Foucault, M. (1978) *The history of sexuality, volume 1: An introduction* (R. Hurley Trans.), New York: Pantheon Books.
Gergen, M. and Gergen, K. (2003) 'The social construction of the real and the good', in: M. Gergen and K. Gergen (Eds.) (2003) *Social constructivism. A reader*, London: SAGE.
Giardiello, P. (2014) *Pioneers in early childhood education*, Abingdon: Routledge.
Gilroy, P. (1993) 'Reflections on Schön: An epistemological critique and a practical alternative', in: P. Gilroy and M. Smith (Eds.). *International analyses of teacher education*, Abingdon: Carfax Publishing Company, p.125–142.
Grieshaber, S. and McCardle, F. (2010) *The trouble with play*, Berkshire: Open University Press.
Grundy, S. (1987) *Curriculum: Product or praxis*, Oxford: Routledge Falmer.
Hassan, Z. (2005) *Connecting to source*. Retrieved 24 July 2010 from: www.world changing.com.
Headington, R. (2000) *Monitoring, assessment, recording, reporting and accountability: meeting the standards*, London: David Fulton.
Hendrick, H. (1990) 'Constructions and reconstructions of British childhood: An interpretative survey, 1800 to the present', in: A. James and A. Prout (Eds.) *Constructing and reconstructing childhood*, London: Falmer Press, p.35–59.

Jeffrey, B. and Woods, P. (2009) *Creative learning in the primary school*, London: Routledge.

Kalliala, M. (2011) 'Look at me! Does the adult truly see and respond to the child in Finnish day-care centres?' *European Early Childhood Education Research Journal*, 19(2), p.237–253. DOI: doi:10.1080/1350293X.2011.574411.

Kamii, C. and Ewing, J.K. (1996) 'Basing teaching on Piaget's constructivism', *Childhood Education*, 72(5), p.260–264. DOI: doi:10.1080/00094056.1996.10521862.

Kemmis, S. (2010) 'What is to be done? The place of action research', *Educational Action Research*, 18(4), p.417–427.

Kernick, D.P. (1998) 'Lies, damned lies, and evidence-based medicine', *The Lancet*, 351June 13(9118), p.1824. DOI: doi:10.1016/S0140–6736(05)78797–78793.

Kingdon, Z., Gourd, J. and Gasper, M. (2017) *Flourishing in the early years: Contexts, practices and futures*, Oxon: Routledge.

Kohan, W.O. (2013). 'Plato and Socrates: From educator of childhood to a childlike educator?' *Studies in Philosophy and Education*, 32(3), p.315–325.

Kristjansson, K. (2013) 'There is something about Aristotle: The pros and cons of Aristotelianism in contemporary moral education', *Journal of Philosophy of Education*, 48(1), p.48–68.

Kuyinia, A.B. and Alhassanb, A.R.K. (2016) 'Caring for blind parents: Cost to the education and well-being of children in Tamale, Ghana', *Journal of Social Work in Disability & Rehabilitation*, 15(1), p.22–41. DOI: doi:10.1080/1536710X.2016.1124252.

Lowe, R.J. (2012) 'Children deconstructing childhood', *Children and Society*, 26(4), p.269–279.

Lundy, L. (2007) '"Voice" is not enough: Conceptualising Article 12 of the United Nations Convention on the Rights of the Child', *British Educational Research Journal*, 33(6), p.927–942.

MacNaughton, G. (2005) *Doing Foucault in early childhood studies: Applying poststructural ideas*, London, England: Routledge.

Marshall, J. (2017) *Contemporary debates in education studies*, Abingdon: Routledge.

May, V. (2011) *Sociology of personal life*, Basingstoke: Palgrave.

Mayall, B. (2002). *Towards a sociology for childhood: Thinking from children's lives*, Buckingham: Open University Press.

McDade-Montez, E., Wallander, J. and Cameron, L. (2017) 'Sexualization in U.S. Latina and white girls' preferred children's television programs', *Original Article*, (77), p.1–15. DOI: doi:10.1007/s11199–11016–0692–0.

McDowall-Clark, R. (2017) *Exploring the contexts for early learning – Challenging the school readiness agenda*, Oxon: Routledge.

McLeod, N. (2016) 'Education as a philosophical endeavour', in: *Philosophy for children in teacher education: Creating the conditions for learning*, Oxon: Routledge.

McLeod, N. (2015) 'Reflecting on reflection: Improving teacher's readiness to facilitate participatory learning with young children', *Professional Development in Education*, 41(2), p.254–272.

McLeod, N. (2011) 'Exploring early years educators' ownership of language and communication knowledge and skills: a review of key policy and initial reflections on Every Child a Talker and its implementation', *Education 3–13 International Journal of Primary, Elementary and Early Years Education*, 39(4), p.429–445. DOI: doi:10.1080/03004271003776850.

McLeod, N., Wright, D., McCall, K. and Fuji, M. (2017) 'Visual rhythms: Facilitating young children's engagement at Tate Liverpool', *European Early Childhood Educational Research Journal*, 26(1), 1–15. DOI: doi:10.1080/1350293X.2017.1380888.

Millei, Z. (2005) 'The discourse of control: Disruption and Foucault in an early childhood classroom', *Contemporary Issues in Early Childhood*, 6(2), p.128–139.

Montessori, M. (1965) *Dr. Montessori's own handbook* (F. Simmonds Trans.), London: Schocken Books.

Moss, P. (2017) 'Power and resistance in early childhood education: From dominant discourse to democratic experimentalism', *Journal of Pedagogy*, 8(1), p.11–32. DOI: doi:10.1515/jped-2017–0001.

Moss, P. (2014) *Transformative change and real utopias in early childhood education: A story of democracy, experimentation and potentiality*, London: Routledge.

Moss, P. (2013) 'Beyond the investment narrative', *Contemporary Issues in Early Childhood*, 14 (4), p.370–372.

Moss, P. (2010) 'We cannot continue as we are: The educator in an education for survival', *Contemporary Issues in Early Childhood*, 11(1), p.8–19.

Moss, P. (2010) 'What is your image of the child?' *United Nations Educational Scientific and Cultural Organisation (UNESCO) Policy Brief on Early Childhood*, 47 / January – March 2010, p.1–2.

Moss, P. (2006) 'Early childhood institutions as loci of ethical and political practice', *International Journal of Educational Policy, Research and Practice: Reconceptualising Childhood Studies*, 7, p.127–136.

Muncie, J. and Goldson, B. (2006) *Comparative youth justice: Critical issues*, London: SAGE Publications.

Murray, J. (2015) 'Early childhood pedagogies: Spaces for young children to flourish', *Early Child Development and Care*, 185(11–12), p.1715–1732. DOI: doi:10.1080/03004430.2015.1029245.

Murris, K. (2013) 'The epistemic challenge of hearing a child's voice', *Studies in the Philosophy of Education*, 32, p.245–259.

Noddings, N. (2003) *Happiness and education*, Cambridge: Cambridge University Press.

Norling, M., Sandberg, A. and Almqvist, L. (2015) 'Engagement and emergent literacy practices in Swedish preschools', *European Early Childhood Education Research Journal*, 23(5), p.619–634.

Nussbaum, N. (2010) *Not for profit: Why democracy needs the humanities*, Princeton, NJ: Princeton University Press.

Nygård, M. (2017) 'The Norwegian Early Childhood Education and Care institution as a learning arena: Autonomy and positioning of the pedagogic recontextualising field with the increase in state control of ECEC content', *Nordic Journal of Studies in Educational Policy*, 3(3), p.230–240.

Ofsted (2017) *Bold beginnings: The reception curriculum in a sample of good and outstanding primary schools*, Manchester: The Office for Standards in Education, Children's Services and Skills.

Orlandi, K. (2014) 'Addressing the attrition between the conflicting influences experienced by teachers on the interface between Foundation Stage and Key Stage One', *Journal of Early Childhood Research*, 12(3), p.294–307.

Palmer, S. (2007) *Toxic childhood: How the modern world is damaging our children and what we can do about it*, London: Orion House Publishing.

Pascal, C. and Bertram, T. (2009) 'Listening to young citizens: The struggle to make real a participatory paradigm in research with young children', *European Early Childhood Education Research Journal*, 17(2), p.249–262. DOI: doi:10.1080/13502930902951486.

Piaget, J. (1965) *The language and thought of the child*, London: Routledge and Kegan Paul.

Piaget, J. (1954) *The construction of reality in the child*, New York: Basic Books. (Original work published 1937).

Piaget, J. (1952) *The origins of intelligence in children*, New York: Basic Books. (Original work published 1936).

Postman, N. (1983) *The disappearance of childhood*, London: W.H. Allen.

Prout, A. (2005) *The future of childhood*, London: Routledge.

Qvortrup, J., Bardy, M., Sgritta, G. and Wintersberger, H. (Eds.) (1994) *Childhood matters*, Vienna: European Centre.

Reed, M. and Canning, N. (2010) *Reflective practice in the early years*, London: SAGE.

Rinaldi, C. (2006) *In dialogue with Reggio Emilia: Listening, researching and learning*, London: Routledge.

Rokeach, M. (1973) *The nature of human values*, New York: The Free Press.

Roe, R.A. and Ester, P. (1999) 'Values and work: Empirical findings and theoretical perspective', *Applied Psychology: An International Review*, 48(1), p.1–21. DOI: doi:10.1080/026999499377646.

Rogoff, B. (2003) *The cultural nature of human development*, New York: Oxford University Press.

Sahlberg, P. (2016) 'Professional autonomy, trust and collaboration in educators' work', Philosophy of Education Society of Great Britain. Annual ConferenceNew College, Oxford1–3 April 2016. Retrieved on 26 May 2017 from: www.philosophy-of-education.org/dotAsset/bc4f09b5-a27f-4306-9966-3aa1fa2cf12c.pdf.

Sahlberg, P. (2010) 'Rethinking accountability in a knowledge society', *Journal of Educational Change*, 11(1), p.45–61.

Schön, D.A. (1987) *Educating the reflective practitioner toward a new design for teaching*, San Francisco, CA: Jossey-Bass.

Schön, D.A. (1983) *The reflective practitioner: How professionals think in action*, New York: Basic Books.

Schwartz, S.H. and Bilsky, W. (1987) 'Toward a universal psychological structure of human values', *Journal of Personality and Social Psychology*, 53(3), p.550–562.

Shahar, S. (1990) *Childhood in the Middle Ages*, London: Routledge.

Slater, A. and Tiggemann, M. (2016) 'Little girls in a grown up world: Exposure to sexualized media, internalization of sexualization messages, and body image in 6–9 year-old girls', *Body Image*, 18, p.19–22. Available from: https://doi.org/10.1016/j.bodyim.2016.04.004.

Smidt, S. (2011) *Introducing Bruner: A guide for practitioners and students in early years education*, Oxon: Routledge.

Smidt, S. (2009) *Introducing Vygotsky: A guide for practitioners and students in early years*, Oxon: Routledge.

Smith, R. (2010) *A universal child?*London: Palgrave Macmillan.

Stenhouse, L. (1983) 'The relevance of practice to theory', *Theory Into Practice*, 22(3), p.211–215.

Stenhouse, L. (1975) *An introduction to curriculum research and development*, London: Heinemann Educational.

Sorin, R. and Cook, J. (2005) 'Changing images of childhood: Reconceptualising early childhood practice', *International Journal of Transitions in Childhood*, 1(12), p.12–21.

Taylor Allen, A. (1988) 'Let us live with our children: Kindergarten movements in Germany and the United States, 1840–1914', *History of Education Quarterly*, 28(1), p.23–48.

United Nations (1989) *Convention on the rights of the child*, New York: United Nations.

Urban, M. (2017) 'We need meaningful, systematic evaluation, not a preschool PISA', *Global Education Review*, 4(2), p.18–24.

van Huizen, T. and Plantenga, J. (2015) *Universal child care and children's outcomes: A meta-analysis of evidence from natural experiments*, Utrecht: Utrecht School of Economics.

Wadsworth, B.J. (1996) *Piaget's theory of cognitive and affective development: Foundations of constructivism*, 5th ed, New York: Longman.

Wasmuth, H. and Nitecki, E. (2017) 'Global early childhood policies: The impact of the global education reform movement and possibilities for reconceptualization', *Global Education Review*, 4(2), p.1–17.

Whitty, G. and Wisby, E. (2007) 'Whose voice? An exploration of the current policy interest in pupil involvement in school decision-making', *International Studies in Sociology of Education*, 17(3), p.303–319. DOI: doi:10.1080/09620210701543957.

Wilkins, C. (2011) 'Professionalism and the post-performative teacher: New teachers reflect on autonomy and accountability in the English school system', *Professional Development in Education*, 37(3), p.389–409. DOI: doi:10:1080/19415257.2010.514204.

Winch, C. (2015) 'Assessing professional know-how', *Journal of Philosophy of Education*, 4(50), p.554–572.

Wood, E. and Atfield, J. (2005) *Play, learning and the early childhood curriculum*, London: Paul Chapman.

Woodrow, C. (1999) 'Revisiting images of the child in early childhood education: Reflections and considerations', *Australian Journal of Early Childhood*, 24(4), p.7.

Yelland, N. and Kilderry, A. (2005) 'Postmodernism, passion and potential for future childhoods', in: N. Yelland (Ed.) *Critical issues in early childhood education*, New York: Open University Press.

2

THE REFLEXIVE EDUCATOR

Naomi McLeod

In the context of developing a professional identity, I start by looking at what is understood by critical reflection and reflexivity, and why such approaches are so important within the current climate of today's western 'top down' approach to early childhood education, which prioritises outcomes and high stakes testing (Moss, 2017). I explore how being open to engaging in an internal process of critical reflection and reflexivity can enable a consciousness of personal views and beliefs and how this in turn can facilitate multi-layered complex connections, which open up new ways of seeing and being. To do this I make links with a Reflexive Framework (McLeod, 2015), which developed as part of my doctoral research, working collaboratively with early years teachers. This is offered as a practical set of principles for applying critical reflection in a sustainable way. Different theoretical models that explain the different dimensions of reflexivity are included. For example, Dewey's attitudes (1933a), Pollard's reflexive competencies (2002), Brookfield's lenses (1995), Schön's 'new epistemology' for praxis (1987) and Scharmer's Theory U (2009). In addition, by examining the life and experiences of Paulo Freire, connections are made with his ideas and thinking, specifically in relation to questioning unjust dominant discourses (or models) evident in early childhood educational structures and practices today (Smidt, 2014). By engaging in a process of critical reflection, I demonstrate how educators are then better positioned to take responsibility, make informed decisions about every day developmental and outcome-driven models of practice (Dahlberg and Moss, 2005; McLeod, 2011, 2015; McLeod, 2017). It then becomes possible to understand why different pedagogical approaches are more effective for enhancing participation with young children. The chapter concludes with prompts for reflection.

The need for a 'bottom-up' approach

In promoting quality early childhood education that empowers both children and educators, participatory approaches that focus on positive dispositions to learning and imaginative play are essential (Norling et al., 2015; Orlandi, 2014). This is in contrast to the focus on standardisation, a narrowing curriculum, high stakes testing and accountability for teachers and schools, which has resulted in a low risk, outcomes-based approach that is deficit in design and deficit in output. A detrimental effect of this outcome obsession is the 'objectification of the child to be controlled' (Wasmuth and Nitecki, 2017, p.5–6) rather than respected and valued.

Being aware of this top-down approach in early childhood practice is the first step in questioning dominant outcome-driven discourses. The need to be open to questioning is of paramount importance here. For example, questioning around 'what matters' rather than 'what works' is necessary alongside thoughts about 'what difference does my practice make' over 'what is the measurable effect'. In doing so, the process of learning needs to be valued rather than the outcomes. Looking at 'How can I improve' and asking 'What is right for children' shows a deeper self-awareness around quality rather than thinking about 'how the score can be improved'.

In response to the English government's troubling emphasis on evidence-based positivist research, Pascal and Bertram (2012, 2018) advocate the importance of collaborative, practice-led (bottom-up) inquiry, so educators are empowered in their knowledge of early childhood. As a way of authenticating the robustness of this, educators need to have a 'more astute awareness about power (politics) and a sharpened focus on values (ethics) as part of learning and teaching' (ibid.). At the heart of collaborative inquiry is the need for reflexivity (phronesis) (as discussed in Chapter 1). This mix of phronesis, praxis, ethics and power is referred to as 'praxeology' by Pascal and Bertram (2012, 2018), which enables an authentic worldview of modern early childhood: necessary for supporting deep self-awareness of the bigger picture and a change in habits of mind and being (Pascal and Bertram, 2012, 2018). In Chapter 10 we look at this in more detail.

Defining reflexivity and its relevance in the current climate

To become critically reflective or reflexive, we first need to understand what these terms mean and their value in the current climate of early childhood education. While reflection upon practice can help in terms of finding meaning and making sense of '*what*' is happening (Ghaye and Ghaye, 1998), for a deeper understanding there needs to be a willingness to be 'open' to internal questioning regarding 'how' and 'why'. In its basic form, critical reflection or reflexivity is a process that involves a metacognitive (reflexive) course of action. This requires an internal personal awareness and self-examination of what is thought and done, which can then result in a conscious change (Bolton, 2010; McLeod, 2015). It is an ongoing entangled fluid process involving the head, heart and will. It comprises becoming conscious of knowledge, which in turn facilitates multi-layered complex thought processes and connections with underpinning personal views, values, principles, assumptions and beliefs. This can open up new ways of seeing and offers insight around individuals' multiple identities and interpretations of situations (Smith, 2016). Put more simply, reflexivity offers insight around 'working out how our presence influences knowledge and actions' (Bolton, 2010, p.7). Most essentially is a willingness or readiness to question personal values, beliefs and assumptions so it is possible to examine the influence on actions (pedagogy practiced) (McLeod, 2015) and make appropriate changes (Derrida, 1999; Moon, 2008). Reflexivity then, in relation to early childhood educators (and the participation of young children), means having an awareness of issues of power and control (as considered in Chapter 1). This leads to a more deliberate scrutinising of the values and assumptions that underpin pedagogy as a whole, which can be done through viewing different 'lenses' (Brookfield, 1995). In a sense, this willingness to be open and question becomes an ongoing, fluid 'learning journey' of inter-relationships as part of professional development for empowering educators to see and do differently (Edwards et al., 2002; McLeod, 2011; Reed and Canning, 2010). Indeed, van Manen (1995) refers to reflexivity as 'finding oneself' through open questioning, which as an experience can be both difficult and uncomfortable.

Becoming a 'critically' reflective or reflexive professional as an agent of change (Price and Valli, 2005) can be gained by looking at difficulties or critical incidents as part of our daily practice and 'standing back' to see and appreciate different lenses (Etherington, 2004). However, my argument as a necessary starting point for critical reflection and reflexivity is for the need for open-mindedness and a readiness to see differences (McLeod, 2015). As Hassan (2005) notes, 'failure to see is the biggest barrier towards tackling our challenges' (p.6). In the current climate of marketisation and a product-driven view of education, often associated with Western practice (Moss, 2008), reflexivity through questioning, then, offers an alternative approach that has the capacity to empower educators as it enables an awareness and understanding of *why* different approaches are ethically appropriate.

As Dimova and Loughran (2009) note, open-mindedness requires being ready to listen to alternative perspectives. This means being prepared to hear views and ideas that may be contrary to our own and being able to admit that a prior belief may be incorrect particularly in relation to pedagogy (Rinaldi, 2006). To start this 'opening process' there is the need for authentic readiness (Dewey, 1933; McLeod, 2015, 2017) by which I mean a genuine willingness to be open to developing self-awareness.

As explained in the Reflexive Framework as follows (McLeod, 2015), 'readiness' was acknowledged as the first necessary step by the group of teachers who participated in a research project with me. The focus was on 'critical reflection as a tool for developing pedagogical participation with young children' (McLeod, 2011). While it was not until the end of the research process that this realisation became apparent, they felt very strongly that 'readiness' was the key to becoming critically reflective. For this reason, it is the first principle as part of the framework that I discuss next. I have included it here so different models and ideas about critical reflection can be compared and contrasted.

Introducing McLeod's reflexivity framework

In 2011, I carried out a participatory action learning project that involved working with a group of early years teachers who were interested in exploring how to enhance the participation of young children in their learning. Together we engaged in a series of open, collaborative workshops (McLeod, 2012) (where uncertainty could be embraced, and risks could be taken; for example, sharing uncertainties about participatory practice) (McCormack and Boomer, 2007; McIntosh, 2010). The teachers began to examine the influences on their views, beliefs and understandings in relation to listening, consulting and participating with young children. Over a six-month period of working collaboratively, the teachers developed new ways of 'seeing and being' (Kemmis, 2010). They felt part of something that mattered to them that made a difference for the children they taught and for themselves both personally and professionally. As part of the research process, nine reflective features or 'steps' as we initially referred to them developed. These are presented in Figures 2.1a and 2.1b. Together we considered whether participatory practice could be sustained through a process of critical reflection by embedding the framework as part of daily practice.

Figures 2.1a and 2.1b are the same framework, just in a different format to accommodate different preferences.

Reciprocal Relationship

- **Readiness** to be **open,** self-aware and conscious of own practice
- **Recalling a critical incident** accurately as part of own practice
- **Recognising personal** views, biases, assumptions, understandings, (stand back, after and during) (*on, in*)
- **Reflecting** from a **child's / another person's** perspective. What are their feelings? How do you know?
- **Reviewing together** comparing own understandings
- **Relating to reading** / research
- **Reappraising the relevance** and implications for own practice
- **Responding** with **appropriate changes**
- **Remembering** the **benefits** so critical reflection is sustainable.....

FIGURE 2.1A Reflexive Framework
(McLeod, 2015)

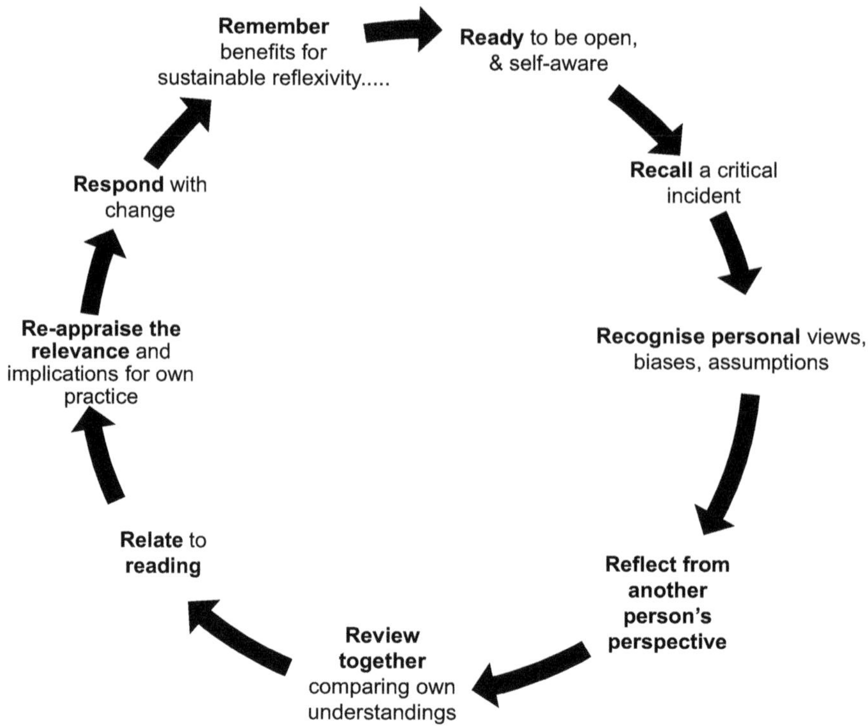

FIGURE 2.1B Reflexive Framework
(McLeod, 2015)

Details of how the framework emerged are explained next.

The project took place over a six-month period and involved myself and a small group of teachers engaging in a series of weekly collaborative action learning workshops. It was not a 'quick fix' to achieving changes in practice, but rather an approach that enabled self-awareness, internal questioning and a deconstruction of entangled assumptions around the purpose of education in the context of their work. By engaging in continuous ongoing interactions, a new concientisation, personal awareness and appreciation around cultures of participatory learning developed (Karlsson Häikiö, 2018; McCormack and Boomer, 2007). It was an opportunity that nurtured ownership and understanding of their own situation, which in turn enhanced their self-confidence and personal efficacy. Consequently, there was a reconfiguration and shifts in habits of mind, enabling an empowerment to make necessary ethical changes as part of their teaching (Lange, 2004; Taylor, 2007).

As Hassan (2005, p.6) points, it can be hard to perceive the whole but, 'when we don't have a picture of the whole, when we're not even questioning what part of the picture we're seeing, we end up arguing strenuously from our own position of "truth"'. We are often unable to understand why others do not see the same point of view as ourselves, when actually the reality is that we need to critically reflect on self, other and relationships in order to see the whole structure that we are part of (Lange, 2004).

At the end of each hour-long action learning workshop, together we agreed on a follow-up task that involved and enabled the teachers to question different aspects or critical incidents that occurred as part of their practice. One example included disagreements between children and the expectation for the teacher to sort things out. Alternatively, another example looked at adults serving children at lunch time rather than children serving themselves. Another example involved questioning prioritising planned activities with pre-determined outcomes.

Teachers were encouraged to keep a reflective journal that captured the essence of their critical incidents using the following guidance:

- Recall: a critical incident that occurs as part of your practice
- Recognise: personal views, assumptions, understandings that this is based on
- Reflect: from the child's / another person's perspective: what is their experience?
- Reappraise: what this shows you

The intention was for the teachers to use the emerging features as a structure for keeping a reflective journal in relation to their practice. The focus was on children's participation (Moon 2006, 2008). Through their journal writing and engagement in the reflective and collaborative nature of the workshops, they became more self-aware and open to change. Their ability to see personal influences on their practice and appreciate the child's experience was enhanced. Quite early in the project, the reading I provided for the teachers offered a sense of purpose and authority in relation to justifying participation with young children (Eun, 2011; Givvin and Santagata, 2011; McLeod, 2011).

As the project developed, and the process of collaborating and sharing together was valued by the teachers as protected time, so *Reviewing together* was added as a principle for critical reflection.

The first necessary feature or principle of being 'ready' was only added towards the end of the project when we reflected together on the essential nature of being open and aware of the influence of past experiences on practice (Scharmer, 2009). Together, the teachers became more expert at evaluating and *Reappraising the relevance* of their teaching in relation to participatory learning for young children (Shier, 2001). They became more reflexive in relation to their own practice recognising personal challenges and the need for risk taking as a means of enabling higher levels of participation for the children as part of their practice (Shier, 2001). Consequently, *Responding* was added as a principle. Finally, at the end of the study, *Remembering* the benefits and the empowered impact was important for maintaining participation as part of future teaching.

The evolving features were a practical way for supporting the teachers in their reflexive journey and also acted as a framework around which they each constructed written reflections as part of a journal. As Barad (2007) notes, there was an awareness that ethics, epistemology and ontology cannot be separated when they are engaged with knowledge, production and with the world.

The *framework* therefore developed as part of ongoing engagement by the teachers and myself in an organic, open and reflexive research process. The steps are offered as a way of supporting other early childhood educators, in questioning their practice and becoming critically reflective (Corbin and Holt, 2005, p.51). The arrow represents 'Reciprocal Relationships' as a 'golden thread' that connects the process as a whole rather than a particular pattern that should be followed. It demonstrates the ongoing entangled, fluid process of becoming conscious of knowledge, which in turn facilitates multi-layered complex thought processes and connections with underpinning personal views, values, principles, assumptions and beliefs (Karlsson Häikiö, 2017). It also demonstrates how the head, heart and will are central in valuing reflexivity as a process. In doing so, the framework should not be seen as a prescriptive set of criteria to be followed rigorously. The process of becoming reflexive can begin with any of the features and for these reasons, the following diagram (Figure 2.1c) to some extent reflects the entangled, multi-layed nature of the framework.

In Chapter 3 I explain how this framework has been slightly adapted to reflect the reflexive process I have engaged in as part of writing this book. A revised version of the framework includes the need to not just reflect from human perspectives, but also to value the non-human lens.

FIGURE 2.1C Reflexive framework (McLeod, 2015)

Examples of the teachers' experience of becoming reflexive are summarised as follows using poetic haikus. They capture the essence of their experience before, during and after the research project.

Watching in the known and safe (before the project)
Collaborative spaces (during the project)
Opening up and letting go (moving forwards)

Purposeful movement (before the project)
Authentic knowing (during the project)
Personal transformations (moving forwards)

These indicate the empowering and transformative nature of becoming critically reflective and the new possibilities as part of future practice (Dewey, 1933). There is a sense of real purpose and hope (Freire, 1996, 1972, 1970) as different perspectives are valued (Brookfield, 1995; Scharmer, 2009). Rather than seeing targets as the driver of their practice, the teachers valued the participatory process more (Moss, 2010). As one of the participants said, '*I love where the project has brought us . . . . I love the freedom we've found*'. Another participant commented, '*I think that until you go through this process you don't realise how important it is*'. Through the collaborative process, they began to recognise the influence of personal experience and background as significant (Ashworth, 2004) and the importance of questioning power imbalances so that they could begin to examine habits of mind and being (Hassan, 2005; McLaren, 1993; Scharmer, 2009). As another teacher noted, '*Once we recognise our own values, then we can see the child's perspective and how they feel*'.

In this way, learning is a continuous changing process that is rhizomatic and transformational (Karlsson Häikiö, 2017, 2018; Mezirow, 1997). It can take different unpredictable routes, becoming a challenge for the educator who needs to relate to curricula and other governing documents.

Another participant teacher recognised personal influences and the consequential challenges: '*I need to make sure I take the risk because that definitely benefits the children*'. Here the teacher sees herself as a potential barrier to participation. While they valued the importance of following children's interests, they felt restricted by the time available due to curriculum pressures attributed by Ofsted and local authorities (Dimova and Loughran, 2009; Tickell, 2011). They became aware of the value of participatory agentic practice for both the children and themselves. They commented how, '*Learning expands and explodes; it's huge*'. Together they identified the following collective benefits for the children:

- More interaction and discussion between the children
- More making sense of learning and seeing real life learning
- Enjoyment and excitement
- Children thinking together and sharing their ideas which provided a sense of self-worth and empowerment
- Taking turns and supporting each other

- Children's ideas valued and not dominated by adults
- Children saw their ideas develop from beginning to end
- Learning was valuable and meaningful
- Increased self-esteem and self-worth
- Children understood themselves
- Children feel valued
- Children seeing adults are interested
- Children's delight
- Achieving the '*deeper scale points*'
- Children becoming independent and responsible for their decisions

There was a close association between the adult taking risks and the children benefiting. By the end of the project the teachers viewed the Early Years Foundation Stage framework (DCSF, 2008) as a means for supporting participation rather than a means to an end. The importance of 'letting go' (Scharmer, 2009) of paradigms of the past was reinforced, and being comfortable with an understanding of what is good or what makes for human flourishing (Kemmis, 2010). One teacher noted, '*I can see the benefits for the children, and for us and I can justify why*'. An indication of how the benefits far outweighed the barriers became transparent when she said, *'I love where the project has brought us. I love that you know we dedicate time to just being with the children. I love the freedom we've found'*.

In this way, Lenz Taguchi considers that in becoming reflexive, our self-understanding and identity can be transformed in an ongoing material-discursive co-constitution (2012, p.18, 42–43). Such a postmodern transformative view of learning challenges the traditional view of children as having to adapt to adult expectations, and instead views children as agentic in the way they are able to challenge the adult and so create change that is dynamic and in motion (Dahlberg, Moss and Pence, 1999). In this way the child can become uncomfortable for a controlling adult.

Collectively the creation of McLeod's Framework (2015) demonstrates reflexivity in practice. The teachers learning was transformed, which in turn led to the children's active participation being enhanced.

Having shared how this framework developed, the chapter continues by building on the core principles and requirements of reflexivity for openness. Different theoretical perspectives about 'how' to become critically reflective are explored.

Dewey's attitudes for becoming critically reflective

John Dewey's (1929) theory of knowing and his concept of reflection (1933a) together offer practical ways for promoting thinking about the purpose of education in practice. Dewey's concept of reflection is a purposeful and conscious act, involving a reconstruction of an experience by looking and thinking back over one's practice. According to Dewey, critically reflective action is 'careful consideration of any belief or supposed form of knowledge in light of the grounds that support it and the further consequence to which it leads' (Dewey, 1933, p.9). In layman's terms, this means questioning why different pedagogical approaches are used and an awareness of the implications. For Dewey (1933a), critical reflection involves a state of uncertainty or a problem that results in questioning to make sense of the concern. Loughran (2006) notes how the word 'problem' can have negative connotations for educators associated with mistakes, and instead suggests seeing a problem as an opportunity or a puzzle that can promote curiosity and questioning.

Dewey (1933a), explains how critical (or reflexive) thinking supports the purpose of education as a process for behaving wisely, so practice is meaningful and purposeful. Connections between actions and consequences are made so educators learn from experience, therefore developing further knowledge and improving problem-solving skills. As such, Dewey's understanding of critical reflection starts by seeing a situation as a cause for concern or a problem with a variety of open possibilities. This is then considered in light of previous experiences or understandings with an intentional and committed action, for behaving morally 'for the good of humankind' (praxis) (Kemmis, 2010, p.419). At the heart of this ethical and socially just perspective is the metacognitive (reflexive) course of action that Bolton (2010) refers to. Dewey's attitudes (1933a) offer a practical way of supporting the application of critical reflection and behaving wisely in relation to early childhood education today. At the heart of this process are three essential attitudes: firstly an open-minded attitude, secondly a responsible attitude and thirdly a wholehearted attitude.

An open-minded attitude

For Dewey (1933a), open-mindedness involves an 'active desire to listen to more sides than one' (p.30) and in doing so question the reliability of the source so that alternative can be considered. At the heart of this initial attitude is the requirement to acknowledge the fact that our 'dearest' beliefs and values may possibly be wrong. As Hassan (2005) recognises, this is a very complex and challenging requirement, mainly because of the lifetime of biases and beliefs attached to our own perceptions. In this context, Scharmer (2009) refers to the 'blind spot', which is the part we often do not see or recognise because of our inability to see 'the inner place (source) from which our attention and actions originate' (p.464). Still today, Dewey's (1933a) attitudes are used and viewed as essential by many current writers on critical reflection such as Moon (2008), Pollard (2002) and Brookfield (1995), who refer to Dewey's work in creating the right attitude for critical reflection. As part of Western culture, Levinas raises a concern over the danger of 'not seeing' and the tendency to associate or turn any new knowledge into something familiar, rather than seeing and appreciating fresh and different ideas (Critchley, Peperzak and Bernasconi,1996).

As Scharmer (2009, p.xiv) explains:

> When we listen, we usually hear very little other than what we have heard before . . . . [We] selectively hear only what we recognise, interpret what we hear based on our past views and feelings and draw conclusions much like those we have drawn before.

Hassan echoes the words of Scharmer in his recognition that 'failure to see is the biggest barrier towards tackling our challenges' (2005, p.6). The requirement to be open also resonates with Brookfield and his four lenses of critical reflection (1995), which are explored a little later.

A responsible attitude

Taking responsibility is Dewey's second attitude necessary for valuing education as praxis (as an intentional action with a moral intent). For example, taking responsibility can result in making informed decisions about everyday developmental and outcome-driven models of practice in early childhood education (Dahlberg and Moss, 2005; McLeod, 2011, 2015). In this way, praxis is an intentional moral action and as such embodies a commitment to human well-being and the search for truth and respect for others (Bernstein, 1983).

A wholehearted attitude

The third of Dewey's necessary attitudes is wholeheartedness, which he suggested required energy and enthusiasm. As Boydston and Rorty (2008, p.136) note, 'there is no greater enemy of effective thinking than divided interest'. A genuine enthusiasm that operates as an intellectual force involves a passion that drives a deep passion, determination or a commitment. Shier (2001) refers to this as an obligation to follow through with an action. In maintaining such a wholehearted attitude, Moon (2008) emphasises the importance of appropriate conditions or a supportive environment. Given the current climate of externally imposed political high stakes testing and outcome-driven pressures, Wilkins (2015) acknowledges how this can prevent educators from asking open questions about the purpose of education (Hassan, 2005; Marcos, Miguel and Tillema, 2009; Scharmer, 2009). While Moon (2008) acknowledges the value of Dewey's attitudes (of being open, responsible and wholehearted) as crucial is developing a critically reflective approach, she also recognises the complexities and associated difficulties of committing to Dewey's attitudes.

Pollard's competencies for nurturing critical reflection

In relation to Dewey's concept of reflexivity, Andrew Pollard (2002) offers three types of competence necessary for education as phronesis. These are: i) empirical competence, ii) analytical competence and iii) evaluative competence. Empirical competence relates to being aware of two types of observations: i) objective, being what is seen, and ii) subjective, what we feel or think. Being aware of both of these is important but difficult when enquiring into our own practice (Davies and Artaraz, 2009; Hassan, 2005). Often the two are connected in that our feelings about what is important will influence what we see as important and therefore objective. Deconstructing these influences is therefore key in terms of becoming self-aware (reflexive). Next, analytical competence relates to deciding how to interpret observations in context (for example, in relation to participation with young children or promoting democratic practice). As Dewey (1933a) notes, the focus should involve something that we are uncertain about or a feature that we would like to explore further. Thirdly, evaluative competence refers to being aware of one's own values in order to understand and appreciate the experience of others. Only by being aware of our own views, biases and assumptions in relation to knowledge can we then begin to see and value those of others and see afresh (Clough and Nutbrown, 2007; Davies and Artaraz, 2009). As already discussed, this can be difficult given personal cultural experiences that become embodied (Leitch, 2006; Rinaldi, 2006).

As part of the reflexive principles (McLeod, 2015) (and ongoing research I engage in), the influence of educators' personal views, biases and assumptions on practice is recognised, and included as part of the framework. This notion is explained next as part of Brookfield's lenses.

Brookfield's lenses for critical reflection

Drawing on Stephen Brookfield (1995), four distinct but interconnecting 'lenses' are presented as necessary for educators to achieve the level of insight, critical reflection and wisdom that Aristotle (1925) and Dewey (1933a) refer to. The four lenses of reflection are i) personal self-reflection, ii) reflection from a child's perspective, iii) the lens provided by colleagues as critical friends and finally iv) viewing practice through the lens of literature.

The most distinguishing feature of Brookfield's first lens, indeed of the reflective process as a whole, is the essential requirement to seek out underpinning assumptions (Brookfield, 1995; Davies and Artaraz, 2009), which he notes as 'taken for granted beliefs about the world, and our place within it' (Brookfield, 1995, p.2). Such views are so obvious to us as that we do not see the need to explicitly be aware of them or articulate them. For example, in England the focus on literacy and numeracy in both primary and early childhood education is so common that it is often viewed as normal and thus not questioned and sit as part of our sub-conscious. In such instances, Brookfield uses the term 'hunting' to reinforce the need for a self-appraisal so that an awareness of biases and embedded beliefs can be made explicit (Hassan, 2005). Unknowingly, it is these that give purpose to who we are and what we do. Failure to uncover an awareness of underpinning influences creates a superficial engagement with critical reflection and can result in a fragmented understanding of the true value of critical reflection (Brookfield, 1995).

As Marcos, Miguel and Tillema (2009) warn, this tends to be the norm today and is visible when attention is given to *'what'* reflection is, rather than *'how'* to embed it as a meaningful process. Once a genuine openness and willingness to examine personal beliefs and assumptions has been nurtured, it is possible to view practice from a child's perspective, and likewise value the reality of other lenses such as a parent's perspective. As Brookfield (1995) stresses, seeing 'through a child's eyes' makes the educator aware of those actions or assumptions that either confirm or challenge existing power relationships in the classroom. Likewise, Ashworth (2004) stresses how a lack of attunement to the 'other' person (such as a child / parent) as part of dialogue has a subverting effect on participation. While Ashworth (2004) recognises the risk that this can involve for educators in terms of fears over losing control, appreciating an experience from a child or parent's perspective can really demonstrate the value of critical reflection and new insight. For example, Western early childhood practice often involves expecting children to sit on a carpet area with their legs crossed, listening to a teacher for considerable lengths of time. By simply considering how this feels (and trying it out ourselves), it soon becomes clear how uncomfortable it is after a few minutes. With additional questioning around 'why' this has become the norm, it becomes apparent how 'copied' expectations are passed from one professional without any questioning of power imbalances. Only by asking children (and parents) how they feel about an experience do we get a true insight. For this reason, McLeod's (2015) framework encourages 'Reflecting' '*on*' and '*in*' a child's, or / and another person's experiences so an alternative and often different perspective is appreciated.

The third lens offered by Brookfield (1995) for supporting the process of becoming critically reflective involves sharing with colleagues as critical friends. During conversations about various challenges associated with practice, incidents can be viewed differently. In this way, sharing becomes an opportunity to see practice in a new light that perhaps previously was hidden (that is, if educators are ready and open to new ways of seeing). The value of collaboration is recognised and included as part of McLeod's reflexivity framework (2015) as part of 'Reviewing together' and sharing personal understandings about practice. Likewise Ashworth (2004) stresses the need for attunement to the other person as part of dialogue so there is not a subverting effect. During reflective conversations about practice, colleagues therefore need to be very sensitive about aspects of each other's practice that were previously hidden. At the heart of this process, a trusting, safe, open environment is essential for facilitating consciousness, self-awareness and new ways of being for children, and educators alike. In Chapters 3 and 10 these conditions are explored further.

Another lens offered by Brookfield (1995), Dewey (1933a) and Hofkins (2009) essential for embedding reflexivity is '*the act of teaching together with its attendant theory and discourse*' (Hofkins, 2009, p.10). The consideration of practice in relation to 'literature' can support and enhance understanding and enable educators to justify decisions about different approaches as part of their practice, which adds a dimension of ownership and empowerment (McLeod, 2011; Volpe, 1981). In addition, Moss (2014) claims that in order for teachers in England to regain ownership over what happens in the classroom, there is a need for practitioners to reflect on the more holistic approaches from European perspectives using literature as a source of informing knowledge and understanding. According to Roberts (2013), Friere notes how our understanding of the world is enhanced or liberated by reading, which is further enriched by dialogue or conversation. As already identified, this relies on educators being open to questioning in the first place, let alone finding time for reading and reflection (Dimova and Loughran, 2009). Given the enhanced understanding, empowerment and sense of ownership that can come from relating practice to relevant reading and research, this is also included in McLeod's Framework (2015) as necessary for becoming reflexive.

POINTS FOR REFLECTION

- Dewey's attitudes include being 'open', 'responsible' and 'wholehearted'
- What are the underpinning beliefs and values of your ECE practice / philosophy?
- Are you open to new ways of seeing and being?

The roots of Dewey's (1933) approach to critical reflection remained until the 1960s when there was a re-conceptualisation by Schön in relation to experience and application in practice. Schön built on and extended Dewey's foundations of critical reflection in his focus on 'action' so that a reflexive approach was promoted. The next part of this chapter examines the legacy of Schön and his optimistic proposal for self-reflection as a powerful tool for improving daily practice (Dimova et al., 2009). It is only through a genuine openness and willingness to examine personal beliefs, values and experiences that we are able to put ourselves in the position of 'another' (such as a child or another adult) and appreciate other perspectives.

Schön's practical application of reflection

The influence of Aristotle's philosophical thinking about educational praxis can be seen in Schön's (1983, 1987) work, in particular the requisite attitudes necessary for a practical application of critical reflection. Schön's (1983) views on critical reflection were closely linked with the notion of self-reflection and an optimistic vision of the power of individuals to better understand their work and improve their practice. For Schön, critical reflection was a medium for the acquisition of professional knowledge: a means of understanding 'tacit knowledge' (1983, p.54), ordinary practical knowledge (knowing-in-action) which he claimed could be understood through two forms of reflection which were central to his thinking: reflection-*in*-action, and reflection-*on*-action.

Reflection-*on*-action is comparable to Dewey's concept of reflection as a purposeful and conscious act, a reconstruction of an experience by looking and thinking back over one's practice.

Reflection-*in*-action was what Schön referred to as a new epistemology of practice, that would stand the question of professional knowledge on its head (1983, p.xi). According to Schön (1983), reflection-*in*-action is more about 'thinking on your feet, keeping your wits about you, and learning by doing suggest [ing] not only that we can think about doing but that we can think about doing something while doing it' (p.54). Reflection-*in*-action involves consideration of experiences, connecting with personal feelings, and attending to theories used as part of practice. In addition, reflection-*in*-action also entails building new understandings to inform personal actions in the situation that unfolds so that:

> The practitioner allows himself to experience surprise, puzzlement, or confusion in a situation, which he finds uncertain or unique. He reflects on the phenomenon before him, and on the prior understandings, which have been implicit in his behaviour. He carries out an experiment, which serves to generate both a new understanding of the phenomenon and a change in the situation.
>
> *(Schön, 1983, p.68)*

As such, reflection-*in*-action is about how educators create new knowledge as part of dealing with and appreciating problematic situations in action. Grimmett (1988, p. 13) notes how it is the emphasis on the 'crucible of action' that sets Schön's (1983) work apart. The process of reflection-*in*-action was an idealised one and rare according to Schön. In proposing his 'new epistemology', Schön claimed what he called a 'convergence of meaning' (1987, p.99). By convergence of meaning, Newman (1999) clarifies Schön's interpretation of openness as an agreed meaning of what is understood as part of communication between the master and the student (or in the case of this book, the educator and the child). This depends on and occurs as a result of dialogue having three essential features; i) communication has to take place in context; ii) there is an understanding of language consisting of interwoven words and actions; and iii) reciprocal reflection-*in*-action on tacit knowing-*in*-action (Schön, 1987). Schön (1983) considered that when the educator experienced something unexpected or unfamiliar, through 'convergence of meaning', reflection-*in*-action led to a rethink in-action so that there was an 'on the spot experiment of trying out new actions to explore newly intended phenomena or occurrences' (p.28).

An example from the research project from which the Reflexive Framework emerged is provided as follows.

> Children in a Reception class (aged 4 and 5 years old) are invited by the teacher to come and sit on the carpet in preparation for a literacy input by the teacher. Three boys stay seated at the play-dough table close to the carpet when all of the other children are sat on the carpet. The teacher asks the children again if they are ready to sit with the other children (i: communication takes place in context). The children tell the teacher that they'd rather

> stay at the play dough table. They are all engaged in using the dough. The teacher recalls how sometimes when sitting on the carpet these 3 children are easily distracted and find it hard to concentrate. They tend to fidget. The teacher wonders whether the boys will engage more effectively as part of the literacy activity if they stay sitting at the dough table, so she does not pursue her request for them to join the other children any further. (ii: here there is an understanding of language consisting of interwoven words and actions). As the teacher continues with the rest of the children, she notices how the 3 children continue to play with the dough but also participate in the whole group literacy session. They listen and turn their bodies so they can see the illustrations as part of the story. As the teacher asks different questions, the 3 boys are keen to respond and give their views. The teacher realises that the physical engagement with the dough supports their concentration and engagement in the literacy activity, (iii: reciprocal reflection-*in*-action on tacit knowing-*in*-action).
>
> *(Schön, 1987)*

An affirmation of these actions enabled changes to be made for the better, for both the child and the educator, as Kemmis says 'for the good of humankind' (2010). In this way 'convergence of meaning' involves asking 'How do I know?' or 'How can I be sure?' in relation to interpreting dialogue accurately. In this example, the teacher could quite easily have misinterpreted the boys' choice to stay at the dough table, perhaps misbehaving or even as defiant behaviour. Accommodating the boys' needs and allowing them to remain at the table could have resulted in other children wanting to join them. This is where critical reflection then in relation to early childhood educators (and the participation of young children) involves having an awareness of issues of power and control. In this way, Schön's 'convergence of meaning' acts consciously and is collectively develops *wisdom,* what Aristotle referred to as *phronesis.*

Schön's reflection-*on*-action and reflection-*on*-action as a new epistemology is embedded in McLeod's Framework (Recognising personal influences, and Reflecting (*on, in*) a child's / another person's experience from their perspective). By asking 'How do I know' or 'How can I be sure what a child's experience involves', Schön's 'convergence of meaning' is visible, and in doing so, raises awareness of issues of power and control.

In reality, van Manen (1995) is dubious about how realistic reflexivity is as part of teaching, and explains how attempting to do just this can become an 'obstacle' to teaching effectively (p.39). Instead, the question for van Manen is 'where and how does reflection enter the reality of the pedagogical lifeworld' (1995, p.36). Similarly, Levinas also queries the reality of Schön's reflection-*in*-action over concerns that the unfamiliar is taken (by the educator) and turned into the same or familiar (Critchley, et al., 1996). Likewise, Gilroy (1993) is dubious about the reality of reflecting-*in*-action and his interpretation that 'the knowledge produced by critical reflection can only be recognised by further reflection, which in turn requires reflection to recognise it as knowledge, and so on' (p.138). In essence, Gilroy is saying educators need time to stand back and reflect on action before responding. In this way Schön's new epistemology of practice, through convergence of meaning, is challenging because the educator has to recognise or interpret what is 'known'. In many respects, Schön draws on Aristotle's different forms of knowledge and the educator who aspires to be more than a technical worker (Moss, 2010): a process that draws on ancient wisdom and multiple forms of knowing offering an authentic connection with the self and a shift in awareness. As already noted, this process begins with a willingness to question personal values, beliefs and assumptions so we can examine the influence on actions (pedagogy practiced). This willingness to be 'open' and to question, ultimately determines our ability to welcome difference and new knowledge so we are 'ready' to change (Derrida, 1999; Moon, 2008).

Next, Theory U (Figure 2.2; Scharmer, 2009) is presented as an alternative model for exploring the complex and challenging internal processes involved as part of being ready and open to engaging in a process of self-awareness (Hassan, 2005).

This figure indicates, how an open mind, heart and will is the nucleus for embodied readiness; essential for critical reflection. It is a journey that can be uneasy and involve feeling uncomfortable as part of a reflexive process of coming to know oneself (Lincoln and Guba, 2000).

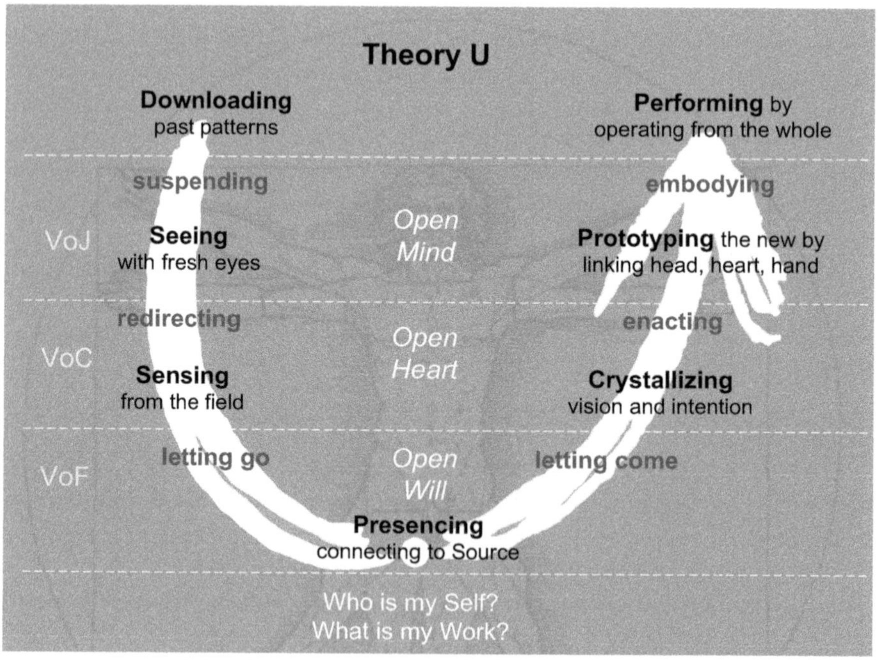

FIGURE 2.2 Theory U: Becoming open and ready

An open mind

Alongside McLeod's (2015) recognition of the complexities of being open and the difficulties because of a lifetime of biases and beliefs, Hassan (2005) clarified the added complexity which he refers to as 'the voice of judgement' (VoJ) which can cause a person to play safe, follow the imposed rules (Scharmer, 2009, p. 42; Wilkins, 2011) and not take risks, which as a result can prevent a participatory teaching approach. For example, in the context of early childhood education in England, this might involve educators not questioning the appropriateness of outcome-driven curriculum and high stakes testing.

An open heart

Having an 'open heart' entails accessing personal emotions which relate to empathising with others and a person's ability to see from another perspective or 'through the eyes' of someone else (Scharmer, 2009). This is central to critical reflection and is also central in helping teachers to explore and understand their identities (Hargreaves, 2001; Nias, 1996; Noddings, 1996). While emotion can distort critical reflection and the need that teachers can feel to be right (De Bono, 1983), cultivating an open heart by being vulnerable and honest, can promote trust. Here Scharmer (2009) warns of the voice of cynicism (VoC) or scepticism, which can prevent a person putting his/herself in a vulnerable position such as being open and honest. For example, while early childhood educators in England may question the inappropriateness of an outcome-driven curriculum and high stakes testing, the feelings and experiences of children may not be fully appreciated and / or personal fears over not complying with expectations may dominate. Recognising the value of emotions strengthens the significance of an open heart through self-awareness and the sometimes unquestioning acceptance of life experience and assumptions.

An open will

An open will refers to 'letting go' and being true and honest. This is crucial but ultimately depends on being able to drop the 'habitual self' (Scharmer, 2009, p.41). Often 'the voice of fear' (VoF) can block an open will, for example the fear of being in the minority and not complying. As Scharmer (2009) outlines the journey to openness is 'always the road less travelled' (p.42) because of the complex and difficult inner work it involves in relation to self. This embodied openness is situated at the heart of a series of fluid spaces which facilitate the uncomfortable process of coming to know oneself. In essence, as educators we need to be ready to take responsibility and examine daily practice in terms of political influences and ethical values (McLeod, 2015; Pascal and Bertram, 2012, 2018) so we can make informed decisions about accepted developmental and outcome models and respond appropriately (praxis). For example, recognising the inappropriateness of planned outcomes and high stakes testing as part of early childhood education in

England can result in educators making an informed decision to value and adopt more ethical and participatory pedagogical approaches as part of practice (Dahlberg and Moss, 2005; McLeod, 2011, 2012, 2015). In response to this crisis of domination in education and in an attempt to think differently and reject the dominant discourse that prevails, the question asked by Ball (2016) (cited in Moss, 2017) is 'what kind of self, what kind of subject have we become, and how might we be otherwise?' (p.5). Moss (2017) calls for 'an openness to uncertainty, unpredictability and wonder' (p.20) for where there is a will and a desire, there is power, and 'where there is power, there is resistance' (Foucault, 1978, p.95). In this respect, Smidt (2014) explains how Paulo Freire's thoughts and legacy are particularly relevant when questioning 'what sort of educator we want to be' and what is important about learning as this will influence the pedagogical approach we take with children.

By examining the life and experiences of Paulo Freire, connections can be made with his ideas and his thinking particularly in relation to questioning unjust dominant discourses that are embedded in everyday early childhood educational structures and practices (Smidt, 2014).

Freire and his 'consciousness' theory

In the hope that children grow up with a sense of values that can contribute to making positive changes for society, Paulo Freire's education system is highly relevant as an inspiration for early childhood educators. He is one of the most significant educators during the twentieth century, best known for his support of critical pedagogy for empowering educators. Paulo Freire (1921–1997) as a Brazilian grew up experiencing the Great Depression of the 1930s and experienced first-hand the effects of poverty and hunger on his life and his education.

> I didn't understand anything because of my hunger. I wasn't dumb. It wasn't lack of interest. My social condition didn't allow me to have an education. Experience showed me once again the relationship between social class and knowledge.
>
> *(Freire,* Pedagogy of the oppressed *cited in Gadotti, 1994, p.5)*

As the economic crisis worsened, it became increasingly difficult for his parents to feed and clothe the family and Paulo became acquainted with hardship and extreme poverty around him (Smidt, 2014). He experienced first-hand the lack of empathy that the world had for the frail and needy. Sadly, his father died when he was just 13 years old. This combined with the effects of poverty and the effects that his mother experienced as she attempted to find work in a society hostile to women working outside the home really impacted his failure at school. It was this experience however that really informed his passion and his outrage over how the poor were oppressed and kept ignorant to maintain the status quo (Roberts, 2013). He became acquainted with the daily struggles of life as he watched poor women washing not only their own family's clothes, but also those of more wealthy families. But it was during this time that he learned to play football and swim in the river with the other poor children (Smidt, 2014).

When the economic crisis ended, Freire finished his secondary education and went on to study law and philosophy, more specifically phenomenology, and the psychology of language. As Smidt (2014) highlights, over time the Brazil slave population had been the largest in the world and was central to the colonial economy. Freire began to look at the issue of adult literacy among the poor and rather than practicing law, he dedicated his life to helping educate the very poorest illiterate people of Brazil. He understood how learning to read promotes awareness and liberation. For Freire, real reading is done critically and questioned (through dialogue) so that it is made sense of (Smidt, 2014). Freire referred to 'reading the word as reading the world', that is, our understanding of the world is enhanced or liberated by reading. We become conscious through reading, and this is enhanced by dialogue or conversation (Roberts, 2013).

Freire's (1970, 1994) approach to education is predominantly informed by the need to develop a consciousness or 'conscientization' of oppressing professional customs (Jacobs and Murray, 2010). It is based on the need for dialogue, (including listening), principles of empowerment, social justice, emancipation and freedom. He promoted dialogue as the most effective way to strengthen the relationship between teacher and child (Roberts, 2013) and promote meaningful learning. This was seen as a very liberal approach in Brazil at that time as literacy was a requirement for voting in presidential elections. With literacy came power.

In 1961, Freire became the director of the Department of Education at a local institution and set out to promote intensive support for thousands of farm workers learning to read and write. But in June 1964, Paulo was imprisoned as a traitor for exercising democracy in lectures. In 1967 his book *Education as the practice of freedom* was published followed by *Pedagogy of the oppressed* in 1968. As an advocate of democracy, his identification of the need for developing a consciousness or 'conscientization' (Por. conscientizaçâo) of oppressing professional practices is at the heart of his philosophy of education. Only through the development of this conscientizaçâo are we able to question the nature of our historical and social situations. He is recognised as having a profound impact on educational thought and practice across the world (McLaren and Leanard, 2001). For Freire, there is no such thing as a neutral education process (Mayo, 1999). Education either functions as an instrument which is used to facilitate the integration of generations into the logic of the present system and bring about conformity to it, or it becomes the 'practice of freedom', the means by which men and women deal critically with reality and discover how to participate in the transformation of their world (Mayo, 1999, p.5).

In *Pedagogy of the oppressed* (1972, 1996), Freire advocates that education should (and can) allow the oppressed to regain their sense of humanity, so in turn they become empowered and overcome their situation. Nevertheless, he acknowledges that for this to occur, the oppressed person must play a role in their emancipation, be willing to consider new ways of seeing (in relation to education) and examine their own role in the power relationship between teacher and child for true liberation to take place. For this reason, Freire believed education was political in its link with pedagogy, and identified this as the main principle of critical pedagogy. Only when educators are aware of the 'politics' that surround education does education makes sense. This is because developing self-awareness enables us to take responsibility for knowing what is important (McLaren and Leanard, 2001). His perspective of developing consciousness or cultivating 'concientization' (Taylor, 1993, p.52) requires a critically reflective attitude in relation to education with the aim of action for social justice and fairness (Darder, et al., 2003). Learning is a collaborative, problem-posing process of enquiry which starts by questioning assumptions that have been taken for granted and raises awareness of unequal power relationships as part of teaching and learning. New knowledge that leads to personal action can then transform oppressive or inequitable teaching and learning processes (McLaren, 1993; Roberts, 2013).

In recent years, several early childhood scholars (for example, Alloway, 1997; Boldt, 1997; Boldt, 1997; MacNaughton, 2005; Moss, 2017) have shown how early childhood institutions embody inequitable power relationships particularly in terms of how adults understand young children and in addition how such institutions separate children from participating fully as part of wider society. MacNaughton (2005) argues that early childhood educators need to draw on critical reflection and an ideology critique in order to question, explore pedagogy and see how entrenched forms of inequality and unfairness appear in the everyday practice of learning and teaching. This knowledge can then be used to empower and transform understanding and teaching. Critical reflection that is informed by a critique of today's Western 'top-down' approach to early childhood education which prioritises outcomes and high stakes testing (Moss, 2017) can create social change, because it involves political questioning and being skeptical about power imbalances as part of the learning context (McTaggart, 1992). Once power relationships as part of an ideology are understood as a means to oppress and constrain, an understanding of what needs to change and why is possible. MacNaughton (2005) suggests that this can be done by asking questions such as 'Who benefits from the way I teach?', 'How and why do they benefit?', 'Why do I take this particular approach?', 'Whose interests does my approach support?' and 'Do I want to continue this way?' In this way we can increase our choices about how to think and operate against actions that are inequitable and unfair.

In relation to educational practice and liberation, Freire has left a significant mark on thinking about progressive practice. He was concerned with action through dialogue which was not just about deepening understanding but was part of making a difference in the world. Dialogue in itself is seen as a co-operative activity involving respect. Freire (1970, 1994) offers his pedagogy of hope (or critical theory) as a hopeful process in the context of education and its relationship with democracy. Freire contended that the basic importance of education is not only in the content of education but in the 'act' of cognition, through questioning *why*. Provided with appropriate dialogic conditions for this encounter, an individual can gradually perceive and construct their personal and social reality as well as the contradictions in it. In becoming conscious of personal perceptions of reality, it is possible to deal critically with it.

Freire and praxis

In the same way that Aristotle recognised the need for praxis as a moral disposition to act truthfully and rightly and have a concern to further human well-being and the good life (as discussed in Chapter 1), Freire (1972) speaks of 'praxis' as action supported by reflection (examining one's own experiences and views) but requiring theory to illuminate it. In praxis, there is a continual interplay between ends and means so that action is informed with a moral intent. In just the same way there is a continual interplay between thought and action.

When resistance is combined with movement, there is hope, in the same way that Freire (1970, 1994) promoted in his *Pedagogy of hope*. Hope is the necessary ingredient for being successful in the future success of the future directory of early childhood education in England and in contesting the narrow perception of outcome driven focus on developmental learning and standardised testing, so a new reality of an alternative discourse of quality determined by democratic entitlements and structures becomes the norm (Moss, 2017).

This brief examination of the life and experiences of Paulo Freire has demonstrated how connections can be made with his ideas and his thinking in relation to questioning unjust dominant discourses that are embedded in everyday educational structures and practices today (Smidt, 2014).

Chapter 3 explores how appropriate conditions for participatory and democratic learning are created as part of a safe trusting environment. However, as Moon (2008) notes, no one person can make another person reflect, they can only facilitate or foster a critically reflective approach through appropriate conditions. As we have seen, this involves a very complex and challenging internal process of being open and ready to become critically reflective (McLeod, 2017). Such conditions were nurtured as part of creating the 9 Rs of Reflection (McLeod, 2015). As acknowledged throughout this chapter, the tendency for educators today in England is to accept different approaches to early childhood education as truth without questioning the validity or researching alternative views (Rogoff, 2003). Western socio-cultural influences can have a 'silencing' effect on professionals, resulting in feelings of powerlessness (Brookfield, 1995; Hanson, 2011).

POINTS FOR REFLECTION

- Becoming critically reflective requires being prepared to let go, take risks and make changes.
- Is there anything about the process of critical reflection you are 'sceptical' about?
- Are you ready to commit time and enthusiasm to becoming critically reflective?

Summary

In conclusion, this chapter has demonstrated how critical reflection and reflexivity are essential elements of professional identity. Rather than being viewed as an add-on, reflexivity is a state of mind and a way of being that can enhance professional confidence, autonomy and can be empowering. In doing so different theoretical underpinnings and practical frameworks have been explored as alternative approaches for questioning the mechanistic product-driven view of teaching often associated with Western practice (Moss, 2010) in the hope that critical reflection can become a meaningful part of daily practice.

References

Alloway, N. (1997) 'Early childhood education encounters the postmodern: What do we know? What can we count as true?' *Australian Journal of Early Childhood*, 22(2), p.1–5. DOI: doi:0001605LO.

Ashworth, P. (2004) 'Understanding the transformation of what is already known', *Teaching in Higher Education*, 9(2), p.147–158. DOI: doi:10.1080/1356251042000195385.

Aristotle (1925) *The Nicomacheon ethics*, Oxford: Oxford University Press.

Barad, K. (2007) *Meeting the universe halfway. Quantum physics and the entanglement of matter and meaning*, Durham – London: Duke University Press.

Bernstein, R.J. (1983) *Beyond objectivism and relativism: Science, hermeneutics and praxis*, Oxford, England: Basil Blackwell.

Boldt, G. (1997) 'Sexist and heterosexist responses to gender bending', in: J. Tobin (Ed.) *Making a place for pleasure in early childhood education*, New Haven, CT: Yale University Press, p.188–213.

Bolton, G. (2010) *Reflective practice: Writing and professional development*, (2nd edn.) London: SAGE Publications.

Boydston, J.A. (Ed.) (2008) *The later works 1925–1953 John Dewey, Vol. 8, 1933 Essays and how we think, revised edition (Collected works of John Dewey)*, Carbondale: Southern Illinois University Press.

Brookfield, S.D. (1995) *Becoming a critically reflective teacher*, San Francisco, CA: Jossey-Bass A Wiley Company.

Cannella, G.S. (1997) *Deconstructing early childhood education: Social justice and revolution*, New York: Peter Lang Publishing.

Corbin, J. and Holt, N.L. (2005) 'Grounded theory', in: B. Somekh and C. Lewin (Eds.) *Research methods in the social sciences*, London: SAGE, p.49–55.

Critchley, S., Peperzak, A.T. and Bernasconi, R. (Eds.) (1996) *Emmanuel Levinas: Basic philosophical writings*, Bloomington: Indiana University Press.

Dahlberg, G. and Moss, P. (2005) *Ethics and politics in early childhood education*, Abingdon: Routledge Falmer.

Davies, S. and Artaraz, K. (2009) 'Towards an understanding of factors influencing early years professionals' practice of consultation with young people', *Children and Society*, 23(1), p.57–69. DOI: doi:10.1111/j.1099–0860.2008.00142.x.

De Bono, E. (1983) *Practical thinking*, Harmondsworth, Middlesex: Penguin.

Department for Children, Schools and Families (DCSF) (2008) *Practice guidance for the early years foundation stage*, Crown copyright, Department for Children, Schools and Families.

Derrida, J. (1999) *Adieu to Levinas*, Stanford, CA: Stanford University Press.

Dewey, J. (1933a) *How we think: A restatement of the relation of reflective thinking to the educative process*. New York: Heath and Company.

Dewey, J. (1933b) *The later works of John Dewey, volume 8, 1925–1953: Essays and how we think*, Revised Edition (*Collected works of John Dewey, 1882–1953*) J. Boydston and R. Rorty (Eds.) (2008) Carbondale: South Illinois University Press.

Dewey, J. (1929) *The later works of John Dewey, volume 4, 1925–1953: The quest for certainty* (*Collected works of John Dewey*) J. Boydston and S. Edelston Toulmin (Eds.) (2008) Carbondale: South Illinois University Press.

Dimova, Y. and Loughran, J. (2009) 'Developing a big picture understanding of reflection in pedagogical practice', *Reflective Practice*, 10(2), p.205–217. DOI: doi:10.1080/14623940902786214.

Edwards, A., Gilroy, P. and Hartley, D. (2002) *Rethinking teacher education, collaborative responses to uncertainty*, London: Routledge Falmer.

Etherington, K. (2004) *Becoming a reflexive researcher: Using our selves in research*, London: Jessica Kingsley.

Eun, B. (2011) 'A Vygotskian theory-based professional development: Implications for culturally diverse classrooms', *Professional Development in Education*, 37(3), p.319–333. DOI: doi:10.1080/19415257.2010.527761.

Foucault, M. (1978) *The history of sexuality, volume 1: An introduction* (R. Hurley Trans.), New York: Pantheon Books.

Freire, P. (1996) *Pedagogy of the oppressed*, London: Penguin.

Freire, P. (1994) *Pedagogy of hope*, New York: Continuum.

Freire, P. (1972) *Pedagogy of the oppressed*, Harmondsworth: Penguin.

Freire, P. (1970) *Cultural action for freedom* (M. Bergman Trans.,) Middlesex: Penguin.

Gadotti, M. (1994) *Reading Paulo Freire: His life and work* (M. Gadotti Trans.), New York: New York Press.

Ghaye, A. and Ghaye, K. (1998) *Teaching and learning through critical reflective practice*, London: David Fulton.

Gilroy, P. (1993) 'Reflections on Schön: An epistemological critique and a practical alternative', in: P. Gilroy and M. Smith (Eds.), *International analyses of teacher education*, Abingdon: Carfax Publishing Company, p.125–142.

Givvin, K.B. and Santagata, R. (2011) 'Towards a common language for discussing the features of effective professional development: The case of a US mathematics program', *Professional Development in Education*, 39(3), p.439–451. DOI: doi:10.1080/19415257.2010.527711.

Grimmett, P.P. (1988) 'The nature of reflection and Schön's conception in perspective', in: P.P. Grimmett and G.L. Erickson (Eds.) *Reflection in teacher education*, New York: Teacher College Press, p.5–15.

Hanson, K. (2011) '"Reflect": Is this too much to ask?', *Reflective Practice: International and Multidisciplinary Perspectives*, 12(3), p.293–304.

Hargreaves, A. (2001) 'Emotional geographies of teaching', *Teachers' College Record*, 103(6), p.1056–1080. DOI: doi:10.1016/S0883–0355(02)00006-X.

Hassan, Z. (2005) *Connecting to source*. Retrieved 24 July 2010 from: www.world changing.com/.

Hofkins, D. (2009) 'Eight letters start with P', *General Teaching Council Magazine*, 17, p.10–11.

Karlsson Häikiö, T. (2018) 'The Atelier as Potential Space for Transformative Learning Processes', in: T. Karlsson Häikiö and K.G. Eriksson (Eds.) *Art-based Education: An Ethics and Politics of Relation. Making Narratives, 3/2018*, HDK, Academy of Design and Crafts, University of Gothenburg, p.71–91.

Karlsson Häikiö, T. (2017) 'Dokumentation, transformation och intra-modala materialiseringar [Documentation, transformation and intra-modal materialisations]', in: B. Bergstedt

(Ed.) *Posthumanistisk pedagogik; Teori, undervisning och forskningspraktik* [*Posthuman pedagogics; Theory, education and research practice*], Gleerups: Malmö.

Kemmis, S. (2010) 'What is to be done? The place of action research', *Educational Action Research*, 18(4), p.417–427. DOI: doi:10.1080/09650792.2010.524745.

Kemmis, S. (2001) 'Exploring the relevance of critical theory for action research: Emancipatory action research in the footsteps of Jürgen Habermas', in: P. Reason and H. Bradbury (Eds.) *Handbook of action research: Participative inquiry and practice*, London: SAGE, p.91–102.

Kemmis, S. and McTaggert, R. (1990) *The action research planner*, Melbourne, Victoria: Deakin University Press.

Lange, E. (2004) 'Transformative and restorative learning: A vital dialectic for sustainable societies', *Adult Education Quarterly*, 54, p.121–139. DOI: doi:10.1177/0741713603260276.

Leitch, R. (2006) 'Limitations of language: Developing arts-based creative narrative in stories of teachers' identities', *Teachers and Teaching*, 12(5), p.549–569. DOI: doi:10.1080/13540600600832270.

Lenz Taguchi, H. (2012) *Pedagogisk dokumentation som aktiv agent: introduktion till intra-aktiv pedagogik* [*Pedagogical documentation as active agent; introduction to intra-active pedagogics*], 1. uppl. Malmö: Gleerups utbildning.

Lincoln, Y.S. and Guba, E.G. (2000) 'Paradigmatic controversies, contradictions and emerging confluences', in: N.K. Denzin and Y. S. Lincoln (Eds.) *Handbook of qualitative research*, (2nd ed.) London: SAGE, p.191–216.

MacNaughton, G. (2005) *Doing Foucault in early childhood studies: Applying poststructural ideas*, London: Routledge.

Marcos, J.J.M., Miguel, E.S. and Tillema, H. (2009) 'Teacher reflections on action: What is said (in research) but what is done (in teaching)', *Reflective Practice*, 10(2), p.191–204. DOI: doi:10.1080/14623940902786206.

Mayo, P. (1999) *Gramsci, Freire and adult education: Possibilities for transformative action*, London: Zed books.

McCormack, B. and Boomer, C. (2007) *Creating the conditions for growth. Report on the Belfast City Hospital and The Royal Hospitals Collaborative Practice Development Programme*, Belfast: Belfast Health and Social Care Trust.

McIntosh, P. (2010) *Action research and reflective practice. Creative and visual methods to facilitate reflection and learning*, London: Routledge.

McIntosh, P. (2009) 'The puzzle of metaphor and voice in arts-based social research', *International Journal of Social Research Methodology*, 12, p.1–13. DOI: doi:10.1080/13645570902969357.

McLaren, P. (1993) *Life in schools: An introduction to critical pedagogy in the social foundations of education*, New York: Longman.

McLaren, P. and Leanard, P. (2001) *Paulo Freire A critical encounter*, Oxon: Routledge.

McLeod, N. (2015) 'Reflecting on reflection: Improving teacher's readiness to facilitate participatory learning with young children', *Professional Development in Education*, 41(2), p.254–272.

McLeod, N. (2012) *Critical reflection as a tool for developing pedagogical participation with young children in their learning*, EdD Thesis, University of Sheffield library.

McLeod, N. (2011) 'Exploring early years educators' ownership of language and communication knowledge and skills: A review of key policy and initial reflections on Every Child a Talker and its implementation', *Education 3–13 International Journal of Primary, Elementary and Early Years Education*, 39(4), p.429–445. DOI: doi:10.1080/03004271003776850.

McTaggart, R. (1992) 'Principles for participatory action research', *Adult Education Quartely*, 41(3), p.168–187. DOI: doi:10.1177/0001848191041003003.

Mezirow, J. (2000) 'Learning to think like an adult: Core concepts of transformation theory', in: J. Mezirow and associates (Eds.). *Learning as transformation*, San Francisco, CA: Josey-Bass, p.3–33.

Mezirow, J. (1997) 'Transformative learning: Theory to practice', in: P. Cranton (Ed.) *Transformative learning in action: Insights from practice: new directions for adult and continuing education*, (74) San Francisco, CA: Jossey-Bass, p.5–12.

Montessori, M. (1967) *The discovery of the child* (M.J. Costelloe, Trans), New York: Ballantine. (Original work published 1948).

Moon, J. (2008) *Critical thinking: An exploration of theory and practice*, Oxford: Routledge.

Moon, J. (2006) *Learning journals: A handbook for reflective practice and professional development*, London: Routledge.

Moon, J. (2004) *A handbook of reflective and experiential learning*, London: Routledge Falmer.

Moon, J. (1999) *Reflection in learning and professional development*, London: Routledge Falmer.

Moss, P. (2017) 'Power and resistance in early childhood education: From dominant discourse to democratic experimentalism', *Journal of Pedagogy*, 8(1), p.11–32. DOI: doi:10.1515/jped-2017–0001.

Moss, P. (2014) *Transformative change and real utopias in early childhood education: A story of democracy, experimentation and potentiality*, London: Routledge.

Moss, P. (2013) 'Beyond the investment narrative', *Contemporary Issues in Early Childhood*, 14 (4), p.370–372.

Moss, P. (2010) 'We cannot continue as we are: The educator in an education for survival', *Contemporary Issues in Early Childhood*, 11(1), p.8–19.

Newman, S. (1999) 'Constructing and critiquing reflective practice', *Educational Action Research*, 7(1), p.145–163. DOI: doi:10.1080/09650799900200081.

Nias, J. (1996) 'Thinking about feelings: The emotions in teaching', *Cambridge Journal of Education*, 26(3), p.293–306. DOI: doi:10.1080/0505764960260301.

Noddings, N. (1996) 'Stories and affect in teacher education', *Cambridge Journal of Education*, 26(3), p.435–447. DOI: doi:10.1080/0305764960260311.

Norling, M., Sandberg, A. and Almqvist, L. (2015) 'Engagement and emergent literacy practices in Swedish preschools', *European Early Childhood Education Research Journal*, 23(5), p.619–634.

Orlandi, K. (2014) 'Addressing the attrition between the conflicting influences experienced by teachers on the interface between Foundation Stage and Key Stage One', *Journal of Early Childhood Research*, 12(3), p.294–307.

Pascal, C. and Bertram, T. (2018) 'Effective early learning: A praxeological and participatory approach to evaluating and improving quality in early childhood education', *FAEEBA Magazine: Education and Contemporaneity* [online], 27(51), p.105–120. Available at: http://revistas.uneb.br/index.php/faeeba/article/view/4969/3176 [Accessed: 12 November 2018], DOI: doi:10.21879/faeeba2358–0194.2018.v27.n51.p105–120.

Pascal, C. and Bertram, T. (2012) 'Praxis, ethics and power: Developing praxeology as a participatory paradigm for early childhood research', *European Early Childhood Education Research Journal*, 20(4), p.477–492. DOI: doi:10.1080/1350293X.2012.737236.

Pollard, A. (2002) *Reflective teaching*, London: Continuum.

Price, J.N. and Valli, L. (2005) 'Pre-service teachers becoming agents of change. Pedagogical implications for action research', *Journal of Teacher Education*, 56(1), p.57–72. DOI: doi:10.1177/0022487104272097.

Reed, M. and Canning, N. (2010). *Reflective practice in the early years*, London: SAGE.

Rinaldi, C. (2006) *In dialogue with Reggio Emilia: Listening, researching and learning*, London: Routledge.

Roberts, P. (2013) *Paulo Freire in the 21st century: Education, dialogue and transformation*, London: Paradigm.

Rogoff, B. (2003) *The cultural nature of human development*, London: Oxford University Press.

Sahlberg, P. (2015) *Finnish lessons 2.0. What can the world learn from educational chance in Finland?* (2nd edn.) New York; London: Teachers College.

Sahlberg, P. (2011) 'The fourth way of Finland', *Journal of Educational Change*, 12(2), p.173–185.

Sahlberg, P. (2010) 'Rethinking accountability in a knowledge society', *Journal of Educational Change*, 11(1), p.45–61.

Scharmer, C.O. (2009) *Theory U: Leading from the future as it emerge*, San Francisco: Berrett-Koehler Publishers.

Schön, D.A. (1987). *Educating the reflective practitioner toward a new design for teaching*, San Francisco, CA: Jossey-Bass.

Schön, D.A. (1983) *The reflective practitioner: How professionals think in action*, New York: Basic Books.

Shier, H. (2001) 'Pathways to participation: Openings, opportunities and obligations', *Children and Society*, 15(2), p.107–117. DOI: doi:10.1002/CHI.617.

Smidt, S. (2014) *Introducing Freire: A guide for students, teachers and practitioners*, Oxon: Routledge.

Smith, J. (2016) 'Sailing through social LA GRRAACCEESS: Tool for deconstructing and facilitating reflective and reflexive practice', *Reflective Practice*, 17(5), p.570–582.

Taylor, E.W. (2007) 'An update of transformative learning theory: A critical review of the empirical research (1999–2005)', *International Journal of Lifelong Education*, 26(2), p.175–191. DOI: doi:10.1080/02601370701219475.

Taylor, P. (1993) *The texts of Paulo Freire*, Buckingham: Open University Press.

Tickell, C. (2011) *The early years: Foundations for life, health and learning. An independent report on the early years foundation stage to her majesty's government*, London: Department for Education.

van Manen, M. (1995) 'Epistemology of reflective practice', *Teachers and Teaching: Theory and Practice*, 1(1), p.33–50. DOI: doi:0001607LO.

Volpe, R. (1981) 'Knowledge from theory and practice', *Oxford Review of Education*, 7(1), p.41–57. Available at: www.jstor.org/pss/1050088.

Wasmuth, H. and Nitecki, E. (2017). 'Global early childhood policies: The impact of the global education reform movement and possibilities for reconceptualization', *Global Education Review*, 4(2), p.1–17.

Wilkins, C. (2011) 'Professionalism and the post-performative teacher: New teachers reflect on autonomy and accountability in the English school system', *Professional Development in Education*, 37(3), p.389–409. DOI: doi:10:1080/19415257.2010.514204.

3

DEMOCRACY AND PARTICIPATION IN EARLY CHILDHOOD EDUCATION

Naomi McLeod and Tarja Karlsson Häikiö

This chapter builds on Chapters 1 and 2. Having engaged in a meta-cognitive course of action that begins with being ready to question and develop a self-awareness of personal values and beliefs about the purpose of education, an appreciation of the wider political and cultural pressures on early education can be understood. It then becomes possible to see imbalances of power in learning and teaching which are particularly relevant to participation, as this involves sharing power based on mutual respect (Carr, 1998; 2006, 2012). Often, though, we are too busy responding to such power forces to recognise and question them (Beijaard et al., 2004; Scharmer, 2009).

We begin this chapter by defining democracy and participation in the context of early childhood as a social construction and educators as advocates for children grounded in the United Nations Convention of the Rights of the Child (UNCRC) (1989). In particular Articles 12 (children's views) and 13 (freedom of expression) are used as benchmarks for respecting children's right to express themselves about matters that concern them and for their views to be taken into account. Articles 12 and 13 are used as a lens to critically examine the quality of participatory practice and children's rights to a voice as we draw on Hart's (1992) 'ladder of participation'' and Shier's (2001) 'Pathways to participation' model for democratic practice. The relevance of 'listening' and a 'respectful reciprocal relationship' are explored and examples of what this looks like in practice and reflective prompts are provided throughout. Different challenges and potential benefits for both children and early childhood educators are also explored. In the context of international approaches and quality early education, we draw on a posthuman perspective. Ultimately, for democratic and participatory learning and teaching in early education to become sustainable as a meaningful part of everyday practice, we reinforce the need for a commitment to reflexivity and participatory practice as a pedagogy of hope (Moss, 2017).

Defining democratic learning

The word democracy comes from the ancient Greeks who combined the words *demos* (people) and *krates* (rule) to create the idea of people-power or rule by the people. Democratic, respectful practice relates to educators' awareness of power dynamics between themselves and the child so children are viewed positively as rich, capable, independent decision-makers (Dahlberg and Moss, 2005; MacNaughton, 2005; Moss, 2013, 2014). In contrast to an outcome-driven, deficit model of education (Dockett and Perry, 2007), an open form of praxis as an intentional and committed democratic action with a moral intent is advocated (Kemmis, 2010). Here a social constructivist philosophical approach, committed to phronesis, is promoted where children interpret for themselves, make connections, question and make sense of situations (Hultman and Lenz Taguchi, 2010; Lenz Taguchi, 2012; Häikiö, 2017; Olsson, 2012; Rautio, 2014; Rogoff, 2003). Such a pedagogy is a hallmark of a critical perspective on traditional education and draws on participatory and collaborative approaches where children are viewed as competent learners and encouraged to take responsibility and make decisions about things that are important to them (MacNaughton et al., 2007; McNeish, 1999; McLeod, 2011, 2015; Morrow, 1999; Rinaldi, 2006, 2012). Given that adults can be the most significant barrier to children's participation (Kellett, 2011), to demonstrate democracy within the context of early childhood education we draw on Shier's (2001) conceptual model of participation, which involves adults and includes five levels, namely listening, consultation and participation.

These are defined as follows:

Listening:

1. Children are listened to
2. Children are supported in expressing their views

Consultation:

1. Children's views are taken into account
2. Children are involved in decision-making processes

Full participation:

1. Children share (some) power and responsibility for decision-making

Listening to children

There is much interest in the field of listening and its importance (for example by Bath, 2009; Clark, 2004, 2005, 2017; Cutler, 2002; Lancaster, 2003; MacNaughton et al., 2007; McNeish, 1999; Rinaldi, 2006, 2012).

Clark's (2017) definition of listening begins with the understanding that 'listening is an active rather than passive process . . . . which involves children and adults discussing meanings' (p.491) and is a crucial factor in understanding children's experiences. Listening to children means taking their perspectives seriously and valuing the contribution of talk. Likewise McLeod (2008) interprets authentic listening with children as involving both respect and a willingness to empower them as agents of change, that is, the author of one's own actions (Hilppö et al., 2016). Such quality approaches are very often adopted from international perspectives (Leather, 2017; Nutbrown, 1996). For example, Danish early years outdoor pedagogy and the *Reggio Emilia* approach involve children being supported through interaction with their peers and adults, who place more emphasis on open constructive thought and communication than on the transmission of knowledge and skills (Malaguzzi, 1992; Villen, 1993). Similarly, in relation to early childhood education, the Te Whāriki curriculum of New Zealand is based on responsive learning contexts and reciprocal interaction which lies in the ecological model based on Bronfenbrenner (1979, 2004). Further detail and examples will be provided in Part 2, where we look at specific '*International philosophies and practical interpretations of early childhood education*'.

Without effective participation with children, we cannot access their viewpoints, anxieties, or experiences and provide adequately for their needs and show respect for them. Kellett (2011) reminds us how oblivious as educators we can be to the hurdles that divide adults' and children's worlds. She draws on Laurie Lee's (1975) novel *Cider with Rosie*, and Lee's account of his first day at school, in which he describes how his teacher pointed to an empty chair in the classroom and told him to '*sit there for the present*'. Lee obeyed respectfully. Later, when his mother asked how his first day at school had gone, he shared his disappointment: *'the teacher told me to sit there for the present and I sat there all day but I never got one'*. While this is amusing the miscommunication illustrates how often adults' and children's communication operates on parallel lines but how children's perspectives and priorities are not considered or visible to adults. Communicating with children therefore starts with viewing children as rich in potential (Moss, 2017; Rinaldi, 2006) and valuing their views. When children are not listened to, they can feel frustrated and disappointed (Brookes, 2018). Not listening to children can have serious consequences, linked to identity, a sense of self, belonging and well-being (Bath, 2009). More generally though, it prevents us from understanding children's lived experiences.

Consultation

Building on listening as a foundation, consultation is defined by Borland (2001) as a process which involves listening with the purpose of determining the views of children as a guide to action. However, Alderson (2000) notes how the term consultation implies a power imbalance, as those who consider the views of others do so based on their own conditions, because they select the decision they make or the questions they ask (Myhill, 2006). The adult chooses whether or not to act on what they find (Davies and Artaraz, 2009). It is important that children's voices do not simply reinforce adult perspectives and adult authority (Wyness, 2006).

Consequently, Kelley (2006) argues that the quality of children's involvement is dependent on and determined by the openings and responses made by the adult. Young children require supportive adults who are respectful of them and encourage a listening approach, which can be a challenging process for adults because of their underpinning values and attitudes. Consultation, then, is a process that opens up a whole new experience of self-awareness and reflection on the adult's part (Lancaster, 2003; Moss, Petrie, and Poland, 1999). As Feldman and Weiss (2010, p.29) claim, 'significant change' in teaching can only happen as a result of realising and developing a consciousness about oneself as an educator (Wall, 2008, 2016)

Participation

In comparison to listening and consultation, the word 'participation' implies that power is shared between all those involved (Bath, 2009; Hart, 1992; Miller, 2003; Shier, 2001). Kellett (2011) argues that unless involving children is accompanied by a commitment to developing a personal awareness of underpinning assumptions and values and to organisational change, children's participation will remain controlled and ornamental rather than respectful and genuine. Participation, as Bath (2009) indicates, involves addressing issues of power imbalance. May (2005) questions how realistic this is as ultimately 'publications empower practitioners to ascertain, manage and represent the pupil's voice, rather than encouraging practitioners to empower the pupils themselves' (p.30). As such, May considers power imbalances as inevitable, unless educators engage in a process of self-awareness of personal values and beliefs about the purpose of education and an appreciation of the wider political and cultural pressures on early education (as discussed in Chapter 2).

While consultation and participation with older children has become more common, this is not generally the case for younger children (Bath, 2009; Kellett, 2011). In reality, listening, consultation, and participation is still often tokenistic because adults can choose whether to listen and / or consult with children or ignore what children say and not involve them in decision-making. Ultimately it is adults who hold the power and decide. Concerns such as these have led to an awareness of active participation of children in decision-making processes and the importance of children's rights to a voice.

Why listening, consultation, and participation are so important

Listening to a child and valuing their voice at a basic level shows respect for another human being. Having a voice can also be empowering for children as it develops self-belief, a sense of belonging, feeling valued, and confidence in making independent decisions. Such agentic opportunities enable children to take responsibility, deal with uncertainties in life, and be authors of their own actions and so influence the world around them (Davis and Elliot, 2014). When children's voice is ignored, they can feel upset, disempowered, and unvalued (Fisher, 2013). This may also develop feelings of incompetence which may affect their self-belief to make decisions (Clarke, 2017). In the long term this can impact negatively on the ability to develop their own initiative, to think for themselves and question (Fisher, 2013). Ultimately this may affect how children cope in difficult situations (Brookes, 2018).

Children's participation (including voice) in their learning is also a sign of quality (Norling, Sandberg, and Almqvist, 2015) and enables opportunities for young children to make connections as they talk their ideas through and make sense of their learning. In a participatory context, children are encouraged to collaborate, make independent choices, share responsibility, and follow through their own independent ideas to make sense of their learning and develop deeper conceptual understandings (Clark, 2004, 2005, 2017; Lancaster, 2003; Landsdown, 2005; Nutbrown, 2011). In this way, 'the hundred languages of children' and the recognition of the 'multiplicity' of language drawing on the *Reggio Emilia* approach is key (Rinaldi, 2006, p.193), so language is not just seen as verbal or spoken but as a means of expression. Metaphorically the hundred languages can be interpreted as a symbol for otherness, multiplicity, or from a multicultural perspective on learning and relationships with the purpose of understanding others and creating the ability for communicative skills beyond the linguistic barriers (Karlsson Häikiö, 2018a).

Here, active listening skills are required by the adult alongside an openness for welcoming possibilities as part of a trusting environment. At the heart of such learning spaces, children are respected as individuals, and learning is supported through interaction with their peers and adults. In addition, there is an emphasis on constructive thought and communication rather than on the transmission of knowledge and skills (Malaguzzi, 1992; Villen, 1993). Such approaches are based on responsive learning contexts and reciprocal interaction (Bath, 2009) and are central to an ethical, socially just approach to learning. An emphasis on the 'process' of learning enables opportunities for young children to engage more in enjoyable experiential opportunities. An end product can be a significant part of learning but how children get there and the decisions they make along the way are what give the process of participation the ability to engage at a deeper level, with opportunities for expanding thoughts and possibilities (Beetlestone, 1998; Craft, 2002; Jeffrey and Woods, 2009). In this way, participation and respecting children's views enables a sense of worth and agency as they make decisions about things that are important to them. This is fundamental to the well-being of children and them developing as capable, confident learners, and active citizens (Bath, 2009). Ultimately this requires children to be viewed as capable, so their views are respected as part of normal everyday practice rather than the exception (Chan, 2011). Here an awareness of children's rights is crucial.

The importance of participatory and democratic learning in early education then is based on the following components:

1. firstly, the recognition of the importance of young children's talk and voice as part of learning (McLeod, 2011, 2017; Myhill, 2006; Rinaldi, 2006);
2. the right children have as part of Article 12 and 13 of the United Nations Convention (UNCRC) (1989) to express themselves in relation to things that

are important to them and or information they have received, and for their views to be taken into account;

3. a move to build respectful and democratic communities as part of everyday routines with young children (MacNaughton, 2005), and in recognition of this as a growing interest in the field of listening to children as a hallmark of democratic practice and a critically reflective and empowering education (Cutler, 2002; Karlsson Häikiö, 2017; MacNaughton et al., 2007; Morrow, 1999; McNeish, 1999; Rinaldi, 2006);
4. participation provides a sense of belonging, which is fundamental to the well-being of community members (Bath, 2009);
5. 'significant change' in teaching can only happen as a result of realising and developing a consciousness about oneself as an educator (Feldman and Weiss, 2010, p.29).

For educators to be respectful and confident enablers of participatory learning so children have a voice, Lancaster (2003) stresses the importance of starting with taking children's perspectives seriously, in line with Articles 12 and 13 of the UNCRC, so that they are encouraged to express themselves and contribute if they wish to. Developing a participatory approach therefore requires an understanding of how to share adult power (including sharing responsibility).

Children's rights and early education (children's voice)

The foundations of contemporary ethical / participatory principles

It is only within the past few decades that society has begun to recognise and respect the rights of young children and support principles that enable their voice and participation in learning and the wider context, such as part of research (Moore, 2008; UNICEF, 1995). In considering young children rights and implications, it is helpful to take a brief look back into history so that the foundations can perhaps be better understood. During the Second World War (1939–1945), many excessive and horrendous experiments were carried out by Mengele, a Nazi doctor who conducted inhumane medical experiments on prisoners in Auschwitz.

The aim was to advance knowledge for the benefit of the Aryan community, but at the expense of children and adults who were considered of an inferior race. His methods were inhumane, torturous, and frequently resulted in death (Greig, Taylor, and MacKay, 2007). Rather than viewing this behaviour as warped and misguided, Katz (1992) presents the view that the actions of those involved in such atrocities can be explained by the overriding regime which was seen as supreme and was therefore not questioned. While it could be argued that this has little relevance on our behaviour today, according to Müller-Hill (1992) the messages about ethical implications which emerged were clear.

> The attempt of science to provide acceptable values and ethics had failed. Medicine and science should never again be trusted when they promise to deliver their own ethical values; these values have to come from other sources.
>
> *(1992, p.48)*

Following the Second World War and the Nuremburg Trials, there was horror and disgust at the revelation of what happened under the pretence of so-called research. With the resolve that such atrocities would never happen again, regulations and legal principles were established by the judiciary (Greig, Taylor, and MacKay, 2007). The emerging outcome was The *Nuremburg Code* of 1947 which outlines moral, ethical, and legal principles relating to research with all human participants requiring that voluntary consent by participants is given and ensuring that the research is for the good of society (ibid.). From this emerged the Universal Declaration of Human Rights (1948). At the time, children were overlooked as rights bearers which eventually led to the United Nations Convention on the Rights of the Child (UNCRC) (1989), which makes it clear that human rights apply to children. MacNaughton, Hughes, and Smith (2007) highlight how this made children's rights, including the right to have a voice in decisions about them, legally binding. It was an overt commitment to acknowledge and respect the rights and status of all children as individuals. In particular, Article 12 states the right for children to express their views freely in all matters affecting them and their views being given due weight (UNCRC, 1989). This means that not only should children be able to give their views, and be listened to, but their views and ideas should be taken seriously. This would imply children are consulted appropriately and there is a response or an action (Borland, 2001) in relation to things that are important to them. Likewise, Article 13 recognises children's right to share information in any way they choose, including by talking, drawing, or writing. As a starting point, Articles 12 and 13 are therefore concerned with ensuring children feel able to express themselves comfortably. This is reliant on adults respecting children, valuing their views, and listening to them. In this way children are viewed as agentic, which Pascal and Bertram (2009) note as an important part of their right to act on their own terms, give voice, have power, to make choices, and explore the world on their own conditions. Children who learn to participate in society in the early years are more likely to develop into engaged citizens with respect for the principles of democratic values (Pascal and Bertram, 2009, p.254).

While consultation with older children has become more common in England, this is not always the case for younger children (Davies and Artaraz, 2009; Kellett, 2011). In England, Wales, and Northern Ireland, children's rights have been partly addressed with legislation in the Children Act (2004) and the Childcare Act (2006), which place an obligation on adults to ensure that children are enabled and encouraged to contribute their views on relevant matters, *if* they wish to participate. However, with such legislation Manful and McCrystal (2010) note how the Convention is mentioned but not used as a guiding framework in relation to the development of strategies for children. They highlight the need to review how early childhood professionals conceptualise children's rights so they are not just viewed as a means of protection in the interest of the children, but also so opportunities for meaningful choices can be made by children. Indeed the 2014 Children and Families Act does not even mention children's rights. Likewise, previous Early Years Foundation Stage frameworks supported children's voice, noting the importance on 'making time to listen to children's views and to act on them even when they do not match adult views' (DCSF, 2008, Principles into Practice cards 2.3). However, the fact that this statement was located under the heading '*Challenges and Dilemmas*' rather than '*Effective Practice*' 'implies caution about the idea that children may wish to express a contrasting view from that of an adult' (Giardiello, 2014). Sadly, this statement no longer appears in more recent frameworks (DfE, 2017). While the rights of the child are mentioned, it does so in a protective stance that emphasises safety rather than participation.

Kellett (2011) reminds us how oblivious educators can be 'to the barriers that divide adults' and children's worlds. As Grimsci notes, the attempts to develop child centered practices, so children's perspectives or voices are heard, are continuously inhibited by conventional teachers who often prioritise pre-planned activities particularly with a focus on literacy and mathematics and so have a very technical approach to children's learning (cited in MacNaughton et al., 2007). This is reinforced by recent reports such as *Bold beginnings* (Ofsted, 2017) which prioritises a formal, very instrumental and linear model of teaching based on a transmission and reproduction of knowledge rather than an aptitude and love of learning based around children's interests and engagement (McLeod, 2017; Orlandi, 2014). *Bold beginnings* (Ofsted, 2017) is an example of how children's learning in England is viewed (politically) as being ready for formal education with 'reading, writing and mathematics' as the priority through 'direct teaching time everyday' (p.4). This implies a didactic transfer of knowledge as a priority rather than valuing the uniqueness of individual children's learning needs and interests. In this respect, children's voice and participatory learning is not valued. Similarly, the Statutory Framework for the Early Years Foundation Stage (DfE, 2017) in England sets out the requirements from birth to 5 years of age and promotes children's 'learning for ensuring school readiness' and stipulates 'expected levels, and their readiness for Year 1' (p.14).

Authentic participation needs to involve a respectful response by adults to children's voice so children are respected as agents of change (the authors of their own actions) (Hilppö et al., 2016). For this to happen Thomson (2008) explains how educators need to ensure children are given time, appropriate tools, and are trusted (i.e. viewed as capable), 'so they can rise to the challenge and offer us valuable insight into their worlds of experience and meaning-making' (p.25). Essentially, Lundy (2007, p.933) explains how children's voice requires their views being listened to and acted on by adults which involves addressing power relations that are inherent in adult – child relationships. Developing a participatory approach then requires an understanding of how to share power.

Whichever perspective of childhood is taken will be reflected in the practice offered to young children as part of their learning. Respectful participation of young children then 'attempts to take their views seriously as they experience their lives in the here and now' (Morrow and Richards, 1996, p.92). As Percy-Smith and Thomas (2009) remind us, a rights-based concept of participation may represent an entitlement to have a say, but it is not enough. The most effective participation is where children work 'as members of a community where roles and responsibilities are shared, where "agency" rather than "voice" is the key concept' (Percy-Smith and Thomas, 2009, p.359). As Graham and Fitzgerald (2010) and Rinaldi (2006) contend, participation is about respectful relationships and shared responsibility that takes place through dialogue.

As discussed in Chapter 1, protective and passive perceptions of children and childhood perpetuate an imbalance of power between the educator and child rather than a reciprocal respectful relationship. Only by being ready to question 'why' different approaches are ethically appropriate can alternative views be appreciated (McLeod, 2017).

POINTS FOR REFLECTION

- Why are children asked to put their hands up if they would like to speak or to cross their legs when sitting on the carpet?
- Why do educators prioritise planned activities based around literacy and mathematics?
- How do timetabled events (such as assembly, and break / lunchtimes) limit children's participation and choices?
- Is listening to children important to you?

Different models of participation

Hart's Ladder of Participation

Hart's (1992) 'Ladder of children's participation' was the first substantial attempt to visualise children's participation (Kellett, 2011). It is designed on eight levels or rungs of participation from 'manipulation' to 'shared decision-making'. The bottom three rungs describe youth involvement that is not participatory, whereas the top three rungs progress in their levels of participation (see Figure 3.1).

Participation involves children having an initial idea. Adults are available but do not take the lead and wait to be invited by children to join in the decision-making process. What is not clear, however, is how adults progress so their practice can become more participatory, for example, what 'not taking charge' involves and how decisions can be shared. This is not helpful in terms of developing an understanding of the participatory process and the entangled nature involving self-awareness and the various influences. It also to some extent simplifies participation by implying the adults need only wait for an invitation by children. The reality is that adults tend to be the main barrier to

Step 8	Shared Decision Making	Full Participation	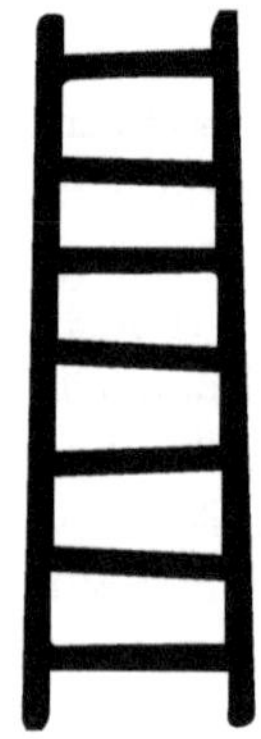
Step 7	Children Lead	Degrees of Participation	
Step 6	Adults Initiate		
Step 5	Consult and Inform		
Step 4	Assign		
Step 3	Tokenism	Non Participation	
Step 2	Decoration		
Step 1	Manipulation		

FIGURE 3.1 An adaption of Hart's 'Ladder of participation'

children's participation. This is often displayed in the context of data-driven priorities and normative pedagogical practices (such as in England) where adult planned practice dominates, and where is a distinct power imbalance. How an educator relinquishes power for participation in such circumstances is central to this chapter.

Shier's conceptual model of participation

Shier's (2001) alternative model (see Figure 3.2) focuses on the role of the educator so children's participation can be enhanced in line with Article 12 and 13 of the United Nations Convention on the Rights of the Child (UNCRC).

Shier's (2001) *model of participation* is a conceptual framework that recognises the need for self-awareness by the educator and a respect for children's voice as a starting point. Only if the adult is open and ready to listen to young children will opportunities for children to express themselves be facilitated so they share in the decision-making process. Shier's framework is a practical tool that can pinpoint the level of adults' participation, so they can see what they need to do to enable full participation. Standing back and evaluating their role in this process can support planning by identifying changes that need to be made to encourage children's views and their level of participation. Shier's model, in comparison to Hart's 'Ladder' (1992), is based on

> five levels of gradual participation: 1. children are listened to, 2. children are supported in expressing their views. 3. children's views are taken into account, 4. children are involved in decision-making processes, 5. children share power and responsibility for decision-making. In addition, three stages of commitment are identified at each level: 'openings', 'opportunities' and 'obligation'.
>
> *(p. 107)*

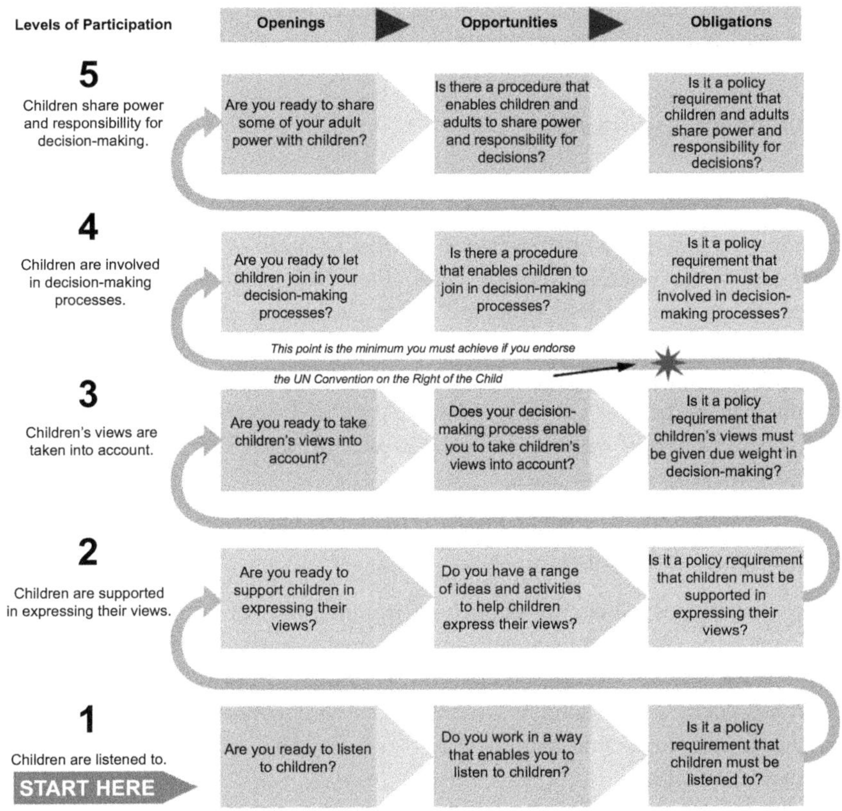

FIGURE 3.2 'Pathways to participation' indicates key responses by educators for facilitating varying levels of participation for children.

In addition to the five levels of participation (progressing from listening to consultation and participation), three stages of 'dedication' are acknowledged at each level: 'openings', 'opportunities', and 'obligations' as indicated in Figure 3.2. At each level, a personal 'opening' attitude and commitment is required by the educator, without which the second stage of creating an 'opportunity' will not occur.

Facilitating an opening

The first stage of Shier's (2001) 'Pathways to participation' model as a means of addressing power imbalances begins when listening to children is valued by an adult and they are ready to listen. An 'opening' requires an awareness of personal behaviours in relation to listening, so they can listen and respond appropriately. For example, on a very basic level if a young child asks if they can do something for themselves such as dressing themselves or selecting the necessary colours for doing a painting, the adult has a choice of facilitating the child's request. The normal practice for the adult may be to select the child's clothes or paints. Being ready to listen acts as an opening for the child.

Facilitating an opportunity

As Shier (2001) explains, an opportunity builds on an opening and will occur if the adult responds and supports a child in facilitating an opening. For example. responding by offering a child a choice of what to wear or which paint colours to use, results in an opening for the child. Here the adult will need to provide appropriate resources such as time and space. Facilitating an opportunity may also require the development of new skills such as self-awareness, knowledge understandings and approaches by the educator. For example, the automatic response by an adult may be to make decisions for children and not include choice. Recognising this can result in making choices available and adopting more of a facilitation role and physically standing back.

Facilitating an obligation

Finally, according to Shier, an 'obligation' is understood as an agreed policy of the setting (or as the participant teachers who engaged in research using this as a tool to support participation with young children, preferred to call it '*a commitment as part of everyday practice*'). In doing so, consultation with children and participation is recognised, respected, and honoured by teachers as an integral daily part of the organisation or setting.

By using each prompt as part of the Shier framework, educators can identify their current position in relation to participation and can see the next steps that needs to be taken in order to further participation as part of their everyday teaching. In reality, different experiences can result in different levels or stages of participation. What Bath (2009, p.103) stresses as being important as part of this process is that a participatory approach is not viewed as 'an optional extra but as a vital tool to transform children's educational experiences, and the experience of the adults who work with them'. Central to this is self-awareness and a willingness to change. While Kirby and Gibbs (2006) criticised both Hart and Shier's models on the basis that different experiences can result in different levels or stages of participation, they are useful in highlighting the complex and challenging roles involved in facilitating children's voice as part of participation (Lundy, 2007).

Pedagogy of relationships and listening

Clearly, the nature of a participatory approach begins when adults take children's perspectives seriously in line with Article 12 of the UNCRC and adults offer young children opportunities that are active rather than passive in processes that matter to them (Clark, 2005, 2017; Lancaster, 2003). This procedure involves addressing power relations that are inherent in adult-child relationships and opens up the development of self-awareness and readiness to see differently on the adult's part (Lancaster, 2003; Rinaldi, 2006) so that respectful and democratic communities as part of everyday teaching can be built with young children (MacNaughton, 2005; MacNaughton et al., 2007).

For Rinaldi (2006) understanding *how* to share power is based on the principles and pedagogy of listening and relationships associated with the *Reggio Emilia* (Malaguzzi, 1994) approach, the inspirations of which are based on contextual reflections and insights from different theories and theorists (Rinaldi, 2006). For example, the importance Vygotsky (1978, 1986) attached to the relationship between thought and language and the active process through open dialogue is adopted alongside Montessori's (1967 / 1948) recognition of the need for children to become independent and autonomous learners. Further detail is provided in Chapter 4. The *Reggio Emilia* approach has widened the idea of communication into what is known as 'the hundred languages of children' and the recognition of the 'multiplicity' of language (Rinaldi, 2006, p.193). In this way, language is not just seen as verbal or spoken but as a means of expression.

Adult active listening skills

For pedagogy of listening, active listening skills are required by the adult in order to hear accurately what is being communicated by a child. As Scharmer (2009) states, we tend to resort to selective hearing, i.e., what is familiar to us based on our views, experiences, and feelings. Similarly, in reality 'very little is heard other than what we have heard before' (ibid., p.xiv). Most situations remain the same because our awareness 'renders it invisible' (p.xiv). There is a lack of response to the subtle powers that are influencing us. As a result, when we listen, we selectively hear or over generalise what is familiar to us based on our views, experiences, and feelings, so the 'other' (the new) is taken and turned into the familiar (Critchley et al., 1996). For Rinaldi, the pedagogy of listening requires openness at its core and a welcoming of differences by the teacher, or as Donald Schön (1987) called it, there is a 'convergence of meaning', an honest and accurate interpretation. This entails / includes three main elements: i) internal listening, ii) multiple listening, and iii) visible listening.

i) Internal *listening*

Internal listening requires a meta-cognitive course of action that begins with being ready to question and develop a self-awareness of personal values and beliefs about the purpose of education. This is the beginnings of critical reflection which (as discussed in Chapter 2) can enable new ways of seeing and being (Rinaldi, 2006). Links can then be made to everyday pedagogical practice as a sustainable embedded reflexive approach, which results in a conscious 'opening' by the educator to children's voice (McAlpine and Weston, 2000; Shier, 2001). Similarly, Price and Valli (2005) note the need to continuously reflect back on personal beliefs, thoughts, and actions which occur when critically reflecting. Van Manen (1995) warns about the dangers of trying to bolt a reflexive approach as part of practice, which can become 'highly frustrating', and an 'obstacle' to teaching effectively (p.39). Instead, the question for van Manen is 'where and how does critical reflection enter the reality of the pedagogical lifeworld' (1995, p.36).

ii) Multiple *listening*

The second aspect required as part of Rinaldi's (2006) pedagogy of listening is multiple listening or openness to the 'other', which is essential in creating an atmosphere for a listening approach (Rinaldi, 2006). This requires an open-mindedness or as Dewey (1933) noted an

> active desire to listen to more sides than one, ... to give full attention to alternative possibilities, to recognise the possibility of error even in the beliefs which are dearest to us.
>
> *(p.30)*

Given the tendency to selectively hear what is familiar to us, there is a need for honesty in the interpretation of 'other' perspectives or knowledge. Levinas refers to a need to check the accuracy of our interpretation so there is not a mis-representation and a merging of new knowledge with old (and recognisable knowledge). Levinas refers to this as 'the ethics of an encounter' (Rinaldi, 2006, p.14). Critchley, et al. (1996) advocate that by accepting 'the ethics of an encounter' (p.14), there is openness to the 'other' and an attempt to make meaning of the 'other' without fixed ideas of what is appropriate. This requires a reflexive attitude by examining those influences that determine our ability to welcome difference and new knowledge (Derrida, 1999) and corresponds with the process of critical reflection, in particular the McLeod's Reflexive Framework (2015) and Brookfield's four 'lenses' (1995, 2017). This second stage of multiple listening also draws a parallel with Shier's 'Pathways to participation' (2001) and the openings that are created as a result of openness to 'other' (in this instance, opportunities for children). According to Schön (1983; 1987) and Carr and Kemmis (1986), the overall benefit of multiple listening is an enhanced professional knowledge and practice. Once again though, van Manen (1995) is cautious and considers that 'even with the best of intentions, things do not [always] happen this way' mainly because 'life in classrooms . . . is dynamic [and] ever changing every moment, every second' (p.40). As such multiple listening is more complex than perhaps it sounds.

iii) Visible *listening*

Thirdly, visible listening is required for Rinaldi's (2006) pedagogy of relationships which includes a response or a 'demonstration' of commitment. There is an evaluative process by the educator which recognises the relevance and the need to consider the implications for future practice and as a result adopt a new approach. In this way Shier's (2001) 'obligations' as part of his 'Pathways to participation' model offers a means of demonstrating participatory 'visible listening' and also 'Remembering' from McLeod's Reflexive Framework, so critical reflection is sustainable. In essence, what is needed is for educators to take responsibility and make informed decisions about every day practice so that the accepted developmental and outcome model is challenged (Dahlberg and Moss, 2005; McLeod, 2011, 2012, 2015). Only by questioning every day practice in terms of personal values, beliefs, and the influences on it can moral and socially just pedagogical approaches be valued and nurtured. In response to this crisis of domination in education and in an attempt to think differently and reject the dominant discourse that prevails, the question asked by Ball (2016) (cited in Moss, 2017) is 'what kind of self, what kind of subject have we become, and how might we be otherwise?' (Ball, 2016, p.5), Moss (2017) calls for 'an openness to uncertainty, unpredictability and wonder' (p.20) for where there is a will and a desire, there is power, and 'where there is power, there is resistance' (Foucault, 1978, p.95).

The fundamentals of the pedagogy of listening closely resemble Shier's (2001) participation model, Dewey's (1933) attitudes, Brookfield's (1995, 2017) lenses, Pollard's (2002) competencies, and Scharmer's (2009) Theory U core elements. In this way, there is a close relationship between Rinaldi's 'pedagogy of listening' and 'critical reflection' and a need for openness and self-awareness. Table 3.1 highlights the reciprocal relationship between critical reflection and participation which together can support and reinforce one another. Put more simply, the facilitation of participatory practice can be empowering for both child and educator.

Such practice offers hope for a renewed culture of childhood and establishes schools as part of a democratic society where there is an ethical awareness driven by curiosity, openness and a desire and willingness to question and reflect critically (Dahlberg and Moss, 2005). When resistance is combined with movement, there is hope, in the same way that Freire (1970, 1994) promoted in his *Pedagogy of Hope*. Hope is the necessary ingredient for being successful in the future success of the future directory of early childhood education and in contesting the narrow perception of outcome driven focus on developmental learning and standardised testing, so a new reality of an alternative discourse of quality determined by democratic entitlements and structures becomes the norm. In this way early childhood education challenges the traditional and conventional idea of knowledge development and can promote a social constructivist interpretation of learning, where knowledge is generated by complex and multidimensional processes simultaneously moving in different directions (Karlsson Häikiö, 2017, 2018a, 2018b, 2018c), and children are empowered to act as social agents (make decisions about things that are important to them as part of daily life). Such approaches involve complex internal awareness by children as discussed next.

TABLE 3.1 Reciprocal relationship between critical reflection and participation

The relationship between critical reflection and participation

Participation Shier (2001)	Awareness of power relation-ships	Dewey's Attitudes	Pollard's Competencies	Brookfield's Lenses	McLeod's Reflexive Framework	Scharmer's Theory U
	Openings	**Open mindedness** self awareness & assess-ment open to recognise & see new ways **Responsibility** to consider consequences as part of everyday practice **Wholeheartedness** – genuine energy & enthusiasm	**Empirical** – (objective & subjective) **Analytical** inter-pretation of observations **Evaluate** accurately through an aware-ness of own values and views	**Own view** **Child's** **Other adult / Colleague** **Literature**	**Readiness** to be **open** **Recalling** a **critical incident** **Recognising personal** views **Reflecting** from a **child's / another person's** perspective	Open mind
	Opportu-nities	**Open mindedness** to see children's view in new ways **Responsibility** to con-sider consequences of an action for the child **Wholeheartedness** – genuine energy & enthusiasm	**Empirical** – (objective & subjective) **Analytical** inter-pretation of observations **Evaluate**	**Own** **Child's** **Other adult / Colleague** **Literature**	• **Readiness** to be **open**, • **Recalling** a **critical incident** • **Recognising personal** views • **Reflecting** from**child's /** another perspective • **Reviewing together** • **Relating** to **reading** / research • **Reappraising the relevance** and implications • **Responding** with appropriate changes • **Remembering** the **benefits**	Open mind and heart

Obligations	**Open mindedness** to change **Responsibility** to consider consequences as part of everyday practice **Wholeheartedness** – genuine energy & enthusiasm	**Empirical** – (objective & subjective) **Analytical** inter-pretation of observations **Evaluate**	**Own** **Child's** **Other adult / Colleague** **Literature**	• **Readiness** to be **open**, • **Recalling** a **critical incident** • **Recognising personal** views • **Reflecting** from a **child's /** another perspective • **Reviewing together** • **Relating** to **reading** / research • **Reappraising the relevance** and implications • **Responding** with appropriate changes • **Remembering** the **benefits**	Open mind, heart and will

Children's agency and internal awareness

In comparison to the internal, multiple, and visible listening that is required by adults for a pedagogy of relationship (Rinaldi, 2006), Hilppö et al. (2016) and Gallagher (2012) highlight the complex internal relationship that children experience as part of agency. This involves connections between the underlying structure of different socio-cultural contexts, and the relationship with different internal functions, such as thought, language, feelings, aspirations, and the confidence required to take action. Roth (2010) sees children's sense of agency as related to individual children's 'capabilities, aspirations, and perceived opportunities and limitations to take action' (p.159).

In educational situations such inner processes are not always observable from an extrinsic position. Hilppö et al. (2016) refer to this concept as 'radical passivity': an unconscious idea which transforms into a more conscious intentional process. For Roth (2010) this influences a child's intent about whether to act or not (p.160). The drive for a child to do something comes from an inner experience (intrinsic motivation) of wanting to do something (an extrinsic action). This want is not always observable, but can still create a radical force lying behind a becoming action or a choice not to act. In particular, Hilppö et al. (2016) identify the need for a desire by a child to 'want to', plus a belief that 'I can' and a confidence in it being 'possible' (p.165). This is comparable with Vygotsky's socio-cultural theory, a higher consciousness, and an awareness of actions, involving thinking and reflecting on as different levels in the conscious or not yet conscious learning process (Karlsson Häikiö, 2017, 2018b, 2018c). Such internal awareness or 'radical passivity' is useful in understanding the complexity of children's agency and how educators in an early childhood environment in different ways can support the children's awareness of their agency, and so play an important role in facilitating children's agency or not. It is comparable with Levinas's 'ethics of an encounter' (Rinaldi, 2006, p.14) and the need for open and accurate interpretation by educators as part of encounters with children. Given that adults can act as a potential barrier to children having a voice and participation, the following case study has been selected as a way of demonstrating how participation and 'the ethics of an encounter' plays out in practice. Various associated issues and tensions are revealed.

The following conversation provides an insight into an educator's internal awareness and how this facilitated children's participation.

It is written by Julie, a Reception teacher in England who engaged in McLeod's (2012) doctoral research which was entitled: 'Critical reflection as a tool for developing pedagogical participation with young children' (2011). The conversation is part of a creative evaluation and includes Julie's thoughts and views about participation before she engaged in the project, during, and afterwards. To do this, she selected creative picture cards that captured her experience. The following text is the narrative spoken by Julie.

> ***Before the project:*** *I felt like I had a huge mountain of things and everything was going on and really I just needed to understand that there are a huge amount of benefits that come out of listening to children. Letting go was scary because you leave a lot behind, so it's making sure the scary doesn't take over.*
>
> ***During the project:*** *To some people it seems out of the ordinary to follow what children would like to do but actually it's so important that we listen to the children, but it goes against the norm. Sometimes we don't realise the easiest path to meeting children's interests and we try to go around it the wrong way when really as long as we have that basic desire to listen and participate it's easy.*
>
> ***Forwards into the future:*** *The way I see it, the journey's not finished yet, we've got further to go and I don't think we'll ever be finished . . . We need to share with other people and to help them realise the importance of participation with children. The benefits are huge. Just by listening to children, their self esteem is heightened, they see we really are interested in their ideas and the feeling of self-worth and achievements coming through by being interested in them is incredible. In terms of their learning – it just explodes into so many different areas than the narrow planning I was doing with learning objectives. It's just a case of opening the door really and letting the water in. Where did that come from? . . . . Participation has got to be a process whilst we're doing things, and, reflecting in and not just on, and hopefully I'll move more into that as part of my process of teaching a lot more.*
>
> *. . . I love where the project has brought us. I love that we dedicate time to just being with the children and sharing their experiences and ours with them and each other and giving them time so that they are just with us and not having to do a focussed activity every second. I love the freedom we've found.*

This extract tells Julie's story of genuinely growing to value reflexivity and participation with children. She recognised the benefits for both herself and the children but was aware of initial uncertainties and the importance of being open. She realised the importance of sharing what she had learnt with others and had a newfound confidence in being able to do this. This in turn enabled her to see the potential of participatory practice as an integral part of her current and future teaching (Kemmis, 2010).

A final part of the creative evaluative session together included creating a creative collage and poetic haikus as a way of sharing and seeing visually the collective knowing and experience of the whole project. Simons and McCormack (2007) suggest using approaches and resources that participants are familiar with, in particular the use of creative arts, which 'does not make assumptions about prior knowledge; but instead helps the participant to convert their tacit knowledge (knowledge we know but cannot tell) into a different context' (p.34). The teachers were invited to create a collage that captured their impressions of engaging in the project. A variety of creative resources were presented as stimuli to choose from, such as buttons, feathers, straws, stars, glitter, material, sticks, and different coloured paper. Each collage created captured the teachers' views and assumptions associated with children's participation, 'before' the project, 'during', and 'afterwards'. As each teacher shared their story, I (Naomi) noted key words and metaphorical phrases spoken. These illuminated the various experiences of taking part in the study and were used to create a poetic haiku that summarised each participant's overall experience. Three haikus are shared as follows:

Freedom to question (before)
Seeing as a whole (during)
The sky's the limit (moving forwards)

Stuck in a box
Journey of reflection
Participation through openness

Safe, open but unsure,
Inspired, open and sure,
Ready to share, empowered.

Each haiku provided a visual means of remembering the relevance and benefits of participation and, as Mitchell and Weber (1999) note, remembering serves to 'illuminate and transform the present' (p.1–2).

A posthuman perspective on children's participation

While the postmodern perspective on early childhood education (as discussed previously) is concerned with society and culture and strives to equate the child and the adult in the learning process (Dahlberg, Moss, and Pence, 1999), a posthuman perspective in turn is not interested in equality. Instead it has a completely different starting point: an anthropocentric (nature, cosmos, and culture) position where the child or the adult becomes equivalent to everything else in the educational situation (materials, objects, phenomena), all of which exert influence. To understand how this relates to children's participation, we draw on Barad's term intra-activity (2007) in comparison with the term interaction. Interaction requires interplay between individuals, that is a positioning where individuals are the starting point. In intra-action, the different agents do not work independently; they are not juxtapositioned, and do not work as opposites. Rather they involve co-operation as a starting point. For example, children often come up with interesting ideas and suggestions because they look at things in an unfiltered way. From an early educational perspective this requires a difference in how we view the child and value their individual contributions as part of a collective entity that creates change in understanding through intra-actions and relationships between child-child and child-things (Karlsson Häikiö, 2017; Lenz Taguchi, 2012). In this way entangled and multi-layered thought processes (or rhizomatic learning) and non-linear planning procedures are necessary (Deleuze and Guattari, 1988; Karlsson Häikiö, 2017, 2018c; Lenz Taguchi, 2012; Olsson, 2014).

In relation to postmodern and posthuman perspectives concerning education and teaching, Alexandersson (1994) explains the relationship between a child's individual achievements and common strategies for learning as a way of continued professional development. While teaching is often characterised as a linear way of thinking – for example in relation to planning children's learning – instead, this needs to be viewed as a more non-linear, open and holistic process (Alexandersson, 1994). A posthuman perspective presents a rhizomatic interpretation of knowledge creation, where learning takes place through unexpected ways and steps in interlaced, entangled processes (Deleuze and Guattari, 1988; Olsson, 2012, 2014; Åsberg, Hultman, and Lee, 2012). In this way there is a need for the educator to reposition (McLeod, 2017). Posthumanism therefore promotes a view of educational practice where learning can be seen as variations in an equivalent spectrum of differences, which contradicts a traditional step-by-step and measurability-adapted developmental thinking. From a posthuman perspective, each child's change in understanding, bodily development, widening of knowledge is seen as the child making difference in him- / herself as an ongoing transformation process of thought and body in space and time. The focus is not on the comparison with others based on a standardised scale, but as a process. From a pedagogical point of view, this means that all events, discoveries, and answers can be seen as valuable in an educational situation, which creates completely different conditions for learning if compared to a system based on permanent knowledge or the search for given answers (Olsson, 2014, 2012).

According to a posthuman interpretation, theories are seen as navigation instruments, where the criticism is about questioning without negativity. Barad (2012) (cited in: Dolphijn and van der Tuin, 2012) suggests the need for diffractive reading, or a reading of material where attention is given to patterns of differences that become significant (2012, p.49–52). A diffractive reading of collected materials provides tools to study both the method of observation and analysis and the object of observation. A diffractive reading of documented material can be used to create an equalisation of hierarchies and power structures in the educational activities by creating awareness among educators about their approach to children and on differences in reading of the documentation between the educators.

Through the impact of Barad's theories, and physics as her underpinning theoretical view of knowledge, physics have come to have relevance to early childhood education in the Nordic countries in recent years. Barad uses a wave as a metaphor to make clear intra-action as a phenomena of interference and describes the relationship between human and matter as an onto-epistemological entanglement (cited in Dolphijn and van der Tuin, 2012). The example of a wave shows how visible matter and invisible energy interacts or is intertwined. Intra-action is a term presented by Barad (2003, 2007) to explain her theory and why there is no distinction between objects and individual persons since everything consists of energies and relationships. From this viewpoint, no distinction is made between, for example, the researcher who regards an occurrence and what the researcher considers, or between the child who uses a material and the material per se. Everything is coherent, or interwoven on an imminent, intrinsic plane (Deleuze and Guattari, 1988). Even though we perceive the things we have around us as separate from us, the separation on the sub-nuclear level is an illusion. Basically, we are in touch with everything in our environment, and even things, like ourselves, consist of the same matter but in different forms (Karlsson Häikiö, 2017). Barad however is aware of the difficulty of releasing ourselves from humanistic thinking and the difficulty of seeing people and matter as equivalent. For this reason, she suggests that at the heart of internal dialogue, and questioning of self, avoiding the term 'agent' is recommended because this 'works against the relational ontology' proposed by Barad (cited in Dolphijn and van der Tuin, 2012). Put simply, in the granting of agency by humans, this pulls us back into a familiar unequal power balance as it is the adult who gives agency to the child. Barad therefore advocates a relational and dialogic process so knowledge is created in an intra-active process (Karlsson Häikiö, 2017).

As a result of the deep collaborations and the reading we have engaged in as part of writing this book, we recognise and appreciate the relationship between human and non-human matter and the importance of being in touch with our environment. This is reflected in the following adapted version of McLeod's Framework, so that it now includes the need to not just reflect from human perspectives, but also to value the non-human lens, such as the environment. Figures 3.3a, 3.3b, and 3.3c depict this.

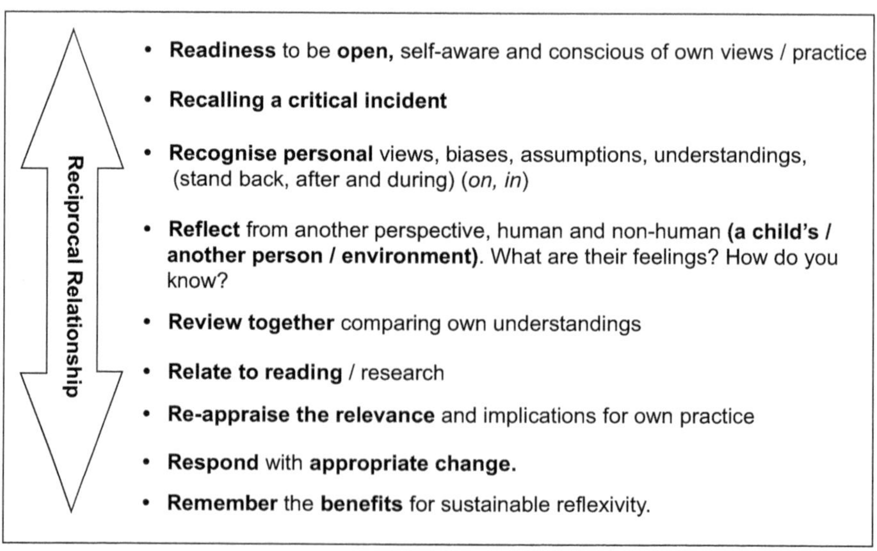

FIGURE 3.3A Reflexivity Framework.

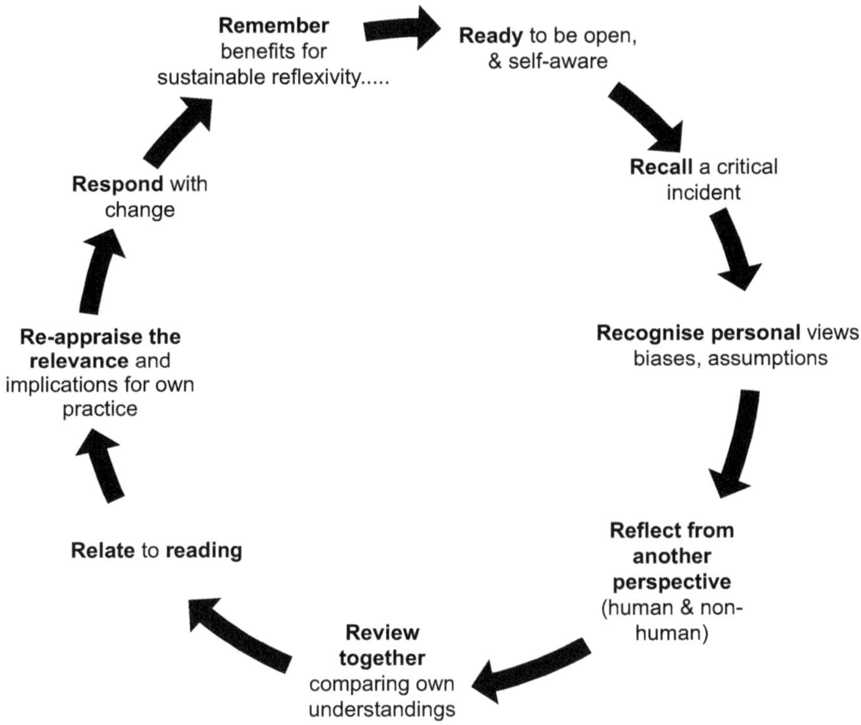

FIGURE 3.3B Reflexivity Framework.

FIGURE 3.3C Reflexivity Framework.

Barriers to voice and participation: A way forward

Unless involving children is accompanied by a respect and commitment to genuine and true openness through internal dialogic awareness, young children's participation, voice, and agency will remain tokenistic (May, 2005).

MacNaughton et al. (2007) note three barriers that can prevent participation. Firstly, educators can be dubious about the possibility of having meaningful consultations with young children if they are not viewed as capable. Secondly, educators can lack in confidence or competence about how to ask young children questions (anxiety and a lack of skills), and third, even if educators can overcome the two barriers, there is often insufficient time to enable meaningful conversations. Finding time for reflection can often be a stumbling block for educators in England alongside the political demands of accountability required by settings from Ofsted and Central Government (Marcos, Miguel, and Tillema, 2009). In addition, Ashworth (2004) recognises that for many educators, the fear of losing control can act as a barrier to participation. Scharmer (2009) refers to this as 'the voice of fear' which can block an open will essential for 'letting go' and being able to drop the 'habitual self'. Consequently practice suffers. As Bath (2009, p.34) suggests, in the context of early childhood policy and education, an opening up is essential by educators as part of a critically reflective approach.

Summary

What has emerged from this chapter is an understanding of the reciprocal nature between participation and critical reflection. The integral concepts of ethical openness, authentic engagement, and honesty at the heart of each process can facilitate deep self-awareness and self-examination, thus enabling a reflexive new position as advocated by Aristotle, Dewey, Schön, and Barad. We conclude by proposing that together as a reciprocal relationship, the processes of reflexivity and participation support and strengthen each other. In theory, this suggests that collectively they are more likely to be successful as a sustainable practice that is empowering for both educators and children.

POINTS FOR REFLECTION

- In what ways do you respect and value children's ideas and interests / voice and agency?
- Listening, consulting, and participating with children needs to be identified as
- a personal area of development so it becomes a commitment.
- What might the benefits of participation be for children and yourself?
- Are there aspects of your practice that are habitual rather than participatory?
- How might you overcome any barriers that prevent children's agency?
- How may non-human as well as human features be relevant as part of your own practice?

References

Alderson, P. (2000) *Young children's rights*, London: Jessica Kingsley.

Alexandersson, M. (1994) *Styrning på villovägar; Perspektiv på skolans utveckling under 1990-talet* [*Steering our of track: Perspectives on school development in the 1990s*], Skolverket.

Åsberg, C., Hultman, M. and Lee, F. (2012) *Posthumanistiska nyckeltexter* [*Post-human key texts*], Lund: Studentlitteratur.

Ball, S. (2016) 'Subjectivity as a site of struggle: Refusing neoliberalism?' *British Journal of Sociology of Education*, 37(8), p.1–18.

Barad, K. (2007) *Meeting the universe halfway: Quantum physics and the entanglement of matter and meaning*, Durham, NC: Duke University Press.

Barad, K. (2003) 'Posthumanist performantivity: Towards an understanding of how matter comes to matter', *Signs*, 28(3), p.801–831.

Bath, C. (2009) *Learning to belong: Exploring young children's participation at the start of school*, London: Routledge.

Beetlestone, F. (1998) *Creative children, imaginative teaching*, Buckingham: Open University Press.

Beijaard, D., Meijer, P. and Verloop, N. (2004) 'Reconsidering research on teachers' professional identity', *Teaching and Teacher Education*, 20(2), p.107–128. DOI: doi:10.1016/j.tate.2003.07.001.

Borland, M. (2001) *Improving consultation with children in relevant aspects of policy making and legislation in Scotland*, Edinburgh: Scottish Parliament.

Bronfenbrenner, U. (2004) *Making human beings human: Biological perspectives on human development*, London: SAGE Publications.

Bronfenbrenner, U. (1979) *The ecology of human development: Experiments by nature and design*, Cambridge, MA: Harvard University Press.

Brookes, L. (2018) 'Why we need to listen to children of prisoners', *European Journal of Research, Development and Policy*, 53(3), p.271–274.

Brookfield, S.D. (2017) *Becoming a critically reflective teacher*, (2nd edn.) San Francisco: Jossey-Bass A Wiley Company.

Brookfield, S.D. (1995) *Becoming a critically reflective teacher*, San Francisco: Jossey-Bass A Wiley Company.

Carr, W. (1998) 'The curriculum in and for a democratic society', *Curriculum Studies*, 6(3), p.323–340. DOI: doi:10.1080/14681369800200044.

Carr, W. and Kemmis, S. (1986) *Becoming critical: Education, knowledge and action research*, Lewes, England: Falmer Press.

Chan, K.H. (2011) 'Rethinking children's participation in curriculum making: A rhizomatic movement', *International Critical Childhood Policy Studies*, 4(1), p.107–122.

Clark, A. (2017) *Listening to young children: A guide to understanding the Mosaic Approach*, (3rd edn.) London: Jessica Kingsley Publishers LTD.

Clark, A. (2005) 'Listening to and involving young children: A review of research and practice', *Early Child Development & Care*, 175(6), p.489–505. DOI: doi:10.1080/03004430500131288.

Clark, A. (2004) 'The Mosaic Approach and research with young children', in: V. Lewis, M. Kellett, C. Robinson, S. Fraser and S. Ding (Eds.) *The reality of research with children and young people*, London: SAGE.

Clark, A. and Moss, P. (2001) *Listening to young children: The Mosaic Approach*, London: National Children's Bureau and Joseph Rowntree Foundation.

Craft, A. (2002) *Creativity and early years education: A lifewide foundation*, London: Continuum.

Critchley, S., Peperzak, A.T. and Bernasconi, R. (Eds.) (1996) *Emmanuel Levinas: Basic philosophical writings*, Bloomington: Indiana University Press.

Cutler, D. (2002) *Taking the initiative*, London: Carnegie United Kingdom Trust.

Dahlberg, G. and Moss, P. (2005) *Ethics and politics in early childhood education*, Abingdon: Routledge Falmer.

Dahlberg, G., Moss, P. and Pence, A. (1999) *Beyond quality in early childhood education and care: Postmodern perspectives*, London: Falmer Press.

Davies, S. and Artaraz, K. (2009) 'Towards an understanding of factors influencing early years professionals' practice of consultation with young people', *Children and Society*, 23(1), p.57–69. DOI: doi:10.1111/j.1099–0860.2008.00142.x.

Davis, J. and Elliot, S. (2014) *Research in early childhood education for sustainability: International perspectives and provocations*, Abingdon: Routledge.

Department for Children, Schools and Families (DCSF) (2008) *Practice guidance for the early years foundation stage*, Crown copyright 2008, Department for Children, Schools and Families.

Department for Education (DfE) (2017) *Statutory framework for the early years foundation stage: Setting the standards for learning, development and care for children from birth to five*, London: Crown copyright.

Deleuze, G. (1994) *Difference and repetition* (P. Patton Trans.), New York: Columbia University Press.

Deleuze, G. and Guattari, F. (1988) *A thousand plateaus: Capitalism and schizophrenia*, London: Athlone Press.

Derrida, J. (1999) *Adieu to Levinas*, Stanford, CA: Stanford University Press.

Dewey, J. (1933) *How we think: A restatement of the relation of reflective thinking to the educative process*, New York: Heath and Company.

Dockett, S. and Perry, B. (2007) 'Trusting children's accounts in research', *Early Childhood Research*, 5(1), p.47–63. DOI: doi:10.1177/1476718X07072152.

Dolphijn, R. and van der Tuin, I. (2012) *New materialism: Interviews and cartographies*, University of Michigan: Open Humanities Press.

Feldman, A. and Weiss, T. (2010) 'Understanding change in teachers' ways of being through collaborative action research: A cultural-historical activity theory analysis', *Educational Action Research*, 18(1), p.29–55. DOI: doi:10.1080/09650790903484517.

Fisher, J. (2013) *Starting from the child: Teaching and learning in the foundation stage*, (4th edn.) Maidenhead: Open University Press.

Foucault, M. (1978) *The history of sexuality, volume 1: An introduction* (R. Hurley Trans.), New York: Pantheon Books.

Freire, P. (1994) *Pedagogy of hope*, New York: Continuum.

Freire, P. (1970) *Cultural action for freedom* (M. Bergman Trans.), Middlesex, England: Penguin.

Gallagher, S. (2012) 'Multiple aspects in the sense of agency', *New Ideas in Psychology*, 30(1), p.15–31. DOI: doi:10.1016/j.newideapsych.2010. 03. 00doi:3.

Giardiello, P. (2014) *Pioneers in early childhood education*, London: Routledge.

Graham, A. and Fitzgerald, R. (2010) 'Progressing children's participation: Exploring the potential of a dialogical turn', *Childhood*, 17(3), p.343–359.

Greig, A., Taylor, J. and MacKay, T. (2007) *Doing research with children*, (2nd edn.) London: SAGE.

Hart, J. (2009) 'Charting change in the participatory setting of childhood', in: N. Thomas (Ed.) *Children, politics and communication: Participation at the margins*, Bristol: Policy Press.

Hart, R. (1992) 'Children's participation: From tokenism to citizenship', UNICEF Innocenti Essays. Florence, Italy: UNICEF.

Hart, J., Newman, J., Ackerman, L. and Feeney, T. (2004) *Children changing their world: Understanding and evaluating children's participation in development*, Woking: Plan International.

Her Majesty's Stationery Office (2014) *The Children and Families Act*. Parliament of the United Kingdom / Crown copyright.

Her Majesty's Stationery Office (2006) *The Childcare Act*. Parliament of the United Kingdom / Crown copyright.

Her Majesty's Stationery Office (2004) *The Children Act*. Parliament of the United Kingdom / Crown copyright.

Hilppö, J.Lipponen, L.Kumpulainen, K. and Rainio, A. (2016) 'Children's sense of agency in preschool: A sociocultural investigation', *International Journal of Early Years Education*, 24 (2), p.157–171. DOI: doi:10.1080/09669760.2016.1167676.

Hultman, K. and Lenz Taguchi, H. (2010) 'Challenging anthropocentric analysis of visual data: A relational materialist methodological approach to educational research', *International Journal of Qualitative Studies in Education*, 23(5), p.525–542.

Jeffrey, B. and Woods, P. (2009) *Creative learning in the primary school*, London: Routledge.

Karlsson Häikiö, T. (2018a) 'Cultural participation for, with and by children: Enhancing children's agency through art pedagogy, visual knowledge-building and learning', *InFormation – Nordic Journal of Art and Research*, 7(1), p.19. Available from: https://doi.org/10.7577/information.v7i1.2630.

Karlsson Häikiö, T. (2018b) 'The atelier as a potential space for transformative learning processes', in: T. Karlsson Häikiö and K. G. Eriksson (Eds.) *Art-based education; An ethics and politics of relation. Making Narratives*, Vol. 3/2018. HDK, Academy of Design and Crafts. University of Gothenburg.

Kalsson Häikiö, T. (2018c) 'Förskolan som visuell kultur [Preschool as visual culture]', in: M. Bendroth Karlsson, T. Karlsson Häikiö and L.O. Magnusson, *Skapande verksamhet i förskolan; Kreativt arbete med analoga och digitala redskap* [*Creative activity in preschool through use of analogue and digital tools*], Lund: Studentlitteratur.

Kalsson Häikiö, T. (2017) 'Dokumentation, transformation och intra-modala materialiseringar [Documentation, transformation and intra-modal materialisations]', in: B. Bergstedt, *Posthumanistisk pedagogik; Teori, undervisning och forskningspraktik* [*Post-human pedagogics: Theory, education and research practice*], Malmö: Gleerups.

Katz, J. (1992) 'Abuse of human beings for the sake of science', in: A.L. Caplan (Ed.) *When medicine went mad: Bioethics and the Holocaust*, Totowa, NJ: Humana Press.

Kellett, M. (2011) 'Engaging with children and young people', Centre for Children and Young People: Background Briefing Series, no. 3. Lismore, NSW, Australia: Centre for Children and Young People, Southern Cross University.

Kelley, N. (2006) 'Children's involvement in policy formation', *Children's Geographies*, 4(1), p.37–44. DOI: doi:10.1080/14733280600577145.

Kemmis, S. (2010) 'What is to be done? The place of action research', *Educational Action Research*, 18(4), p.417–427. DOI: doi:10.1080/09650792.2010.524745.

Kirby, P. and Gibbs, S. (2006) 'Facilitating participation: Adults' caring support roles within child-to-child projects in schools and after-school settings', *Children and Society*, 20(3), p.209–222.

Lancaster, P. (2003) *Listening to young children*, Maidenhead, England: Open University Press.

Landsdown, G. (2005) *Can you hear me? The right of young children to participate in decisions affecting them*, Working paper 36, The Hague: Bernard van Leer Foundation.

Leather, M. (2017) 'A critique of forest school: Something lost in translation', *Journal of Outdoor and Environmental Education*, Council of Australia. p.2–10.

Lee, L. (1975) *Cider with Rosie*, London: Penguin Books.

Lenz Taguchi, H. (2012) *Pedagogisk dokumentation som aktiv agent: Introduktion till intra-aktiv pedagogik* [*Pedagogical documentation as active agent: Introduction to intra-active pedagogics*], Malmö: Gleerups utbildning.

Lundy, L. (2007) 'Voice is not enough: Conceptualising Article 12 of the United Nations Convention on the Rights of the Child', *British Educational Research Journal*, 33(6), p.927–942.

MacNaughton, G. (2005) *Doing Foucault in early childhood studies: Applying poststructural ideas*, London: Routledge.

MacNaughton, G., Hughes, P. and Smith, K. (2007) 'Early childhood professionals and children's rights: Tensions and possibilities around the United Nations General Comment No. 7 on Children's Rights', *International Journal of Early Years Education*, 15(2), p.161–170. DOI: doi:10.1080/09669760701288716.

Malaguzzi, L. (1992) *A charter of rights*, Municipality of Reggio Emilia: Italy.

Manful, E. and McCrystal, P. (2010) 'Conceptualisation of children's rights: What do child care professionals in Northern Ireland say?' *Child Care in Practice*, 16(1), p.83–97. DOI: doi:10.1080/13575270903381744.

Marcos, J.J.M., Miguel, E.S. and Tillema, H. (2009) 'Teacher reflections on action: What is said (in research) but what is done (in teaching)', *Reflective Practice*, 10(2), p.191–204. DOI: doi:10.1080/14623940902786206.

May, H. (2005) 'Whose participation is it anyway? Examining the context of pupil participation in the UK', *British Journal of Special Education*, 32(1), p.29–34. DOI: doi:10.1111/j.0952–3383.2005.00366.x.

McAlpine, L. and Weston, C. (2000) 'Reflection: Issues related to improving professors' teaching and students' learning', *Instructional Science*, 28(5), p.363–385. DOI: doi:10.1023/A:1026583208230.

McNeish, D. (1999) 'Promoting participation for children and young people: Some key questions for health and social welfare organizations', *Journal of Social Work Practice*, 13, p.191–204. DOI: 10.doi:1080/026505399103403.

McLeod, A. (2008) *Listening to children: A practitioner's guide*, London: Jessica Kingsley Publishers.

McLeod, N. (2015) 'Reflecting on reflection: Improving teacher's readiness to facilitate participatory learning with young children', *Professional Development in Education*, 41(2), p.254–272.

McLeod, N. (2012) *Critical reflection as a tool for developing pedagogical participation with young children in their learning*, Thesis (EdD). University of Sheffield library.

McLeod, N. (2011) 'Exploring early years educators' ownership of language and communication knowledge and skills: A review of key policy and initial reflections on Every Child a Talker and its implementation', *Education 3–13 International Journal of Primary, Elementary and Early Years Education*, 39(4), p.429–445. DOI: doi:10.1080/03004271003776850.

Miller, J. (2003) *Never too young: How young children can take responsibility and make decisions*, London: Save the Children.

Mitchell, C. and Weber, S. (1999) *Reinventing ourselves as teachers: Beyond nostalgia*, London: Falmer Press.

Montessori, M. (1967) *The absorbent mind* (C. Claremont Trans.), New York: Dell Publishing. (Original work published 1949).

Montessori, M. (1966) *The discovery of the child* (M. Johnstone Trans.), Madras, India: Kalakshetra Publications. (Original work published 1948).

Moore, T. (2008) 'Little voices and big ideas: Lessons learned from children about research', *International Journal of Qualitative Methods*, 7(2), p.77–91. Accessed on 7 July 2008. Available from: http://creaivecommons.org/licenses/by/2.0.

Morrow, V. (2008) 'Ethical dilemmas in research with young children and young people about their social environments', *Children's Geographies*, 6(1), p.47–61. DOI: doi:10.1080/14733280701791967.

Morrow, V. (1999) 'It's cool . . . cos' you can't give us detentions and things can you?: Reflections on research with children', in: P. Milner and B. Carolin (Eds.). *Time to listen to children: Personal and professional communication*, London: Routledge, p.203–215.

Morrow, V. and Richards, M. (1996) 'The ethics of social research with children: An overview', *Children & Society*, 10(2), p.90–105. DOI: doi:10.1111/j.1099–0860.1996.tb00461.x.

Moss, P. (2017) 'Power and resistance in early childhood education: From dominant discourse to democratic experimentalism', *Journal of Pedagogy*, 8(1), p.11–32. DOI: doi:10.1515/jped-2017–0001.

Moss, P. (2014) '*Transformative change and real utopias in early childhood education: A story of democracy, experimentation and potentiality*', London: Routledge.

Moss, P. (2013) 'Beyond the investment narrative', *Contemporary Issues in Early Childhood*, 14(4), p.370–372.

Moss, P., Petrie, P. and Poland, G. (1999) *Rethinking school: Some international perspectives*, York, England: Joseph Rowntree Foundation.

Müller-Hill, B. (1992) 'Eugenics: The science and religion of the Nazis', in: A.L. Caplan (Ed.) *When medicine went mad: Bioethics and the Holocaust*, Totowa, NJ: Humana Press.

Myhill, D. (2006) 'Talk, talk, talk: Teaching and learning in whole class discourse', *Research Papers in Education*, 21(1), p.19–41. DOI: doi:10.1080/02671520500445425.

Norling, M., Sandberg, A. and Almqvist, L. (2015) 'Engagement and emergent literacy practices in Swedish preschools', *European Early Childhood Education Research Journal*, 23(5), p.619–634.

Nutbrown, C. (Ed.) (1996) *Respectful educators – capable learners: Children's rights and early education*, London: Paul Chapman.

Ofsted (2017) *Bold beginnings: The reception curriculum in a sample of good and outstanding primary schools*, Manchester: The Office for Standards in Education, Children's Services and Skills.

Olsson, L.M. (2014) *Rörelse och experimenterande i små barns lärande; Deleuze och Guattari i förskolan [Movement and experimentation in small children's learning: Deleuze and Guattari in preschool]*, Lund: Studentlitteratur.

Olsson, L.M. (2012) 'Eventicizing curriculum; Learning to read and write through becoming a citizen of the world', *Journal of Curriculum Theorizing*, 28(1), p.88–107.

Orlandi, K. (2014) 'Addressing the attrition between the conflicting influences experienced by teachers on the interface between Foundation Stage and Key Stage One', *Journal of Early Childhood Research*, 12(3), p.294–307.

Pascal, C. and Bertram, T. (2009) 'Listening to young citizens: The struggle to make real a participatory paradigm in research with young children', *European Early Childhood Education Research Journal*, 17(2), p.249–262.

Percy-Smith, B. and Thomas, N. (Eds) (2009) *A handbook of children and young people's participation: Perspectives from theory and practice*, Abingdon: Routledge.

Price, J.N. and Valli, L. (2005) 'Pre-service teachers becoming agents of change: Pedagogical implications for action research', *Journal of Teacher Education*, 56(1), p.57–72. DOI: doi:10.1177/0022487104272097.

Rautio, P. (2014) 'Mingling and imitating in producing spaces for knowing and being: Insights from a Finnish study of child–matter intra-action', *Childhood*, 21(4), p.461–474.

Rinaldi, C. (2012) 'The pedagogy of listening: The listening perspective from Reggio Emilia', in: C. Edwards, L. Gandini and G. Forman (Eds.) *The hundred languages of children: The Reggio Emilia experience in transformation*, Oxford: Praeger, p.233–246.

Rinaldi, C. (2006) *In dialogue with Reggio Emilia: Listening, researching and learning*, London: Routledge.

Rogoff, B. (2003) *The cultural nature of human development*, New York: Oxford University Press.

Roth, W.M. (2010) *Language, learning, context: Talking the talk (Foundations and futures of education)*, (1st edn.) New York: Routledge.

Scharmer, C.O. (2009) *Theory U: Leading from the future as it emerges*, San Francisco, CA: Berrett-Koehler Publishers.

Schön, D.A. (1987) *Educating the reflective practitioner towards a new design for teaching*, San Francisco, CA: Josset-Bass.

Schön, D.A. (1983) *The reflective practitioner: How professionals think in action*, New York: Basic Books.

Shier, H. (2001) 'Pathways to participation: Openings, opportunities and obligations', *Children and Society*, 15(2), p.107–117.

Simons, H. and McCormack, B. (2007) 'Integrating arts-based inquiry in evaluation methodology: Challenges and opportunities', *Qualitative Inquiry*, 13(2), p.292–311.

Thomson, P. (Ed.) (2008) *Doing visual research with children and young people*, London, New York: Routledge.

UNICEF (1995) *The convention on the rights of the child: Official text know your rights! Translation for young people*, UK Committee for UNICEF.

United Nations (1989) *Convention on the rights of the child*, New York: United Nations.

van Manen, M. (1995) 'Epistemology of reflective practice', *Teachers and Teaching: Theory and Practice*, 1(1), p.33–50. DOI: doi:0001607LO.

Villen, K. (1993) 'Pre-school education in Denmark', in: T. David (Ed.) *Educational provision for our youngest children: European perspectives*, London: Paul Chapman, p.18–34.

Vygotsky, L.S. (1986) *Thought and language*, Cambridge, MA: MIT Press.

Vygotsky, L.S. (1978) *Mind in society: The development of higher psychological processes*, Cambridge, MA: Harvard University Press.

Wall, J. (2016) 'Children and the future of human rights: From saving to child empowerment', *Growing w/ Design. Making Narratives, volume 1*. HDK – Academy of Design and Crafts. University of Gothenburg.

Wall, J. (2008) 'Human rights in light of childhood', *International Journal of Children's Rights*, 16, p.523–543.

Wyness, M. (2006) 'Children, young people and civic participation: Regulation and local diversity', *Educational Review*, 58(2), p.209–218.

PART 2

Five international pedagogies as provocation

Part 2 lies at the heart of the book and builds on the ideas and provocations of the previous three chapters. Chapters 4 to 8 examine the distinctive philosophical, theoretical and practical interpretations of five international approaches: the Maria Montessori method, the Reggio Emilia project, the Finnish perspective, Te Whāriki and Danish outdoor nature pedagogy using a critical lens, alongside case studies from Sweden, Finland, Denmark, New Zealand and England. As each is evaluated in relation to contextual historical, socio-cultural and political influences, we ask how the different approaches can be useful within one's own culture and the varying early childhood education programmes and what can be learned. Through this process the intention is for the reader to develop a personal philosophy of education that is valuable within their own context.

4

MARIA MONTESSORI (WITH PERSPECTIVES FROM SWEDEN)

Patricia Giardiello and Kerstin Signert

The most important period in Montessori's curriculum are the formative years:

> At birth, the child leaves a person – his mother's womb – and this makes him independent of her bodily functions. The baby is next endowed with an urge, or need, to face the out world and to absorb it. We might say that he is born with 'the psychology of world conquest.' By absorbing what he finds about him, he forms his own personality.
>
> *(Montessori, 1985, p.84)*

Given the sentiment expressed in this quote it is worthwhile examining Montessori's formative years to begin to understand what "psychology of world conquest" led to her distinct philosophy, values and beliefs that have left a lasting legacy on early childhood education.

Montessori was born into a middle-class family on the 31st August 1870 in the town of Chiaravalle, in the province of Ancona, Italy, during a time of political turbulence. In a land for centuries divided into separate states, Italy had finally become a unified country with Rome newly elected as its capital in 1871. Montessori, who as a child was talented, headstrong, self-confident, optimistic and stimulated by change, found an ally in her mother Renilde, who was an educated person and loved Italian literature. Renilde was a constant support for her daughter's innovative ideas and unusual lifestyle choices for that era, in contrast to a certain conservatism from her father. Kramer (1976, p.28) reports that Montessori became seriously ill at age 10, greatly concerning her mother. Maria told her, "Don't worry, Mother, I cannot die: I have too much to do."

When Montessori was still attending infant school, a left-wing government came to power, responsible for inaugurating social and educational reform (Chisnall, 2008). This had a direct bearing on Montessori's own educational journey as up to this time girls were not encouraged to receive more than a basic elementary school education. Thus, at the age of 13, Montessori began secondary education and excelled in mathematics. To fulfil her desire, at the time, to become an engineer, Montessori's next step was to enrol at the local Technical College. However, these were times when medicine, rather than other disciplines, provided a platform on which to speak out across a broad agenda including the physical, moral and social regeneration of the recently created Italian nation. Furthermore in Italy, as in most other European countries at the time, the medical degree provided an early point of access for women to enter universities (Babini, 2000). Consequently in 1889, in a sudden change of direction, Montessori enrolled in the Faculty of Medicine of La Sapienza the University of Rome and although she was not, as is generally claimed, the first female medical graduate in Italy, she was the only female during her time at La Sapienza to graduate with a degree in medicine (Giardiello, 2014). In 1896, on completion of her medical degree specialising in psychiatry, a choice based on her passion for scientific research and the social implications of psychological research, Montessori began her work in the public medical clinics in Rome whilst at the same time entering the political arena as a proponent of socialist policies arising from the Italian feminist movement. These early experiences influenced her later pedagogical philosophy.

An examination of contextual socio-cultural, historical, political influences

Montessori saw feminism, politics and social medicine as inextricably intertwined and in the public eye she increasingly became the "face" of her causes, one which was how best to care for the "feeble minded" children who at best were being kept back in elementary schools and weighing heavily on municipal finances (Babini, 2000, p.50). In current times, a major concern amongst early childhood educationalists is the way in which globalised education trends mix with national and local politics and social-culture influences to explain the unfolding of policy, as noted in Chapter 1 which examines cultural influences and how children are viewed. Montessori believed that if mankind was going to create a new order of society, with morality and social values rather than conquest, power and profit at its core (Duckworth, 2006), then adults, including educators, "should have faith in the fresh vitality and uncluttered vision of the child as a messiah" (Montessori, 1972, p.14).

Wyness (2006) asserts that educational practices and policies (which are explored in detail in Chapter 1) are the products of how society views children and the purpose of education; such views contribute to regarding children as future "products" whose worth will be evaluated by their later performance as adults. In her time and concerned about the perception and social status of children (Treganza, 2008, p.1), Montessori wrote that:

> A child . . . is condemned by adults to . . . places of exile until he reaches an age when he can live in an adult world without causing others distress. It is

only then that a child is admitted to society. Prior to this he has to obey adults like a person deprived of civil rights.

(1965, p.193)

Current challenges in early childhood education in England need alternative ways of thinking, acting and accommodating, and it is argued in the next part of this chapter that Montessori's distinct philosophy, values and beliefs can contribute meaningfully to this process.

The distinctive philosophical underpinning principles

Montessori gave attention to ideas of the early philosophers and educators in the formulation of her own method of education. Valuing a child-centred approach to the education of children, as espoused by Montessori, can be traced back to the ideas of Aristotle, Quintilian, Comenius, Rousseau, Locke, Pestalozzi and Froebel (see Giardiello, 2014). An ethical and democratic approach to learning and development is fostered through the child's sensory experience of the materials and didactic equipment, specifically, the child's sensory understanding of what the objects are made of, their design, their use and their aim. These four features are reminiscent of Aristotle's (384–322 BCE) list of the four causes which shape processes: matter (the material cause), pattern (the formal cause), agency (the efficient cause) and goal (the final cause) (Feez, 2007). Quintilian (1920), drawing on his own experiences as a teacher emphasised the value of observing children and recognising individual strengths, thus providing a strong connection to Montessori's principle of carefully carried out observations. Comenius also found favour with Montessori through his focus on learning through the senses, first-hand experiences and learning by doing (Comenius, 1628–1632/1907). The key ideas of Locke (1632–1704) and Rousseau (1712–1778) were also an influencing factor in the thinking behind Montessori's approach. Locke's view of the development of consciousness from concrete experience to abstraction is realised in Montessori's principle of the absorbent mind (Feez, 2007). Locke's idea of a child's mind being that of a *tabula rasa* (blank slate) upon which experiences make their mark and the importance of the child's environment in influencing thought and experiences resonated strongly with what Montessori set out to achieve in her work with children. However, Montessori went beyond Locke's *tabula rasa* theory as she believed that every child is born with some particular strength that could be uncovered and developed individually given the right conditions for learning. Practically this involves giving attention to the prepared environment in the way that the classroom is organised with large carpeted spaces punctuated by low shelves, to the manner in which the educators follow the child's lead and the way in which they interact with minimum discourse creating a sense of liberty and freedom. Rousseau, in his fictional work *Emile* (1762), presented profound ideas on education as a liberating force and a medium with which to reform society. He believed that education should take its cues from nature and allow time for children to develop and learn should self-discovery and natural unfolding of their abilities. Montessori's thinking was influenced by Rousseau in relation to her criticism of the adult world, which in her opinion gives no consideration to children (Röhrs, 1994). The Agazzi sisters, Rosa (1866–1951) and Carolina (1870–1945), well-known Italian Nursery teachers from Trieste, were also an inspiration with regard to the development of the whole child through their child-initiated practical life experiences which Montessori re-shaped and adapted using a more methodical and scientific approach (Röhrs, 1994). Although sharing a theoretical kinship with Rousseau, Pestalozzi and Froebel, Montessori believed that the existing pedagogy, handed down from these three philosophers, was incomplete and vague as it failed to embrace the importance of studying the child before educating him. Montessori adopting a positivist stance argued that merely deducing what it was like to be a child had resulted in a philosophical rather than scientific view of the child (Montessori, 1964).

In the design of her new education system Montessori formulated a multifaceted and dynamic blend of existing ideas, theories and pedagogy with new insights gained from her innovative empirical study of child development. Montessori went to explain that:

> If education is to be reformed, it must be based upon children. No longer is it enough to study great educators of the past: as Rousseau, Pestalozzi and Froebel; the time for that is over . . . what I have done is merely study the child, to take and express what he has given me and that is called the Montessori Method.
>
> *(Montessori, 1948, p.17).*

The Montessori Method

The overarching guiding principle of Montessori's revolutionary pedagogical approach, which became known through her writings as the Montessori Method, is freedom and structure. Montessori's belief was that freedom and discipline were intertwined and each could not be achieved without the other. Viewed in this way, discipline was not something imposed from the outside by an adult. but rather a challenge to become worthy of freedom (Röhrs, 1994). Seeing education as a process in setting children free, Montessori demonstrated that within a carefully structured environment children could be free to teach themselves, first through the senses and then through the intellect (Duckworth, 2006). Montessori argued for the liberty of the child, not that of pure indulgence as advocated by Rousseau, but a freedom that should permit a development of individual, spontaneous manifestations of the child's nature (Montessori, 1965, p.28). Furthermore embedded in this notion of liberty was Montessori's discovery, based on countless hours of observation, that children were not motivated by extrinsic rewards, but rather their intrinsic motivation and persistence at a task, driven by their desire to work at the task itself. For this reason, Montessori placed great emphasis on a prepared environment in which freedom was more akin to self-discipline and under the direction not of the teacher but rather a self-correcting pedagogy through the use of didactic material, a practice that Montessori describes as 'auto education' and which is at the core of her scientific pedagogy (Montessori, 1964, p.370). From a non-Montessorian perspective to some extent freedom for the child is curbed, for example, by means of the prepared environment the adult could be in control with expected outcomes in the way resources are made available to the child. On the other it could be argued that the adult responds to the child's interests in the way the environment is prepared and a Montessori classroom is uncluttered and meticulously prepared before the children arrive in the morning, with only as much material as the children need to further their development. "Overabundance debilitates and retards progress" (Montessori, 1964, p.79). This view is echoed in current times as the idea of helping young children to learn by creating calm spaces that are less like the traditional classroom (the teacher instructing from the front of the classroom to pupils sitting at desks) fits in with Early Years Foundation Stage framework (DfE, 2017) and its principle of an enabling environment Montessori's underpinning pedagogy is imbedded in the *Reggio Emilia* approach (see Chapter 5) which refers to the environment as the *Third Teacher* confirming the importance they place on creating the right environment for children to construct their own learning and development.

Although critically disposed towards Froebel's specifically designed materials which he referred to as gifts and occupations (Froebel, 1826/1906, p.205), Montessori derived inspiration for her didactic equipment predominately from Jean Itard (1775–1838) and his student Eduard Seguin (1812–1880), who both believed in educating children through their senses.

Montessori believed that "the education of the senses must be of the greatest pedagogical interest" (Montessori, 1964, p.215) particularly during the period of rapid development from birth to 7 years of age. Montessori's sensorial materials helped the young children attending her centres (known as *Case dei Bambini*) to isolate and develop the five senses of sight, sound, smell, taste and touch. These included sound boxes and bells to develop the auditory sense; food preparation and smelling bottles for the olfactory sense; colour, shape, size and form resources to develop visual sense. To promote the tactile sense, rough and smooth boards and sandpaper shapes where provided. Montessori designed further activities so that young children could combine and integrate the tactile with vestibular (balance) and proprioceptive (body awareness) stimuli. Montessori's pedagogic approach included Practical Life Exercises which worked for the vestibular and proprioceptive senses through children's care of self. These activities included: washing, brushing hair and teeth, dressing, tying of shoelaces and of care of the immediate environment, for example, polishing brass objects, washing up, watering the plants and pouring water into bowls. Through "grace and courtesy," children learnt to move gracefully, to greet each other, to lift objects carefully and to receive various objects from each other politely (Montessori, 1964). Montessori wrote "this sense training prepared the ordered foundation upon which he [the child] may build up a clear and strong mentality" (Montessori, 1964, p.216). According to Bone (2005, p.312) "in terms of sociocultural theory this 'alloy of speech and action' begins to shape a sense of self as children are involved in the experience of offering and accepting with grace in a scenario that will be repeated endlessly in life." With her scientific training and constructivist leanings, Montessori was to produce equipment that was methodically designed to exploit the progressive order in which she believed young children develop. Montessori (1967, p.27) wrote "the hands are the instruments of man's intelligence . . . He constructs his mind step by step till it becomes possessed by memory, the power to understand, the power to think."

Adaptations of Montessori's great array of sensory and sensory-motor didactic materials can be found in most early childhood settings across the world today. However, the mere presence of the materials would not be enough for Montessori, who believed that only under proper guidance would they be educationally effective (Giardiello, 2014). This rested on the principles of recognising children's growth at crucial developmental moments which Montessori referred to as Sensitive Periods. Montessori proposed that if these periods are given proper consideration, they can be exploited to promote episodes of intense and efficient learning, but if advantage is not taken of them, then those opportunities are irretrievably lost. This developmental sequence of children's mental growth attracted the attention of Jean Piaget (1954) who would eventually move beyond Montessori's concepts to formulate his own theory of developmental psychology (Feez, 2009; Giardiello, 2014; Kramer, 1976).

The role of the educator – *Direttrice*

When considering the role of the educator, Montessori differed from that found in a traditional school where the teachers were the focal point of the child's attention. Montessori preferred the term: *direttrice,* a directress who had three roles in respect of the pupils, which were to prepare the environment with meticulous attention to detail; careful use of space and separate work areas; to act as a guide and demonstrate procedures and show the correct use of the didactic materials (after this introduction, self-correcting learning would take place). Another hallmark of teaching: remain in the background directing the flow of routine classroom living, observing and keeping records of the children's activities, but never intervening or interfering (Montessori, 1964). These essential virtues of concentration, coordination, order, independence, and respect are all evident when the triangle of interactions between pupil, teacher and environment is viewed through the lens of ritual (Cossentino, 2005).

The idea that children could learn for themselves, referred to today as child-initiated learning, was quite startling at the time for those teachers who considered it their 'bounden duty' to plan for whole group learning (Burnett, 1962, p.73). In contrast to Froebel (1826/1906), who suggested that his teachers should live and play with the children leading and directing them, Montessori believed that her teachers should remain in the background, watching and facilitating but leaving the initiative entirely to the children by means of a carefully planned environment. In this respect Montessori's sense of democratic values and social justice influenced her thinking as she believed that through the development of self-discipline children would be able to act ethically and handle conflict with maturity. The essential elements of Montessori's philosophy regarding the role of the adult and the learning environment can be found in early childhood education approaches where the practitioners are skilled in "following" the child; fostering independence through a carefully prepared environment; responding to the changing interests, needs and democratic rights of the child. For example, ideas about the democratic rights of the child and the importance of a prepared environment are fundamental to what the protagonists of the internationally renowned *Reggio Emilia* Approach feel are at the centre of their educational vision. Loris Malaguzzi (1920–1994) founder of the *Reggio Emilia* Approach in Northern Italy said that they meditated on the work of Montessori, describing her reverentially as 'Montessori – she is our mother, but as all children, we have had to make ourselves independent of our mothers' (as cited in Rinaldi, 2006, p.7). Thus, Montessori's objectives for an education that promoted children's democratic freedom through a right based approach were reworked by the *Reggio Emilia* community and are at the centre of their educational vision.

Adopting a post-modernist perspective that is based on the premise that education is entering a new phase, Montessori's philosophy has much to offer early childhood education in the twenty-first century. For example, as an alternative approach to managing young children's behaviour using extrinsic rewards and sanctions, Montessori viewed order in the environment as a basic human need that could combat children's stress and instil a sense of calm. In a Montessori school prosocial interaction is fostered through grace and courtesy practices between peers and between children and adults cultivating a sense of respect (Kuh, 2014).

As climate change coupled with overpopulation and inequalities has begun to take its toll on our planet and on global human development, sustainability has become increasingly important for a prosperous future (MacDonald, 2015). According to Siraj-Blatchford et al. (2010), young children have rights and shared responsibilities in achieving a sustainable future. This was recognised by Montessori and in reverence for the natural world she maintained that "we serve the future by protecting the present" (1967, p.x). Montessori used the word "cosmic" to draw attention to the "orderly arrangement" of the universe in which children lived (Feez, 2009, p.143). The Montessori classroom provides the child with resources and materials that allow for exploration and discovery of the planet.

As educators in England contemplate the purpose of early childhood education beyond pre-determined goals for learning and doing well in tests, Montessori's distinctive philosophical principles of early childhood education might provide some guidance for an alternative route that can nurture wiser, kinder and more knowledgeable human beings.

A closer theoretical examination of two key elements of the Montessori Method

The purpose of this section is to isolate certain key elements of the Montessori Method in order to better understand why an educational method that originated over 100 years ago, in a world that was different in many ways to today's is still seen as, by many educationists, an effective approach (Marshall, 2017).

As discussed earlier, two important aspects of Montessori's educational method are the sensorial materials and the self-directed nature of children's engagement with those materials. These will now be discussed in turn with connections made to variation theory which resonates strongly with Montessori's scientific pedagogical approach.

Sensorial materials

One of the most important features of the Montessori Method are the sensorial materials which she developed from the writings of French Physicians Jean Itard (1775–1838) and Edouard Seguin (1812–1880), who believed in educating children through their senses. With her scientific training and constructivist leanings, Montessori produced equipment that was methodologically designed to exploit the progressive order in which children develop (Giardiello, 2014). Montessori observed that given the opportunity, children would rather correct themselves than depend on an adult to do it for them; this she theorised as "control of error." For example, the *cylinder block* is a clear example of Montessori's control of error. A child would not be able to fit all the cylinders properly into a cylinder block if one cylinder is out of place (each cylinder has an increasing dimension). As the sensory material is self-correcting, Montessori intended that the child needed insight and not correction. It was their own inner development that enabled the child to see the differences in the materials. Correction would therefore, according to Montessori, be made by the child independently. Children's learning is facilitated by a cumulative structure, in turn, helping children gradually develop their cognition. In this respect Montessori's sensory materials are designed to be used in a certain sequence. As the child learn to distinguish the finer differences between objects and aspects of the properties of the objects, the difficulty increased. By seeing, hearing, feeling, smelling or tasting, the child is guided to discover differences and similarities using their senses. The intention is that the child eventually learns to perceive and appreciate very small differences and as a result also learns to recognise and to manage his or her surroundings more effectively.

By learning to make distinctions between different concrete objects and their characteristics, Montessori (1948) believed that the children, in their work with the sensory materials, not only became better in observing and arranging in order their physical environment, but also generally becoming more susceptible to and skilled in processing new and unknown content in their learning.

In order to inspire the child to work with the sensory materials, one of the principles of the material was that the different objects would be aesthetically appealing by colour and shape. Montessori's idea was that the material should attract the child's attention, "'Take me' the material says," she writes (Montessori, 1948, p.83). Furthermore, by presenting carefully crafted attractive materials the child benefited holistically from an active selection process; a process where hands, eyes, ears, mouth and nose are either used to investigate objects or to selectively apply useful information of the dimensions, aspects and characteristics that are highlighted in each situation. Many of these materials are made of smooth polished wood. Others are made of enamel, metal, wicker, and fabric.

Montessori's way of creating order and avoiding a chaos of impressions is through setting limits in the classroom. The materials are placed on special shelves and only one item of each variety should be on the shelves according to Montessori (1964).

Montessori's thoughts about sensory training using concrete materials also characterised the post-war thoughts of knowledge and democratic education; the idea that citizenship is first and foremost a matter of individuals and their knowledge, skills, dispositions and individual responsibilities. For example, children, by being actively engaged with the materials, enhance their learning according to their own specific developmental needs (Arfwedson, 2000).

Montessori strongly believed that even very young children needed to have precise language labels (nomenclature) for the objects and concepts in their world Montessori (1964). To ease the difficulty, when learning new concepts she used the *three-period lesson*. First developed by Edouard Seguin, it is a theoretical method for teaching vocabulary alongside concepts using a variety of Montessori materials or objects. The items are usually presented in groups of three, and is a process that is still in use in Montessori classrooms to this day.

What follows is an example of a three-period lesson:

THREE-PERIOD LESSON ON PRIMARY COLOURS

Period 1. Naming (Introduction) "This is the colour red."

Using the colour tablets, the direttrice presents two or three different colours on the table, and then points to these and says: "This is red. This is blue. This is yellow."

Period 2. Recognising (Identification) "Show me the colour red, the colour blue, the colour yellow."

To maintain the child's interest, the direttrice sets challenges by saying "Hand me yellow, put blue in your lap, hold red above your head, hide yellow behind your back. Move blue to this corner."

Period 3. Remembering (Cognition) "What is this?"

If the child makes a mistake at any point (pointing to blue instead of red), the direttrice does not correct the child or point out the error, but simply goes back briefly to the first period of the lesson. Similarly, if the child makes a mistake in the third period of the lesson, the direttrice does not make any comment to point out the mistake, but just goes back and repeats the second period of the lesson.

For a visual demonstration visit www.youtube.com/watch?v=T0BzZycy91Y

The three-period lesson resonates with variation theory as a way of supporting the child's learning processes which is briefly discussed next.

The self-directed nature of children's engagement and variation theory

Montessori's sensory materials and objects that are used to train the senses have many different characteristics, such as weight, structure, colour or shape. To distinguish and put a single property in the foreground, the child learns to separate this property from the others by making it varied. For example the blocks in the *Pink Tower* (iconic in a Montessori classroom) have the same form and colour, but differs in size, or the *Red Rods* which also have the same form and colour, but differs in length. Montessori perceived that knowledge is possible to develop by systematically using the variation between different objects or phenomena.

Montessori's use of sensory materials can be linked to variation theory (Marton and Booth, 1997), which is a learning theory grounded in phenomenography which, put simply, is the different ways in which people experience, conceptualise, realise and understand various aspects of phenomena in the world around them. When working within the framework of variation theory, "a feature critical to understanding a phenomenon (concept) is varied, while other features of the phenomenon are held invariant" (Pramling Samuelsson and Pramling, 2016, p.290). This links closely to Montessori's approach in the use of the sensory materials.

In summary, these aspects of the Montessori Method, on close examination, are different to conventional classrooms. The features of the sensorial materials themselves are designed to be used in a certain sequence, for example, the many different characteristics of the objects and links to variation theory used to train the senses; each piece of material isolating just one concept at a time, each containing a control of error that allows for self-correction, and the child-led manner of engagement with those materials self-selection, repeated and active engagement, is argued by Montessorians as benefiting development and learning over the teaching of the conventional classroom.

Montessori and outdoor learning

Maria Montessori also talked about the importance of nature as a significant part of her method (Montessori, 2013). Montessori believed that children are born predestined to have a relationship with nature, so they can appreciate it, take responsibility for it and contribute to society as everything on earth is connected. For example, if soil becomes polluted, plants, animals and humans will be affected so it is important to care of and take responsibility for the environment (Montessori,

1965). As children observe the environment using sensory didactic material, they develop a true understanding, which Montessori valued as essential. To live well, she believed children need to be in touch with nature and that less healthy children gain strength by being exposed to the sun's rays or by lying stretched out on the grass. She noted how one of the greatest instincts of childhood is to be able to run in the rain. For Montessori, cultivating plants and caring for animals was an important part of education. Rather than directing children to observe nature, Montessori (1948, p.73) wanted to leave children to observe by themselves believing that "the child more than anyone else is a spontaneous observer of nature and needs to have at his disposal materials with upon which he can work."

In the first *Casa dei Bambini* in Via Marsi, Rome, the ground was not landscaped as a garden and remained as a large patch of fenced in land. There were however pots with flowers placed around a large terrace. When Montessori observed the children playing freely, she saw how they chose to move around in small spaces which went against the conviction that it is better to give children limitless space. As a result, she believed that if it was not possible to have a garden, there should be window boxes and tubs of soil in the outdoor areas as a substitute (Montessori, 1948). She also noted the importance of children taking responsibility for pets such as rabbits, pigs, mice and hamsters and taking turns to feed and take care of them. Montessori valued children being taken out regularly for walks and expeditions in the country so the teacher could encourage children to learn the names (and botanical names) of all trees, flowers, birds and butterflies they saw, and collect leaves which could be pressed. Children could then use books in the classroom to find out more details and label plants. She suggested they also brought back caterpillars in boxes so they could care for them and see the transformation from chrysalis to moth or butterfly. Collecting frogspawn so the change into tadpoles and little frogs could be observed was important, after which children could return them to the pond (Montessori, 1988). During the summer months, Montessori suggests children study flowers and observe how they are pollinated. In autumn, looking for fruits and seeds was encouraged with attention to how they were distributed. Montessori believed that by passively describing flowers and plants, children would soon become disengaged. Instead, by offering minimal information, the children through such self-directed nature-based experience would be motivated to discover for themselves using all their senses. (Montessori, 1965).

During such learning opportunities, Montessori emphasised the importance of the adult encouraging children to treat living things with care and respect and that no litter should be left behind when the children were out and about in nature:

> Let the children be free; encourage them; let them run outside when it is raining; let them remove their shoes when they find a puddle of water; and, when the grass of the meadows is damp with dew, let them run on it and trample it with their bare feet.
>
> *(Montessori, 1948, p.71).*

Debates around the Montessori Method

The Montessori Method arouses much debate and her focus on freedom of inquiry and a scientific approach to early years pedagogy have found many supporters as well as detractors in Italy and across the world. When Montessori published the first edition of her book on the method in 1909, the interest in her teaching methods grew rapidly. The first time she presented her teaching methods in the United States was in 1913, and while Montessori received many followers for her methods, critical voices were also heard. Her education system was criticised by psychologists and educators. One thing that was criticised was the individualisation, which was so important in Montessori's work as it allowed each child to progress in his or her own rate of work and rhythm of learning, but understood by her critics as a lack of opportunity, through group activity, for social development and interaction. Proponents of the Montessori Method would argue that the prepared environment used in the classroom allows for students to interact more freely, rather than at set times of the day as it would be in a traditionally-styled classroom.

Another criticism was Montessori's intentions of social equalisation through education, which reflected Marxist views that there should be a society in which everyone would be able to improve themselves within fields that suited them (Ferreira and Bittar, 2008). This went against the predominating capitalist view in the United States that equality is impossible, since education is about the development of quality labour power rather than the equalisation of labour power per se (Kumar, 2010). In addition, William Heard Kilpatrick (1914), a student of Dewey and later a professor of pedagogy at Columbia University, USA, believed that Montessori's methods, including sensory training, was based on obsolete psychological theories, and that Montessori thus became ignorant of the latest developmental thinking in psychology. Kilpatrick criticised Montessori's emphasis on the child's independence and individuality at the expense of group work and her assumption of children's development in a predetermined order with sensitive periods. Kilpatrick also questioned Montessori's view of the teacher's role as an observer and that the child's interest would be ruling in teaching, an approach contrary to the dominant American thought at this time, that children in order to cope with their everyday problems would learn this in social situations. Montessori was also accused of commercialism by Boyd (1914), who criticised that Montessori, when the impending materials were being manufactured, gave the rights to a chosen manufacturer.

All these criticisms, especially those which came from Kilpatrick, contributed to the fact that Montessori's pedagogy, despite its major initial successes, soon lost its supporters in the United States. Kilpatrick's criticism of Montessori remained untouched until Campbell (1970) analysed them further. Campbell believed that the content of Montessori's theories had a different perspective, more physiologically than psychologically, which, according to Campbell, was due to Montessori's medical background. Montessori (1939/1998) believed that the child, by being free to decide how long and when he wants to work with an object, learns to take responsibility for himself, his thoughts and actions. These thoughts were strongly provocative when Montessori launched them in the early twentieth century and were also criticised by Calkins (1975), who found that Montessori's methods prevented social adjustment. Calkins said that when they chose what they wanted to work with, children had little opportunity for cooperation with others and thus did not learn to work in groups. Another viewpoint came from Susan Isaacs (1885–1948), an English pioneer in early childhood education, who shared Montessori's philosophy that everything educators need to know about children is learnt from the children themselves. There was also a strong connection to the idea of the child have the freedom to choose, but Isaacs felt that this freedom was somewhat inhibited by the perceived extreme didacticism brought about by the implementation of the Montessori materials (Giardiello, 2014; Graham, 2009; Smith, 1985).

Despite these critiques Montessori's philosophy of teaching, which has provided a lasting legacy to early childhood education, is best précised in her own words:

> The basis of our teaching is that . . . the child has to acquire physical independence by being self-sufficient; he must become of independent will by using in freedom his own power of choice; he must become capable of independent thought by working alone without interruption . . . We have to help the child to act, will and think for himself. This is the art of serving the spirit, an art which can be practiced to perfection only when working among children.
>
> *(Montessori, 1967, p.281)*

International case studies

The following section presents two case studies from England and from Sweden.

CASE STUDY 1: WE HEAR FROM A MONTESSORIAN FROM ENGLAND.

Firstly, I don't teach. I would never feel qualified to do so. I work within a community of children where education is a natural, spontaneous process evolving from real experiences in the environment. This is the way in which human beings have adapted to their environments since they evolved to do so. This is an evolutionary view, where I am attempting to help prepare the child for a better, more peaceful world than ours. I am a tool for the child's (and society's) developing potential.

My personal philosophies became apparent to me through an accidental catalyst moment. As a young parent, my first child had been content within the 'baby room' at my local nursery. I went along to visit the nursery when my child was transitioning into the 'toddler room' and observed the children running around the small, cramped room regardless of others who were playing with plastic toys on the floor. At that moment I knew there must be more to early childhood education than this. My journey began with the humble acknowledgement that I wanted my young child to be treated seriously and listened to as a human being with thoughts and feelings just like any adult. The realisation that not all adults felt the same way was shocking at the time and after much research led me to read Montessori's work where my views felt valued and drove me to qualify in Early Childhood Montessori Pedagogy.

As a Montessorian for the last 15 years, I have had many bitter struggles with theoretical practice and practical experience. I can see now that these have generally led me to study further and research more. Underlying issues with some dogmatic practices ensured that I gained my EYPS (Early Years Professional Status) and then left Montessori practice after 10 years to study for my QTS (Qualified Teacher Status) and worked within mainstream EYFS (Early Years Foundation Stage) settings with children from birth to 5. However, within 2 years I was back working within a Montessori elementary community. I had missed a certain something that I continue to struggle to qualify. It is a way of being that affects everything I do. A respectful and absolute belief in the child's knowing and individual understanding which is more important than any piece of knowledge that I could 'teach'. It is this connection or alignment with Montessori that drives me to struggle with the other pedagogical implications the philosophy brings. I find that criticisms such as the play/work issue, collaborative thinking, disputes regarding Montessori's claims to new thinking or summative assessment require a wider lens. I don't discount some of these issues, I just learn to live with them. This is my forgiving, philosophical view if you like.

I struggle to vocalise my own issues in collaborative CPD (Continued Professional Development) meetings with traditional settings as I know I am lucky to be able to follow my beliefs about pedagogical practice whereas for some there is a political dichotomy between what the practitioner believes and what is practically possible within a narrow curriculum and culture of assessment. More recently, online Montessori communities have enabled me to feel less isolated and discuss pedagogical issues openly and with less perceptible judgment or Montessori dogma. Of course, collaborative working as part of an 'educating' team is my most helpful pedagogical learning tool. As I continue to further my understanding of pedagogical practice I have started my MA studies in the hope of understanding my practice further.

I feel passionately that my Montessori practice strives to provide a respectful, nurturing environment which every unique individual is entitled to. My practice is made up of more than the activities to promote concentration, freedoms of self-expression, movement and choice, care of the environment and the 'three period lesson'. Children and adults have the right to learn together, follow their dreams and have the time and space to do so. It is a spiritual journey for all involved. In our community we name it 'Montessori' however I personally view it as a practical environment for an evolutionary journey; a continual series of adaptations towards a peaceful future.

Provided by Julie Butterfield

CASE STUDY 2: REFLECTIONS OF A SWEDISH MONTESSORI TEACHER TAKEN FROM A CONVERSATION HELD IN NOVEMBER 2017.

The location is Casa Montessori (Montessoriskolan Casa) an independent Free school located in Bö Herrgård, in Gothenburg. There is a very long waiting list – and parents travel from as far as 50km away.

There are children with a variety of special educational needs and those with different languages. Although we wanted to enrol them there are no new immigrant children because of the long waiting list.

There are 36 children and 7 adults in the Pre -school. The focus in the Montessori pre-school – for children aged (2½–5) is to prepare them to value and respect nature, plants/seeds. The school is for the child – every child is different and valued as a person for being unique – "I want him or her to be what is for them." We do it just for the child.

Practical life space is what we start with – sensory.

Placed so children use it in a way that is meaningful for children, brush teeth / buttoning / ordering / pouring / floor exercise / rolling out mat / play dough / selecting and putting away / mopping / filling / REAL life. Each activity is modelled by the teachers. For example, in the Kitchen children help to set the table and to get the knives and food out and wash up.

When the children are aged 6 they start the next stage of school in, usually in Spring but our philosophy is to respect when children are ready and to follow their personal plan.

We work in age- integrated groups, 6–9 years and 9–12 years. The Montessori philosophy permeates all our teaching: "Help me think of myself". *There are 20 children in each year group with a high child to adult ratio.*

There's a large carpet space for the gatherings and sitting in a circle

The nature is important and the inspiration for learning. It's part of the cosmic plan to create a better world. If everyone knows about the world people will want to take care of it and love it and so nature is part of learning. Embodying is what's important and the experience of the whole, through engaging the senses, the whole body, nature, valuing culture, feelings/caring and the process. As a Montessorian you have to stand with yourself and be ready to listen and to trust to believe in the child and follow the child.

It's a very democratic approach that starts with adults knowing themselves and children knowing themselves and their identity. Helping children to be critical thinkers and to think for themselves is crucial but often teachers seem to feel the need to control to feel safe and accountable – whereas actually we are empowered through self-awareness and a process of reflexivity.

POINTS FOR REFLECTION

- In considering Montessori's legacy are there aspects of her pedagogical approach that you recognise in your own practice and provision?
- In considering Montessori's philosophy of freedom to learn, and given today's emphasis on teacher accountability, how would you go about devolving responsibility to the child?
- In what way and for what purpose would you consider using the three-period lesson in your own pedagogical practice?
- If working within the framework of variation theory, how would you use it to develop children's conceptual understanding of the properties of objects?

Maria Montessori has left a lasting legacy as her method of education has been able to cross cultural boundaries and is still as relevant today as it was as its inception. The spread of her ideas was aided by a series of stimulating lectures held in all parts of the world. In 1929 Montessori established the Association Montessori International to give structure to her work and to ensure, long after her death in 1952, her standards for teacher education would be continued in accordance with her pedagogical and scientific principles (Giardiello, 2016). Montessori placed great value of the processes of learning and was keen to stress the relationship between the teacher and the child.

The essential elements of Montessori's philosophy and her Method can be found in all early childhood education approaches where the educators are skilled in 'following' the child; fostering independence through a carefully prepared environment; responding to the changing interests, needs and democratic rights of the child (Giardiello, 2016, p.34). For example, ideas about the democratic rights of the child and the importance of a prepared environment are fundamental to what the protagonists of the internationally renowned *Reggio Emilia* Approach feel are at the centre of their educational vision as discussed in the following Chapter 5.

References

Arfwedsson, G.B. (2000) *Reformpedagogik och samhälle. En komparativ studie av pedagogiska reformrörelser i USA och Tyskland från 1890-talet till 1930-talet.* Diss. Stockholm: Lärarhögskolan i Stockholm.

Babini, V. (2000) 'Science, feminism and education: The early work of Maria Montessori', *History Workshop Journal*, 49, p.44–67.

Bone, J. (2005) 'Breaking bread: Spirituality, food and early childhood education', *International Journal of Children's Spirituality*, 10(3), p.307–317. DOI: doi:10.1080/13644360500347607.

Boyd, W. (1914) *From Locke to Montessori*, London: George G. Harrap & Company.

Burnett, A. (1962) 'Montessori education: Today and yesterday', *The Elementary School Journal*, 63(2), p.71–77. Retrieved 13 March 2019 from: www.journals.uchicago.edu/doi/pdfplus/10.1086/460015.

Calkins, L.M. (1975) *Lessons from a child*, Portsmouth: Heinemann Educational Books.

Campbell, D.N. (1970) *A critical analysis of William Heard Kilpatrick's the Montessori System examined*, Urbana-Champaign: University of Illinois.

Chisnall, N. (2008) 'Montessori through the eyes of newly qualified teachers in Aotearoa New Zealand', in: P.L. Jeffery (Ed.) *Changing climates: Education for sustainable futures*. Proceedings of the AARE 2008 international education research conference 2008, Queensland University of Technology, Brisbane, Australia: Queensland University of Technology, p.1–12.

Comenius, J.A. (1907) *Comenius's school of infancy: An essay on the education of youth*. Retrieved 4 July 2018 from: http://onlinebooks.library.upenn.edu/webbing/book/lookupid?key+olbp34686 (Original work published 1633)

Cossentino, J. (2005) 'Ritualizing expertise: A non-Montessorian view of the Montessori Method', *American Journal of Education*, 111(2), p.211–244. DOI: doi:10.1086/426838.

Department for Education (DfE) (2017) *The statutory framework for the early years foundation stage*, London: Department for Education.

Duckworth, C. (2006) 'Teaching peace: A dialogue on the Montessori Method', *Journal of Peace Education*, 3, p.39–53. DOI: doi:10.1080/17400200500532128.

Feez, S. (2007) *Montessori's mediation of meaning and social semiotic perspectives*. Unpublished PhD thesis. University of Sydney, Australia. Retrieved 4 March 2014 from: http://ses.library.usyd.edu.au/handle/2123/1859.

Ferreira, J.R. and Bittar, M. (2008) 'Education in a Marxist perspective: An approach based on Marx and Gramsci'. Retrieved 5 July 2018 from: www.scielo.br/scielo.php?script=sci_arttext&pid=S1414-32832008000300014&lng=en&nrm=iso>.

Froebel, F. (1906) *The education of man* (W.N. Hailman Trans.), London: Appleton Ltd. (Original work published in 1826).

Giardiello, P. (2014) *Pioneers in early childhood education: The roots and legacies of Rachel and Margaret McMillian, Maria Montessori and Susan Isaacs*, Abingdon: Routledge.

Graham, P. (2009) *Susan Isaacs: A life freeing the minds of children*, London: Karnac Books Ltd.

Kilpatrick, W.H. (1914) *The Montessori System examined*, Boston: Houghton Mifflin Company.

Kramer, R. (1976) *Maria Montessori*, London: Montessori International Publishing.

Kuh, L. (2014) 'Montessori and classroom management', in: W.G. Scarlett (Ed.) *The SAGE encyclopaedia of classroom management*, London: SAGE Publications.

Kumar, R. (2010) 'Education and the politics of capital: Perspective and agenda for resistance against neoliberalism', *Social Scientist, 38*(9/12), p.51–60. Retrieved from: www.jstor.org.ezproxy.mmu.ac.uk/stable/27896289.

Locke, J. (1910) *Some thoughts concerning education*. Retrieved from: https://play.google.com/books/reader?id=kRJgAAAAcAAJ&printsec=frontcover&output=reader&hl=en&pg=GBS.PP1.

MacDonald, M. (2015) 'Early childhood education and sustainability: A living curriculum', *Childhood Education*, 91(5), p.332–341. DOI: doi:10.1080/00094056.2015.1090845.

Marshall, C. (2017) 'Montessori education: A review of the evidence base', *NPJ Science of Learning*, 2(11). DOI: doi:10.1038/s41539-017-0012-7. Retrieved 13 March 2019 from: http://discovery.ucl.ac.uk/10027542/1/s41539-017-0012-7.pdf.

Marton, F. and Booth, S. (1997) *Learning and awareness*, Mahwah, NJ: Lawrence Erlbaum Associates.

Montessori, M. (2013) *The 1913 Rome lectures*, Amsterdam: Montessori-Pierson Publishing.

Montessori, M. (1985) *The secret of childhood*, London: Sangam Press.

Montessori, M. (1972) *Education and peace* (H.R. Lane Trans.), Chicago, IL: Henry Regnery. (Original work published in 1948).

Montessori, M. (1967) *The absorbent mind* (C.A. Claremont Trans.), New York: Dell Publishing Co. Inc.

Montessori, M. (1965) *Dr. Montessori's own handbook* (F. Simmonds Trans.),London: Schocken Books. (Original work published in 1917).

Montessori, M. (1964) *The Montessori Method* (A.E. George Trans.),New York: Schocken Books. (Original work published 1912).

Montessori, M. (1948) *The discovery of the child* (M.A. Johnstone Trans.), Madras, India: Kalakshetra Publications.

Piaget, J. (1954) *The construction of reality in the child* (M. Cook Trans.),New York, US: Basic Books. DOI: doi:10.1037/11168-000.

Pramling Samuelsson, I. and Pramling, N. (2016) 'Variation theory of learning and developmental pedagogy: Two context-related models of learning grounded in phenomenography', *Scandinavian Journal of Educational Research*, 60(3), p.286–295. DOI: doi:10.1080/00313831.2015.1120232.

Quintilian (1920) *De instituto oratori* (H.E. Butler Trans.), Cambridge: Cambridge University Press. (Original work published circa AD 96).

Rinaldi, C. (2006) *In dialogue with Reggio Emilia: Listening, researching and learning*, Abingdon: Routledge.

Röhrs, H. (1994) *Maria Montessori*. Retrieved 4 July 2018 from: www.ibe.unesco.org/fileadmin/user_upload/archive/publications/ThinkersPdf/montesse.pdf.

Rousseau, J. (1979) *Emile on education* (A. Bloom Trans.), New York: Basic Books. (Original work published in 1762).

Siraj-Blatchford, J., Smith, K. and Pramling Samuelson, I. (2010) 'Education for sustainable development in the early years', Organisation Mondiale Pour l´Education Prescolaire (OMEP): www.omep.org.gu.se/English/news/news_detail//new-book-forpractitioners.cid952209.

Smith, L.A.H. (1985) *To understand and to help: The life and work of Susan Isaacs (1885–1948)*, London: Fairleigh Dickinson University Press.

Treganza, V. (2008) 'Looking back to the future: The current relevance of Maria Montessori's ideas about the spiritual wellbeing of young children', *Journal of Student Wellbeing*, 2(2), p.1–15.

Wyness, M.G. (2006) *Childhood and society: An introduction to the sociology of childhood*, New York:Palgrave Macmillan.

5

REGGIO EMILIA (WITH PERSPECTIVES FROM SWEDEN)

Patricia Giardiello, Tarja Karlsson Häikiö and Pernilla Mårtensson

In Italy, the prosperous city of Reggio Emilia has become famous worldwide for its preschools and infant-toddler centres, attracting study groups from around the world keen to learn more about the innovative art-based processes that constitute the Reggio Emilia Approach. We have seen in the other chapters in Part 2 of this book how different early childhood education and care approaches have developed in response to different social and political agendas. Markedly, the socio-political pedagogical tradition of the Reggio Emilia Approach arose specifically from the municipal socialism of public life in and around the province of Reggio Emilia. Within this context, the Reggio Emilia Approach is a form of progressive early childhood education shaped by Loris Malaguzzi, a psychologist and educator influenced by Dewey's model of progressive education, Montessori's prepared environment, Vygotsky's social cultural theories and the psychological theories of Piaget, Erikson, Bronfenbrenner and Bruner (Cagliari et al., 2016; Rinaldi, 2006). At the same time, though, the protagonists of the approach continue to formulate new interpretations and new hypotheses and ideas about learning and teaching through their daily observations and practice of learning along with children (Gandini, 2003). This chapter begins by considering the influences that shaped the development of the Reggio Emilia Approach, starting with both a geographical and historical perspective, as the two are linked.

An examination of contextual socio-cultural, historical, political influences

Reggio Emilia is located in the Po valley, in the region of Emilia Romagna and is a city at the very center of affluent Northern Italy [between Bologna and Milan]. As a province Reggio Emilia is in the top ranking in Italy as per income per-capita, with its economic strength a result of its long-standing high level of entrepreneurial culture. In fact, Emilia Romagna is the Italian region that reports the biggest immigrant flow, 11.89 percent of the total population of 529,337 (UrbiStat, 2017), with Reggio Emilia being the most favourable destination of migrants both foreign and Italians due to its excellent public services and work opportunities. This increase in immigration, however, has undoubtedly created new challenges for Reggio Emilia, and the town is experiencing a period of transition in terms of cultural awareness. Notwithstanding it is a community that welcomes immigrants, granting them the same rights to early education that all the citizens of Reggio have traditionally been privileged to enjoy for decades. From its inception, the engagement of families and the community was embedded in the Reggio Emilia Approach practices. This can be traced back to its origins immediately after the Second World War when a small group of women set about building a school in a small village called Villa Cella, a neighborhood of Reggio Emilia. The community, working together in employing their entrepreneurial spirit, had raised money from the sale of abandoned war artillery; land had been donated by a local farmer, and bricks and beams salvaged from bombed houses. Coupled with the involvement of Loris Malaguzzi, a young teacher who was working in a public mental health centre for children at the time, they built an infant school from the rubble of war torn buildings. This community impetus whose philosophy was to involve children and parents as equal partners in education, with the support of Malaguzzi, created the basis of the Reggio Emilia Approach. With echoes of Maria Montessori's initial work with children with special educational needs in developing her pedagogical approach, Malaguzzi's own sensitivity led him to recognize children's potential and capabilities in order to develop effective educational programs (Caruso, 2013).

Thus began the start of an educational project which was to eventually spread worldwide; the appeal being that it promotes a rethinking of early childhood education and is a call to the educational community to value children's possibilities, potential, capabilities and competencies (Gibson, 2014).

In the years after the opening of the first school for 3- to 6-year-olds in Villa Cella in 1945 (followed by the opening of eight others in the region), Malaguzzi continued to develop his innovative early childhood pedagogy through constant dialogue and debates with colleagues in the Movement of Educational Cooperation, encouraging the publication of a journal article on educational theories and their potential application in school settings (Caruso, 2013). With the advent of a booming Italian economy and following increasing demands for infant schools, in 1963, with Malaguzzi acting as consultant, the municipality of Reggio Emilia began setting up its network of education services. The Reggio Emilia Approach became firmly established when an article featured on the first page of *Newsweek* in 1991 expressed its recognition of Reggio Emilia for having the best preschools and infant-toddler centers in the world. Today there are 80 Preschools and Infant Toddler Centers belonging to the Istituzione Scuole e Nidi D'infanzia in the municipal of Reggio Emilia (*Reggio Children* Nidi e Scuole).

The friends of Reggio Children International Association

Due to the huge numbers of incoming applications following the *Newsweek* article mentioned previously and because it has been setting its sights increasingly on education, the Municipality of Reggio Emilia decided to set up Reggio Children, a private-public company of which the Municipality is the majority shareholder. Following Loris Malaguzzi's death in 1994, Reggio Children continues to reinforce the underpinning Reggio philosophy (discussed as follows) to promote and defend children's rights. Reggio Children also organizes professional education projects and is involved in the design and management of exhibitions, including the exhibit "The Hundred Languages of Children": a travelling exhibition that has been telling the story of the Reggio Emilia educational experience worldwide to thousands of paying visitors for over 30 years upon invitation from governments, museums, universities and art galleries (Edwards et al., 2012). Accompanying this exhibition is an increasing number of publications about the Reggio Emilia Approach, although most are published in house by Reggio Children, thereby strengthening control over the dissemination of information. According to Dahlberg (2000) through their ongoing dialogue and publications, the protagonists of the Reggio Emilia Approach are challenging the dominating discourse and accepted practices of early childhood pedagogy. This is done by deconstructing the dominant ideas and theories that have shaped the conceptions and images of children and childhood. However, this could be seen as creating a new "regime of truth" as an attempt to colonize early childhood education by means of its ideological stance and key underpinning principles (Johnson, 1999). It is worth noting at this point that Malaguzzi emphasized the importance of dialogue and not seeing the Reggio Approach or any other pedagogical interpretations as true. Instead, he highlighted the importance of continuous questioning of both the educator's own practice and Reggio Emilia's theoretical basis (Häikiö, 2007; Vecchi, 2014).

The Reggio Children's headquarters are located in the Loris Malaguzzi International Centre. Inaugurated in 2006 and completed in 2011, the Centre is supported by the Municipality of Reggio Emilia, Infant-Toddler Centres and Preschools, Reggio Children, and the Loris Malaguzzi Centre Foundation. There are now over 30 international networks around the world where ongoing collaborations oversee several study tours in Reggio Emilia each year, and numerous network-hosted conferences and seminars (Caruso, 2012). In a sector that is often associated with low pay and high staff turnover, only those in a position of privilege who can either pay expensive attendance fees or whom are funded, such as university lecturers, early childhood centre directors, programme administrators and a few fortunate educators, have access and ownership of these study tours, thus creating a "Reggio cargo cult" phenomena as they return from the study tour in a position of power armed with new knowledge about the Reggio Emilia Approach, which they then transmit back to those unable to attend, often the very persons who work on a day-to-day basis with the children (Johnson, 1999, p. 74). Having experienced these study tours, I (Patricia) acknowledge that they do provide an opportunity for deeper investigation into the concepts, contents and values that underpin the educational project of the Municipal Infant-Toddler Centres and Preschools of Reggio Emilia. However, no doubt because of the large numbers of visitors attending, they are carefully orchestrated and keep closely to the "doctrine" that is the Reggio Emilia Approach. For example, any questions from the audience are responded to at the end of each talk, after strict consideration by the panel members of how to respond. In doing so this means there is no deviation from set policies and procedures regarding the dissemination of information about the underpinning principles of the Reggio Emilia Approach. As such this could be viewed as a dominant discourse of control resulting in the Reggio Approach becoming a pedagogical commodity and a product that has been carefully packaged and exported to a number of countries.

The size and the organization of the study tours place natural barriers on the extent of the visitors' opportunity to spend time in Reggio settings seeing what actually takes place with the children. As one Reggio teacher put it to me "These are not children to be goggled at as though they are goldfishes in a bowl" (personal anecdote, 2017). Although this stance is to be respected in considering the rights of the child, this does to some extent impoverish the experience of visiting the Infant-Toddler Centres and Preschools from the viewpoint of being unable to witness first-hand interactions between the co-protagonists and the children as part of the learning processes.

In a similar vein, taking photographs is not permitted during the visits. According to the Reggio protagonists, despite there being no children present, there are many visual images of the children in the documentation displayed on the walls. However, in true Reggio Emilia entrepreneurial spirit, there are brochures and booklets on sale which show images of the children engaging in project work in the settings. This raises ethical issues around the marketization of childhood and appears, at first sight, paradoxical. On the one hand, there is a desire to protect the rights of the child through exercising control over who gains access. On the other hand, there is a desire to profit from the learning processes children engage with. At this point it is worth reflecting on experiences of those visiting Reggio Emilia which should not be to solidify the habits of teaching in schools, but rather to show the complexity and multiplicity of ways of doing and being with young children (Parnell, 2012). Likewise, Malaguzzi (1998) also advised that as well as knowing theories on childhood, we should also keep an ever-widening eye to the children and practice themselves, as they will change our minds and make us see in new ways. Furthermore and leaving aside the concerns mentioned previously, it is also highly questionable as to whether it is possible to transfer or replicate the Reggio Emilia approach or any other ECEC system. As Moss and Petrie (2005, p.149) state:

> The uniqueness of that context [Reggio Emilia] is woven from numerous threads, coloured by a particular time, place and history: the social actors, both children and adults; the social, political, cultural and economic conditions; the understandings, discourses and values; and the political and ethical choices

made in answer to particular questions. Carlina Rinaldi states this singularity clearly when she says of the early childhood provision in Reggio Emilia: "We do not offer a recipe, nor a method, our work is not to be copied because values can only be lived not copied."

The distinctive philosophical underpinning principles

It is a challenge to sort out and identify the underpinning key principles of the Reggio Emilia Approach as each one is inextricably entwined and influenced by the other. In the following table (Table 5.1), informed by Reggio Children, are some of the main key principles.

At the centre of the Reggio pedagogy is the child with potential, who is seen as a competent learner, able to build relationships; who holds firm to his or her own values; who respects others; who embodies a curiosity and open-mindedness to all that is possible (Gandini, 2003). Everything that takes place in Reggio infant and toddler centres in terms of teaching and learning stems from the overriding factor which is "the image of the child." As Malaguzzi asserted (1993, p.10), the image of the child is "rich in potential, strong, powerful, competent, and most of all connected to adults and other children." This connectivity or relationship that children develop with peers, material and the environment does not happen within compartmentalized lessons but rather through multiple encounters over an extended period of time (McNally and Slutsky, 2017). Reggio educators recognize, as did Montessori, that learning is not a direct result of teaching but instead is related to how children interpret the interactions they have with people, places, materials and ideas (Hendrick, 1997; Malaguzzi, 1998; Rinaldi, 1998). Just as Montessori placed great emphasis on the prepared environment, one of the principles that sets the Reggio Emilia Approach apart is the importance it places on the spaces within the school environment. The spaces are described as symbols for the philosophy that mirrors the emotional, relational and communicative aspects of the approach. In establishing the multisensorial and emotive spaces, light, sound and other factors (i.e., transparency, tactility, osmosis, olfactory) are taken into account (Häikiö, 2007). It is the configuration of space and how young children perceive and use space to create meaningful encounters that is valued in a Reggio Emilia setting. So important was this belief, that Malaguzzi defined the environment as the third teacher (Gandini, 2012). At the center of each Reggio Emilia setting is an open and large common space called the "piazza" (town square), reflective of those found in the city where citizens either pass through or congregate as part of their daily activities. Classrooms which are consciously arranged into small open areas or activity zones (Caruso, 2013; Häikiö, 2007) are placed at a distance from the "piazza", but are connected to it so children are free to move between the piazza and the classroom throughout the day. The piazza of the school is a place for "encounters, friendships, games and other activities that compete with the classroom" (Malaguzzi, 1998, p.64).

Pieces of documentation are displayed in the spaces in order to make the children's feelings, ideas and actions visible as part of the public culture of the Infant-Toddler Centres and Preschools of Reggio Emilia (Caruso, 2013). An important

TABLE 5.1 Reggio Emilia Principles

All children have potential	From birth the child has the need and the right to communicate and interact with others. Through energy and curiosity, the child constructs his/her own learning.
Children are connected	The child is a member of a family and a community rather than an isolated individual. The child learns through interaction with peers, adults, objects and symbols. Preschool centres are seen as a system of relations embedded in a wider social system.
The reciprocity of children	"Children are very open to exchanges and reciprocity as deeds and acts of love which they not only want to receive but also to offer. These form the basis of their ability to experience authentic growth, dependent on the elements listed above, as well as on conflict and error." (Rinaldi, 2006, p.57)
Children are communicators	Children have the right to use many forms of symbolic representation: words, movement, drawing, painting, building, sculpture, shadow play, collage, dramatic play, music (the "hundred languages"). In this way children are able to explore and communicate ideas in many different ways and are able to link ideas across different media.
The environment is the third teacher	Space is designed to encourage encounters, communication and relationships. There is order and beauty in the organization of materials; every corner of space has an identity and purpose. The piazza and the atelier are at the heart of the preschool centre.
Educators are partners, nurturers and guides	Educators and artists (*atelierista*) facilitate children's exploration of themes—short- or long-term projects—and guide experiences of open-ended discovery and problem-solving. They observe and listen closely to children in order to deepen their understanding of the children's ideas and their ways of working together. They reflect in groups to analyze their observations and decide how to further support the children's learning.
Educators are researchers	The educators work together, sharing their observations and interpretations about how the children are exploring and interacting. They develop their own research based around how best to support particular aspects of children's learning.
Documentation as a learning tool	Careful consideration and attention are given to the presentation of the thinking of the children and the adults who work with them. Transcriptions of children's words and dialogues, photographs and drawings are used for groups of adults and children to reflect on the learning that is taking place. The documentation enables children, educators and parents to share each other's learning, not just at the end of a learning process but as an aid to a continuing group idea.
Families as partners	Families have an active role in children's learning experience. They are encouraged to share their ideas and experiences of their children's learning and are able to see what has been happening in school through documentation and discussions.

(Source: Sightlines Initiatives, UK reference agency for Reggio Children, 2018.)

note, however, is that the documentation is not always permanent or in panel form, for as technology advances so does the way in which projects and other work is documented, revisited and presented to the public (ibid.). In Reggio schools, documentation is both "noun and verb" and is the unique process of carefully recording, revisiting and communicating the socially constructed ways in which knowledge is created (McNally and Slutsky, 2017, p.1931). Consequently, documentation plays an important part in the environment as an informative, aesthetic and visual factor in the construction of the spaces. In the environment there are also documentation panels, and triangular mirrors and other material described to be an integral part of the pedagogical work with children's formation of their identity and body-conception, communication and exploration (Karlsson Häikiö, 2017, 2018). Educational documentation that follows the child's learning process from a child-centered perspective can, according to Dahlberg and Elfström (2015), function as a contrast to the dominant discourse of measurement. A further development of the educational documentation model adopts what can be seen as a rhizomatic approach (see Chapter 3), through providing space for relationships and process-ontological inputs when reviewing children's learning (Åsberg et al., 2012; Olsson, 2014). Through a rhizomatic interpretation of knowledge creation, learning takes place through unexpected ways and steps in inter-woven processes (Åsberg et al., 2012; Deleuze and Guattari, 1988; Olsson, 2014). Olsson (2014, p.59–60) describes how educators "through rhizo-analysis can review the documented materials critically, as well as deconstruct and reconstruct the learning processes." By documenting how the work flows in different directions, this mirrors the children's rhizomatic learning processes (Lenz Taguchi, 2012; Olsson, 2014). Furthermore, by including the children in the documentation process they can be involved in self-evaluation of the learning process and thus in the decisions about the content and results.

Vallberg-Roth (2010) describes educational documentation as a post-constructionist way of working and believes that documentation is employed from many different starting points and methods (multi-documentation). She describes transformative assessment as being different forms of evaluation of learning processes that can be seen as a transforming and interactive assessment in movement between different actors, forms, content and functions. Lenz Taguchi (2012) writes about transformational movements or links between "organisms, materialities, discourses and people between participating agents" (p.61, Häikiö Trans.) The documented material consists of "materialized and actualized events" that "merge into knowledge production through the educational documentation" (ibid., 2012, p.63, Häikiö Trans.). Thus, in the documentation, transformative potentials arise through observation as performative agents (ibid.). A transformative approach to learning means that knowledge is generated and transformed during the learning process in constantly renewing situations (Stirling, 2014). Learning processes can be seen as transformative, where different forms of creation and communication is used simultaneously through use of different expressive forms as cultural tools, but also tools for learning (Häikiö, 2007; Karlsson Häikiö, 2017). Radical thinking about transformative pedagogy can be derived from a longer tradition of socio-cultural enthusiasm and liberative pedagogy (Giroux, 2011; Kurki, 2000).

There are nevertheless critical voices concerning documentation that describe this practice from a problematic perspective (Emilson and Pramling Samuelsson, 2014; Lindroth, 2018). Both Swedish and international studies show that there is a risk that the adult perspective dominates and that the teachers emphasize the benefits of educational documentation without considering potential disadvantages such as over surveillance (Lindroth, 2018). For example, a great deal of documentation in Reggio settings is created using photographic images and videos of the children's learning processes. According to Flannery Quinn and Manning (2013) in applying a post-structural lens to the use of photographs in early childhood education, we position photography as a source of knowledge and power which is situated within the contexts of possibly contradictory ideas about what is normal, desired, and possibly "best" for children. "But the question of the interests or even 'best' interests of children is one that needs to be questioned within the framework of ethical values and power relations" (ibid., p.273). When deciding what the best interests of children are and how to act in those interests, it is useful to turn to Clark and Moss' (2001) who contend that observing children is not an adult's right, and we should question whether uncovering the details of children's lived experiences really is in their best interests.

Sparrman and Lindgren (2010) call the use of visual documentation a normalizing practice and see it as a new discourse of visibility in preschool and refer to this as a "growing field identifying the importance of visual documentation" (2010, p.249; Buckingham and Jones, 2001; Edwards, Gandini and Forman, 1998). They link the use of documentation to surveillance (Foucault, 1979; Rose, 2001, p.166), and problematize the concept of child-perspective in relation to the use of documentation. Halldén (2003) describes the child-perspective to be ambiguous. Visual documentation can be considered to make each child seen and heard and give voice to children, but can also be a way for adults to "adopt" a child perspective and use it for political or other purposes, or to give an image of an ideal preschool rather than showing what actually happens during the activities carried out, thus functioning as a way to market a profile of the preschool (Lindroth, 2018), as discussed earlier. Furthermore, Emilsson and Pramling Samuelsson (2014) describe the pressure that educators can feel when being constantly required to document the daily practice. Sandberg, Sheridan and Williams (2012) have shown that the documentations are seldomly used as a basis for analysis, whilst other studies describe that what is documented is often on a relatively high abstraction level which can hinder analysis (Emilson and Pramling Samuelsson, 2014; Lindroth, 2018). Löfdahl and Pérez Prieto (2009) report that it is the more clearly visible elements of the activities that are documented and that other more complex parts of the practice are omitted, which in turn is linked to the importance of the appearances of the preschool profile.

Alnervik (2003) also found the documentation process to be complex as a concrete method, but still positive to using documentation, although they also problematized the documentative practice. Several studies have pointed out that documentation can be used to take a child's perspective and include children (Clark and Moss, 2001; Kumpulainen et al., 2013). According to these studies, educational documentation is believed to contribute to increased awareness and understanding of the learning processes of children and their strategies of learning (Bjervås, 2011; Dahlberg, 2012; Elfström, 2013; Hultman, 2011; Rintakorpi, 2018), as well as to visualize invisible learning (Häikiö, 2007; Lenz Taguchi, 2000). According to the Swedish National Agency for Education (Skolverket, 2012), in Sweden there has been a change from a traditional observational documentative practice to a use of a more analytical stance to educational documentation. This means a closer relationship to the children, their perspectives and participation in the documentation of the learning processes.

Within the concept of meaning-making, educational documentation is a continuous and exacting learning process with "a lot of experimenting on the part of the pedagogue, a lot of dialogue with other pedagogues in which multiples perspectives can be introduced" (Moss, 2008; Dahlberg et al., 1999, p. 149). Reggio settings have created an archive of documentation that makes "pedagogical work visible and subject to dialogue, interpretation, contestation, and transformation" (Dahlberg, 2012). All members of the community, be they children, parents, educators, politicians and other citizens, have access to pieces of documentation about the schools and they are encouraged to discuss and debate the content (McNally and Slutsky, 2017). In this context documentation is interpreted and used for its value as a tool for recall and critical reflection. As discussed in detail in Chapter 2, the ability to question and grapple with what exists before one's eyes is sharpened by reflexive practice. An integral part of listening to children's ideas to inform planning is the use of *progettazione*. This term is lost in translation, but the closest translation would be "project work". Drawing on the philosophies of Pestalozzi, Dewey and Isaacs (see Giardiello, 2014), active experiential learning, based on the child's interest in learning about a topic, constitutes a large part of the time children spend in Reggio settings. For Malaguzzi (1998) and Rinaldi (1998, 2006) *progettazione* is something different from curriculum. Instead of formal teaching of a predetermined curriculum to be evaluated using testing procedures, through reflection and self-reflection both educators and children embark on a learning journey that has many twists and turns; the intention being to help children interact with people, objects and the environment in ways that have personal meaning to them.

In the Reggio Emilia municipal educational system educators and families of each school are supported by a *pedagogista* (pedagogue) who could be compared to a mentor, coach and/or advisor in UK schools. These pedagogical coordinators support the professional development of educators and collaborate with them to make choices and decisions about their ongoing work with children and families. A *pedagogista* is someone who asks questions and is devoted to thinking about pedagogical possibilities. Their work with the educators, *atelieristas* (see the following) and families opens up spaces for reflection on habits and presuppositions, and the difficult and sometimes painful understandings that result (Vintimilla, 2018). With the *pedagogista* as the liaison between the schools and the municipality there is a system of open communication that helps the whole community work in harmony providing a means for democratic participation and in the discussion and evaluation of pedagogical practice (Rinaldi, 2006). Here lies the genesis of the "pedagogy of relationships and listening" a metaphor that distinguishes the Reggio Emilia Approach (ibid., p.64). The educators in a Reggio setting use a pedagogy of relationship and listening to unearth the questions, theories and interpretations children have about their experiences and then work with them to express their ideas (McNally and Slutsky, 2017). Listening to children's ideas enhances the possibility of discovering how children think and how they both question and develop a relationship with reality. Rinaldi (2006, p.113) concedes that this way of working is by no means original but "originates precisely from the idea that children are the most avid seekers of meaning and significance and that they produce interpretative theories." These thought processes extend Vygotsky's arguments (1978, 1986), that dialogic practice plays a pivotal role in children's conceptual development.

Another special component of every Reggio Emilia setting is the atelier: a workshop or art studio where children can work out their ideas using "intelligent materials," so-called because they are not neutral but are imbued with learning potential and expressive qualities. The explorative method used in the Reggio Emilia Approach is intended to develop the children's abilities where there is no separation between creative play, artistic activities, construction play, etc. In creating sustainable education, work on art, culture and visual skills are important strategies. Thereby, the focus on the art studio, or atelier, have become a symbol for the development of social participation and analysis of society by visual means (Häikiö, 2007; Karlsson Häikiö, 2018). By learning to reflect on what is seen, by exercising ability to express and communicate thoughts and opinions, the child becomes competent and reflective. In the Reggio Emilia preschools a symbolic function (Vygotsky, 1978) is used as a mediator of metaphoric levels that creates bridges between concepts and memories that function as links between the experiences of the children and their learning processes. Vygotsky (1978) defines the symbolic function as a basis for and mediator of learning that is generated in play, creative and artistic activities and self-motivated learning. According to Vygotsky (1978) artefacts, signs and language have a symbolic function in the mediation and transformation from a level of understanding to a higher level. This in turn helps the children to understand the relation between concrete and abstract levels in their understanding of the world (Häikiö, 2007).

According to Vecchi (2010) the creative process reinforces and deepens learning at many different levels, both thought and emotionally, through the processing of various materials and techniques. It is in the play, in the exploration and the creation, in the exchange between children, that the learning that takes place with the guidance and challenge of the educators. Through work with perception, optical phenomena, light and projections, mirrors, color and shape and with a variety of materials and techniques the children's abilities grow. Through these experiences involving different phenomena and meeting different kinds of materials, a repertoire of experiences is created; the materials offer a framework for what can be developed. As Vecchi (2010, p.12) points out "we must go beyond materials and techniques to stop and look at processes of empathy and intense relations with things. . ." Facilitated by the *atelierista* (an expert artist in residence), "children's different languages could be explored by them, unstudied using a favourable and peaceful atmosphere" (Malaguzzi, 1998, p.74). In this way the children learn the qualities and predictability of the materials in a hundred different ways, with hundreds of different languages (Vecchi, 2010). A mini-atelier is also connected to each classroom which allows for extended *progettazione* (see the following) (Malaguzzi, 1998). This space resembles the central atelier and provides the opportunity for children to work in small groups with or without a teacher (Gandini et al., 2005). A key principle of the Reggio Emilia approach is that children engage with a hundred languages. Notably, the exponents of the Reggio Emilia approach do not refer to a hundred aspects of a language, but a hundred distinct languages (Vecchi, 2010); although they do not see these languages as tightly tied to specific disciplines, implicit within this principle is a recognition that a cultural context involves multiple knowledge systems, multiple ways of understanding and acting, and multiple modes of communication (Stone, 2012).

The philosophy which underpins the Reggio Approach serves to remind us of the importance of acknowledging the interlinked nature of young children's learning, and how this in turn affects the intellectual growth of the child. The Approach gives the child a voice and the curriculum stems not from pre-determined learning outcomes as seen in the English Early Years Foundations Stage (DfE, 2017), but from the learning intentions of the child. The influence of the Reggio Emilia Approach impacts on how early childhood educators listen to the children's questions, follow their interests and ideas, observe and document their learning and build the curriculum around them.

As alluded to, the Reggio Emilia Approach has not been without criticism, not so much for the underpinning principles that it works with, but for the ways in which the Approach has been marketed. Criticism of the Approach is also raised by Johnson (1999) who points out the potential "cargo cult" where the implementation of Reggio threatens to undermine a school's own unique identity. However, as Wright (2000, p.224) points out "the perpetuation of cargo-cultism in Reggio Emilia by academics, teachers and so forth, in no way invalidates the philosophy and practice of the Reggio Emilia schools."

While many early childhood educators from across the world attribute their philosophy and practices to the Reggio Approach, they cannot replicate the exact circumstances found in Reggio Emilia, which exists in a unique historical, cultural, political and economic context. Rather than it being used as a blueprint to be copied, it is more authentic when it is culturally contextualised as a local project (Moss, 2018). The next section of this chapter demonstrates this viewpoint. In doing so we use Sweden as an example.

The Reggio Emilia Approach within a Swedish context

According to Häikiö (2007), the interest in Reggio Emilia in Sweden can be explained by the radically new and inspiring pedagogy developed in the Reggio Emilia preschools, but also by the common historical background of the European early childhood education, which means a dialectical and activity-oriented tradition based on Froebel's and Dewey's theories among others, and by the similar social political views in the Emilia Romagna region which corresponds with the Swedish democratic aspirations of the educational system. In Sweden the Reggio Emilia preschools are renowned as being part of community based regional thinking with strong roots in the Emilia Romagna history of solidarity and cooperation. The inspiration from Reggio Emilia has evolved over time and is today a powerful influence in the design of preschools and schools. Reggio Emilia helped educators to renew concepts and values that opened up a new way of thinking and influenced preschool provision and day to day practice. The design of preschool environments, both outdoors and indoors, became significant. Project thinking emerged as a tool to highlight meaningful learning where observation and pedagogical documentation was used to visualise ongoing learning processes. The metaphor of the "hundred languages of children" became additional characteristics of the Reggio Emilia inspiration.

In Sweden the Reggio Emilia Approach has had a major impact and according to Moss (2008), it is apparent in government policy, teacher education and the network of preschools linked to the Reggio Institute in Stockholm and all engaged in co-constructive dialogue. This can be traced back to a momentous meeting which took place in Reggio Emilia in 1978 between Loris Malaguzzi and art teacher Karin Wallin, and nursery assistant Anna Barsotti, also authors, that resulted in two visiting exhibitions from Reggio Emilia "One child has one hundred languages" in 1981 and a revised version "More about one hundred languages" 1986, both set up in Stockholm, Sweden. The exhibitions led to the development of a strong wish among educators in Sweden to travel to Reggio Emilia to experience for themselves Loris Malaguzzi's philosophy of learning and knowledge that mediated a democratic perspective. The inspiration from the Reggio Emilia's pedagogical philosophy soon began to make a difference in Swedish preschools and schools. Various networks emerged around the country where collaborative learning was in focus. Educators who visited Reggio Emilia participated in these contexts and found new tools for listening and observing their educational activities, promoted by changeability and a transformative approach (Dahlbeck and Lagrell, 2014; Häikiö, 2007). Barsotti (2007, p.57) argues that the idea of Reggio Emilia's creative, hypothetical and problem-oriented approach is, as she sees, not to try to speed up the children's cognitive development, but to allow them access to their own thinking. By this, the individual may have the opportunity to "swim" in all of his or her personality, take possession of him-/herself, in becoming a citizen. Barsotti (2007, p.58) further states that "when the children are born they are immediately transformed by an ocean of words and signs" and that "communication encompasses the whole life of the child, of man: the logic of thought, communication as a basis for socialization, emotions and sensorial experiences transforming into communication."

At the same time as the Reggio Emilia inspiration came to Sweden in the 1980s, some preschools and schools received children and families from other parts of the world. These families were largely placed in suburbs of the major cities. Even if this immigration period was not of the size that Europe has experienced today, but for the educators who worked at these preschools and schools, educational work was a challenge, because knowledge and research on multilingualism was lacking at this time. Malaguzzi's philosophy and writing of "the rich and unique child" therefore became essential in the educational discussions that followed. These discussions are relevant even today and are still ongoing. For a collegiate struggling with these questions, the trips to Reggio Emilia and the meeting with the Reggio preschools and Malaguzzi were a power source, contributing to a change in the view of the child, and the educators saw an opportunity to re-evaluate their preschool / school culture in relation to what they saw and experienced in Reggio Emilia. Being aware of what a relational approach stands for in theory and practice gave the educators new ways of thinking and reflecting on their professional roles. The development of learning environments helped the children to express themselves with different poetic and various verbal languages. Parents and educators collaborated in the building-up of a platform from where they could relate to each other, to the school and the outside world. The educators chose listening as an input to make these relationships function. The experiences of the children and cultures of the parents were visualized through project work. Through the Reggio Emilia Approach and Malaguzzi's voice, we can see into a mirror of self-reflection. Malaguzzi condensed the many connections between creativity, democracy and learning into three words: exploration, participation, and connectivity which he reflects on in the following passage:

> The first flower we encounter along our path is in connection with space, with the moon, with the stars. The discussion builds up the connection through different processes. A school and preschool that is receptive to creativity is a preschool / school that have freedom as a base. The interaction that flows in the children's life in preschool and school is a social type of interaction. This interaction is also above all a respect for the other. Thus we have already come to a very important core point, the inevitable alliance between the adult and the little child. This term connects, puts together, it is a term that is very important to us. The basis for our logical ability is the possibility to connect multiple things to each other at the same time, put together several things, even those things that seem to contradict each other one should approach and tie together. This

> picture provides an instant picture of solidarity. Think about what relationships mean when it comes to relationships between adults working with children. There can be no connection without discussion. It is the discussion that builds the connection through different processes.
>
> *(Malaguzzi,* Modern barndom, *2012, Karlsson Häikiö, Trans.).*

The following case study illustrates the way in which inspirations from Reggio Emilia prompted rethinking of place and didactic choices for change. This case study draws on ethnography and visual documentation of children's everyday activities in the indoor classroom and outdoor environment at a Reggio Emilia in a primary school in Sweden. The children in foci were 6 and 7 years old and attend a combined pre-primary and primary school.

REGGIO INSPIRATION IN A PRE-PRIMARY AND PRIMARY SCHOOL IN SWEDEN

At one of the multilingual pre-primary and primary schools in a suburb of a Swedish city, the Reggio Emilia philosophy gave inspiration to "developing a more rhizomatic thinking about learning" (Dahlberg et al., 2015, p.274). This meant that the design of the educational work branched out, just as a ginger root, in all directions with new roots growing out in a way that made the learning process unpredictable. Where learning that was previously seen as something linear and predetermined had to give way. Near to the preschool flows a waterfall which gathers into small ponds. The discovery of animals and plants in its surroundings created amazement and wonder in the children. An exploration of various natural materials taken in to the school created new learning opportunities, where hypotheses on phenomena in nature emerged. Educators and children observed and documented with the help of photography memorising what they learnt in verbal text both individually and collectively. The reciprocity and dependency of one another in dialogue and discussions became clear both for the children, educators and parents. A book made from the documentation materials of what the children have gathered from the outdoor environment was communicated and became a tool for parental participation. The parents encountered the children's hypotheses and questions at the school. The content of the project became contextualised and part of mutual experiences in the homes, which built new knowledge, as parents' different cultures and experiences were woven together with the children's experiences. These different authentic environments also reinforced the multilingualism of the children as they were able to use their sensibilities and their different verbal languages in the activities they were part of. Educators functioned as co-constructors (Dahlberg, Moss and Pence, 1999) in this process to create a meaningful context.

The frequent visits to the pond created new, wonderful and exciting questions about which way the water flows. The map shows two directions, inland and out to the sea – should we take left or right? Through negotiation with the children it was decided to first follow the water flow to the left. The educators listen to the children who want to know where the water flow comes from. As a preparation, the children presented their hypotheses about how the water is flowing. These hypotheses were gathered at a collective wall that visualized the different proposals. In this way the children and the educators experienced the hypotheses as an unpredictable process.

When stimuli become weak enough, one thing suddenly and surprisingly can be something else. The world becomes immediately uncertain and indeterminate. Rather like sailing in fog. But at the same time the unspeakable feed us possibilities (Öquist, 2003, p.13).

A crisp winter morning a few miles from school, our steps led us towards the origin of the flow, a small curve of water flowing out of a lush lake became the discovery that once again raised new questions. This moment in the woods gave energy to new orientations, word-scopes, pictures, sounds, stories in close relation to the nature that re-appeared in the classroom in different ways. The children decided to follow the water flow in the other direction to the right and encounter the city's treatment plant. To promote deeper understanding and to further develop the children's positive attitudes to their environment the educators arranged a visit to the plant.

Later on in the project the parents became involved and were asked to share their memories from their childhood homelands of their relationship to water through conversations, images and text. The watercourses continued, becoming a river reaching the city by the sea. The focus of the project changed to discovering the city. Over a period of time the city's surroundings around the river was explored including parks, statues, famous and less well known buildings, museums, libraries, theaters. Relationships were created with the city's citizens in different parts of the city. The children and educators were met with respect and assurance everywhere. The observations the children made in the city were documented with various tools by both the children and the educators through the "hundreds languages" in the learning processes where reality and imagination interact. This approach confers on drawings, designs, models and other forms of representation a particular kind of responsiveness and originality which would be rarely found otherwise. As Vecchi (2014, p. 8) affirms: "An empathetic attitude, the sympathy or antipathy towards something we do not investigate indifferently, produces a relationship with what brings us to introduce a 'beat of life' into explorations we carry out. This beat of life is what often solicits intuitions and connections between disparate elements to generate new creative processes."

This part of the project ended with the children choosing to present the different places in the city to which they had developed a close relationship.

Differing groups of children created mini-projects around the places they had chosen and presented their experiences and learnings in different forms of expressions. The parents visited the exhibition at the preschool, where both the children's and educators' processes that were reflected upon and analysed with use of educational documentation were presented and discussed as part of natural conversations. A city tour was arranged, and finally came the day when a coach fetched the children and their families to visit the chosen places with the children being the guides with Swedish and other languages the children speak in their homes being used. The city visit is rounded off by a visit to a vantage point where the suburb can be seen in the distance and where the river unites with the sea.

New, vigorous energy flows into all that is unexplained, unstructured and merely hinted at. This is where the desire, the longing and the impulse to understanding arise. Daring to base our experience on soft signals, without the ambition of reshaping this experience into something specified and confirmed is one of the secrets to a deeply satisfying life. In the nooks and crannies that surround us in our lives resides that which cannot be articulated. It is simply a matter of halting, opening our senses and allowing ourselves to be astonished, like children. Suddenly we experience a sense of wonder, those priceless moments when life flashes and twinkles like sparklers. All we need, quite simply, is something to be astounded over, in order to access that sensation of wonder (Öquist, 2003, p.12) (L. Schenk Trans.).

From the very beginning, Malaguzzi (1998) taught us not to copy Reggio Emilia's philosophy and practice. Theory and practice must be constructed and enlivened in close relationship with the culture and society, the context in which the preschool / school has its profession and activities (Personal communication, Mårtensson, April, 1981 with Malaguzzi)

The following case study is an unfolding narrative of the practice, pedagogy and policies of a Swedish ecological preschool inspired by the Reggio Emilia Approach.

A FALL FROM THE TREE: THE EMERGENCE OF AN ECOLOGICAL PRESCHOOL

A preschool in Sweden has an ideology that is based on an ecological and sustainable pedagogical approach; this can be seen in the creation of the learning environment, the construction of the building, its work with the children and in the contact with parents and families. The new preschool building was developed in collaboration with architects and is totally ecologically standardised (Green flag-certified according to the national organisation Håll Sverige rent (Keep Sweden clean]; www.hsr.se/gron-flagg) when it comes to building materials and energy consumption. In an interview with the preschool manager and the *pedagogista*, they emphasise the value-base of the preschool, where the daily work is applied through documentation, as well as activities at all levels, supported by various theories where power-relations and norms are continually re-assessed. This gives the driving force and changeability to create opportunities for meeting all the children in their learning processes on individual as well as group levels. An innate belief in equal value and everyone's unique contribution to the common good requires curious and trustworthy educators. The role of the *pedagogista* is to facilitate connections between the children, groups of children and to visualize the connections between theory and practice.

The preschool practice is inspired by the Reggio Emilia Approach and one of the contributors to learning besides the children and the environment is seeing the educators as co-constructors (Dahlberg, Moss and Pence, 1999), as opposed to being seen as the source of knowledge (Dysthe, 1996). Their work is based on a socio-cultural approach to learning, where learning takes place through social interactions and in dialogue with others (Vygotsky, 1978); through physical meetings but also in interaction with literature; or through information that is shared through social media. The work starts with a philosophical view that children and educators create knowledge together, a so-called collaborative approach where relationships and knowledge is shaped (Palmer, 2011).

A renewal of the preschool, or what the preschool manager and the *pedagogista* refer to as a process of transformation, started with a collective reflection and process initiated by the educators regarding where they felt that a change was required to meet each child's right to meaningful learning. The earlier environments at the preschool were not in relation to the children or to the surrounding society, and did not support the work of the educators. A dramatic experience at the preschool came to influence the educators to move in a new direction. One of the educators was injured during pre-school hours by falling from a tree they were climbing, which was an unexpected incident and the educators were surprised at the interest of the children in this event. While in the UK, this would have been viewed as a health and safety issue, in Sweden, it was seen as an opportunity for a new project where indifference was replaced by glowing eyes of curiosity. The incident of "the fall from the tree" resulted in a return to active participation of the children. Together the children and educators created an empathetic community-based project with opportunities for exploration, visualisation and meaningful learning. The educators became aware that this children's group respected and loved being engaged in the community, evident in the way they viewed the children as rich and competent. Visits to the teacher in convalescence became part of involving the community, all driven by the children's empathy and their care for the educator.

During this period, a new preschool building was taking place involving both the outer architecture of the preschool and the inner pedagogical content as a result of the unexpected event of the fall from the tree. The educators were given a legitimacy to influence the new environment. There was a renewed energy shared by educators. A relational pedagogy and dialogue-based approach became significant (Aspelin and Persson, 2011) for the educators. Throughout the emergence of the new preschool the children and educators were involved in the construction process. The children and educators dreamed, imagined, sketched, planned, and visualised a miniature model version of the desired preschool with different aesthetic languages. This was produced using material from visits to the construction site. The preschool became designed in close interaction with the children and educators, in relation to and in dialogue with nature and questions of sustainability. Parts of the façade towards the yard were designed as bird cages.

When the new preschool was ready, all participants, parents and children met and were involved in conversations about how the children's environments should be adjusted to the experience of daily life and towards a sustainable future.

At the preschool the kitchen and the cook have a central function, where children participate in the ordering, preparation and distribution of ecological food. Also, the parents are involved in the preparation of the menu at the preschool. Since the preschool is situated in an area with families from multi-ethnic backgrounds, the work with the kitchen as a pedagogical approach contributes to the participation of families. The cook in this way has an important role as educator. Next to the kitchen there is situated an atelier, with an *atelierista*, or studio teacher. The atelier is part of the collaboration with the kitchen, and vegetables and food are used in the atelier as inspirational and creative materials.

In the preschool atelier, the use of aesthetic expressions has a strong relationship to the activities and projects in the setting. Sensory learning, and interaction between the atelier and the kitchen reinforces creativity which stimulates children's communication. The children become co-creators in food culture with a sustainable future perspective, through use of both verbal and aesthetic languages.

The preschool is today a flexible learning environment, consisting of interior and exterior settings, with a rich variety of materials that act as provocations for the children to respond to and interact with, since things are not just insignificant objects, but in relation to the children. As Nordin-Hultman (2004) states, creating such environments is important in ensuring children's interest and meaningful participation. At the preschool this kind of thinking is evident, which also becomes clear in the documentations of different project work, where transparency, memories, well-being, relationships, subjectivity and exploration are important themes in the project work (as discussed earlier).

FIGURE 5.1 Image representations of a Reggio-inspired preschool.
Note: *In the pictures can be seen the ideology of the preschool and a photo of an activity zone for investigations on nature from the preschool (Picture compilation).*
Photographs: Pernilla Mårtensson and Tarja Karlsson Häikiö.

POINTS FOR REFLECTION

- In considering your own practice, do you pay enough attention to developing relationships with the children, their families and the community?
- How would you ensure that every space in your provision enables a "pedagogy of listening" and are there any aspects that you would change?
- How do you plan to ensure that children are following their own interests?
- How would you involve children in assessing their own learning?

FIGURE 5.2 Aesthetic expressions in the preschool atelier.
Note: *This image is in the atelier where the children can create with different techniques, often with natural materials as fruit juice from berries, and with different creative materials combined with work with light tables, light projections and with other visual perceptively challenging material. Photograph: Pernilla Mårtensson.*
Photographs: Pernilla Mårtensson.

As shown in our discussions the fundamental principles of the Reggio Emilia Approach are deeply embedded in their own social-cultural history and environment. The collaboration between the children in the Infant-Toddler Centers and Preschools and those protagonists who support their educational journey, at every level, including families and the wider community, has influenced early childhood education worldwide. "Reggio Inspired" has become a familiar term for those settings who seek to incorporate or feature aspects of the Reggio Approach into their own programs. According to Murphy et al. (2016, p.313) "the aesthetic aspects of the environment and the presence and work of the *atelierista* . . . is perhaps one of the aspects that is the most striking to the visitor, and one that is the most difficult to replicate elsewhere." However, as we have seen in the two case studies from Sweden, many aspects of the Reggio Emilia Approach have been found to be well matched to their own socio-cultural ideas and thinking. The idea of engaging in long term projects based on children's interests is not a new idea, but one that has resonated with many of the early key thinkers and pioneers of early childhood education (Giardiello, 2014). What Malaguzzi and the Reggio Emilia settings have accomplished is to bring together into a whole the key ideas and bedrock principles of early thinkers, philosophers and educators, adding strong values towards children and families, a work ethic based on collaboration and the financial resources of the municipality. A final thought is the way the Reggio Emilia Approach encourages educators to critically reflect on their own practice and provision and to move away from a purely technical stance towards a democratic and ethical way of working with children.

References

Alnervik, K. (2003) *Men så kan man ju också tänka! Pedagogisk dokumentationsom förändringsverktyg i förskolan* [*You can also think like this! Pedagogical documentation as a tool for change in early childhood education*]. Dissertation. Jönköpings universitet.

Åsberg, C., Hultman, M. and Lee, F. (2012) *Posthumanistiska nyckeltexter* [*Post-human key texts*], Lund: Studentlitteratur.

Aspelin, J. and Persson, S. (2011) *Relationell pedagogik* [*Relational pedagogics*], Malmö: Gleerups förlag.

Barsotti, A. (2007) *D-som Robin Hoods pilbåge. Ett kommunikationsprojekt pådaghemmet Diana i Reggio Emilia* [*D as in Robin Hood's bow: A communication project at the pre-school Diana in Reggio Emilia*], Stockholm: HLS förlag.

Bjervås, L.-L. (2011) *Samtal om barn och pedagogisk dokumentation som bedömningspraktik i förskolan; En diskursanalys* [*Dialogues on children and pedagogical documentation: A discourse analysis*]. Dissertation. Utbildningsvetenskapliga fakulteten, Institutionen för pedagogik, kommunikation och lärande. Göteborgs universitet.

Buckingham, D. and Jones, K. (2001) 'New labour's cultural turn: Some tensions in contemporary educational and cultural policy', *Journal of Educational Policy*, 16(1), p.1–14.

Cagliari, P., M. Castagnetti, C. Giudici, C. Rinaldi, V. Vecchi and P. Moss (Eds.) (2016) *Loris Malaguzzi and the schools of Reggio Emilia: A selection of his writings and speeches, 1945–1993*, Abingdon: Routledge.

Caruso, F. (2013) 'Embedding early childhood education and care in the socio-cultural context: The case of Italy', in: J. Georgeson and J. Payle (Eds.) *International perspectives on early childhood education and care*, Maidenhead: Open University Press.

Clark, A. and Moss, P. (2001) *Listening to young children: The Mosaic Approach*, London: National Children's Bureau for the Joseph Rowntree Foundation.

Dahlbeck, P. and Lagrell, K. (2014) *En skola som berör* [*A school that makes a difference*], Lund: Studentlitteratur.

Dahlberg, G. (2012) 'Pedagogical documentation: A practice for negotiation and democracy', in: C. Edwards, L. Gandini, and G. Foreman (Eds.) *The hundred languages of children: The Reggio Emilia experience in transformation*, (3rd edn.) Santa Barbara, CA: Praeger, p.225–232.

Dahlberg, G. (2000) 'Everything is a beginning, and everything is dangerous: Some reflections of the Reggio Emilia experience', in: H. Penn (Ed.) *Early childhood services: Theory, policy and practice*, Buckingham: Open University Press, p.175–183.

Dahlberg, G. and Elfström, I. (2015) 'Pedagogisk dokumentation i tillblivelse [Pedagogical documentation in becoming]', *Pedagogisk Forskning i Sverige [Pedagogical Research in Sweden]*, 19(4–5), p.268–296.

Dahlberg, G., Göthson, H. and Jonstoij, T. (2015) *Hundra sätt att förundras [Hundred ways to wonder]*, Stockholm: Liber AB.

Deleuze, G. and Guattari, F. (1988) *A thousand plateaus: Capitalism and schizophrenia*, London: Athlone Press.

Dahlberg, G., Moss, P. and Pence, A. (1999) *Beyond quality in early childhood education and care: Postmodern perspectives*, London: Falmer Press.

Department for Education (DfE) (2017) *The statutory framework for the early years foundation stage*, London: Department for Education.

Dysthe, O. (1996) *Det flerstämmiga klassrummet - Att skriva och samtala för att lära*, Lund: Studentlitteratur.

Edwards, C., Gandini, L. and Foreman, G. (1998/2012). *The hundred languages of children: The Reggio Emilia experience in transformation*, (3rd edn.) Santa Barbara, California: Praeger.

Elfström, I. (2015) 'Pedagogisk dokumentation som del i ett systematiskt kvalitetsarbete i förskolan [Pedagaogical documentation as part of systematic quality work]', in: Åsén, G. (Ed.) *Utvärdering och pedagogisk bedömning i förskolan [Assessment and evaluation in preschool]*, Liber: Stockholm.

Emilsson, A. and Pramling Samuelsson, I. (2014) 'Documentation and communication in Swedish preschool', *Early Years: Journal of International Research & Development*, (34), p.175–187.

Flannery Quinn, S. and Manning, J.P. (2013) 'Recognising the ethical implications of the use of photography in early childhood educational settings', *Contemporary Issues in Early Childhood*, 14(3), p.270–278.

Foucault, M. (1979) *Discipline and punish: The birth of the prison*, New York: Vintage Books.

Gandini, L. (2003). 'Values and principles of the Reggio Emilia Approach', in: L. Gandini, S. Etheridge and L. Hill (Eds.) *Insights and inspirations from Reggio Emilia: Stories of teachers and children from North America*, Worcester, MA: Davis Publications, p.25–27.

Giardiello, P. (2014) *Pioneers in early childhood education: The roots and legacies of Rachel and Margaret McMillan, Maria Montessori and Susan Isaacs*, Abingdon: Routledge.

Gibson, M. (2014) 'Reggio Emilia: How a city in Italy started an education trend', *The Conversation*. Retrieved 29 November 2018 from: https://theconversation.com/reggio-emilia-how-a-city-in-italy-started-an-education-trend-25809.

Giroux, H.A. (2011) 'Rethinking education as the practice of freedom: Paulo Freire and the promise of critical pedagogy', in: *On critical pedagogy*, New York:Continuum Publishing, p.152–166.

Häikiö, T. (2007) *Barns estetiska lärprocesser; Atelierista i förskola och skola [Children's aesthetical learning processes: Atelierista in pre-school and school]*. Dissertation. *Gothenburg Studies in Art and Architecture*, nr 24. Acta Universitatis Gothoburgensis. Göteborgs Universitet.

Halldén, G. (2003) 'Barnperspektiv som ideologiskt och/eller metodologiskt begrepp [Child perspective as ideological and/or methodological concept]', *Pedagogisk forskning i Sverige [Educational research in Sweden]*, 1–2, p.12–23.

Hendrick, J. (1997) *First steps toward teaching the Reggio way*, Upper Saddle River, NJ: Prentice-Hall.

Hultman, K. (2011) *Barn, linjaler och andra aktörer: Posthumanistiska perspektiv på subjektskapande och materialitet i förskola/skola* [*Children, rulers and other actors: Posthuman perspectives on subject creation and materiality in preschool*]. Dissertation. Stockholms universitet.

Johnson, R. (1999) 'Colonialism and cargo cults in early childhood education: Does Reggio Emilia really exist?' *Contemporary Issues in Early Childhood*, 1(1), p.61–78.

Karlsson Häikiö, T. (2018) 'The atelier as potential space for transformative learning processes', in: T. Karlsson Häikiö and K. G. Eriksson (Eds.) *Art-based Education: An Ethics and Politics of Relation. Making Narratives*, 3/2018, HDK, Academy of Design and Crafts. University of Gothenburg, p.71–91.

Karlsson Häikiö, T. (2017) 'Dokumentation, transformation och intra-modala materialiseringar [Documentation, transformation and intra-modal materialisations]', in: B. Bergstedt (Ed.) *Posthumanistisk pedagogik - Teori, undervisning och forskningspraktik* [*Posthuman pedagogics: Theories, education and research*], Lund: Studentlitteratur.

Kumpulainen, K., Lipponen, L., Hilppö, J. and Mikkola, A. (2013) 'Building on the positive in children's lives: A co-participatory study on the social construction of children's sense of agency', *Early Child Development and Care*, 184(2), p.211–229.

Kurki, L. (2000) *Sosiokulttuurinen innostaminen* [*Sociocultural animation*], Tampere: Vastapaino.

Lenz Taguchi, H. (2012) *Pedagogisk dokumentation som aktiv agent: introduktion till intra-aktiv pedagogic* [*Pedagogical documentation as active agent: Introduction to intra-active pedagogics*], Malmö: Gleerups utbildning.

Lenz Taguchi, H. (2000) *Emancipation och motstånd; Dokumentation och kooperativa läroprocesser i förskolan* [*Emancipation and resistance: Documentation and cooperative learning processes in preschool*]. Dissertation. Stockholm: LHS Förlag.

Lindroth, F. (2018) *Pedagogisk dokumentation – en pseudoverksamhet? Lärares arbete med dokumentation i relation till barns delaktighet* [*Pedagogical documentation – A pseudo-practice? Educators work with documentation in relation to children's participation*], Licentiatuppsats, Institutionen för pedagogik, Linnéuniversitetet.

Löfdahl, A. and Pérez Prieto, H. (2009) 'Institutional narratives within the performative preschool in Sweden: "If we write that we're no good, that's not good publicity!"' *Early Years*, 29(3), p.261–270.

McNally, S.A. and Slutsky, R. (2017) 'Key elements of the Reggio Emilia Approach and how they are interconnected to create the highly regarded system of early childhood education', *Early Child Development and Care*, 187(12), p.1925–1937.

Malaguzzi, L. (2012) 'En människa som gör skillnad [A person who makes a difference]', *Modern barndom*, nr 2/12Malaguzzis seminar nr 5,24/5 1993.

Malaguzzi, L. (1998) 'History, ideas, and basic philosophy: An interview with Lella Gandini', in: C. Edwards, L. Gandini and G. Forman (Eds.) *The hundred languages of children: The Reggio Emilia Approach – Advanced reflections*, (2nd edn.) Westport, Connecticut: Ablex Publishing, p.49–99.

Malaguzzi, L. (1993) 'For an education based on relationships', *Young Children*, 49(1), p.9–12.

Moss, P. (2008) 'Toward a new public education: Making globalization work for us all', *Child Development Perspectives*, 2(2), p.114–119.

Moss, P. and Petrie, P. (2002) *From children's services to children's spaces: Public policy, children and childhood*, Abingdon: Routledge.

Murphy, R.Ridgway, A.Cunneen, M. and Horgan, M. (2016) 'Reggio Emilia', in: T. David, K. Goouch and S. Powell, (Eds.) *The Routledge international handbook of philosophies and theories of early childhood education and care*, Abingdon: Routledge.

Nordin-Hultman, E. (2004) *Pedagogiska miljöer och barns subjektskapande* [*Pedagogical environments and children's subject construction*], Liber: Stockholm.

Olsson, L.M. (2014) *Rörelse och experimenterande i små barns lärande; Deleuze och Guattari i förskolan [Movement and experimentation in small children's learning: Deleuze and Guattari in preschool]*, Lund: Studentlitteratur.

Olsson, L.M. (2012) 'Eventicizing curriculum: Learning to read and write through becoming a citizen of the world', *Journal of Curriculum Theorizing*, 28(1), p.88–107.

Öquist, O. (2003) *Tyst erfarenhet [Silent experience]*, Helsingborg: Carlsson.

Palmer, A. (2011) *Hur blir man matematisk? Att skapa nya relationer till matematik och genus i arbetet med yngre barn [How to be mathematic? To create new relationships to mathematics and gender in early years education]*. Dissertation. Stockholm: Liber.

Parnell, W. (2012) 'Experiences of teacher reflection: Reggio inspired practices in the studio', *Journal of Early Childhood Research*, 10(2), p.117–133.

Reggio Children Nidi e Scuole (Online Newsletter). Retrieved 13 March 2019 from: www.reggiochildren.it/i-nidi-e-le-scuole-del-comune-di-reggio-emilia/.

Rinaldi, C. (2006) *In dialogue with Reggio Emilia: Listening, researching and learning (Contesting early childhood)*, Abingdon: Routledge.

Rinaldi, C. (1998) 'Projected curriculum, constructed through documentation – Progettazione: An interview with Lella Gandini', in: C. Edwards, L. Gandini and G. Forman (Eds.) *The hundred languages of children*, Norwood, NY: Ablex, p.113–115.

Rintakorpi, K. (2018) 'Dokumentoinnin mahdollisuudet ja haasteet esi- ja alkuopetuksen kuvataiteellisessa toimintakulttuurissa [The possibilities and challenges of documentation in visual work culture in early education]' in: Rusanen, S., Kuusela, M., Rintakorpi, K. and Torkki, K. *Mun kuvista kulttuuriin - kuvataidetta esi- ja alkuopetukseen [My images becoming culture: Visual art in early and pre-primary education]*, Helsinki: Lasten Keskus ja Kirjapaja OY.

Rose, G. (2001) *Visual methodologies*, London: SAGE.

Sandberg, A., Sheridan, S. and Williams, P. (2012) 'Systematic quality work in preschool', *International Journal of Early Childhood*, 45(1), ISSN: 0020–7187 DOI: doi:10.1007/s13158–13012–0076–0078.

Sightlines Initiatives, Encounters (2018) Retrieved 13 March 2019 from: www.sightlines-initiative.com/in-dialogue-with-reggio-emilia.html.

Skolverket [National Agency for Education] (2012) *Uppföljning, utvärdering och utveckling i förskolan – pedagogisk dokumentation [Follow-up, evaluation and development in preschool – Pedagogical documentation]*, Stockholm. Available from: www.skolverket.se.

Sparrman, A. and Lindgren, A.-L. (2010) 'Visual documentation as a normalizing practice: A new discourse of visibility in preschool', *Surveillance & Society*, 7(3/4), p.248–261. Available from: www.surveillance-and-society.org ISSN: 1477–7487.

Stirling, A. (2014) *Emancipating tranformations: From controlling 'the transition' to culturing plural radical progress*, STEPS, Working Paper 64. Brighton: STEPS Centre.

Stone, J. (2012) 'A Vygotskian commentary on the Reggio Emilia Approach', *Contemporary Issues in Early Childhood*, 13(4), p.276–289.

UrbiStat (2017) Retrieved 25 November 2018 from: https://ugeo.urbistat.com/AdminStat/en/it/demografia/stranieri/emilia-romagna/8/2.

Vallberg-Roth, A.-C. (2010) 'Att stödja och styra barns lärande – tidig bedömning och dokumentation [To support and steer children's learning – Assessment and documentation in early years]', in: Skolverket, *Perspektiv på barndom och lärande i förskolan och grundskolans tidigare år: En kunskapsöversikt [Perspectives on childhood and learning in early childhood, pre-primary and primary education: An overview]*, Stockholm: Fritzes.

Vecchi, V. (2014) *Blå cikoriablommor; Ateljén i Reggio Emilias pedagogiska verksamhet [Blue cicoria-flowers: The atelier in the pedagogical philosophy in Reggio Emilia]*, Lund: Studentlitteratur.

Vecchi, V. (2010) *Art and creativity in Reggio Emilia: Exploring the role and potential of ateliers in early childhood education*, Abingdon: Routledge.
Vintimilla, C.D. (2018) 'Encounters with a pedagogista', *Contemporary Issues in Early Childhood*, 19(1), p.20–30.
Vygotsky, L.S. (1986) *Thought and language*, Cambridge, MA: MIT Press.
Vygotsky, L.S. (1978) *Mind in society: The development of higher psychological processes*, Cambridge, MA: Harvard University Press.
Wright, S. (2000) 'Why Reggio Emilia doesn't exist: A response to Richard Johnson', *Contemporary Issues in Early Childhood*, 1(2), p.223–226.

6

A FINNISH PERSPECTIVE OF EARLY CHILDHOOD EDUCATION

Patricia Giardiello, Tarja Karlsson Häikiö, Ulla Härkönen, Liisa Lohilahti and Naomi McLeod

Introduction

Currently there is worldwide interest in the Finnish education system as politicians, policy-makers and educators search for successful approaches. This is mainly due to international achievement studies such as the Programme for International Student Assessment (PISA), which has an increasing influence on education policy worldwide. Finland performs well in PISA and is often cited as an example of both efficient and equitable education. In the past decade, 15-year-old Finnish students have been among the highest-performing in all the 34 OECD (Organisation for Economic Co-operation and Development) countries. In Finland, children start their nine-year basic schooling in the autumn term of the year when they turn 7. This is the highest school starting age in the OECD countries.

'In Finnish early education (up to the age of 7), creative play and physical activity traditionally have occupied most of children's time' (Pulkkinen, 2012a, p.326). Although Finland's PISA success and its connection to early childhood education are less studied, some features can perhaps be named as effective behind the success of older children (Määttä and Uusiautti, 2012). Finnish early education typifies the EDUCARE model, which means the interconnectedness of education and care, as well as learning as the foundation of pedagogical action. This chapter starts by illuminating the socio-cultural and historical understanding of the dominant educational idea in Finland, which is education for equality (Lundkvist et al., 2017). Also, it explores how the distinctive nature of Finnish early childhood education and care system is embedded in the development of Finnish society. Finland follows a typically Nordic societal system where the state is responsible for the citizens and where early childhood education and care is part of the social welfare system offering social services to families (Hujala et al., 1998; Määttä and Uusiautti, 2012). Finnish family policy continues to rest on three pillars: 'child-oriented society, thriving families with children and the prevention of social exclusion', first established in 2006 by the Ministry of Social Affairs and Health (MSAH, 2006, p.2–3).

The distinctive nature of Finnish ECEC

Finland is a Nordic nation bordered by Sweden to the north, Russia to the west, Estonia to the south and the Gulf of Finland to the west. With a population of 5.5 million, Finland is one of the more sparsely populated European countries whilst being one of the most prosperous economically (Sahlberg, 2012). The roots of Finland are very diverse and influenced from a range of historical, political and socio-cultural perspectives. As in most European countries, Finland has strong international roots which offer a wide socio-cultural and historical basis for early childhood pedagogy. Beginning in the twelfth century, Sweden controlled most of what is present-day Finland, continuing its dominance over the area until 1809 when Finland became a grand duchy of the Russian Empire. Having achieved independence in 1918, Finland remained a mostly rural, agrarian society until after World War II. According to Sahlberg (2012) the post-war era was a time of political instability and economic transformation which also gave rise to new social ideas and policies, in particular, the idea of equal educational opportunities. After 1950, Finland rapidly industrialised and fuelled a southern migration, enlarging Helsinki and turning some formerly rural villages into small cities with the proportion of women in the non-agricultural labour force also seeing a steady increase (Haavio-Mannila, 1971). This was mainly due to the labour force policy initially expecting contributions from women rather than immigrant workers. However, these expectations took a few decades before social support for households with small children in Finland began to draw more attention. The absence of such support for child day care in the 1950s and 1960s led to a situation wherein working mothers often relied on informal care for their small children, namely by seeking help from friends and relatives (Takahashi, 2008).

The question of publicly funded child day care in Finland was highlighted by the Social Democrats and women's organisations in the late 1960s as a way of enhancing gender rights and facilitating labour participation of mothers (Campbell-Barr and Nygård, 2014). According to Takahashi (2008, p.45) 'it was not until 1973 that the act on child day care was promulgated in Finland, clarifying the responsibility of municipal governments (kunta in Finnish) for providing child day care services to local residents'. In the early 1980s, due to a continuing shortage of day care facilities, home care allowance was introduced to aid the child day care scheme and was seen as a watershed in Finnish childcare policies. Home allowance provided cash benefits to parents raising their small children below 3 years of age at home on the condition that the child did not use municipal day care services.

However, at the start of the 1990s, Finland also suffered the deepest economic recession since World War II. The effects of the recession manifested in the form of mass unemployment and as tax revenues diminished, the State and the local authorities also reduced their services (OECD, 2016). However, fundamental to Finland's educational mission is the idea that equality is vital to economic success and societal wellbeing, as well as the belief that a small nation, reliant on creativity, ingenuity and solidarity to compete in the global economy, cannot afford inequality or segregation in schooling or health (Butler, 2016). Therefore, in light of this, since the late 1990s, the perspective on children's rights attracted more social attention with respect to early childhood education (ibid.). In the relocation of children's rights in Finnish childcare policy, the issue of social justice is no longer limited to concerns about parents' (mothers') working status; rather, it is associated with concerns about access to early childhood education for small children, for example, how to guarantee opportunities for children with respect to early childhood education prior to basic education in primary school attracted increasing social attention (Takahashi, 2008). It was during this time that preschool education became increasingly highlighted as an important element of Early Childhood Education and Care (ECEC) services. In 1997 the universal right to full-day childcare was extended to children under the age of 7 (Forssén, Jaakola and Ritakallio, 2008; Hiilamo, 2002), and as a way of strengthening children's early learning and childhood education, a voluntary year of early education for 6-year-olds ('pre-school') was introduced in 2001 (STM, 2002). The aim of pre-school education was to prepare children for statutory basic education by providing systematic education in a playful form one year before school-age at 7. The main motive for introducing a pre-school year was to strengthen learning capacities, but it also built on ideas of education as a leveller of unequal life conditions of children (Campbell-Barr and Nygård, 2014). The Finnish system of ECEC policy may be described with the concept of 'EDUCARE' (OECD, 2016) where education, care and teaching have been combined to form an integrated whole and where play is a central pedagogical tool.

Nowadays, the day care centres perform the dual functions of childcare and early childhood education provided by kindergarten teachers with formal qualifications. However, there is regional disparity in the availability of municipal day care centres, as they tend to concentrate on urban areas. Also, in rural settings it is childcare nurses and not early childhood teachers who take care of children. Finnish day care centres and pre-schools are carefully designed to meet the academic, social, emotional and physical needs of children. Unfortunately, according to Pulkkinen (2012, p.166) 'the tendency has spread into Finland of calculating the short-term cost-effectiveness of education'. This has resulted in larger groups of children in ECEC settings, cuts in resources and policy changes are being made irrespective of the research results, which show the effects that these changes have on children (ibid.). Reassuringly, despite Finnish education undergoing the biggest financial cuts in its history, with the latest round cutting two billion Euros or 8 per cent off the budget, early years and primary schools have been relatively protected, according to the OAJ, the Finnish teaching union (Butler, 2016).

As indicated previously, Finland has a legal obligation to provide an ECEC place for all children aged 0 to 6 (given that the starting age of compulsory school is seven in Finland) with maximum hours of ten hours a day. In Finland, it is also possible to attend ECEC services 24-hour care at the weekend and during holidays when parents are working (OECD, 2016). At the same time, however, the global financial crisis of 2007–2008 changed the economic and political landscape for family policy in Finland with recent governments pressing for cost containment in family policy, such as cuts in child benefits (Eurofound, 2015). Furthermore, the newly enacted law on ECEC was amended in late 2015, shortly after its enactment, so that the right to full-day ECEC for children without both parents in full-time work, education or on family leave was restricted to 20 hours per week (Suomen säädöskokoelma, 2016). Not only was this restriction controversial, but it also implied a gradual shift away from an ECEC ideological rationale focussing on children's development, early learning, social mobility and wellbeing, to an economic neo-liberal rationale that emphasises mothers' labour market participation and cost containment (Lundkvist et al., 2017).

An overview of the Finnish education system

The history of Finnish pre-school provision began with the opening of the first kindergarten and crèche in the city of Jyväskylä in 1863 with the first Finnish-speaking teacher seminary held at the University. The first publicly funded kindergartens opened in Helsinki in 1888 soon to find their place in society, taking care of children from the poorest environment whilst their parents were at work (Salminen, 2017). As in most European countries, Finland has strong international roots which offer a wide socio-cultural historical basis for early childhood pedagogy in Finland. From a historical perspective, the most noted influence in early childhood education has come from Germany, through the work of Friedrich Froebel's principles on children's growth (Salminen, 2017). Finland in the main is influenced by Swedish pedagogical theories such as Dialogpedagogik (dialogic pedagogy) (Schyl-Bjurman and Strömberg-Lind, 1976) and Ansvarspedagogik (problem-based pedagogy) (Bladsjö et al., 1984). In the 1970s, Sukhomlinsky (2016), a Ukrainian teacher drawing inspiration from Pestalozzi's head, heart and hand pedagogy (see Giardiello, 2014), was also an influence and known in many parts of the world as the creator of the 'School of Joy', a preschool programme that was conducted almost totally outdoors and addressed all the needs of growing children: physical, emotional, intellectual and spiritual (Cockerill, 2016).

The goals of Finnish day care (päivähoidon) education were defined in policy 40 years ago, based on the work of the parliamentary Committee for Educational Goals in Day Care, (cited in Ojala, 2005, p.85) which emphasised the view of the child, society and culture based on educational objectives of 'physical, social, emotional, aesthetic, intellectual, ethical, and religious education, taking into consideration for each domain the care and educational environments, the quality of care and education, and the child's own play activity' (Pulkkinen, 2012, p. 328).

In Finland today, education is organised and structured through the Finnish Agency for Education. There is no statutory testing until children reach upper secondary education (Finnish Agency for Education, 2017). Early childhood education and care in Finland runs from birth up to the age of 6 (ibid.). At the end of this phase children then move into a compulsory year called 'pre-primary'. The implications of a longer period of early childhood education are the allowance of more time for the development of the individual child, language and independence. Upon completion of the pre-primary year, children move into 'basic education' from the age of 7 up to the age of 16. The National Core Curriculum for Basic Education (Finnish Agency for Education, 2017) comprises main objectives to be taught to children by educators. Finnish educators assess children's progress and development through formative assessment to aid them in supporting children and their next steps to development (Finnish Agency for Education, 2017).

The early childhood education and care 'curricula' in Finland is offered through 'six orientations' (Finnish Agency for Education, 2017). These 'orientations' have no prescribed content, unlike England's Early Years Foundation Stage (DfE, 2017), and as such there is greater autonomy given to educators to enable them to follow the interests of children in their care, focusing on the holistic development of the child (Lee et al., 2014). No statutory testing equates to less pressure on teachers to fulfil requirements and achieve goals. A focus on the development of language runs through each orientation, with a focus on encouraging children to interact with adults and their peers. Each orientation has a set of values and educators are encouraged to consider individual needs and the interests of children when choosing the content of the curriculum (Finnish Agency for Education, 2017).

In Finland the new Early Childhood Education and Care Act came into force on 1st September, 2018. It speaks of a new concept of early childhood education and care, and less about day care. The most recent curriculum is the 2017 National Core Curriculum for Early Childhood Education (2017) which has attracted international interest. The values that underpin the Finnish Early Childhood Curriculum are based upon the United Nations Convention on the Rights of the Child (UNCRC, 1989) and includes giving due weight to the views of the child (Finnish Agency for Education, 2017).

As identified in the curriculum document, the primary task of the pre-school educator is to promote personal wellbeing of children, to strengthen forms of behaviour, to consider ways to relate to other people and to gradually increase the independence of children (Rantala, 2016; Utbildningsstyrelsen, 2016). In the ECEC guidance plan, there is an emphasis on the individual child in addition to descriptions about group activities and the learning environment. Different thinking and practices are discussed openly and constructively as a way of working together. The new Finnish Early Childhood Education Act (2018) aims at raising the professional competence of educators for the benefit of high quality early childhood education. In addition, directives in the involvement of the child in the daily work have been added, raising this issue to a more prominent level (as clarified in the new Early Childhood Education Act (2018)). Early childhood education is viewed as a whole involving a systematic and goal-oriented pedagogy with particular emphasis on play. The objectives are clearly defined in the law as follows, where early childhood education must:

1. promote the holistic growth, development, health and well-being of each child according to age and development;
2. support the conditions for the child's learning and to promote lifelong learning as well as the implementation of educational equality;
3. arrange multi-layered pedagogical activities based on play, movement, artistic and cultural heritage, and enable positive learning experiences;
4. ensure a developing, learning-promoting, healthy and safe early childhood educational environment;
5. ensure a respectful approach to children and establish lasting and interactive relations between children and early childhood educators;
6. create equal opportunities for all children, promoting equality and gender equality, and capacity to understand and respect the general cultural heritage as well as the linguistic, cultural, religious and religious background of each child;
7. identify the need for individual support for the child and provide appropriate support in the education through cross-sectoral cooperation;
8. to develop child co-operation and interaction skills, to promote the child's role in a peer group and to guide ethically responsible and sustainable activities, respect for other people and membership of society;
9. ensure that the child has the opportunity to participate and influence matters concerning him-herself;
10. work together with the child and the child's parents or other care-takers to benefit the balanced development of the child and overall wellbeing and to support the child's parents or other care-takers in the upbringing.

Cultural institutions play an important role in Finland, and research on children's access to public spaces, as well as cultural experiences, has since the 2000s a stronger position in Finnish art educational practice. The role of education is to enforce children's knowledge of the cultural heritage, and encounters with art works as well as architecture or artefact design enrich the daily life of children (Rusanen, 2007; Rusanen et al., 2014).

Key aims and principles of the Finnish ECE curriculum

The main aims and principles of the ECE curriculum are reflective of the concepts of a democratic and multi-cultural society, and tolerance (as referred to in the National Core Curriculum for Early Childhood Education and Care (2017) and the new Early Childhood Education and Care Act (2018)).

According to Härkönen's pedagogical systems theory (2009, 2013; Georgiou, 2007; Kettukangas, 2017; Kouvo-Suutari, 2016) laws, curricula and many political, economic, and religious documents are influenced directly by the culture of a society. They each have very strong and powerful influence in various areas of ECE. Härkönen sees the need for ECE to be seen as a strong independent science, a more determining factor than is currently happening. This view reinforces what

Pulkkinen (2012b, p.328) sees as '— an important issue to be discussed in Finland and elsewhere (which) is how to connect the science of child development to public policy in order to promote supportive, nurturing, and child-friendly communities'. Today politics and funding are dominating the quality of ECE. According to Pulkkinen (2012b, p. 328):

> Unfortunately, the trend toward calculating the short-term cost-effectiveness of education has spread into Finland. This has resulted in large schools and cuts in schools′ resources. Such policy changes take place irrespective of research results about their effects on children.

In ECE, the amendments to Early Childhood Education and Care legislation in 2016 (8.5.2015/580) was part of creating financial savings. This has been at the expense of quality ECE and the associated benefits for children. Pulkkinen (2012b) notes the need to 'stand up for educational philosophy and resist (the) pressure for standardization and test-based accountability' (p.328), which as Puroila and Kinnunen (2017) show has contributed to a deteriorating in quality of ECE in Finland. Today test-based learning and standardisation is evident in Finnish ECE as well as schools. Due to the school readiness agenda, there is more pressure for children to begin formal schooling at 6 rather than 7 years of age, and preschool at the age of 5 rather than 6. Many professionals and educators in Finland are concerned about these pressures. As Pulkkinen (2012a) recognises, age 7 is appropriate for starting teacher-directed learning particularly from the perspective of brain development, which aligns with Finland having the highest school starting age of 7 in the OECD countries – which for Pulkkinen is the first pillar for a good childhood in Finland.

In Finland the percentage of educators with a degree is lower compared to other Nordic countries, but higher than in many OECD countries (OECD, 2012). The trend is that there will be less educated staff in the future, including some day care centres which will affect the quality and the pedagogical core of professionalism traditionally associated with kindergarten teachers (Karila, 2012).

Härkönen's pedagogical systems theory (2009, 2013) provides an awareness of historical pedagogical perspective and the complexity of ontological, epistemological and social principles. It supports what Pulkkinen (2012b) says in relation to developing action models to involve the public, politicians and media, both nationally and internationally. Härkönen (2006, 2011; Virkki, 2015) identifies key categories and content pertinent to historical views on early childhood education and extrapolates categories from different theorists or pedagogical thinking, for example from Montessori, Freinet, Sukhomlinsky, Neill, Malaguzzi and Freire. Systems theory demonstrates the complexity and holistic nature of early childhood education and pedagogy and is useful for understanding the various multilayers and complexity of the historical, philosophical, socio-cultural and political construction and de-construction in relation to early childhood education in Finland.

The following case study provided by Liisa Lohilahti as the manager of a Day-Centre in Eastern Finland demonstrates the various professional composition and the importance of core values in sharing good practice with interested international visitors who are keen to understand not only what is involved but how and why it is effective.

We have noticed an increasing interest by international visitors, particularly from Asian countries, mainly China and Japan. During the visits, visitors explain how Finnish early childhood education is being implemented because of its quality on a practical level. Of course, such an international interest in early childhood education is part of a meaningful sharing of high-quality education practices and pedagogical ideas. On the other hand, you can contemplate on, and even raise questions about, the impact of realising the same practice in different cultures. We know, for example, that the ratio of adults per children is a major factor in the realisation of high-quality early childhood education, as well as the size of the groups of children. In Finnish early childhood education the ratio of children under 3 years is 4 children per 1 educator (max group size 12), and 8 children per 1 educator (max group size 24), in a group of over 3 year-olds. In accordance with the new Finnish Early Childhood Education Act, the child groups cannot be larger than supported by an educator rate of 3 adults. Also the professional composition of the staff team must be at least two thirds of the educators having a Degree in Early Childhood Education, Primary Education or in Socionomy. In Asian countries the size of the groups is higher and the number of early childhood educators is less in relation to the number of children. Also the content of the education differs from the content in Finnish early childhood education.

The educational background of educators also differs between countries, which is of great importance to the quality of early childhood education. One of the most striking features of Finnish Early Childhood Education is multi-professional and highly trained staff. This is considered to be both a guarantee of quality, and at the same time a problem (Karila, 2016)*. The advantage is that educators, that have a higher education level, can influence the staff with a lower educational level in the work community. In practice, however, the problem in Finland seems to be the fact that educational staff are not always structured in such a way that the work community, with its own and specific competence in the work culture with different responsibilities and obligations in various professional groups, can manage to make this transfer of knowledge. Educators that are unaware or unsure of the core values in the own profession, have problems in benefiting from a variety of competencies and perspectives in relation to other professionals (also reinforced by* OECD, 2012).

The following case study demonstrates how in Finland, studying early childhood education, and pre-primary education takes inspiration from Reggio Emilia's pedagogical philosophy. Liisa Lohilaht explains how and why this inspiration is embedded as part of preschool educational culture and how in Finland Reggio Emilia *pedagogicla* philosophy is well known in early childhood education (from birth to 6 years) and pre-primary education (aged 6–7 years). It also demonstrates how in basic elementary education (age seven–16), the philosophy of Reggio Emilia is relatively unknown.

The application to our basic curriculum (Finnish Agency for *Education, 2017) is therefore challenging. Due to this, work has (for my own part as a Head of both a private day care centre and elementary school), required much developmental work for the elementary education unit teachers / educators. First, my focus elaborates on the problem of the basic elementary education curriculum from a Reggio perspective. This is because the earlier Finnish curriculum in basic education (grades one–six) (children aged seven–16 years) is clearly different from a Reggio perspective in the methodology of teaching, concerning the role of the child and the teacher, as well as of the subject-based work. In early childhood education (birth to six years) in Finland and for a long time, pre-primary education (aged six–seven) focused on integrating thematic learning units through implementing early education pedagogy as much as possible through knowledge of early childhood education. For example teaching mathematics, mother tongue and music involved an integrated thematic approach of subjects so learning was meaningful for the children. Such an approach has been unproblematic, since Finnish basic pre-primary teachers have access to by very high-quality teaching materials to support planning learning content for pupils. In Finland, it is now customary with older children (ages seven–16) to focus on subject-based education. This influence is becoming more obvious today, and is having a negative impact on pre-primary education (children aged between six and seven years) where the class teacher draws on their subject specialisation as part of their teacher training.*

Thematically oriented subject studies are typically implemented in the form of project work in both early childhood education (birth to six years) as well as in pre-primary, (age six–seven). Project work requires a teacher's active engagement (from the side) throughout the project. Teachers start project work by observing children, gathering information on children's interests, depending on the individual development, areas of expertise, but also challenges of each child or pupil. The dynamics of the children's or pupil's group is a leading force during the project work. With the observations as a base, the educators and teachers can proceed with the project planning and the practical implementation together with the children/pupils. The central task of the educators/teachers is to observe the child's processing and the progress during the project work. The process of the children/pupils is also evaluated, in the preschool through documentation and in the school environment in relation to grading. Through evaluation and observation, the educator/teacher makes a follow-up plan to advance in the project through a pre-visioning model, through a pre-project (Häikiö, 2007; Vecchi, 2014) that works spirally as a continuous circular process (Lenz Taguchi, 2012), until the project has come to a decision point. A separate project may take days, weeks, months or even years, and simultaneously there may be several projects in parallel. In my own unit we do not ordinarily support two or more projects at the same time, but in practice every year we carry out a year-long sustainability project alongside with thematic projects, as we are a green-flag preschool/school unit.

In theme-based project work children learn in specifically set learning situations and environments, where the learning processes are contextually conducted through active learning and in relation to the world view of the children. The creating of a context starts with the children's daily life and their interests, and also generates understanding and application of knowledge in practice. In learning, a variety of senses is used to support learning, the learning processes and to create more opportunities for learning to take place. As we know, the process of memorizing and recalling information from memory is supported when a variety of sensory stimuli is combined in the learning situation. Various sensory stimuli give different learners a wider opportunity to master and make sense of their knowledge acquisition.

In our education plan for the preschool/school, inspired by Reggio Emilia, we implement a flexible class structure independent of division in a traditional school year. This means that children have an individualised learning curve and the goals of teaching are achieved individually. The first linkage in our primary school is in the second class in the Spring, when the pupil should have attained at least the minimum level of knowledge of one–two graders based on the national educational goals. This is an indication that he or she can be transferred to the third grade. A flexible structure in basic education supports the individual learning path of each child. This makes the teacher responsible of the knowledge processes taking place in the classroom, and therefore in the setting I manage, we have maintained a class size of 16 to 17 pupils / children, especially in the lower grades. The class sizes should be preferably less than 20, so the teacher can interact with all the pupils.

Recent changes in Finland

In Finland today, in basic education (ages 7–16) classes can easily encompass more than 25 pupils. In some schools in Finland, for this age group, a trend is prevalent in team teaching where two classes are integrated into the same class with two teachers, which can accommodate up to 50 pupils. This is particularly worrisome, especially from the point of view of individual learning and work expectations. Particularly in lower grades (and elementary education), large group sizes correlate with poor quality and concerning aspects of individuality and child participation. This is a very problematic situation in Finland today, as class sizes of basic education in some districts and cities affects equality. This is in spite of the law stating equal opportunities as a principle for children should be upheld. In the area of early childhood, the situation is better because the maximum group sizes are defined in early childhood education law.

As noted earlier in this chapter, more recently there is an emphasis on preparing children for starting school at 7 years of age and so pre-primary is more frequently being used to work towards defined outcomes. Many ECE teachers and educators are resisting this pressure as depicted in the following conversation with a kindergarten educator in Southern Finland.

A narrative between a group of professionals including the Headteacher of Touhula Day Care Centre, Savonlinna, Finland. Some of the underpinning principles and processes of ECE in relation to pre-primary and primary education, national policies and the work conditions of a municipal day care centre are discussed.

Children aged ten months to six years as well as a pre-school group aged six, are provided for. The focus of is on getting ready for school. Age groups are ten months to three years, three years to five years and age five to six.

The ratio for ten-month-olds and one-year-olds is one adult for four children (1:4). In a group there are 12 children. Adults include one kindergarten teacher and two nurses. All the adults work with all 12 children. In the groups for over three-year-olds the ratio is 1:8 with three adults (one kindergarten teacher and two nurses), and the amount of children is 24. These amounts are as it is said in a statue of ECE. Provision is from 6:30am till 17:00pm to support parents at work. Preschool is about combining creative ways and professionalism so the teacher guides and is aware of subjects, music, gymnastics, arts and so on. Children develop also through basic activities like eating, resting, sleeping, dressing, washing and so on. In Finland, it's a mixed pedagogy of everything, scientifically, it is natural to put the child first, so it is child centred education. Finland is social democracy, egalitarian and equality. This is important, and valuing everyone so life is lived as a democracy. . . It is not usual though to discuss religion and politics. . .despite the curriculum having a focus on democracy. Politics and National administration have limited the time children can attend kindergarten if one or the other of parents is at home.

The focus of preschool is on gymnastics, moving and cognition, which are connected to brain development. In particular the outdoors – moving and going outside each day is important. Very often pedagogues and children walk together to a forest nearby. Children can move inside and outside but it is planned to promote thinking and collaboration to help children make connections. Inside, the focus is on gymnastic activities and active learning. Bits from different approaches are taken for informing pedagogy, but the most important underpinning principle for five–six-year-olds, is play. . . . everything is through play. In Pre-Primary / School, it's more of the same, but there are goals to prepare children for school. . . . However teachers also prepare for children's social, emotional and identity which is really important in developing confidence and cognitive skills for reading, writing and mathematics. Play is embedded throughout. Teaching is play based so the adult facilitates and guides children. In the Finnish national curriculum it does not specify that every child must learn to read before going to school. As a result reading is not taught or pushed. However many of them learn but some children don't. In pre-

school readiness for learning to read is enabled but this really depends on children's interests and ability.

In spring time pre-school children visit the school. They are open to creative learning and social learning but there's a focus on outcomes. The kindergarten approach of play-based doing and experiential learning is respected. Finnish education is influenced by history and different theorists on developmental psychology and social construction. Kindergartens and pre-schools are freer in their interpretation of pedagogy than school teachers because of their constraints as part of the Finnish National Curriculum. Each year pedagogues have to take children forward. In school there is more direct teaching. 'If testing came to Finland though, I think practice would change!'

Child-centred pedagogy in Finland

In child-centred pedagogy in Finland, the size and formation of groups in which children learn is significant. The teacher should have plenty of time to discuss and talk openly with the children in the group. If the size of the group is too large, there will always be children that are less likely to take part in a conversation, which in turn makes the educational situation less meaningful. Child-centred dialogue is an important part of building up of a meaningful educational context (Rinaldi, 2005). The psychological learning environment that maintains a conversational culture supports children's agency and encourages acceptance of each child's voice. It is important to support each individual voice in the group, since it is through this that the child's own knowledge and ideas are brought into the group to enrich the group community (Kumpulainen et al., 2013). Such an approach supports a child's view when no comments or answers are wrong. Rather, all ideas are valued as part of the learning community. The understanding of variety is expanded and a multifaceted learning environment where children learn to accept and affirm each other positively is created, even when there is a difference of opinion. In this way, children learn to accept diversity.

The educator leads and orchestrates the planning, observing, documenting, evaluating and participates in the learning processes with children together. The teacher builds learning situations where children have the opportunity to participate and feel joy in learning (Sukhomlinsky, 2016). The educator's role is to enrich, make learning situations multi-layered and interesting, taking into account the interest of children to increase learning motivation.

The following case study (provided by Liisa Lohilahti) is an example of how a joyful experience is nurtured. She explains how the educators' role is defined with inspiration from Reggio Emilia's pedagogical philosophy.

In the building of a learning community, a warm and genuine interaction is the starting point, where the educator has a key role. Warm interaction creates a safe psychological and mental learning environment, where children can easily communicate and bring forth their voices as equal members of the group. For this reason, we emphasise teamwork where the educators support the formation of a learning environment that supports both individual and group learning. We make sure we provide a great deal of time for open discussions with the children and between us as educators. Together we explore and discuss the objectives of the curriculum at the beginning of the academic year mainly from social and ethical grounds. Our experience has shown that the goals of the subject content is achieved much faster by first building-up a good psychological learning environment. This nurtures children's well-being, and provides a grounding in positive, secure and trusting relationships, which has a positive effect on positive behaviour so less time is dedicated to dealing with problem associated with behaviour. Increasingly we notice a positive impact on children's motivation.

The following 'lunch time' case study is taken from a visit to Asemantie Day Care Centre, a public funded day care centre in Savonlinna, Finland. It demonstrates how lunch time as a community can be used to create a provide a positive learning environment for young children so they take responsibility, develop independence and where educators and children show respect for one another. Susanna Nopanen, the Headteacher of the day care centre, reflects upon the key underpinning principles of her day care centre.

LUNCHTIME AS A COMMUNITY

It is 12.00 and children aged between three and give line up, alongside educators. Each collects a tray and utensils. They decide what they would like to eat from a selection of salads, hot dishes and a variety of seeds (including pumpkin and sunflower). Having selected food using utensils independently and collected a glass of water, they carry their own trays over to where they would like to sit. Educators and children sit together at the same level and engage in conversations that are very natural and respectful. Children are not rushed and can take as long as they need to enjoy their lunch. A glass of water is dropped, but it is not seen as a problem. Children are encouraged to make decisions and take responsibility for themselves so they learn from their experiences, including making mistakes and taking risks. It's is a very respectful environment in the decisions available for children and the positive relationships between children themselves, and educators and children.

Susanna explains that participation and starting with children is what is important as a community. As part of this she identifies the following key principles or features as important for underpinning the practice at the day care centre:Respect
Awareness of underpinning pedagogy
Engagement
Shared planning
Adults playing
Children taking responsibility

Outdoor play (not in a forest) (not easily possible)
Not being rushed
A sense of community
Adults committed to children
Peaceful
Holistic
Kind, positivity, affirmation, constructiveness
Open 24hrs, for the parents in shift work. Children can access 12 hours at any one session

Ways forward for sustaining participation in Finnish ECE

With the introduction of the Finnish Early Childhood Education Act (2018) and the Early Childhood Education Plan (VASU, 2016) a model of child-centred pedagogy is evident in Finland in early childhood education. There is an increasing focus on child participation and giving children voice in education. The child has been brought to the centre of his / her own learning as an active agent and participant, whose interests are utilised as part of the planning and implementation of pedagogical activities.

However, with the influence of neo-liberalism and associated pressures for children to begin formal schooling at 6 rather than 7 years of age, and pre-school at the age of 5 instead of 6, many educators in Finland are concerned about the implications. Puroila and Kinnunen (2017) show how standardisation and test-based accountability (p.328), has contributed to a deterioration in quality of ECE in Finland. Given that it is not usual in Finland to discuss political issues within the field of ECE, and question different theorists openly (Härkönen, 2009), there is a risk that effective ECE could be eroded, in a similar way to the trend in England. Consequently there is a need for educators to engage in reciprocal dialogue and challenge their thinking from a reflexive perspective so that they can 'stand up' for appropriate values in early childhood education (Pulkkinen, 2012) and maintain the world renowned view of quality ECE in Finland.

POINTS FOR REFLECTION

- How would you interpret or recognise 'the joy of learning' in your setting?
- What key principles would be important as the foundations for this?
- What would be your reaction to providing 24-hour day care?
- What would you say is the answer in maintaining the high quality of ECE in Finland?

References

Bladsjö, A., Holmbom, A., Johansson, B., Lagrell, K. and Nelander, L. (1984) *Ansvarspedagogik [Pedagogy of responsibility]*, Stockholm: Liber Förlag.

Butler, P. (2016) 'No grammar schools, lots of play: The secrets of Europe's top education system', *The Guardian*, 20 September 2016. Retrieved 2 January 2019 from: www.theguardian.com/education/2016/sep/20/grammar-schools-play-europe-top-education-system-finland-daycare.

Campbell-Barr, V. and Nygård, M. (2014) 'Losing sight of the child? Human capital theory and its role for early childhood education and care policies in Finland and England since the mid-1990s', *Contemporary Issues in Early Childhood*, 15(4), p.346–359.

Cockerill, A. (2016) 'Vasily Sukhomlinsky: The teacher who changed the world', Retrieved 19 January 2019 from: www.abc.net.au/radionational/programs/conversations/vasily-sukhomlinsky-educating-the-heart/7878410.

Department for Education (DfE) (2017) *Statutory framework for the early years foundation stage*, London: Department for Education.

Eurofound (2015) *Families in the economic crisis: Changes in policy measures in the EU*, Luxembourg: Publications Office of the European Union. Retrieved 30 January 2019 from: www.eurofound.europa.eu/sites/default/files/ef_publication/field_ef_document/ef1556en_1.pdf.

Finnish Early Childhood Education and Care Act (2018) Retrieved 30 January 2019 from: https://eacea.ec.europa.eu/national-policies/eurydice/content/national-reforms-early-childhood-education-and-care-21_en.

Finnish Agency for Education (2017) *National core curriculum for early childhood education and care*. Retrieved 30 January 2019 from: www.oph.fi/english/curricula_and_qualifications/early_childhood_education_and_care.

Forssén, K., Jaakola, A.M. and Ritakallio, V.M. (2008) 'Family policies in Finland', in: Ostner, I. and Schmitt, C. (Eds.) *Family policies in the context of family change*, VS Verlag für Sozialwissenschaften.

Giardiello, P. (2014) *Pioneers in early childhood education: The roots and legacies of Rachel and Margaret McMillan, Maria Montessori and Susan Isaacs*, Abingdon: Routledge.

Georgiou, I. (2007). *Thinking through systems thinking*, Abingdon: Routledge.

Haavio-Mannila, E. (1971) 'Convergences between East and West: Tradition and modernity in sex roles in Sweden, Finland and the Soviet Union', *Acta Sociologica*, 14(1), p.114–125.

Häikiö, T. (2007) *Barns estetiska lärprocesser; Atelierista i förskola och skola [Children's aesthetical learning processes; Atelierista in pre-school and school]*. Dissertation. Gothenburg Studies in Art and Architecture, nr 24. Acta Universitatis Gothoburgensis. Göteborgs Universitet.

Härkönen, U. (2013) 'Pedagogical systems theory as a cornerstone of sustainable early childhood and preschool education', in: Proceedings of the 10th international JTEFS/BBCC conference. *Publications of the University of Eastern Finland Reports and Studies in Education, Humanities, and Theology*, 7, p.411–449. Finland: University of Eastern Finland. Retrieved 10 April 2018 from: http://urn.fi/URN:ISBN:978-952-61-1112-4.

Härkönen, U. (2011) 'The process of creating the pedagogical systems theory for early childhood and preschool education', in: M. Veisson, E. Hujala, P.K. Smith, M. Waniganayake and E. Kikas (Eds.) *Global perspectives in early childhood education: Diversity, challenges and possibilities*, Frankfurt am Main: Peter Lang, p.47–66. (Retrieved from: Library of University of Eastern Finland).

Härkönen, U. (2009) 'Pedagogical systems theory and model for sustainable human development in early childhood education and care (ECEC)', *Journal of Teacher Education for Sustainability*, 11(2), p.77–86. DOI: doi:10.2478/v10099–10009–0042–0041. Retrieved

23 September 2018 from: https://content.sciendo.com/view/journals/jtes/11/2/article-p77.xml.

Härkönen, U. (2006) 'Diversity of early childhood theories a democratic society', *Journal of Teacher Education and Training*, (6), p.103–115. Daugavpils: Daugavpils University, Institute of Sustainable Education. Retrieved 14 March 2019 from: www.oppi.uef.fi/wanda/users/uharkone/tuotoksia/Diversity_JTET_pdf.pdf.

Hiilamo, H. (2002) *The rise and fall of Nordic family policy?* Research Report 125. Helsinki: Stakes.

Hujala, E., K. Karila, V. Nivala and A.-M. Puroila (1998) 'Towards understanding leadership in Finnish context of early childhood education', in: E. Hujala and A.-M. Puroila (Eds.) *Towards understanding leadership in context of early childhood: Cross-cultural perspectives*, Acta Universitatis Ouluensis. E35. Oulu: Oulu University Press, p.147–170.

KarilaK. (2012) 'A Nordic perspective on early childhood education and care policy', *European Journal of Education*, 47(4), p.584–595.

Kettukangas, T. (2017) 'Perustoiminnot-käsite varhaiskasvatuksessa [The concept of basic activities in early childhood education]', in: *Publications of the University of Eastern Finland. Dissertations in education, humanities, and theology*, 110. Retrieved 25 August 2018 from: http://urn.fi/URN:ISBN:978-952-61-2574-9.

Kouvo-Suutari, A. (2016) 'Work education in family day care', Poster at the EECERA Conference, Dublin, Ireland.

Kumpulainen, K., Lipponen, L., Hilppö, J. and Mikkola, A. (2013) 'Building on the positive in children's lives: A co-participatory study on the social construction of children's sense of agency', *Early Child Development and Care*, 184(2), p.211–229.

Lee, D.H.L., Hong, H. and Niemi, H. (2014) 'A contextualized account of holistic education in Finland and Singapore: Implications on Singapore educational context', *The Asia-Pacific Education Researcher*, 23(4), p.871–884.

Lenz Taguchi, H. (2012) *Pedagogisk dokumentation som aktiv agent: Introduktion av intra-aktiv pedagogic*, Malmö: Gleerups. (Translated into Norwegian.)

Lundkvist, M., Nyby, J., Autto, J. and Nygård, M. (2017) 'From universalism to selectivity? The background, discourses and ideas of recent early childhood education and care reforms in Finland', *Early Child Development and Care*, 187(10), p.1543–1556. DOI: doi:10.1080/03004430.2017.1295041.

Määttä, K. and Uusiautti, S. (2012) 'How do the Finnish family policy and early education system support the well-being, happiness, and success of families and children?' *Early Child Development and Care*, 182(3–4), p.291–298. DOI: doi:10.1080/03004430.2011.646718.

Ministry of Social Affairs and Health (MSAH) (2006) *Finland's family policy*, Helsinki: Ministry of Social Affairs and Health. Retrieved 30 January 2019 from: www.stm.fi/en/publications/publication/_julkaisu/1058023#en.

Ojala, M. (2005) 'How Finland is researching early childhood education', in: O. Saracho and B. Spodek (Eds.) *International perspectives on research in early childhood education*, Portland, OR: Information Age Publishing, p.79–117.

Organisation for Economic Co-Operation and Development (OECD) (2016) *Starting Strong IV, early childhood education and care, data country note, Finland*. Retrieved 4 January 2019 from: www.oecd.org/education/school/ECECDCN-Finland.pdf.

Organisation for Economic Co-Operation and Development (OECD) (2012) *Education at a glance 2012: Highlights*, OECD Publishing. Available from: http://dx.doi.org/10.1787/eag_highlights-2012-en.

Pulkkinen, L. (2012a) 'Ten pillars of a good childhood: A Finnish perspective', *Childhood Education*, 88(5), p.326–330. DOI: doi:10.1080/00094056.2012.718680. Retrieved 11 May 2018 from: http://dx.doi.org/10.1080/00094056.2012.718680.

Pulkkinen, L. (2012b) *Goals for the decade of childhood 2012–2022, based on ten pillars of a good childhood: A Finnish perspective*. Retrieved 2 January 2019 from: www.allianceforchildhood.eu/files/Book2013/QOC13-Chapter5-Pulkinnen.pdf.

Puroila, A.-M. and Kinnunen, S. (2017) *Report on the impacts of amendments to early childhood education and care legislation, Publications of the Government's analysis, assessment and research activities* 78/2017. Prime Minister's Office, 18 December 2017. Retrieved 10 October 2018 from: https://tietokayttoon.fi/en/frontpage and http://urn.fi/URN:ISBN:978-952-287-487-0.

Rantala, A. (2016) *Snälla du! Kan du sätta dig? Om vägledning i förskolan*. Dissertation. Umeå Universitet, Umeå.

Rusanen, S. (2007) *Taidekasvattajaksi varhaiskasvatukseen: Kuvataiteen opintojen kehittaäminen lastentarhanopettajien koulutuksessa*. Dissertation. Helsinki: Taideteollisen korkeakoulun julkaisusarja.

Rusanen, S., Kuusela, M., Rintakorpi, K. and Torkki, K. (2014) *Musta tuntuu punaiselta: Kuvataiteellinen toiminta varhaisiässä*. Helsinki: Lasten keskus, Kirjapaja OY.

Sahlberg, P. (2012) 'A model lesson: Finland shows us what equal opportunity looks like', *American Educator Online*. Retrieved 3 January 2019 from: https://files.eric.ed.gov/fulltext/EJ971754.pdf.

Salminen, J. (2017) 'Early childhood education and care system in Finland'. Prace z warsztatu. Nauki o wychowaniu. *Studia interdyscyplinarne*, 2(5). DOI: doi:10.18778/2450-4491.05.09.

Schyl-Bjurman, G. and Strömberg-Lind, K. (1976) *Dialogpedagogik*, Sverige. Lund: Br. Ekstrand, LiberLäromedel.

STM (2002) *Valtioneuvoston periaatepäätös varhaiskasvatuksen valtakunnallisista linjauksista* [*Decision in principle of the Council of State concerning the national policy definition on early childhood education and care*], Julkaisuja: Sosiaali- ja terveysministeriö [Ministry of Social Affairs and Health], p.9.

Sukhomlinsky, V. (2016) *My heart I give to children*, ERJ Language Service Pty, Limited.

Suomen säädöskokoelma (2016) *Laki varhaiskasvatuslain muuttamisesta, 108/2016* [*Statute concerning the change of the law on early childhood education and care, 108/2016*], Annettu Helsingissä 29 päivänä tammikuuta 2016. Helsinki: Suomen säädöskokoelma.

Takahashi, M. (2008) 'Challenges in Nordic childcare policies: With special reference to Finland', *The Journal of Comparative Economic Studies*, 4(1), p.41–55.

Utbildningsstyrelsen [Board of Education] (2016) *Grunderna för planen för småbarnspedagogik 2016*, Helsingfors: Utbildningsstyrelsen.

Vecchi, V. (2014) *Blå cikoriablommor; Ateljén i Reggio Emilias pedagogiska verksamhet* [*Blue cicoriaflowers; The atelier in the pedagogical philosophy in Reggio Emilia*], Lund: Studentlitteratur.

Virkki, P. (2015) Varhaiskasvatus toimijuuden ja osallisuuden edistäjänä, *Publications of the University of Eastern Finland. Dissertations in education, humanities, and theology* 66. Helsinki. Retrieved 7 August 2018 from: http://urn.fi/URN:ISBN:978-952-61-1735-5.

7

TE WHĀRIKI

Patricia Giardiello, Geraldine Leydon and Annette Hargreaves

An examination of contextual socio-cultural, historical, and political influences

> Ehara taku toa i te toa takitahi engari he toa takitini.
>
> "I come not with my own strengths but bring with me the gifts, talents and strengths of my family, tribe, and ancestors".
>
> *Te Whāriki (2017, p.12)*

First published in 1996, the Te Whāriki early childhood curriculum in Aotearoa (New Zealand) has come of age and after 21 years in existence it was revised and refreshed in 2017. Reflecting the Māori tradition of viewing children, no matter what their age or ability, as inherently competent, the opening statement of the revised *Te Whāriki* continues to reassure that:

> children are competent and confident learners and communicator healthy in mind, body and spirit, secure in their sense of belonging and in the knowledge, that they make a valued contribution to society.
>
> *(Te Whāriki, 2017, p.6).*

Aotearoa (New Zealand) is a small country in the South Pacific with 4.7 million people, 15 per cent of whom are Māori, the Indigenous peoples of this land. After 200 years of British colonisation, te reo Maori, the Māori language, has become endangered therefore one of the goals of the Te Whāriki early childhood curriculum (New Zealand Ministry of Education, 1996, 2007, 2017) is that all children should "experience the stories and symbols of their own and other cultures" (New Zealand Ministry of Education, 1996, p.16). For this reason, early childhood care and education in Aotearoa (New Zealand) has a strong narrative approach to both pedagogy and assessment.

To understand the Te Whāriki approach, it is essential to look back at its origin and discover the roots and underpinning influences in motivating the formulation of this unique curriculum, unique due to its bicultural framework. Many current curriculum frameworks around the world are inspired by a vison of another approach or approaches. But Te Whāriki, which translates as a woven Māori mat for all to stand on (see the following), takes its inspiration from the cultural and spiritual identity of the inhabitants and is the first bicultural early childhood curriculum in New Zealand that includes the dual perspectives of both Māori, and Pākehā (non-Māori) who are mainly European immigrants, but include a large Pacific Islands population and an increasing Asian population. In traditional Māori *raranga* (weaving) processes "the master weavers attest that each of the strands must be skilfully interwoven to serve its purpose in maintaining the integrity of the Whāriki and its shape" (Erueti and Rangikoepa Palmer, 2014, p.1066). As a metaphor, Te Whāriki enables the diverse early childhood services and centres, their teachers, families and children, to "weave" their own curriculum pattern shaped by different cultural perspectives, the developmental phase of the children, and the philosophy or structure of the programme.

The landscape of early childhood education in New Zealand stems from the Kindergarten movement which arrived in the new colony, via Europe, and the United States in the 1870s. Typical early kindergarten programmes in New Zealand echoed those of Froebelian kindergartens (May, 1997), which included art and craft in the curriculum. Creative art activities were part of the "gifts" and "occupations" that characterised a Froebelian kindergarten (see Chapter 8, Danish Outdoor Nature Pedagogy). The Kindergarten movement continued to expand during the first half of the twentieth century but remained closely aligned to traditional Froebelian ideas (Terreni, 2010). The Progressive Education Movement, founded on the educational ideas of John Dewey (1859–1952) around the importance of free play, began to have an impact in New Zealand educational settings. Progressive educators believed that children learn best "by doing", not by being passive listeners, and that the teacher's role was to be a facilitator of learning in classrooms where children's interest helped to provide appropriate developmental learning experience. Dewey "built upon and critiqued the scripted play pedagogy devised by Froebel and constructed his own notion of play that he argued fostered experiential learning, voluntary participation, and social order" (Beatty, 2017, p.424). Dewey's ideas called attention to the necessity of children's play being grounded in "the child's experiences of the real world" (May, 1997, p.113) and learning by doing ideas such as these began to be embraced by the newly emerging Playcentre movement. The movement was spurred on by Susan Isaacs, who gave a series of keynote lectures at the New Education Fellowship conferences held around New Zealand and Australia in 1937. The ensuing development of the playcentre movement, informed by Isaacs' ideals around the value of open-ended free play combined with the importance of observing children's skills and understanding, supported the move towards a less formal structure with greater opportunities for children to explore their own ideas and interests, (Giardiello, 2014; Sewell and Bethall, 2009). The playcentres also reflected Isaacs' focus on developing the whole child and by involving parents and the community in the process of learning (Alvestad and Duncan, 2006). The playcentre movement also connected with Māori organisations such as the Māori Women's Welfare League (Bushouse, 2008). Although free play was central to the playcentres during the 1960s and 1970s "the boundaries of what had been defined as free play were beginning to be pushed...free play was now being conceived in more political terms as having to do with the rights and autonomy of children" (May, 1997. P.118).

By the 1970s early childhood and care (ECEC) had become a focus of campaigns associated with women's rights, children's rights and Māori rights. A network of advocacy organisations for ECEC emerged, which gradually built its capacity for effecting change (Tearney, 2016). As a response to New Zealand women's increasing emancipation and their demand for increased child-care, a growing desire for Māori self-determination and language preservation, as well as other ethnic minorities seeking first language and cultural maintenance, a range of early childhood services sprang into existence (Terreni, 2010).

Following a series of early childhood conventions in the 1980s and 1990s, the report of the Early Childhood Education Project, Future Directions: Early Childhood Education in New Zealand, was published in 1996 (NZEI Te Riu Roa, 2016), which led to the first ECEC curriculum Te Whāriki (Ministry of Education, 1996). Aotearoa New Zealand research and narratives on early childhood curriculum can be mapped back to the introduction of Te Whāriki in draft form in 1993 with the first final version appearing in 1996 (Carr and May, 1993; Cullen, 1996).

Previously, discussions about early childhood education used the dominant discourse of "aims and objectives" with the terminology "curriculum first appearing in the title of an early childhood official document in 1988" (Dalli, cited in Georgeson and Payler, 2013, p.153). In the post-modern era, not only in New Zealand, but across the developed world it began to look rather outmoded to focus only on content and objectives. A curriculum came to be seen as a powerful instrument to make the educational system more effective in the development of the human potential. Though according to Laevers (2005) it also can engender processes that bring us farther away from this main goal because they go against the principles of good practice. In a symposium organised by the OECD in Stockholm in 2003 (OECD, 2004) four approaches were discussed as examples of good practice in the field of early childhood education; the selected approaches were: Te Whāriki, Reggio Emilia, the High Scope Model from Michigan in the United States (highscope.org) and the philosophy of Experiential Education from Flanders. All have a holistic approach in common, which is: respect for the child, an open framework approach, a rich enabling environment, emphasis on communication, interaction and dialogue and an appropriate mapping of children's competencies.

What makes Te Whāriki a unique curriculum is the way in which it embraces the aspirations, pedagogy, values and beliefs of its bicultural heritage enshrined in the Treaty of Waitanga between the indigenous chiefs and the British crown (May and Carr, cited in David, Goouch and Powell, 2016). The treaty was the result of a political process of restoring lands and resources (still in process today) to *tangata whenua* (literally, people of the land, i.e., Māori). Within the Te Whāriki framework, Māori values and belief systems based on the cultural and political beliefs of the minority Indigenous people sit alongside a Western humanist tradition. The positioning of the Māori oral tradition, with its spiritual commitments, histories and theories, alongside a Pākehā written tradition resulted in an unusual document, with two of its authors, Tamiti and Tilly Reedy, implying that it is explicitly about self-determination "Toku Rangatiratanga na te manamatauranga – knowledge and power set me free" (Reedy, cited in Nuttall, 2013, p.43). At its inception Te Whāriki emphasised developing reciprocal partnerships between families, early years professionals and the wider community. It is grounded in socio-cultural theory (Rogoff, 1990; Vygotsky, 1978) that places the learning experiences of children in a broader social and cultural context. This self-confessed ground-breaking approach was to later inform the structure of the English Birth to Three Matters (2002) and the Curriculum Guidance for the Foundation Stage (2000), precursors to the current English Early Years Foundation Stage (EYFS) (DfE, 2017).

After Te Whāriki's publication in 1996, the initial response from many early childhood teachers was supportive, and as a pedagogical tool Te Whāriki was widely accepted without much criticism or even critical engagement. The underlying ontology of Te Whāriki, as an open curriculum, enabled educators to use the guidelines of the Te Whāriki framework to weave their own early years centre's Whāriki or curriculum. However, whilst Nuttall (2002) argued that this approach was a strength, as it allowed maximum regard for centre contexts in teacher decision-making it may also be its greatest weakness as the structure and language of Te Whāriki can be easily appropriated to legitimate practice that is ideologically at odds with the theoretical bases of the document. A counter argument is that because of its sociocultural stance, Te Whāriki is not and can never be a "one size fits all" curriculum, and this is shown both implicitly and explicitly throughout the document (Zhang, 2015). For example, Te Whāriki states that "[T]he list of (learning) outcomes in this document is indicative rather than definitive. Each early childhood education setting will develop its own emphases and priorities" (Ministry of Education, 1996, p. 44).

Coming from a different angle, another criticism is that the bicultural nature of Te Whāriki frames biculturalism within a monocultural perspective (Duhn, 2006), reinforcing the discourse of cultural diversity which assumes that cultures have universal and identifiable characteristics. An assumption, according to Farquar (2015), that limits our understanding of difference to the extent that it can only be interpreted according to Westernised cultural values, i.e. in terms of progress, rationality and what is normal. Duhn (2006) in her analysis of the bicultural child in Te Whāriki, suggests that the child, as portrayed in this curriculum is neither Māori nor Pākehā, instead the portrayal masks a multitude of differences, rather than reflecting and embracing them. The Education Review Office (ERO, 2011,

2016) emphasises in their reviews of early childhood services the importance of recognising what quality provision means from different cultural perspectives. One of the fastest growing cultures in New Zealand's education system comprise Pacific migrants, and concerns have been raised in the reviews of how quality is measured from a predominantly Westernised perspective.

An ERO (2016) review that synthesised 17 national reports identified the following features of effective practice in relation to Te Whāriki:

- Anchors for practice – Te Whāriki and priorities for children's learning
- Designing and implementing a responsive curriculum that responds to children with diverse backgrounds and needs
- Positive foundations for children's learning: social and emotional competency; literacy and mathematics; and transition to school
- Pedagogical leadership
- Effective teaching practice
- Assessment for learning
- Internal evaluation for improvement
- Learning partnerships for a responsive curriculum *(cited in McLachlan, 2018, p.46)*

It was with this backdrop that the revision of Te Whāriki (2017) was undertaken. The chapter now moves on to discuss the distinctive philosophical underpinning principles of the Te Whāriki curriculum including the revisions of 2017.

The distinctive philosophical underpinning principles

> A curriculum must speak to our past, present and future. As global citizens in a rapidly changing and increasingly connected world, children need to be adaptive, creative and resilient.
>
> *(Ministry of Education, 2017, p.7)*

Te Whāriki (2017) or "woven mat" is used as a metaphor for the ECE curriculum, in which four curriculum principles are interwoven with the five curriculum strands. Together these principles and strands set out to give expression to the vision for children that are at the heart of Te Whāriki. The four principles are

- Empowerment / *Whakamana* – the early childhood curriculum empowers the child to learn and grow.
- Holistic Development / *Kotahitanga* – the early childhood curriculum reflects the holistic way children learn and grow.
- Family and Community / *Whānau tangata* – the wider world of family and community is an integral part of the early childhood curriculum.
- Relationships / *Ngā hononga* – children learn through responsive and reciprocal relationships with people, places, and things (see Figure 7.1).

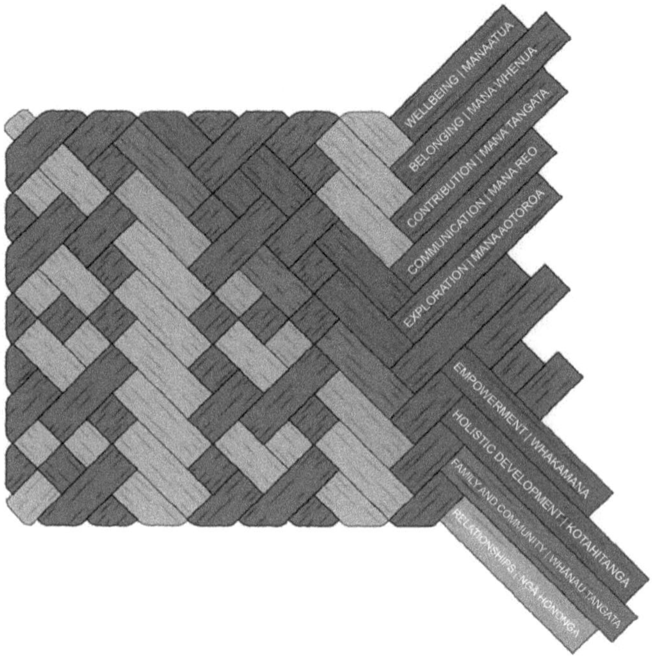

FIGURE 7.1 The four principles of Te Whāriki.

This section discusses the context to the revision of Te Whāriki in 2017. It includes personal experiences of a six-week research journey throughout Aotearoa New Zealand in 2016 which included, though not exclusively, discussions with parents and practitioners from initial teacher education universities and early years practitioners in kindergartens and private settings. The open framework of Te Whāriki discussed later was not only obvious in practice but appeared overwhelming accepted by leaders and practitioners. We observed during our extensive visit it was very unusual for a practitioner to voice any discomfort for any area of Te Whāriki (1996).

For other stakeholders however, there were concerns regarding a perceived insufficient empirical evidence base to support Te Whāriki's world-renowned status with such claims reportedly being based on opinion rather than fact (Blaiklock, 2017). For some, the holistic and generalised nature of Te Whāriki (1996) risked overlooking specific curriculum areas of learning with little evidence to show that ECE programs were enhancing children's learning and wellbeing beyond the development that would naturally occur were they not enrolled in ECE (Blaiklock, 2017). Two parents of children in early years settings, one Pākehā and one Māori, both voiced their ideal of making specific links to learning with specific curriculum areas. Once again, however it was observed that this was at odds with the clear majority of comments from practitioners and leaders in the settings that we visited.

In 2014, Hekia Parata, the Minister of Education, appointed the Advisory Group on Early Learning (AGEL). The group's remit was to recommend improvements in implementing Aotearoa New Zealand's early childhood curriculum framework and to recommend strategies for fostering continuity of learning from birth to 8 years. The AGEL Report (2015) purported that confidence in Te Whāriki varied in practice with practitioners using some parts of Te Whāriki more than others. It concluded that some early years settings were less effective in influencing children's learning and development and links to the curriculum framework were obsolete. The report stated that implementation of the curriculum had steadily drifted away from direct engagement with Te Whāriki and particularly with respect to its bicultural concepts. Similarly, the report echoed some of the suggestions of the ERO review and it became influential in commissioning the update of Te Whāriki. The report highlighted significant variation in curriculum implementation and the quality of pedagogy across the ECE sector. The interpretive nature of Te Whāriki being viewed as both its strength and a challenge could have led to the inconsistency in both understanding and implementing of the curriculum and variability in practice across all dimensions of the curriculum. ERO (2016) identified frequent misinterpretation of Te Whāriki, resulting in misunderstanding within the teaching body of such issues as the child-centred curriculum and the critical role of the teacher within this. This misunderstanding, they claimed, led to occasions of ineffective scaffolding to support children's learning. Furthermore, a narrowing of the curriculum was also seen as reinforcing the opinion that leadership about learning and supporting the curriculum, i.e. pedagogical leadership was lacking in some services (ERO, 2016). As this chapter is being written, ERO is continuing to evaluate what is happening in early learning services as leaders and *kaiako* engage with the updated curriculum. They will report early in 2019 on how well-prepared services are to implement Te Whāriki.

Our visits to early years settings in 2016 resonate in part with the previous discussion. We observed that Te Whāriki (2016) was rarely referred to and only referenced for extracting quotes when formulating learning stories, discussed as follows. This concurs with ERO's (2016) report stating that whilst most services were making some use of the original framework, only 10 per cent were fully employing the underpinning theories and explicitly linking their practice to the principles, strands and goals. The updated document outlines the underpinning theories and approaches in a discreet section (Te Whariki, 2017, p.62–64). These are the Bioecological model, sociocultural theories, Kaupapa Maori theory, Pasifika approaches, Critical theories and Emerging Research and Theory. As this is a discreet section in Te Whāriki (2017), it does not link explicitly to the rest of the document and could be read as a superficial inclusion.

Assessment was a significant component in the discussions leading up to the revision of Te Whāriki (2017). There was a view that centres were struggling with assessment and practitioners were struggling broadly with the learning stories framework (ERO, 2016; McLachlan, 2018). In our research, "Learning Stories" (Carr and Lee, 2012) were used extensively in assessment practice. It was observed that the practitioner usually noted what the child was doing and the learning that was taking place. The practitioner usually formulated broad next steps for the child and/or adult to take (Leydon, 2018). This narrative approach to assessment had been widely adopted by the sector even though the early childhood regulations did not specify the use of particular assessment *approaches*. We were signposted to *Kei Tua o te Pae / Assessment for Learning: Early Childhood Exemplars* (online) which gives guidance on writing learning stories. However, it appeared that settings had developed their own reasons for using learning stories and how they are used upon completion. Significantly, there were no requirements in Te Whāriki (1996) to assess children's learning for particular outcomes. During our discussions, one teacher educator stated that she felt that learning stories had "gone too far", claiming that skills-based attainment was not assessed adequately (Leydon, 2018). This was not a typical response from practitioners, as on the contrary, the view on measuring and quantifying learning outcomes was overwhelmingly voiced as a positive by all practitioners we spoke to across the sector. As one teacher educator explained,

> Compliance kills off personal agency... Something with a heart moves along the continuum to the technical end of the continuum. Spirit gets drained out of activity where compliance is involved.
>
> *(cited in Leydon, 2018, p.26)*

ERO (2016) asserted that children with additional learning needs were being catered for, but there was variability in responses to children with special abilities. Here they reported that some teachers did not appear to have the pedagogical knowledge to extend the learning of these children. During our visits to early years settings in Aotearoa New Zealand, we identified that the curriculum areas were rarely explicitly referred to in planning and that teachers and leaders did not have a shared understanding of the purpose of assessment in the context of the curriculum. ERO (2016) noted that the learning story approach often did not provide evidence of children's learning to inform next steps and this also meant that ERO did not know what the children were learning (Blaiklock, 2017). Reliance on one mode of assessment could be viewed as ignoring other forms of assessment which could shed light on what children are able to do and areas that need further work (ERO, 2016). Conversely, references to dispositions, simply described as characteristics or attitudes to learning that are life skills, e.g. persistence, was common-practice in the learning stories that we read.

When visiting the preschool settings, our observations of the learning stories and educators' engagement with them revealed a wide variety in their rationale and content with individuals often driving the style and content. This could vary from room to room throughout a setting. A manager commented "I am not one for rotas and templates" (Leydon, 2018, p.24). During our discussions, we found that the most consistent rationale for using learning stories was to make learning visible and to share with *Whānau*. When we took opportunities to explore other reasons as to why practitioners used this approach in assessment practice, we noted a common belief that this documentation would be expected by ERO during their inspection. A visit to a Kohanga Reo enlightened us as to the complexity that assessment practices bring to Aotearoa New Zealand. Here, learning stories were used solely to satisfy ERO and they believed that learning stories were more appropriate and useful for mainstream settings.

The revision of Te Whāriki in 2017 resulted after a backdrop of mounting concern that the sector was struggling to implement the curriculum. Our research identified that these concerns were not echoed by practitioners and leaders working in ECE, but rather in ERO and in the AGEL report which was commissioned by a government minister. The report's recommendations arising from the review of AGEL was for the Ministry of Education to commission an update of Te Whāriki. The revision published in 2017 aspired to be reflective of societal changes, shifts in government policy and considerable research around curriculum assessment, pedagogy and practice (McLachlan, 2017).

A primary objective for the update was to focus on providing fewer, clearer learning outcomes whilst the principles, strands and goals remain the same. The learning outcomes have been reduced from 118 indicative outcomes to 20, as discussed in the following. Superficially, this could be seen as a positive move towards a reduction in target setting for children's learning and development, however, a reduction in definitive targets could risk a narrowing of the curriculum leading to an achievement-based approach.

Since the revision, there is now an expectation for teachers to provide a range of methods to assess how children are progressing over time. This increased focus on assessment including stronger guidance on both formal and informal, spontaneous and planned assessment could ensure that children's learning in each strand is assessed. However, coupled with the move to *Kaiko* being portrayed as "intentional" in Te Whāriki (2017), meaning that they act with specific outcomes or goals in mind, these trends could lead to a move away from facilitating child led play towards didactic teaching. This change risks being a shift in focus away from children's individual learning to preparing children for school and to be successful future leaders. Furthermore, the revised document is now linked to the Aotearoa New Zealand primary curriculum (2007) with the danger that this could lead to the schoolification of early childhood education. "The two curriculums are based on similar principles and have similar approaches to valued learning" (Te Whāriki, 2017, p.51). Worryingly, this could result in a narrow tick-based curriculum connecting children's outcomes to the investment the Government makes (Alexander, 2016). Furthermore, this could constitute a paradigm shift in the policy and practice of Te Whāriki as it moves away from the holistic nature of Te Whāriki (1996).

In the revised curriculum, a significant area of debate is the inclusion of the term *Kaiako* which

> ...includes all teachers, educators and other adults, including parents in parent-led services, who have a responsibility for the care and education of children in an ECE setting.
>
> *(Te Whāriki, 2017, p.7)*

Kaiako, rather than teachers, could be viewed as a more inclusive term as it encompasses both qualified and unqualified staff, parents and whānau in ECE centres. However, there are possibilities for tension. During our visit to a Kohanga Reo, we found that in these settings, whānau are highly valued and integral to the setting but may not all be qualified. For this reason they receive less governmental funding. However, Puna Reo are run by registered teachers rather than whānau and receive more funding. It is also problematic as adopting the word 'kaiako' and explicitly defining it to encompass all qualified and unqualified teachers rather than defining *kaiako* as teacher could be viewed as paving the way to de-professionalising early childhood teaching. The question arises as to why it is just early years teachers who are 'kaiako' and not all teachers in schools. This could prove to be a source of contention as the roll-out of the Te Whāriki (2017) unfolds.

In the revised Te Whāriki (2017, p.2), there are now two frameworks of equal status, *Te Whāriki: He whāriki mātauranga mō ngā mokopuna o Aotearoa Early childhood curriculum* and *Te Whāriki a te Kōhanga Reo*. The publication of *Te Whāriki a te Kōhanga Reo* in its own right rather than Part B as in the original document is a major change and reflects an increased valuing in Māori immersion education (McLachlan, 2018). The perceived omission of Pasifika perspectives in the writing group could prove to be critical as they are an integral group in Aotearoa New Zealand. Similarly, the hurried timeline for the revision of the document including rewriting, consultation and finalising has caused concern as it did not provide for a more iterative and inclusive process (Alexander, 2016). As we mentioned earlier, there was an overwhelming embracing of the original framework by those directly engaging and implementing it, so this revision has the potential to lead to disquiet. It is possible that some practitioners may feel disempowered with a lack of ownership which could result in no change to their practice (McLachlan, 2017).

Given that the practice of the Aotearoa New Zealand early childhood educators varied in their implementation of the original Te Whāriki, it is not possible to forecast their responses to the revised framework. Professional development commissioned by the Government is still ongoing and engagement with the documentation is still in the early stages. ERO will be evaluating centres working with Te Whāriki (2017) and then this may give some insight into how centres are interpreting, transitioning and implementing the revised Te Whāriki.

International case studies

The following section presents two case studies from New Zealand.

In the first case study, we hear from a preschool of Tokelauan heritage in the South Pacific. The settings philosophy stipulates that "...the Tokelau language is to be spoken, the culture to be encouraged and nurtured, and for the children to retain the value of Christian principles" (Humble Beginning, online). We hear about the history of the setting and how love continues to permeate through the setting's philosophy and practice.

MATALIKI TOKELAU AKOGA KAMATA

Mr Foa'i and Mrs Feagai Foa'i's educational aspirations were born out of a love for their children and immediate family as well as a desire to serve their community. Aspirations became a reality in the Early Childhood Centre (ECE) 'Mataliki Tokelau Akoga Kamata' [hereby referred to as Mataliki].

Mataliki is a place where children flourish with parents, teachers and staff committed to working together towards a shared vision which has changed little since its inception. Passionate parents dreamt of creating an environment where Tokelauan children are taught using their treasured Tokelauan language (Humble Beginning, 2018). Language connects worlds and in this case a Tokelau [1] ethnic world and the rarity of its worldviews including but not exclusive to the values, language, culture, traditions, geographical context as atolls in the South Pacific.

Historically, Mataliki has been tested many times since its humble beginnings in the 1980s, when a handful of Tokelauan parents living in South Auckland (NZ) decided to band together after teaching their preschool age children and extended family in their home garages. Over 20 years ago, these founding parents had no NZ qualifications, let alone a NZ teaching qualification. All resources had to be created by hand and retranslated from English (or another language) into the Tokelau language, and they had to navigate the NZ Ministry of Education's legal obligations, educational regulations and curriculum guidelines. Other social challenges included Foa'i and Feagai regularly slept on mattresses on the newly purchased preschool building to protect the facilities, contents and land.

Today, resources such as Te Whāriki set a benchmark for curriculum implementation to ensure that ECE's like Mataliki are supported to become their best as an ECE in NZ. Unconditional love is a Tokelauan cultural and Spiritual value which cuts across Te Whāriki principles and strands of learning. A recent visitor to Mataliki wrote of her experience noting "I thought it interesting that when a Samoan school was established next door, staff from the centre went over to help and worked with them developing their learning stories. Inherent in Tokelau culture is the value of unconditional love, giving without any expectation to receive" (Leydon, 2018 , p.21).

Love is a powerful force which is felt in tangible ways by all who are connected to the setting. Families are from a range of Pacific Island ethnic groups including Māori, Tokelau, Samoa, Niue, Cook Islands Maori and Tongan. Children enjoy responsibility during 'lotu' [grace for food, prayers or religious devotions], helping others when participating in daily routines. When values like 'unconditional love' are tested, one prays that love may continue to strengthen and grow. The living legacy of love will be seen through these children and their parents for years to come.

Linda-Teleo Hope

The second case study is a reflection from a centre manager highlighting the challenges she has faced in her role and what has and continues to influence her personal philosophy and pedagogy. She reflects positively on her expectations for the revised Te Whāriki curriculum in the early days of its inception.

Kia ora, my present role as Centre Manager/Curriculum Leader has without a doubt been the most challenging yet most rewarding role I have had in my 20-plus years of teaching. The purpose of my employment was to turn a very run down early learning centre, with tired, unmotivated staff and a sad roll, into a vibrant community of learners, with passionate and joyful teachers, willing to do whatever it takes to ensure as a centre, we live and breathe the teaching philosophy we wholeheartedly believe in.

Inspired by the principles of Emmi Pikler, Reggio Emilia and the Virtues Project (enabled as the New Zealand's early childhood curriculum, is open ended/ unrestrictive), we believe that children are equal human-beings so deserve nothing less than to be treated with the same respect that adults would want to be treated with. The kind of environment we provide is like a home-away-from-home. It feels warm, nurturing, aesthetically pleasing to the eye, it smells and sounds good, nutritionally healthy food is always cooking, and the chatter that can be heard amongst teachers, children and whanau, is kind, caring and loving. As we believe children are very competent and capable and unfold in the way they have been biologically made to do naturally, we allow them the freedom they require to explore their environment in a way that is unhurried or rushed. Educarers are present and ready to assist where necessary, but do not hover over children like a helicopter, ready to catch them if they fall.

Te Whāriki talks about the importance of building trusting, respectful relationships with children and whanau in order for deep, meaningful partnerships to occur. Genuine, authentic, loving, caring, trusting, respectful and reciprocal relationships between teachers, children and whanau, are really needed in New Zealand to address societal problems affecting children. Te Whāriki however does not specifically mention the word love. I believe that the updated Te Whāriki recognises that it's time to take the pressure off our tamariki to learn how to read, write and do maths before school age (which in New Zealand is generally age five). I believe that children in recent years have been robbed of their childhood and all the research tells us right now that children in their early years learn best through play. I was relieved to hear of 'National Standards' in primary schools being abolished as soon as the Labour Government took over in New Zealand. They put pressure on our youngest children, parents and teachers to teach children in their early years, their colours, numbers and letters. What should really be given priority in this country, is allowing children the time they need to learn how to get on with others in an empathetic and compassionate way. As a wise New Zealand woman, Dame Whina Cooper once said, we need to "Take care of our children. Take care of what they hear. Take care of what they see. Take care of what they feel. For how the children grow so will be the shape of Aotearoa".

(McClintock, 2018, p.1)

A consideration of current challenges for educators, children and their families and communities

This chapter now moves on to discuss the challenges early childhood educators face when working with Te Whāriki (2017) which is widely understood as being an inclusive and collaborative curriculum. However, there are concerns that childhood educators may have positioned parents and their communities as "benign outsiders" (Duncan and Te One, 2014). Although early childhood educators seek to maintain best practice of providing an inclusive learning environment, for example, displaying welcome signage in various languages and providing cultural activities, these efforts could be viewed as a token gesture to involving parents, whānau and the wider community. Successful collaboration depends on the early childhood centres' familiarity, interpretation and commitment to working with the family and community strand of Te Whāriki (2017). As mentioned earlier, Te Whāriki (2017) holds a spiritual and symbolic meaning for Māori. Working in this way demonstrates that collaboration is authentic when the educators build and provide culturally appropriate approaches and activities and develop relationships with whānau that are sustainable. Te Whāriki (2017) stipulates that parents and whānau want to trust that the early education centres have their best interests at heart where connection from the family's "whānau" past, present and future are included in daily exchange and routines.

During our travels we found a particularly good example of how an early childhood setting valued parents, whānau and the wider community.

The following are two good working examples of how an early childhood centre had effectively woven Principal 3, Family and community – *Whānau tangata* and the Strand of Wellbeing – *Mana atua* from Te Whāriki (2017).

The Whanganui Central Baptist Kindergarten (CBK), in Wellington, New Zealand, had a vision to go beyond the routine daily exchanges and turn these into opportunities, considering the traditions and beliefs of the community and building a sense of wellbeing. CBK initiated a transition forum between early years educators and new entrant teachers from primary schools. The centre provided a space for these professionals to meet and converse about school transitions. It provided an opportunity for early years educators to explain the new curriculum giving primary teachers an insight into Te Whāriki (2017).

In addition, early childhood educators at CBK understood their success of building relationships with children and whānau was good, and they realised that fathers and grandfathers were largely under-represented. CBK worked with S.K.I.P., a team that focuses on whānau-centred change, to address this. CBK recognised that fathers and grandfathers did not get the quality time they needed with their children due to their irregular and long working patterns. CBK along with S.K.I.P. formed the 'Dads Together' initiative. They worked with fathers and grandfathers through active participation activities, providing a space for them relax and chat. CBK identified trusted community representatives to act as ambassadors that visited fathers and grandfathers in or near their place of work during their lunch break. The group flourished and they met regularly to discuss their feelings and personal insights on child development.

To build on whānau and community unity, CBK began by rearranging the physical space of the classrooms, which meant that parents were 'intentionally' noticed and acknowledged. Children, whānau and early years educators became visible to each other. The centre's pedagogy shifted from that where early years educators were 'seeing' whānau and children to one where whānau experienced 'being seen'. Early years educators were sensitive to recognise and acknowledge whānau values and expectations thus providing an environment with appropriate resources and opportunities to meet psychological and cultural and spiritual needs of all the children in their care.

Te Aroha Nao Community Services Centre ("TANCS") in Palmerston North, New Zealand, started as a small building and now extends along most of the main street in the community. It is a thriving base where children and families are cared for.

Te Aroha Nao Community Services is not only recognised throughout New Zealand but throughout the world. Over the years, it has increased its services that include a multi-disciplinary, integrated early intervention service that helps young families and Whānau.

It was created as an evolution of a modest Playgroup where the primary aim was to build the capacity of whanau to be effective first educators of their tamariki. A secondary aim was to build social connectiveness and a sense of community (*To Turangawaewae* – a place to belong). It was to be a whanau that didn't go away. Thirdly, it was to be a place that promoted the 'MORE', i.e. it was to enhance whanau well-being (*He Ngakau Ora*) through wrap around development services such as adult education, parenting education, counselling and whanau development.

The Te Aroha Nao Community Services Centre focuses on wellbeing of children, families and the community. The early years centre has a team of parents and teachers that are fully involved and work with the curriculum. They encourage a model of 'parents as involved educators' and work creatively to provide a seamless education between home and the centre. The centre focuses on valuing backgrounds, the Mana or power of all families in the community. Teachers at the early years centre appreciate the family dynamics and provide facilities for specific groups. They recently set up an opportunity for fathers to gather at the playcentre in the evening and at the weekends, 'Who let the Dad's Out'. The uptake to this group was slow at first with only a couple of fathers attending but now it is a thriving group where regular initiatives designed by fathers are woven in to the wider curriculum.

The other initiatives at the centre, Te Whare Atawhai, a programme that provides the opportunity for young people to live and learn in a wrap-around environment. These young people are given coaching in day to day from opening their own bank account to paying bills and this is done in a safe and supportive environment. These young people are invited to bring along their children to these sessions. S.K.I.P. (Strategies for Kids, Information for Parents) also runs 'Purposeful Parenting', a forum for parents of all ages to discover their preferred parenting styles and how best to create positive developmental experiences for their children. One parent commented, 'I thought an old dog like myself couldn't learn new tricks, but I've been using this stuff with my kids and it's been helping me with great support in parenting my two girls'.

There has been a continuous development of the centre as the heart of the community. Educational events are continuously held in the centre with Matariki events being a highlight of the year when more than 250 parents and children attend. It is also the venue for many other educational events. It has also been a place for community celebration and community grieving. A tangi was held at the centre for a young girl who passed away through suicide and which created a heightened sense of tension for the community. Te Aroha Noa was able to be a place that could be a container for these raw emotions and create a sense of rangimarie for the whānau involved and the wider community.

POINTS FOR REFLECTION

In this chapter collaboration between the early childhood centre, parents, carers, *whānau* and the community are successful when teaching staff incorporates daily opportunities for interaction.

- What does the word community mean to you in your locality?
- What would an authentic community partnership approach to teaching and learning look like in your setting? How would you develop policy to reflect this?
- How would community partnership benefit a child's holistic development?
- How might you ensure that the community partnership is sustainable?

TABLE 7.1 Glossary of Māori terms

'aiga	(Samoan) 'whānau' or extended family
aroha	love, compassion, empathy, affection
hapū	tribe or subtribe
hinengaro	intellect, the mind
iwi	extended kinship group, tribe, people
kaiako	Includes all teachers, educators and other adults, including parents in parent-led services, who have a responsibility for the care and education of children in an ECE setting (Te Whāriki, 2017, p.7)
kaitiaki	trustee, custodian, guardian, protector
kaitiakitanga	guardianship
Karakia	prayer, ritual chant, incantation
kaupapa Māori	A Māori approach that assumes the normalcy of being Māori – language, customs, knowledge, principles, ideology, agenda
kōhanga reo	Māori-medium early childhood centre with a focus on language and culture retention and revitalisation
kura	school
mana	authority, prestige, power, spiritual power, authority, status and control
manaakitanga	the process of showing respect, generosity, hospitality and care for others
marae	the complex of buildings and land associated with a pan-tribal group, whānau, hapū or iwi
mauri	vital essence, life principle, essential quality
māori	member of the Polynesian indigenous people of New Zealand
mokopuna	grandchild; in the context of Te Whāriki, mokopuna expresses intergenerational connectedness
Papatuanuku	Earth, Earth mother
Puna Reo	Māori-medium early childhood centres led by registered teachers rather than by whānau
pumanawa	inherited talent
raranga	weaving
rangatiratanga	chiefly authority, right to exercise authority, sovereignty, autonomy, control, independence
tangata whenua	People of the land (literal), descendants of the first people to settle Aotearoa New Zealand, indigenous people (used of Māori), person or people with customary authority over an area that may include land and sea. This authority is held by first settlement of an area or by succeeding to an area through active occupation and negotiation with the first peoples
taonga	a highly prized object or possession; includes socially or culturally valued resources, both tangible and intangible, artefact
tamariki	Children

Te Aho Matua	Te Aho Matua o ngā Kura Kaupapa Māori, the document that sets out the principles by which kura kaupapa Māori operate
te ao Māori	the Māori world
Te Marautanga o Aotearoa	The curriculum for Māori-medium schools
te reo Māori	the Māori language
tikanga Māori	Māori ways of doing, including practices, customs and rituals
tinana	physical, body
tinihanga	cunning
tuakana-teina	senior and junior siblings, used where an older or more knowledgeable child supports the learning of a younger or less knowledgeable child
waiata	songs, chants
wairua	spirit
wānanga	educational seminar, institution or forum; (act of wānanga) shared deliberations, discussions, shared learning
whakapapa	lineage, genealogy, ancestry
whakatoi	cheekiness
whānau	extended family, multigenerational group of relatives or group of people who work together on and for a common cause
wharekura	school (often used of kura kaupapa Māori secondary schools)
whatumanawa	heart, mind, seat of emotion

Summary

In this chapter we have explored the differing perspective of Te Whāriki as a curriculum that has historical, social, cultural and educational guiding principles and shown its aspirations for children to develop as competent learners and communicators. A significant strength of Te Whariki is its ability to promote intercultural competence and the emphasis it places upon nurturing children's unique cultural identities. As the case studies have shown the revised Te Whāriki (2017) provides an opportunity for the early childhood sector including educators to reflect and engage in useful discussion about the purpose of curriculum and the nature of the framework in relation to children and families and the guidance needed to achieve this purpose. In the reimagining of Te Whāriki the narrative is clearly ongoing, with its shift from the idea that this is what has been done in the past, to what learning is valued in the future, particularly in relation to increasing globalisation and neo-liberal implications for education. In this respect it is fitting to conclude with the following quote taken from the revised Te Whāriki document:

He pai te tirohanga ki ngā mahara mō ngā rā pahemo engari ka puta te māramatanga i runga i te titiro whakamua.

It's fine to have recollections of the past, but wisdom comes from being able to prepare opportunities for the future.

(Te Whāriki, 2017, p.22)

Note

1 Tokelau comprises three atolls in the South Pacific Ocean between 171° and 173° W longitude and 8° and 10° S latitude, approximately midway between Hawaii and New Zealand. They lie about 500 km (311 mi) north of Samoa.

References

Alexander, S.E. (2016). *Questions hanging over the update of Te Whāriki*. DOI: doi:10.23965/AJEC.42.3.05. Retrieved 8 November 2018 from: www.childforum.com/images/Te_Whariki_update_critique_paper.pdf.

Alvestad, M. and Duncan, J. (2006) '"The value is enormous – It's priceless I think!" Preschool teachers' understandings of the early childhood curriculum in New Zealand – A comparative perspective', *International Journal of Early Childhood*, 38(1), p.31–45.

Beatty, B. (2017) 'John Dewey's high hopes for play: Democracy and education and Progressive Era controversies over play in kindergarten and preschool education', *The Journal of the Gilded Age and Progressive Era*, 16(4), p.424–443. DOI: doi:10.1017/S1537781417000317.

Birth to three matters framework (2002) Retrieved 23 November 2018 from: www.foundationyears.org.uk/wp-content/uploads/2012/04/Birth-to-Three-Matters-Booklet.pdf.

Blaiklock, K. (2017) 'Is New Zealand a world leader in early childhood education? An examination of the empirical evidence in recent reports', *Australasian Journal of Early Childhood*, 42(3), p.38–45.

Bushouse, B. (2008) *Early childhood education policy in Aotearoa / New Zealand: The creation of the 20 hours free programme*, Wellington: Fulbright New Zealand. Retrieved 23 November 2018 from: www.fulbright.org.nz/wp-content/uploads/2011/12/axford2008_bushouse.pdf.

Carr, M. and Lee, W. (2012) *Learning stories: Constructing learner identities in early education*, London: SAGE Publications.

Carr, M. and May, H. (1993) 'Choosing a model: Reflecting on the development process of Te Whāriki, national early childhood curriculum guidelines in New Zealand', *International Journal of Early Years Education*, 1(3), p.7–22.

Cullen, J. (1996) 'The challenge of Te Whāriki for future developments in early childhood education', *Delta*, 48(1), p.113–126.

Dalli, C. (2013) 'A day in the life of a New Zealand kindergarten teacher: A curriculum of open possibilities', in: J. Georgeson and J. Payler (Eds.) *International perspectives on early childhood education and care*, London: Open University Press.

Department for Education (DfE) (2017) *Early Years Foundation Stage (EYFS)*. Retrieved 23 November 2018 from: www.foundationyears.org.uk/files/2017/03/EYFS_STATUTORY_FRAMEWORK_2017.pdf.

DfEE (2000) *Curriculum guidance for the foundation stage*, London: QCA.

Duhn, I. (2006) 'The making of global citizens: Traces of cosmopolitanism in the New Zealand early childhood curriculum, Te Whāriki', *Contemporary Issues in Early Childhood*, 7(3), p.191–202. DOI: doi:10.2304/ciec.2006.7.3.191.

Duncan, J. and Te One, S. (2014) 'Joining the tots: Visual research tools to connect families and community in early childhood education', *Australasian Journal of Early Childhood*, Retrieved 8 November 2018 from: www.earlychildhoodaustralia.org.au/wp-content/uploads/2017/04/AJEC1403.pdf.

Duncan, J., Te One, S., Dewe, R., Te Punga-Jurgens, J., Shaw, L., Easton, S., Thomas, M. and Whanganui Central Baptist Kindergartens and Early Learning Centres' Teaching and Facilitator Teams (2012) *Active adult participation in early childhood education: Enhancing child learning and community wellness, Teaching & learning research initiative*. Retrieved 8 November 2018 from: www.tlri.org.nz/sites/default/files/projects/9279_summaryreport.pdf.

Education Review Office (ERO) (2016) *Early learning curriculum: What's important and what works*. Retrieved 8 November 2018 from: www.ero.govt.nz/assets/Uploads/ERO-Early-Learning-Curriculum-WEB.pdf.

Education Review Office (ERO) (2011) *Early learning curriculum*. Retrieved 15 March 2019 from: www.ero.govt.nz/assets/Uploads/ERO-Early-Learning-Curriculum-WEB.pdf.

Erueti, B. and Rangikoepa Palmer, F. (2014) 'Te Whariki Tuakiri (the identity mat): Māori elite athletes and the expression of ethno-cultural identity in global sport', *Sport in Society Cultures, Commerce, Media, Politics*, 17(8), p.1061–1075. DOI: doi:10.1080/17430437.2013.838351.

Farquar, S. (2015) 'New Zealand early childhood curriculum: The politics of collaboration', *Journal of Pedagogy*, 6(2), p.57–70. DOI: doi:10.1515/jped-2015–0013.

Giardiello, P. (2014) *Pioneers in early childhood education: The Roots and Legacies of Rachel and Margaret McMillan, Maria Montessori and Susan Isaacs*, Abingdon: Routledge.

Highscope. Retrieved 23 November 2018 from: https://highscope.org/.

Humble beginning. Retrieved 31 August 2018 from: www.mataliki.co.nz/humble-beginning/.

Kei Tua o te Pae/assessment for learning: Early childhood exemplars. Retrieved 23 November 2018 from: www.education.govt.nz/early-childhood/teaching-and-learning/assessment-for-learning/kei-tua-o-te-pae-2/.

Laevers, F. (2005) 'The curriculum as means to raise the quality of early childhood education: Implications for policy', *European Early Childhood Education Research Journal*, 13(1), p.17–29, DOI: doi:10.1080/13502930585209531.

Leydon, G. (2018) *Best practice in early years education: Securing the best life chances for young children*, Winston Churchill Memorial Trust. Retrieved 28 August 2018 from: www.wcmt.org.uk/sites/default/files/report-documents/Leydon%20G%20Report%202016%20Final.pdf.

May, H. (1997) *The discovery of early childhood: The development of services for the care and education of very young children, mid eighteenth century Europe to mid twentieth century New Zealand*, Auckland: Auckland University Press, Bridget Williams Books.

May, H. and Carr, M. (2016) 'Te Whāriki: An uniquely woven curriculum shaping policy, pedgagy and practice in Aotearoa, New Zealand', in: T. David, K. Goouch and S. Powell (Eds.) *The Routledge international handbook of philosophies and theories of early childhood education and care*, Abingdon: Routledge.

McClintock, J. (2018) 'Health of our children/tamariki: Wealth of our nation', The Paediatric Society of New Zealand, Submission to the Ministerial Inquiry into Mental Health and Addiction.

McLachlan, C. (2018) 'Te Whāriki revisited: How approaches to assessment can make valued learning visible', *He Kupu The Word*, 5(3). Retrieved 8 November 2018 from: www.hekupu.ac.nz/sites/default/files/2018-05/08%20McLachlan.pd.

McLachlan, C. (2017) *"Not Business as usual": Reflections on the 2017 update of Te Whāriki*. Retrieved 8 November 2018 from: www.aut.ac.nz/__data/assets/pdf_file/0016/180061/EE62_WEB.pdf.

Ministry of Education (NZ) (2017) *Te Whāriki*. Retrieved 8 November 2018 from: https://education.govt.nz/assets/Documents/Early-Childhood/ELS-Te-Whariki-Early-Childhood-Curriculum-ENG-Web.pdf.

Ministry of Education (NZ) (2015) *Report on the Advisory Group on Early Learning (AGEL)*. Retrieved 8 November 2018 from: www.education.govt.nz/assets/Documents/Ministry/consultations/Report-of-the-Advisory-Group-on-Early-Learning.pdf.

Ministry of Education (NZ) (2004) *Kei Tua o te Pae/Assessment for learning*. Retrieved 8 November 8 2018 from: www.education.govt.nz/assets/Documents/Early-Childhood/Kei-Tua-o-te-Pae/ECEBooklet1Full.pdf.

Ministry of Education (NZ) (1996) *Te Whāriki*. Retrieved 8 November 2018 from: www.education.govt.nz/assets/Documents/Early-Childhoood/Te-Whariki-1996.pdf.

New Zealand Educational Institute (NZEI Te Riu Roa) (2016) *History of early childhood education in the context of the union movement*. Retrieved 23 November 2018 from: http://nzei.org.nz/NZEI/Aboutus.aspx.

Nuttall, J. (2002) 'Negotiating the meaning of curriculum—Can we awaken the 'sleeping beauty?' *Early Education*, 28, pp.5–9.

OECD (2004) *Starting strong: Curricula and pedagogies in early childhood education and care. Five curriculum outlines*, Paris: Directorate for Education, OECD.

Reedy, T. (2013) 'Toku rangatiratanga na te mana-matauranga. "Knowledge and power set me free . . ."' in: J. Nuttall (Ed.) *Weaving Te Whāriki: Aotearoa New Zealand's early childhood curriculum document in theory and practice*, Wellington: New Zealand Council for Educational Research, p.35–53.

Rogoff, B. (1990) *Apprenticeship in thinking*, New York: Oxford University Press.

Sewell, A., and Bethell, K. (2009) 'Building interests: A 1940s story of curriculum innovation and contemporary connections', *New Zealand Journal of Teachers' Work*, 6(2), p.93–110.

Strategies with Kids Information for Parents (SKIP) New Zealand. Retrieved 8 November 2018 from: www.skip.org.nz/.

Tearney, F. (2016) *Working paper 2016/03: History of education in New Zealand*, Wellington: McGuinness Institute Limited. Retrieved 15 March 2019 from: www.mcguinnessinstitute.org/wp-content/uploads/2016/08/20161213-Working-Paper-2016%EF%80%A203-History-of-education-in-New-Zealand.pdf.

Terreni, L. (2010) 'A history of visual art education in early childhood in New Zealand: Looking backwards to go forward'. Retrieved 23 November 2018 from: http://artinearlychildhood.org/artec/images/article/ARTEC_2010_Research_Journal_1_Article_2.pdf.

The Evaluation Review Office (ERO) (2011) *Positive foundations for learning: Confident and competent children in early childhood services*. Retrieved 23 November 2018 from: www.ero.govt.nz/publications/positive-foundations-for-learning-confident-and-competent-children-in-early-childhood-services/.

The Evaluation Review Office (ERO). *Early learning curriculum*. Retrieved 23 November 2018 from: www.ero.govt.nz/publications/early-learning-curriculum/.

Vygotsky, L.S. (1978) *Mind in society: The development of higher psychological processes*, Cambridge, MA: Harvard University Press. (Original manuscripts [ca. 1930–1934]).

Zhang, Q. (2015) 'Emergent literacy as sociocultural practice: How well do New Zealand parents fit with Te Whariki?' *Journal of Early Childhood Literacy*, 17(1), p.1–23. DOI: doi:10.1177/1468798415607939.

8

DANISH OUTDOOR NATURE PEDAGOGY

Naomi McLeod

Over the last ten years or so in England, there has been a growing interest in outdoor-nature pedagogy for children in their early years (Constable, 2014; Knight, 2013; Siegfredsen, 2017; Williams-Tennessen and Cimprich, 1996). Being outside and connecting with nature is recognised internationally and valued by educators as an effective learning resource for inspiring children's imaginative play, developing positive relationships, encouraging independence and enhancing children's health, mental health and well-being (Chawla and Cushing, 2007; Dowdell, Gray, and Malone, 2011; Ejbye-Ernst and Stokholm, 2015; Kaplan and Kaplan, 1989; Louv, 2005; Mental Health Foundation, 2005; Stigsdotter and Grahn, 2002).

In England within the contexts of early childhood education there is often an attempt to identify quality outdoor approaches that will raise standards of education and care (often associated with development in children) whilst dealing with diverse issues in our globally changing world (Leather, 2016). In doing so early childhood educators, policy-makers and researchers often look to internationally acclaimed approaches and researchers such as those associated with the Nordic countries. A prominent version has existed for many years in Denmark called the 'skovbørnehaven' (skov-børne-haven) which in Dutch means forest-kinder-garten or 'Skov Børnehus' which translates as Forest Children's House. This is an approach based on an embedded philosophy that informs the socio-cultural pedagogy of Denmark for children aged between 2 and 5 and will be explored in more detail a little later in the chapter. In England the idea of learning outdoors has been interpreted in the steep rise of forest schools (Leather, 2016). While there are some very effective and valuable pedagogical examples, often outdoor learning in England in early childhood is scheduled as 'a turn' for being outdoors and carrying out planned activities outlined as part of different 'levels' of practitioner training. Priority is given to outcome-driven teaching and pressures of accountability (Organisation for Economic Co-operation and Development (OECD) 'Baby PISA', 2018). The outdoors is often viewed as an opportunity to 'let off steam' which sadly is a misinterpretation of a more holistic, embodied approach to nature-outdoor traditions associated with pedagogy in Denmark, Sweden and Finland. Given the current neo-liberal pressures of accountability in England, something is often lost in translation as different international outdoor pedagogical approaches are interpreted. In the hope of reconnecting educators with a sense of ownership and empowerment (Moss, 2010), this chapter looks at the distinctive underpinning philosophy and principles of Danish outdoor nature pedagogy and the various historical socio-cultural, economic and policy influences that inform practice today in Denmark. In doing so I draw on the work of Pestalozzi and Froebel as well as other recent theories (such as Stigsdotter and Grahn, 2002; Ejbye-Ernst and Stokholm, 2015; Kaplan and Kaplan, 1989) to show how they influenced the development of Danish outdoor-nature learning. Comparisons are made with England throughout, supported by various case study examples and conversations to highlight the various political and cultural influences which impact on the different interpretations of forest school that have ensued.

The distinctive underpinning philosophy and principles of Danish outdoor nature pedagogy

Johann Pestalozzi's philosophy (1746–1827)

The foundations of Danish outdoor nature pedagogy can be traced back to Rousseau (1712–1778), Pestalozzi and Froebel (1782–1852) (Williams-Siegfredsen, 2017). As an advocate of autonomy and freedom, Pestalozzi was directly inspired by Rousseau's (*Èmile*) who viewed the child as its 'own creature' with a restored view of education and human nature (Soëtard, 1994, p.1–2). The purpose of education at that time endorsed tendencies to promote work and industry, which contradicted Pestalozzi's belief in the natural freedom of children and a system of education that involved children building their own knowledge as autonomous beings, rather than involving a transition of knowledge. The originality of his method lies in its spirit of freedom and autonomy, which in practice incorporates three elements at its core: heart, head and hand. Pestalozzi recognised the need to detach one's thoughts (in the head) through reflection from the pressures of the world. Being surrounded by others impacts on the heart (natural feelings of what is right), as is often the case today in England, with the pressure of narrow curriculum outcomes and an over emphasis on assessments. Put simply, thinking and being become the same, as thinking is influenced by the constant demand to produce through work. What ought to happen is dominated by an alternative (i.e. pressures), which influences the hand. The head, hand and heart therefore work together and are driven and shaped by human nature within the structure of society. For Pestalozzi, the educator has an awesome moral responsibility to:

> *occupy a special position with respect to the encounter between a child's instinctual desires and the demands society makes on them. They have the power to further the development of autonomy or to cripple it, perhaps for a lifetime.*
>
> *(Pestalozzi, cited in Soëtard, 1994, p.7).*

In this way, Pestalozzi is recognised for fostering the notion of reflective learning for both children and educators (Giardiello, 2014). There is a responsibility to maintain the equilibrium of all three elements (head, heart and hand), so undue advantage is not given to one. A balance within the curriculum is essential so the intellectual, artistic and technical are divided equally. Likewise, the atmosphere for learning needs to value freedom and autonomy. The crux of Pestalozzi's work lies in the question over the purpose of education, either as a means of integrating into society or as developing as individuals to be creative and independent thinkers.

The relevance of Friedrich Froebel's philosophy (1782–1852)

As a pupil of Pestalozzi, Froebel was directly inspired by Pestalozzi's ideas. However, Froebel goes further in his application, offering educators a 'deep philosophy' around education and self-activity based on his childhood experiences, his thinking around nature and his unity with God (Froebel, 1886, p.ix).

Friedrich Froebel was born in 1782 in Oberweissbach, a small town in Thuringian Forest in Germany. When he was just 8 months old his mother died. His father, a strict Lutheran pastor, had little time for Friedrich, so he spent his time with his five older brothers in the care of servants. In his autobiography, Froebel (1886, p.9) writes about his 'gloomy' childhood made worse by his stepmother's coldness towards him and her eventual rejection of him. He spent much of his time on his own in the garden and with nature. It was here that his appreciation of plants, birds and insects first developed and would later inform his ideas on education. When Friedrich was 10, he went to live with his uncle who was also a pastor and a kind and gentle man who provided the love and affection that was missing in Friedrich's earlier life. Again Froebel (1886) writes about the impact of this on his educational ideas (Liebschner, 1992).

At the age of 15, Froebel left school and spent a two-year apprenticeship with a forester studying texts on botany and classifying plants and trees. His appreciation of nature and the spiritual connection with life and existence was becoming more influential on his thinking and the meaning of life. For two years Froebel studied botany, mathematics, architecture and crystallography at Jena University, which at the time was a centre of new and radical philosophical thinking. Eventually after several different occupations, Froebel took up a post teaching in a progressive school, led by a former pupil of Pestalozzi whose ideas on active learning and first-hand experience influenced his own ideas and true passion for educating the very youngest of children, so firm foundations could be established for later years. In 1837 in his mid-50s, he opened his first 'kindergarten'. In naming it, he was mindful of not using the word 'school' or 'institution' so that it represented and was in tune with the natural development of children and in harmony with nature and the community. The word 'kindergarten' was interpreted as a 'garden for children' and a 'garden of children'. It was unlike anything at the time: inclusive and a central part of the community, open from 6am until 7pm to support the needs of working parents and the poorest of children, providing food, clothing and washing facilities (Western, 2000).

Froebel's appreciation of nature

Arguably Froebel was the most significant of the pioneers for early education and care in terms of applying principles into practice. His idea of the kindergarten as a children's garden or a garden for children was a place where children could develop at their own pace in harmony with nature supported by adults who were knowledgeable and respectful of children's needs, ideas and thought processes (Tovey, 2017). Most significantly, Froebel wanted 'to educate men to be free, to think, to take action for themselves' (Froebel, cited in Lilley, 1967, p.41). In his *Education of Man* (1885), the fundamental principles upon which Froebel based his kindergarten are identified. He explains how self-activity through talk and play can nurture meaningful inner connections between a child's thoughts and expression. His key message is 'inner-connectedness' between feelings, thoughts and the action of doing, prompted by a child's initial perception. Through play the mind grows by self-revelation. The child ascertains what he can do and discovers his possibilities of will by exerting his power spontaneously (Froebel, 1886, p.v). Self-activity is the coming together of thought, connections and doing (Froebel, 1886, p.vii). For Froebel, 'self-conquest is the only basis of true freedom' (ibid.). For genuine self-activity, he emphasises spontaneity accompanied by power on the part of the child resulting in joy. Here, Froebel acknowledges the full co-operation of the educator in facilitating children's inner self-consciousness that leads to clarity in thinking and being at peace with oneself and nature. For Froebel, there is a clear connection between the outer influencing the inner and vice versa. In doing so he recognises the need to adapt to a child's nature rather than being prescriptive and attempting to mould children. While plants and animals are given rest and time, Froebel warns about the tendency to see children as a 'lump of clay to be moulded into what the educator pleases' (Froebel, 1886, p.8).

A Froebelian approach views children as capable, curious, adventurous and imaginative, which is enhanced through being at one with nature. Children's individual interests and curiosity is built on and extended by adults. This was at a time when there was no provision for young children; rather they were prepared for work.

> *At present, the popular notions of work and the pursuits of practical industry are unduly false, superficial, untenable, oppressive, debasing and devoid of all elements of life.*
> *(Froebel, 1886, p. 30)*

In contrast, Froebel argued that the earliest years of a child are the most important laying the foundations for later learning. His ideas about nature, self-activity, talk, voluntary participation and play as a spiritual unity, were viewed as radical at the time. Froebel was unique in the way he integrated resources and practices into a purposeful and coherent pedagogical approach (Beatty, 2017). His 'gifts' and 'occupations' include resources and activities that are very familiar today, for example, wooden blocks, sand, water, finger rhymes, stories, singing, painting, sewing, drawing, an appreciation of nature, growing fruit and vegetables, caring for animals and outdoor play. However, the values which underpin Froebel's approach are not so well known or understood, which has led to different interpretations and practices. An awareness of Froebel's philosophy and the underpinning principles are important for it is not just the resources that make a Froebelian approach but rather *how* the resources are engaged with. Understanding *why* such an approach is valuable today as Froebel's principles contradict with the current climate of prioritising school readiness, baseline assessment and pressures around outcomes (DfE, 2017; McDowall-Clark, 2017).

Froebel into practice

Froebel's approach is a whole way of thinking about children and childhood based on a set of values and principles, which include the following:

- **A respect** of young children based on democratic practice, valuing their views and seeing them as capable.
- **Connectedness**: valuing meaningful experiences so children can make sense of their learning. The whole child is important and not splitting areas or subjects so children can make connections with what they already know.
- **Play, talk and first-hand experiences**: valuing play as the highest potential for learning.
- **Creativity**: is fundamental for making connections with inner feelings, imagination and symbolic representation.
- **Freedom and guidance**: autonomy, choice and self-activity involving respectful educators. Children should be free to think and take action for themselves.
- **Outdoor play**: everyday experiences appreciating the natural world.
- **Community**: Democratic and respectful communities where children and adults learn from and with each other.

- **Positive relationships**: between educators and children based on trust that is reciprocal and respectful.
- **Well informed and qualified educators** (a call to arms for women, particularly mothers in a highly patriarchal society): who are critically reflective / self-aware and committed to developing a professional identity and a new understanding through engaging in reflexive, research informed practice. *(Lilley, 1967; Tovey, 2017; Whinnett, 2012)*

Whilst there is no prescribed curriculum as part of the Froebel approach, his kindergarten was resourced with specifically devised materials which Froebel called 'gifts' and 'occupations'. These are designed to support children's playful learning and include the following:

Gifts: which lead to discovery and offer insight.

- Small soft crocheted balls on string
- Wooden sphere, cube and cylinder
- Wooden cubes
- Wooden blocks

Occupations: which lead to invention and offer the child power.

- Stories
- Circle / movement games
- Singing
- Dancing
- Music and finger rhymes
- Materials for weaving, sewing
- Drawing and painting
- Wooden pattern boards
- Threads and punched cards for sewing
- Peas and sticks for constructing
- Clay and wax
- Sticks and stones
- Sand and water

For Froebel, it was not just the resources but the ideas underpinning them (the '*how*' and '*why*') that were important so adults understood the value and purpose of the materials and occupations (Liebschner, 1992; Tovey, 2017). Most importantly, they were inter-connected parts of a whole approach, rather than separate isolated activities (Whinnett, 2012).

In 1871, Erna Emilie Louise Juel-Hansen (née Drachmann) (1845–1922) co-founded Denmark's first outdoor kindergarten, based on Froebel's ideas of children's education.

For genuine self-activity Froebel emphasised spontaneity accompanied by power on the part of the child resulting in joy. These ideas resonate closely with present day Danish outdoor nature pedagogy which is looked at next.

Outdoor nature pedagogy in Denmark today

In Denmark, outdoor nature pedagogy has evolved as an embodied, cultural approach that is part of daily living and early childhood education. Froebel's emphasis on children learning in harmony with nature resonates strongly with the Danish notion of outdoor-nature pedagogy self-activity so confidence and independence is nurtured (Williams-Siegfredsen, 2017). As Ringsmose and Kragh-Müller (2017) note, the first kindergarten to open in Denmark in 1871 was inspired by Froebel.

More recently, other research has been drawn on by Danish outdoor nature pedagogues, alongside Froebel. For example, Kaplan's research highlights the lower stress, better health, well-being and a more balanced approach to life attributed to nature, daylight, fresh air and greenery (Kaplan and Kaplan, 1989). The work of Ejbye-Ernst, 2014; Grahn et al., 1997; and Stigsdotter and Grahn, 2002, reinforces how pedagogical learning in nature has a positive effect on children's concentration, general health and well-being. Through playing outdoors for longer periods, children's self-confidence and risk-taking is enhanced, which reduces accidents and anxieties (Ejbye-Ernst, 2014). The idea of taking a daily hike or in the woods so children can experience plants and animals in context, and chat as they walk and appreciate peace and tranquillity is now commonplace. In relation to practice, Danish pedagogues today have a real appreciation of why the outdoors and the natural environment is valuable as a holistic, meaningful, respectful approach to learning for young children. As Jordet (2007, 2008) notes, Danish outdoor learning is progressive and experiential in nature. There is a recognition that learning is socially constructed and does not happen in a vacuum.

At the heart of this, a child-centred humanistic approach to learning and development has evolved, involving an appreciation of intra-actions. Murris (2016) describes this intra-active pedagogy as entangled relationships between the different languages and physicality of objects and the facilitation of children as agents, so they can make sense for themselves. From within, a relationship is formed between a child and their surrounding objects. According to Murris (2016), when a child selects a physical item to play with, the body and mind work together to decide which to choose. This decision is influenced by different interactions and pre-dispositions around them such as favourite objects, imagination, personal history with the item or the environment (Murris, 2016; Taguchi, 2010). Murris (2016) describes such internal engagements as something that takes place naturally and rather than being stimulated, simply needs to be acknowledged respectfully (by adults). This closely resembles Pestalozzi's ideas around head, heart and hand for educators and Froebel's philosophy of 'inner-connectedness' between feelings, thoughts and the action of doing, prompted by a child's initial perception or interest (Froebel, 1886, p.v)

> *Through play the mind grows by self-revelation. The child ascertains what he can do and discovers his possibilities of will by exerting his power spontaneously.*
>
> (Froebel, 1886, p.vii)

For Froebel, '*self-conquest is the only basis of true freedom*' (ibid.).

Early childhood education and care in Denmark

The early childhood education and care system in Denmark, like other Nordic countries, is based on a social pedagogical approach and is publicly funded by the Danish welfare state. With this comes high expectations around preventing social problems and providing care and learning opportunities for all children. Most Danish ECECs include crèche/nurseries and family day-care providers (0 to 3 years); kindergartens (3 to 6 years); and integrated centres (0 to 6 years) and are open Monday to Friday from 6:30am to 5pm. In Denmark 98 per cent of children from birth to 2.8 years attend nursery and from 2.8 years to age 5.8 kindergarten provision is available. On average 59 per cent of pedagogues have a degree in pedagogy, while the remaining 41 per cent as assistants have some pedagogical education. According to Winther-Lindqvist and Svinth (2018), pedagogical approaches vary, but children tend to spend three to four hours outside each day. Other than 30 minutes each day of adult-initiated activities, children are able to select what to play with themselves. While Ringsmose and Kragh-Müller (2017) provide a comprehensive overview of the distinctive underpinning features of the Danish/Nordic approach, overviews about ECE Danish pedagogy are rare and usually not available in English (Winther-Lindqvist and Svinth, 2018). What is clear is that the Danish ECEC tradition applies a social learning approach that emphasises play, relationships and outdoor life.

As Ringsmose and Kragh-Müller (2017) reinforce, Danish curriculum law stipulates the importance of local setting interpretation so an enabling environment and democracy is promoted. This is in stark contrast to the English Early Years Foundation Stage (DfE, 2017) which prioritises outcomes. From September 2018, the Ministry of Social Welfare in Denmark introduced a new educational curriculum or learning plan (*Pædagogiske læreplan*) for kindergartens, underpinned by the Daycare Acts 2004, 2007 and 2012 (Danish Ministry of Children and Social Affairs). All nurseries and kindergartens are required to use the *Pædagogiske læreplaner* (learning plan) to create a learning and development framework that responds carefully and sensitively to children's own interests, childhood communities and curiosity with a focus on play. In doing so pedagogues and management are required to be reflexive and appreciate the following as part of their work:

- Play
- A childhood, where being a child has value in itself

- Formation and childhood perspectives
- Learning
- *Børnefællesskaber* (children's communities)
- Educational learning environment
- *Forældresamarbejde* (parental co-operation)
- Children in exposed positions
- Coherence in transitions

Six curriculum themes are used for developing content and broad educational objectives as follows:

- All-round personal development
- Social competencies
- Communication and language
- Body, senses and movement
- Nature and natural phenomena (science)
- Culture, aesthetics and community

The curriculum recognises that learning occurs in all types of situations and is used to support pedagogues in offering children opportunities that provide the best conditions for learning and development. Ejbye-Ernst and Stokholm (2015) describe four important focus points or approaches that are important in the pedagogical work with young children particularly in relation to supporting the development of children's personal skills and nature and science skills. The pedagogue must:

- Support and create a rich language environment giving the children access to words and concepts to learn and talk about their observations and experiences
- Support children in looking carefully, seeing details, similarities and differences
- Support children in making their first categories, systems, constructions and models
- Support children in being curious, explore and experiment.

(Ejbye-Ernst and Stokholm, 2015)

The emphasis on children's learning in Denmark so it is in harmony with nature, clearly resonates with Froebel's ideas and his appreciation of self-activity as the coming together of intra-active thought and children making sense as agents for themselves through first-hand, play-based experiences (Ringsmose and Kragh-Müller, 2017). Children's views are valued by educators so they have time and freedom to make choices and connections.

The following two case studies are from conversations I had whilst visiting a private nature-kindergarten called Kalø Skov Børnehus (Forest Children's House) in the summer of 2018. Various insights are provided into every day outdoor experiences that demonstrate respect by pedagogues for young children based on democratic reciprocal relationships. In particular, the idea of 'walking behind, along, and in front of children's playing,' as identified by Ringsmose and Kragh-Müller (2017, p.106) is demonstrated. Various tensions and challenges are also shared.

CASE STUDY 1: WANDERING OFF

A 2-year-old boy is playing outside, absorbed in what he is doing. He stops and walks back to the kindergarten base. He picks up his packed lunch bag, then walks back past the pedagogue and out of the kindergarten area across the fields. A little later, the pedagogue notices he is missing. When the child is located, he is asked why he wandered off. The child explains how he thought it would be nice to have his lunch with his Grandma. The pedagogue reminds him of the (invisible) boundary / line and how he needs to remember to speak with a pedagogue if he wants to go away from the kindergarten base. At the end of the day, the event is shared with the boy's parents, so they are aware of the need to remind him to talk to pedagogues the next time he wants to go beyond the boundary.

CASE STUDY 2: AFTER THE RAIN

After a long spell of dry and sunny weather, there had been thunderstorms and rain through the night and into the following morning. A group of 3-year-olds were outside the kindergarten playing. One child is exploring the trails of water left after the rain. To begin with, he stands watching the water trickle downwards, then he crouches down, squatting and observing more closely. He tries to stop the flow of the water with his hand, but to no avail. He tries using both hands to push the water up the bank; no joy. He creates a barrier with the whole of his arm in an attempt to slow the flow of the water and then he lies down using his body. He is covered in mud, sand and water. Another child (who loves water) has been watching. Next to them is a large tub which is full of rain water. The standing (second) child picks up a bucket and scoops it into the tub of water. He throws it to the ground, adding to the trail of water. The first child looks up and back down, then he stands and gets some water for himself and adds it to the stream of water. After a few attempts of throwing the water to the ground, both boys' attention is turned to throwing water. It becomes a competition of who can throw the water the furthest and then at each other!

A CONVERSATION BETWEEN MYSELF AND THE OUTDOOR-NATURE LEADER MICHAEL JØRGENSEN AT KALØ SKOV BØRNEHUS (KALØ FOREST CHILDREN'S HOUSE)

Headings are prompts for discussion.

Understandings of outdoor-nature pedagogy learning

'It's the way we use the forest and nature that's important. . . It's how to be together with other children so they know themselves, what interests them so they learn how to react. We walk together. It's a special concept of being together in the forest. It's seeing and appreciating the value of the environment and providing children with space, natural noise, clean air and good conversations... and some learning is important. It's about how and why... involving a respectful relationship'.

The role of the pedagogue

'The pedagogue is seen / viewed as an "instructor" who "shares" "with" children and acts as a guide. How this happens is important. It's about a respectful relationship...

- in-front
- by the side
- behind

...When a pedagogue is in front, leading, they provide inspiration, an opening, something to ignite the children's curiosity. What matters is what's happening, how and why. The pedagogue sets the frame, inspires by listening and then responding. The pedagogue uses the Pædagogiske læreplaner (learning plan) which is being introduced in September 2018 to support children's learning and development by listening to them. It's difficult but it's the right thing. . . Pedagogues need to have knowledge but learning is a respectful relationship – learning together. The pedagogue listens to the child (which is difficult) so experiences can be created. There's more of a focus on reflection and self-awareness by pedagogues on what we are doing and why... Ideas and inspiration come from the seasons... We all go into the forest together and use it as inspiration for learning. if a child brings in a toy such as a doll, we look at how it enhances learning, such as family life... Using a knife too is often used which involves sharing the rules before using, but if a child cuts their finger, they learn for next time. The children thrive when they go into school.

It's based on Kaplan's theory and focused attention / spontaneous attention and the link with low stress and well-being' and Grahn's work on how learning in nature has a positive effect on children's concentration and well-being'.

Challenges

'In relation to school / pre-school tensions and preparing for school, there's a focus on defending the uniqueness of kindergartens. This is supported by the political shift focusing on play based learning, nature and science (see the new 2018 learning plan) and the work of Grahn which relates to the whole child'.

'We have more families from Turkey and France so it's important we explain why nature and the outdoors is important. Unfortunately refugee parents don't see forest school as safe. Being outdoors in the cold when it's wet is not part of their culture so we have some work to do building trust and relationships... Essentially there are no pressures from the government as play is supported and parents value nature learning. Having a private setting allows even more freedom'.

In addition, the following case study and conversation as part of my visit to Denmark is provided as a means of comparison. The forest kindergarten involved is Daycare Nord skovbørnehaven which can also be viewed using the following websites: www.daycarenord.dk/

'Kids gone wild' www.youtube.com/watch?v=Jkiij9dJfcw

It provides an insight into every day outdoor experience for one child and demonstrates the underpinning principles and qualities associated with Danish outdoor nature pedagogy as reinforced in the conversation with 'Johan' the leader of Daycare Nord skovbørnehaven.

THE WONDER OF 'STICK'

A child is outside with 'stick'. He came across 'stick' some time ago lying on the floor. Stick is longer than he is with a slight curve to it. He takes stick everywhere with him, when he's playing with his friends and when he's on his own. It has many uses including a mixing tool, a fishing rod, a prop for role play, a troll story, or for an obstacle course, a pole to hang a sign from, a magic wand, a tool to get something that is stuck with, a gate to say 'keep out' and perhaps most importantly, his companion. He talks to his stick as he walks. Stick can be anyone he wants it to be and anything. Stick listens. He is seeing how far stick can reach up a tree. First, he points using stick from an angle. Next, he moves his body closer and notes the increase in height. He stands on his tip-toes and touches a branch. He cheers with delight and attempts it again, this time jumping as he touches the tree with stick at a higher point.

A CONVERSATION WITH JOHAN, DAYCARE NORD'S LEADER ABOUT HIS INTERPRETATION OF OUTDOOR NATURE PEDAGOGY IN DENMARK

'You need to love nature as Niels Ejbye-Ernst says so children experience plants and animals in context in the woods. It's important to give children a real understanding of nature and to touch, feel, smell, see and taste, so they really appreciate the outdoors and value it as an embodied part of them.

There is a view about nature that focuses on not destroying nature which contradicts not touching ... but children need to touch and feel. So children need to be taught to respect plant and animal life.

We use the local area as an inspiration for learning / planning based around fjords, seasons, animals and plants. ... Having fun, playing and being with friends is important, so there needs to be choice for children and trust between the child and the pedagogue. It works both ways. But nature doesn't do it all; we need adults too. But we need to think about why going outdoors matters. Resilience and risk taking are important and children evaluating risks for themselves so they can think for themselves and be resilient and develop a sense of self-identity. If something breaks or goes wrong, it's ok, can think what could I do differently so I learn for next time. It's the same if a child uses a knife and cuts themselves; they learn from it'.

'We co-work with parents in a respectful way. Pedagogues use a coaching approach so rather than telling parents, it's about seeing and appreciating from the child's perspective, so parents answer their own questions.'

'Everyone has to go home happy from kindergarten'.

Theoretical underpinnings

'Our working bible is Patrick Grahn on being outdoors and focused attention / spontaneous attention and the link with low stress and a healthy life balance. Children who are outdoors in the forest are 60% less stressed and at peace compared to normal kindergarten.

Niels Ejbye-Ernst is also an inspiration – a scientist who provided thinking around why the outdoors matters and the ideas of a "Walking Kindergarten", involving a daily hike in the woods as part of the daily curriculum so children experienced plants and animals in context in the woods and as walk, talk / communicate. . .The best resources to include are a stick, water and mud'.

Thoughts on using IT to support nature learning

'There is a camera in a bird box outside in the forest area which is connected to the large screen back in the kindergarten base. This enables children to can watch and observe carefully together how the nest is built, how

the chaffinches / black birds watch over the eggs, how the eggs hatch and how the birds feed the baby birds until they are able to fly and fend for themselves. It's slow learning so the technology is good for tracing the daily changes and capturing intricate parts of the life cycle.'

'With IT, it's important children can use it in the right way; to support group learning, taking turns and listening to one another. Looking at ways to use iPads other than individually or just as a screen is important'.

Johan and the pedagogues identify the following key principles, qualities and experiences as important for underpinning the practice at Daycare Nord. They closely reflect the underpinning philosophies of Pestalozzi and Froebel.

Key principles: Passion
Risk
Freedom
Autonomy / own voice
Respectful relationships
Trust
Embodied
Making connections
Sense of self / identity
Self activity
Partnership with parents (child, family, society and kindergarten)

Pedagogue qualities: Self-awareness
Reflexivity / questioning self
Knowing yourself
Passion for nature
Knowledgeable about nature
Able to listen and respond to children
Respectful
Reflective Practice

Children's experience: Self-activity
Autonomy
Freedom
Sense of self
Knowing self
Having a voice
Responsibility
Risk-taking
Respectful / consideration for others / tolerance
Appreciation of nature and animals

Having visited different nature kindergartens in Denmark, I was keen to meet up with Jane Williams-Siegfredsen (author of '*Understanding the Danish Forest School Approach*') to discuss her understanding of Danish nature pedagogy in comparison to English interpretations. The following conversation took place in the Summer of 2018.

REFLECTIONS BY JANE WILLIAMS-SIEGFREDSEN, INFO@INSIDEOUTNATURE.COM.

Comparisons of forest pedagogy in England and Denmark

'You know the story... we came to Denmark, loved it and brought the idea back to England. I have been in Denmark ever since. We called it 'forest school' but it has been mis-interpreted. You don't need a forest and it's not just about school. Over the last 20 years there have been many changes – not always for the best ... in terms of depth of understanding why, and making connections with underpinning theory... and philosophy. It's different in England; it's changed, which bothers me. The concept of forest school in England has moved away from nature. The level training that is now offered has given it a very narrow output focus resulting in ticking boxes. There's more to offer with outdoors than outputs such as children's imagination and creativity.

Today, in most places, educators have passion... but they're younger and have less experience of life and less experience to draw on. It's a generation that have less experience of risk taking, thinking for themselves, making mistakes. There's a culture of snowflake children and everything is done for them. They're often not able to deal with daily issues or problems. They can't take criticism or deal with challenges. Children today aren't able to be independent, take responsibility or make decisions on their own. It's a different world ... a media one. The pressures and desires are about immediate expectations.

The wonder of nature goes deep... it's a passion. In Denmark, there's trust. It's a cultural thing. Pedagogues step back and trust. In England, it's always "activity" based. The stepping back is missing. There's an obsession with measuring which makes it difficult to step back. As an HMI once said "I've never seen any child grow taller from being measured". It's come from industry – and the focus on output. From the input, the output is decided. The Greek word pedagogue, originated from the Greek word pedagogy "paidagogos", comprising of two parts: "paidos" (child) and "agogos" (leader). Originally in ancient Greek times, the pedagogue accompanied the boy (child) to and from school, rather than teaching him. The pedagogue talked about everything else other than direct teaching. It's a respectful open, relationship'.

Ways forward

'Outdoor educators need an understanding of Froebel's philosophy about nature and outdoor learning so there's an understanding of why it's so

important... but, it's more than academic. It needs to be tacit knowledge too, so they "feel" it. It's good to question "why" and be more reflective ... so there's a deeper understanding. People hide behind health and safety and say they couldn't possibly use different tools deemed to be dangerous or include suggested approaches that involve risk ... such as children climbing, being independent, cooking or whittling'.

'We live in different times. In Denmark, outdoor nature is cultural and valued. In England there are planned activities with measurable outcomes. When I'm asked for a lesson plan or activity plan I say "I'll give it to you after I've done it". In England educators tend to like the security of an activity plan'.

'You can't compare one with the other. It's important to have realistic expectations and take small steps to appreciating and using nature. Educators need to feel comfortable and good about what they are doing with an understanding of why – so they are able to take the next small step. They need to feel secure and safe in their own context ... and know what is right for them. It's good to highlight and help educators see what they've achieved. Memory is an emotional thing and impacts on making it sustainable. It's small steps'.

POINTS FOR REFLECTION

- What are your views on any aspect of the case studies or conversations? Are there any aspects that resonate strongly with your own understanding of outdoor-nature learning?
- What would your response to any aspect of the case studies / conversations be?
- Can you provide your reasons? Where do think your views come from?
- How does your view support children's autonomy, self-activity and choice-making?

While Froebel's emphasis on children learning in harmony with nature, resonate strongly with the Danish notion of outdoor-nature pedagogy (Ringsmose and Kragh-Müller, 2017), interpretations in other counties (such as forest school in England) differ because of contextual economic, political and cultural influences. These effects are discussed next.

Forest school interpretations in England

The notion of learning outdoors is not a new concept in the UK. In the early twentieth century, Rachel and Margaret McMillan founded open-air nurseries in England that influenced early years education for young children in Deptford,

London, so they had access to both indoor and outdoor learning, which included nutritious meals, sleeping outdoors and first-hand experiences so they could explore and make connections for themselves (Giardiello, 2014; Liebovich, 2014).

In the mid-1990s, 'Forest School' practice was introduced to the UK, based on the Danish model, by staff from Bridgewater College (involving Jane Williams-Siegfredsen, as shared previously), having visited Denmark in 1993 as part of an exchange visit. Since then hundreds of forest school leaders have been trained by various validating organisations across Britain using a 'level' / skills-based method. At the heart of the forest school approach in England is 'treating children with respect and viewing them as naturally competent and curious' so they can collaborate, negotiate and make decisions about the experiences they pursue (Maynard, 2007, p.328). As Constable (2014, p.4) implies 'Forest School is actually a return to a form of nursery care that was widespread in the UK early in the twentieth century'. However, Leather (2016) argues that Danish forest school pedagogy is a social construction which educators in England do not always fully appreciate or understand the cultural or theoretical underpinnings of. Maynard (2007) notes that while there are commonalities between the underpinning principles of Bridgewater College and Danish forest school, there are differences in how the core principles are 'interpreted and implemented' (p.328) as part of the numerous forest schools being established across Britain. While being outdoor offers opportunities for encouraging risk taking in natural outdoor areas that are likely to have a positive impact of self-confidence and strengthen positive dispositions to learning, there is a concern with the over-management of children's play and the tight structure around content-focused goals. To some extent, the institutionalised levelled training of educators in English interpretations of forest school has exacerbated the issue around a lack of understandings of theoretical, pedagogical and cultural underpinnings as a social construction (Leather, 2016) and makes it unfair to compare the two interpretations. In Denmark, the Government promotes play (*Pædagogiske læreplaner*, 2018) which is supported by parents who are supportive of outdoor risk as central to learning. Such a 'top-down' 'bottom-up' supportive model makes it easy and natural to foster children's 'self-activity' compared to England where political pressures and economic-marketing priorities focus on a constant measuring of outcomes.

In England it is often the case that young children do not go outdoors in extreme weather conditions (Leather, 2016) and Health and Safety regulations (DfE, 2017) can hinder risk-taking outdoor pedagogical opportunities that children in Denmark experience, such as lighting fires, setting up camps and using real life tools such as knives. Rather than being valued as opportunities for developing independence, confidence, making connections and collaboration, they are often perceived as 'dangerous'. Requirements for risk assessments, close supervision and concerns over litigation can hinder such spontaneous playful learning (Elliot, 2015; Gill, 2007; Leather, 2016). The additional pressures around achieving outcomes (DfE, 2017) and demonstrating progress (Moss, 2017) can result in adult-planned activities with very little 'self-activity' where children are 'free, to think, to take action for themselves' (Froebel, cited in Lilley, 1967, p.41) in a participatory, democratic way.

Generally, a forest school in England is identified as including the following (Austin, Knowles and Sayers, 2013; Austin, Knowles and Sayers, 2017; Knight, 2013; O'Brien 2009; Turtle et al., 2015).

1. Forest School is a long-term approach, where children access a Forest School in regular sessions.
2. Forest School must take place within a wooded environment or natural area (separate from the normal playground – Harris, 2017) for children to become closer to nature.
3. Forest School promotes holistic development, whilst encouraging children to become confident and independent learners.
4. Forest School encourages children to assess, evaluate and take risks in a supportive and safe environment.
5. Forest Schools are run by qualified professionals who are able to assess situations, plan appropriately, observe each child's progress and reflect when necessary.
6. Forest School focuses on the children's learning ability to create positive learning and development for the children and wider community.

Most recently the policy by the Government entitled 'A Green Future: Our 25 Year Plan to Improve the Environment' (2017) indicates an awareness of the need to 'connect people with the environment to improve health and wellbeing' (p.24). In doing so there is a recognition of the need to 'encourage children to be close to nature, in and out of school' (p.24) and 'to make 2019 a year of action for the environment'. The forest school approach is acknowledged as 'encouraging children to explore nature and have a relationship with the outdoors' (p.24). In addition, playing and learning outside is identified as 'a fundamental part of childhood', which 'helps children grow up healthy' (and have) 'a beneficial impact on children's physical and mental health' (p.75).

However, while actions include 'developing a Nature Friendly Schools programme' for schools in the most disadvantaged areas from autumn 2018, this is only noted in relation to older primary-aged children, and is only mentioned as part of science and geography fieldwork. This is far removed from the embodied, holistic approach associated with Danish pedagogy.

As already noted by Tovey (2017), an awareness and appreciation of the underpinning values and asking '*how*' and '*why*' is essential. Leather (2016) suggests that professionals in England lack an awareness of the philosophy or principles underpinning Forest School and an understanding of why the pedagogy of play and nature is relevant. Instead, forest school leaders are required to obtain specific qualifications in order to be in charge of a forest school. Such a skills-based approach would only seem to increase the focus on measuring outcomes and knowledge as part of adult planned activities.

While O'Brien (2009) advocates forest school as child-directed, with children accessing free play opportunities whilst the adults work alongside children or stand back and observe, Leather (2016) found that UK forest school leaders often struggled to stand back and not interfere, therefore making the practice less child-led. Additionally, while forest school play (in Denmark) involves an equal relationship between the adult and the child, and a promotion of children's democratic participation in decision-making, this can be a challenge for many educators in England. Elliott (2015) and Leather (2016) say this is because of a lack of awareness around underpinning pedagogy and general questioning of why different approaches are appropriate in a context of institutional pressures of raising standards and evidencing outcomes.

An English forest school case study

The following case study offers insight into one setting's interpretation of forest school. It involves a small urban primary school situated in a busy built up part of a city in the North West of England. The forest school is set within an enclosed area of the school building surrounded by a high wooden fence and is only accessible through the school. The outdoor space consists of some bushes, a tree, flowerbeds and vegetable 'patches'. The ground is concrete with a mixture of soil and woodchip. Children participate in play-based activities with specific aims in relation to sustainability, socialisation and overall behaviour. The Forest School Leader notes:

> *it is not a proper forest school, because the children don't do proper forest school activities, like lighting fires and working with real tools. They're not dressed appropriately for the cold and wet weather so they need to sit in the 'learning shed' to stay warm… In fact, the sessions are cancelled if the weather is bad.*

ENGLISH FOREST SCHOOL CASE STUDY

The Forest School Leader explains that the children use the outdoor environment for activities to support their different learning stages. Children aged three to four are scheduled for a weekly 20-minute space of time. On entering the forest school, the children are led to a small round wooden table, with wooden stools. This is the meeting place where the children sit and greet each other. There is a white stone in the middle of the table, known as the 'chatting stone', which the children take turns to hold when they are talking about their thoughts and feelings.

The forest school includes a 'mud kitchen' which includes pots and pans and various sized spoons and utensils for digging and filling. There is also a large wooden pallet and several colourful chairs which can be moved and rearranged by the children if they choose to as part of their imaginative play. It is currently 'a bus'. Beside the 'bus' is a 'fire pit' (although no real fires are lit due to health and safety in such a small space). Instead, children use the area to sing songs and tell stories as part of adult-planned activities. Next to this is a low-level flower bed containing plants, shrubs with weeds growing in between. The children are required to tend to the flowerbed and care for the plants following explicit directions. There is a 'musical wall' next to this, with brightly coloured metal and wooden objects for 'making music'. Beside this are an assortment of tires and logs, which the children can use to challenge their building abilities and critical thinking skills. For example, they can work together to use the logs and tyres to get from one side of the path the other without touching the ground. Across from this is 'the den', an area set up by adults using camouflage material attached to a tree for shelter, and a wooden pallet as a base. The space for the den is open, so children can use their imaginations to create any scenario (but it is empty).

Around the tree, adults have placed bird feeders, and bird and bee houses to encourage natural habitats and opportunities for children to care for insects and animals. Opposite this, there are several tyres stacked up to represent a vegetable patch. Each tyre includes something different growing within which the children have planted, such as potatoes, tomatoes, carrots, peas and daffodils. The use of tyres is designed to encourage a positive attitude in children's attitudes towards recycling and creativity and caring for the plants as they water them daily. A water dispenser is positioned so children can access water for different tasks. Most recently, children have made a worm farm so they can observe how worms live in their natural environment. They have also made their own scarecrows and planted flowers that will attract bugs such as ladybirds, bees and butterflies. The final aspect of the forest school area is the 'learning shed', where children can go when it's raining. Inside there are small wooden stools positioned around a table, with a heater and cushions 'to make it cosy'. But, the shed is mainly used to support literacy skills after the 20 minutes of forest school.

The forest school leader states several times that the setting is not a 'proper' forest school setting, despite the school, staff and children referring to it as such. The leader explains how the forest school is used mainly as an intervention aimed at supporting children with behavioural issues or learning needs (but not in the early years).

While children are encouraged to work together when planting, take turns and to be patient with each other, the different elements of adult-planned play offer little choice for children and no free play. This leader's perception supports Leather 's (2016) view that due to the institutionalisation of forest school, practice is adult-planned and structured in relation to specific learning intentions. Just because it is called a forest school and is outdoors does not mean it is a forest school. An awareness and appreciation of the underpinning values is critical.

(Written by Ellen Morgan, MA student)

ENGLISH FOREST SCHOOL CASE STUDY 2

This case study demonstrates the daily pressure of accountability and predetermined Early Years Foundation Stage (EYFS) outcomes and content and the impact on developing a personal philosophy based around responding to and facilitating children's self-activity and intra-actions.

'Today I gathered the morning's Forest School group together to talk about the birds we could hear in the trees. I asked the group of 3 and 4 year olds to close their eyes for a moment and just listen. I asked them what they could hear, and most of the group responded telling me it was the birds up in the trees above us. I then thought I would use the opportunity to talk about what the birds like to eat and where they live, hoping to cover some of the EYFS (For example Understanding the World - 30–50 months 'Shows care and concern for living things and the environment'). While discussing possibly making bird feeders in next week's session, one boy interrupted me and said: "Can we go play now?" followed by him stating to his two friends sat opposite him in the circle: "Let's go play hide-and-seek over there again!" For a moment, I was a little frustrated that my environmentally-based adult-input had been interrupted and cut short, then I quickly remembered the child-led Forest School ethos I had learnt about in my training. I invited the children to go play and enjoy whatever they wanted to go and do for the rest of the session. The boys enjoyed their game of hide-and-seek, other children enjoyed digging and finding worms, and one little girl enjoyed independently climbing a fallen down tree.

We have become so bogged down with planning activities, showing structure and "next steps" that I had forgotten to let the children just be children and play and explore for themselves. I sometimes feel the need for adult input and interaction to the get the most out of the sessions for the children, but sometimes the interaction could actually just be interfering'.

(Reflective diary entry, 18 April, 2018).
Provided by Fern Brooks, Forest School Leader

Conclusion

In Denmark, outdoor pedagogy is very much valued as a fundamental part of learning and life. Pedagogues acknowledge the underpinning philosophy and related theory which in turn is then supported by the *Pædagogiske læreplaner* (2018).

Forest school in England is regarded in principle as a holistic and child-centred approach (Schiro, 2013). The reality, however, tends to result in allowing short time frames for accessing forest school with it often being an additional aspect to the day rather than integrated as part of an underpinning philosophy or mission (Waite et al., 2016). In England forest school tends to be associated with short-term politics, increased standardisation, a narrowing curriculum, pre-determined outcomes and test-based accountability. This has resulted in a low-risk approach with less emphasis on self-activity and play. With such a top-down directed approach, understanding why and valuing an underpinning personal philosophy is superfluous (Dillon and Dickie, 2012; O'Brien, 2009; Waite et al. 2016; Williams-Siegfredsen, 2017).

While the philosophy of Froebel shares similarities with the origins of forest school in Denmark, there are clear differences with forest school interpretations in England (Maynard, 2007; Waite et al., 2016). Bieber and Martens (2011) describe it as comparing apples and pears. The intra-active pedagogy (or self-activity that Froebel referred to) in the context of outdoor nature pedagogy needs to begin with facilitating the child's intra-active agency. Educators embracing a reflexive approach to challenge these views is needed, so children can benefit from intra-actions and self-activity inspired by nature-outdoor learning. While forest schools in England remains popular in the main, it is different to Danish nature-outdoor pedagogy mainly because it operates within the restrictions of an outcomes model of education (Moss, 2013).

Some of the differences between Danish outdoor nature pedagogy and other forms (or 'constructs') of outdoor learning (such as English forest schools) are caused by divergences between (and point of departure in) the Anglo-American curriculum tradition versus the Nordic tradition (Gundem and Hopmann, 1998; Westbury, 2000): a 'social pedagogical approach' versus an 'early education approach' (OECD, 2006), or *friluftsliv* (open air life) versus outdoor education (Henderson and Vikander, 2007).

As Jane Williams-Siegfredsen noted earlier as part of a case study conversation:

> *You can't compare one with the other. It's important to have realistic expectations and take small steps to appreciating and using nature. Educators need to feel comfortable and good about what they are doing with an understanding of why – so they are able to take the next small step.*

As Ringsmose and Kragh-Müller (2017, p.185) conclude, and indeed as do I, the first step requires an open perception and a commitment to respecting children as human beings.

POINTS FOR REFLECTION

- What are the key principles that influence how you view children and your practice with children and families?
- Where do your ideas and views come from?
- Can you make any connections with Froebel's philosophy and principles or perhaps a different theory that helps you to look differently at outdoor practice at your setting?

References

Austin, C., Knowles, Z. and Sayers, J. (2013) 'Investigating the effectiveness of Forest School sessions on children's physical activity levels', The Mercy Forest and Physical Activity Exchange at Liverpool John Moores University.

Beatty, B. (2017) 'John Dewey's high hopes for play: Democracy and education and progressive era controversies over play in kindergarten and preschool education', *The Journal of the Gilded Age and Progressive Era*, 16(4), p.424–443. DOI: doi:10.1017/S1537781417000317.

Bieber, T. and Martens, K. (2011) 'The OECD PISA study as a soft power in education? Lessons from Switzerland and the US', *European Journal of Education*, 46(1), p.101–116.

Chawla, L. and Cushing, D.F. (2007) 'Education for strategic environmental behavior', *Environmental Education Research*, 13(4), p.437–452.

Constable, K. (2014) *Bringing the Forest School Approach to your early years practice*, Oxon: Routledge.

HM Government (2017) *A green future: Our 25 year plan to improve the environment.* Available from: www.gov.uk/government/publications.

Danish Ministry of Children and Social Affairs (2018) *The strengthened educational curriculum* (1 July 2018). Available from: https://socialministeriet.dk/arbejdsomraader/dagtilbud/paedagogiske-redskaber-og-rammer/den-styrkede-paedagogiske-laereplan/.

Danish Ministry of Family and Consumer Affairs (2007) *Law 501. Day Care Act: Act on day care, after-school and club facilities in children and adolescents*, København: Ministry of Family and Consumer Affairs (in Danish).

Danish Ministry of Social Affairs (2004) *Day Care Facilities Act, Social service order 708.* Copenhagen: Socialministeriet.

Danish Ministry of Social Affairs and Integration (2012) *Day-care, after-school and club facilities.* Available from: http://english.sm.dk/social-issues/children-and-youth/daycarefacilities/Sider/Start.aspx.

Department for Education (DfE) (2017) *Statutory framework for the early years foundation stage setting the standards for learning, development and care for children from birth to five.* Crown copyright.

Dillon, J. and Dickie, I. (2012) *Learning in the natural environment: Review of social and economic benefits and barriers*, [online] Natural England Commissioned Reports. Available from: http://publications.naturalengland.org.uk/publication/1321181 Accessed 14/05/2018.

Dowdell, K., Gray, T. and Malone, K. (2011) 'Nature and its influence on children's outdoor play', *Australian Journal of Outdoor Education*, 15(2), p.24–35.

Ejbye-Ernst, N. (2014) *God Praksis? Pedagogersformidling af nature for børn (Good practice? Pedagogues promotion of nature for children)*, Copenhagan: Frilufts Rådet.

Ejbye-Ernst, N. and Stokholm, D. (2015) *Natur og udeliv – uderummet i pædagogisk praksis*, Systime: Aarhus.

Elliot, H. (2015) 'Forest School in an inner city? Making the impossible possible', *Education 3–13*, 43(6), p.722–730.

Froebel, F. (1886) *Autobiography of Friedrich Froebel*, (E. Michealis and H.K. Moore Trans.) London: Swan Sonnenschein.

Froebel, F. (1885) *The education of man* (1986 Reprint), Bath: Cedric Chivers.

Giardiello, P. (2014) *Pioneers in early childhood education*, Abingdon: Routledge.

Gill, T. (2007) *No fear: Growing up in a risk averse society*, London: Caloustie.

Grahn, P., Martensson, F., Lindblad, B., Nilsson, P. and Ekman, A. (1997) 'Ute Pa Dagis (Outside in the day nursery)', *Stad & Land*, 45. Alnarp: Movium, Sveriges Lantbruksuniversitet.

Gundem, B.B. and Hopmann, S. (Eds.) (1998). *Didaktik and/or curriculum: An international dialog*, New York: Peter Lang Publishing, Inc.

Harris, F. (2017) 'Outdoor learning spaces: The case of Forest School', *Area*, 50(2), p.222–231. DOI: doi:10.1111/area.12360.

Henderson, B. and Vikander, N. (Eds.) (2007) *Nature first: Outdoor life the Friluftsliv way*, Ontario: Natural Heritage Books.

Jordet, A.N. (2008) 'Outdoor schooling in Norway – research and experiences', Conference proceedings, Healthier, Wiser and Happier Children. Outdoor Education – Learning with Mind, Heart and Body. Conference at Branbjerg University College, Jelling, 24–25 January 2008.

Jordet, A.N. (2007) *Nærmiljøet som klasserom. En undersøkelse om uteskolens didaktikk i et danningsteoretisk og erfaringspedagogisk perspektiv* [*The nearby environment as classroom*; in Norwegian with English summary]. Doctoral Dissertation. No 80. Oslo: University of Oslo.

Kaplan, R. and Kaplan, S. (1989) *The experience of nature*, Cambridge: Cambridge University Press.

Knight, S. (2013) *International perspectives on Forest School: Natural spaces to play and learn*, London: SAGE.

Leather, M. (2016) 'A critique of Forest School: Something lost in translation', *Journal of Outdoor and Environmental Education*, 21(1), p.5–18.

Liebovich, B. (2014) 'Margaret and Rachel McMillan: Their influences on open-air nursery education and early years teacher education', *FORUM*, 56(3), 529–539.

Liebschner, J. (1992) *A child's work: Freedom and guidance in Froebel's educational theory and practice*, Cambridge: Lutterworth.

Lilley, I. (1967) *Friedrich Froebel: A selection from his writings*, Cambridge: Cambridge University Press.

Louv, R. (2005) *Last child in the woods*, New York: Algonquin Books.

Maynard, T. (2007) 'Forest Schools in Great Britain: An initial exploration', *Contemporary Issues in Early Childhood*, 8(4), p.320–330. DOI: doi:10.2304/ciec.2007.8.4.320.

McDowall-Clark, R. (2017) *Exploring the contexts for early learning: Challenging the school readiness agenda*, Oxon: Routledge.

Mental Health Foundation (2005) *Up and running: How exercise can help beat depression*, London Mental Health Foundation.

Moss, P. (2017) 'Power and resistance in early childhood education: From dominant discourse to democratic experimentalism', *Journal of Pedagogy*, 8(1), p.11–32. DOI: doi:10.1515/jped-2017–0001.

Moss, P. (2013) *Early childhood and compulsory education: Reconceptualising the relationship*, London: Routledge.

Moss, P. (2010) 'We cannot continue as we are: The educator in an education for survival', *Contemporary Issues in Early Childhood*, 11(1): p.8–19.

Murris, K. (2016) *The posthuman child: Educational transformation through philosophy with picturebooks*, London andNew York: Routledge.

O'Brien, L. (2009) 'Learning outdoors: The Forest School approach', *Education 3–13*, 37(1), p.45–60.

Organization for Economic Co-operation and Development (OECD) (2018) *Programme for International Student Assessment (PISA) (OECD)*. Retrieved 14 March 2018 from: www.oecd.org/pisa/.

Organisation for Economic Co-operation and Development (OECD) (2006) *Starting strong II. Early childhood education and care*, OECD Publishing.

Ringsmose, C. and Kragh-Müller, C. (Eds.) (2017) *Nordic social pedagogical approach to early years*, Cham, Switzerland: Springer.

Schiro, M. (2013) *Curriculum theory: Conflicting visions and enduring concerns*, (2nd edn.) Thousand Oaks, CA: SAGE Publications.

Soëtard, M. (1994) 'Johann Heinrich Pestalozzi (1746–1827)', *Prospects: The Quarterly Review of Comparative Education*, 24(1), Paris:UNESCO, International Bureau of Education, p.297–310.

Stigsdotter, U. and Grahn, P. (2002) 'What makes a garden a healing garden?' *Journal of Therapeutic Horticulture, p.* 60–69. *Retrieved*13 June 2018 *from*:http://carstenoerting.dk/wp-content/uploads/2015/09/What_makes_a_garden_a_healing_garden_Stigsdotter_U__Grahn_P.pdf.

Taguchi, H.L. (2010) *Going beyond the theory/practice divide in early childhood education: Introducing an intra-active pedagogy*, Oxon/New York: Routledge.

Tennessen, C.M. and Cimprich, B. (1996) 'Views to nature: Effects on attention', *Journal of Environmental Psychology*, (15), p.77–85.

Tovey, H. (2017) *Bringing the Froebel approach to your early years practice*, Oxon: Routledge.

Turtle, C., Convery, I. and Convery, K. (2015) 'Forest schools and environmental attitudes: A case study of children aged 8–11 years', *Cogent Education*, 2, p.1–14.

Waite, S.Bøllingb, M. and Bentsenc, P. (2016) 'Comparing apples and pears? A conceptual framework for understanding forms of outdoor learning through comparison of English Forest Schools and Danish udeskole', *Environmental Education Research*, 22(6), p.868–892.

Western, P. (2000) *Friedrich Froebel: His life, times and significance*, (2nd edn.) London: Roehampton Institute.

Westbury, I. (2000) 'Teaching as a reflective practice: What might didaktik teach curriculum', in: I. Westbury, S. Hopmann and K. Riquarts (Eds.) *Teaching as a reflective practice. The German didaktik tradition*, Mahwah, NJ: Lawrance Erlbaum Associates, Publishers, p.15–39.

Whinnett, J. (2012) 'Gifts and occupations: Froebel's gifts (wooden block play) and occupations (construction of workshop experiences) today', in: Bruce, T. (Ed.) *Early education practice: Froebel today*, London: SAGE.

Williams-Siegfredsen, J. (2017) *Understanding the Danish Forest School Approach early years education in practice*, Oxon: Routledge.

Winther-Lindqvist, D.A. and Svinth, L. (2017) 'Early Childhood Education and Care (ECEC)', in: *Denmark Oxford bibliography*. Retrieved 13 September 2018 from: www.oxfordbibliographies.com/view/document/obo-9780199756810/obo-9780199756810-0093.xml#obo-9780199756810-0093-bibItem-0006. DOI: doi:10.1093/OBO/9780199756810–0093.

PART 3

A way forward

With a conscious mindfulness of wider issues, we emphasise the need for a shrewder awareness about power inequalities, and an increased focus on values as part of an ongoing reflexive process so professional inquiry can inform our daily practice and challenge the top-down approach associated with government policy.

9

WIDER ISSUES IN EARLY CHILDHOOD EDUCATION

Patricia Giardiello and Tarja Karlsson Häikiö

In this chapter we discuss wider issues affecting childhood and education in the twenty-first century (in particular England, Finland and Sweden) which is characterised by an increasingly globalised, but also more unstable, world economy and recurring financial crises. For example, the beginning of 2008 saw the onset of one of the world's worst financial crises in modern capitalist history (Reinhart and Rogoff, 2011). Because of this economic downturn, the gap between rich and poor families has widened in an alarming number of industrialised countries. For many of these children, place of birth determines their rights and opportunities in life (UNICEF, 2014).

This chapter focuses on four key aspects of wider contemporary issues that have impacted on global childhoods (as identified by UNICEF, 2016b). These are: children's health and well-being, child poverty, English as an Additional Language (EAL) inclusion of migrants and intercultural perspectives. Case studies are used to provide different insights and lenses. In doing so the reader will be invited to consider new ways of seeing and considering alternative possibilities within an ethical framework.

Health and well-being

> The true measure of a nation's standing is how well it attends to its children – their health and safety, their material security, their education and socialization, and their sense of being loved, valued, and included in the families and societies into which they are born.
>
> *(UNICEF, 2007, p. 1).*

It is clear from this message that societies should be judged on how they treat their youngest citizens, and from a UK perspective the health of infants, children and young people has improved dramatically over the last 30 years. The relationship between health and well-being appears to have two-way causality, meaning good health improves well-being and good well-being improves health (De Neve et al., 2013). Many children will lead happy and healthy lives, but the future health and happiness of a significant and growing number of children is under threat. The UK's recent austerity programme with cuts in services, such as Sure Start Children's Centres, has disproportionality affected children and child health and well-being has deteriorated with unprecedented increases in child poverty (ibid.). The Department for Education figures (DfE, 2016) reveal that children's centres have had funding cut from £1.2bn to an estimated £0.6bn over the last six years. Unlike nurseries, where parents leave their children in the care of others, children's centres provide activities, resources and support for disadvantaged families as well as their children. However, these services are now 'hollowed out' and are much more thinly spread, often no longer within 'pram-pushing distance' (Smith et al., 2018, p. 4). We know that promoting positive well-being for children is vital in determining children and young people's life satisfaction and life chances. Early childhood educators will not have failed to notice the increased attention health and mental well-being is receiving, not only in the media but also in research. For example, research conducted by the Children's Society (2017) shows that a significant minority of children in the UK have low levels of well-being, which they argue has the devastating potential to have a severe impact on their childhood and life chances, as well as on the families and communities around them. The research findings identified six priorities that promote positive well-being:

1. the right conditions to learn and develop;
2. a positive view of themselves and an identity that is respected;
3. having enough of what matters;
4. positive relationships with family and friends;
5. a safe and suitable home environment and local area; and
6. opportunity to take part in positive activities to thrive.

The wealth of policy initiatives regarding children's health and well-being and the introduction of the Office for National Statistics (ONS) index of children's well-being (to be updated annually) demonstrate the depth and breadth of concern.

In comparison, the Ten Pillars of a Good Childhood (Organisers of the Decade of Childhood) (ACEI) (cited in Pulkkinen, 2012) are similar but there is an emphasis on nature and respecting children's rights. Pulkkinen (2012) reminds us that human beings are part of nature and that the sense of belonging to nature and its appreciation are strengthened in children and adults who can spend time in the natural environment. By comparison to England, Finnish (and Nordic) children typically begin their outdoor lives at a very early age, when they start to take daytime naps outdoors often in extremely cold sub-zero temperatures and protected by thermal insulted clothing (Tourula et al., 2011). Recurrent exercise in nature has been shown to increase children's emotional well-being and engaging in sufficient outdoor activities has been shown to have positive impacts including higher independent mobility, greater amounts of physical activity and lower prevalence of overweight (Rasi et al., 2017).

Back in 2010, in the UK, the Marmot review (p.6) called for a 'second revolution in the early years', to increase the proportion of overall expenditure allocated there. As was noted, the health and well-being of today's children depends on having the courage and imagination to rise to the challenge of doing things differently, to put sustainability and well-being before economic growth and bring about a more equal and fair society (ibid., p.29). Unsurprisingly, though, given current priorities, there is a neo-liberal quick fix approach in addressing young children's well-being, with its emphasis on human capital and future economic outcomes. This inevitably plays a central role in government policies that relate to well-being. From this, new initiatives such as 'mindfulness' are being operated as a remedy in many early years class rooms in England to rectify the damage of stress and anxiety generated by pressures around achievement and high stakes testing (Huppert and Johnson, 2010). As described in the *Mental Health Foundation Report* (2010, p.8), 'Mindfulness is a way of paying attention. It means consciously bringing awareness to our experience, in the present moment, without making judgements about it'. Although the mechanisms by which mindfulness exerts its effects on well-being are not yet fully understood, there is evidence that mindfulness enhances cognitive control (Tang et al., 2012), which is closely related to emotion regulation (Ochsner et al., 2002).

In considering young children's health and well-being there is strong anecdotal evidence from both the UK and USA of a rising number of children developing a negative disposition towards attending school from as young as 4 years of age (Nitecki and Wasmuth, 2017). Whitebread (2017) affirms that the increase in mental health conditions among children and young people is linked to the decline of free play and that changes in education policy have substantially restricted the amount of learning done through play and increased pressures on children at school, with very high levels of stress related to the narrowing of the curriculum and high stakes testing. As Roberts-Holmes (2015, p.302) indicates, 'the current narrowing of early years assessment, along with increased inspection and surveillance, operates as a policy technology leading to an intensification of "school readiness" pressures upon the earliest stage of education'. From an optimistic perspective, at the time of writing this, there is a new proposed Ofsted framework which identifies a shift in the rebalance of inspections so the focus is on 'what children learn through the curriculum, rather than over-reliance on performance data'. As the new draft Education framework (2019) notes:

> What children learn is too often coming second to the delivery of assessment information. The education inspection framework will put more emphasis on the quality of education and care. It will ensure that we consider children's experiences and how they are being developed, alongside assessments.

If this becomes a reality, the pressure could be eased for both children and educators so that it is less damaging on children's well-being (Ofsted, 2019).

In this era of accountability, early childhood educators need to critically reflect on how they will balance the pressure to prepare young children academically with their personal, social and emotional needs. Effective assessment in the early years cannot be carried out as a one-size-fits-all approach or as a scripted instructional process. The danger is that if tools used for accountability focus of a narrow set of skills, so will the curriculum planning and provision.

Despite recognition of the need to prioritise children's health and well-being in schools in England, the incumbent government's Green Paper on Mental Health: Failing a Generation (House of Commons, 9 May, 2018) has done little to allay concerns; it is not ambitious enough in terms of financial support and resources and there is also little or no attention to prevention or early intervention. Despite the government's recent recognition of the need to prioritise children's health and well-being in schools the National Children's Bureau (Wise Up, NCB online) is urging for a rebalancing of the education system that gives a greater prominence to children's well-being rather than a focusing on academic attainment. As is evident in Part 2 of this book, the focus on evidencing educational outcomes through burdensome data is beginning to infiltrate early childhood pedagogical practice across nations.

Adopting Bronfenbrenner's ecological systems theory (1979), children's lives are embedded within the larger systems of family, community and culture and their values and views are shaped by the worlds of others. According to Ellyatt (2018), no matter where they live in the world all humans have the same core needs as identified in Maslow's hierarchy (1962). This view is optimistic in the sense that knowledgeable educators, given a favourable set of circumstances and in consultation with the children, can change their environments for the better. A tool offered to educators to facilitate this is 'The Flourish Model' developed not only from Bronfenbrenner's ecological systems theory but is also aligned to the ideas of Maslow (1962) and Barret (2017). 'By better understanding and supporting the environments and systems that children and families are exposed to, the model aims to underpin a set of products, services and resources that will help communities to thrive' (Ellyatt, 2018, p.16). These include paying attention to the dispositions, beliefs, values and mindsets that create our individual maps of the worlds. They include security, relationship, independence, engagement, fulfilment, contribution and ongoing growth. In order for children to create their own individual map and be part of the decisions that shape their lives, they should be empowered to put forward their own agendas and be listened to in line with the UNCRC (1989). Children's experience of childhood as reported by them should be counted alongside adult indicators of positive well-being (Ben Ariah, 2008).

It is well documented that well-being is affected if children are poor (Bradshaw, 2015). Taking a child's right and welfare perspective as a starting point, this chapter now moves on to discuss the nature and extent of child poverty and explores the consequences on children's early education and care.

> . . .growing up in poverty can have a detrimental effect on children's long-term outcomes. For instance, there is a recognised link between growing up in poverty and the resulting impact on children's educational attainment, along with poorer physical health outcomes. However, growing up in poverty is still not widely recognised as a substantial risk for the development of mental health problems, which can be a particular problem for families already struggling to maintain the everyday costs of supporting their children.
>
> *(Ayre, 2016, p.6)*

Child poverty

Poverty is a persistent problem throughout the world and has damaging impacts on almost all aspects of family life and outcomes for children. It is associated with material need such as a lack of food, fuel, health care, adequate clothing and housing and lack of resource (usually financial) to meet some or all these needs (European Anti-Poverty Network, 2013). There are 2.2 billion children in the world, and around a half of this figure (1 billion) live in poverty (Global Issues, 2013).

Poverty is often perceived to be closely aligned with worklessness and dependency on the welfare state benefits, especially in developed countries, but more recently there are a considerable number of families who live in working poverty due to low incomes and cuts to welfare (Fraser, Gutiérrez and Pena-Casa, 2011). Child poverty in the UK has been rising since 2011 with 4.1 million children now living in poverty, a rise of 500,000 (15 per cent) in the last five years (JRF, 2018). This despite the UK being the first European country to systematically implement and evaluate policies aimed specifically at reducing child poverty (1999: Ending Child Poverty by 2020). In 1999, the then Prime Minister Tony Blair made a commitment to halve child poverty by 2010 and eliminate child poverty by 2020. After many years of being a neglected issue, child poverty was on the political agenda. In 2001 the Labour government set targets to reduce and eventually 'eradicate' child poverty, within 10–20 years. Though significant progress was made, the 2010 targets to halve child poverty were missed. The current UK government's Welfare Reform and Work Act (2016), repealed the Child Poverty Act (2010) and with it the target to eliminate child poverty by 2020. This new Act has removed the incumbent government's duty to end child poverty by 2020 and has changed the target for child poverty in the UK, moving away from a measure based on income to focusing on the 'root causes' of poverty such as unemployment and family breakdown. This has resulted in many families being caught in the middle of a series of moving currents: stuck in low-paid work, with little chance of progression, subject to high housing costs and using a weakening social security. It is these factors combined that are driving an unprecedented rising tide in poverty among working parents (JRF, 2018). In comparison Nordic countries (Denmark, Finland, Iceland, Norway and Sweden) have long traditions of social welfare policies and have lesser income inequalities than most other countries and high equality with respect to material, educational and health well-being (Raphael, 2011).

In the Nordic countries the growth of ECEC services started earlier and was due to a development in the labour market where women were part of the industrialisation and led to a vast expansion in the 1960s and 1970s (Karila, 2012; Salminen, 2017). This enhanced the possibilities for participation in the labour force for women, contributed to gender equality and social welfare (Sipilä, 1997), and established day care facilities. In the beginning of the 1990s, day care was guaranteed for all children under 3 years in Finland and Sweden, where particular emphasis was put on collaboration with parents since this enhances the child's development and well-being (Karila, 2012; Salminen, 2017). Today, care, development and learning will form a whole in the curriculums in the Nordic countries. Ideologically, there is historically a shared responsibility for care and education between preschool and parents, and at the same time, the preschool is also seen as an institution that will educate the parents in a social responsibility (Lunneblad, 2014, p.118).

Early childhood education and care in Nordic countries has proved to be a decisive factor for social and economic equality and for seeing preschool children as a resource for society (Heckman, 2011; Persson, 2014; UNICEF, 2009). However, research describes great differences between conditions and sees a division between a 'care and social oriented pre-school' and a 'knowledge-oriented and performance-oriented pre-school', often linked to housing, segregation and socio-economic differences (Sernhede and Tallberg Broman, 2014, p.10). In recent years, an increasingly strained economy in society has led to larger groups of children, which in turn increases the risk of social injustice (Salminen, 2017; Williams et al., 2015). In 2016, a decision was made by the Swedish government to reduce the size of the children's groups (SKOLFS, 2018, p.179) after a long time of financial cuts leading to exploitation of ECEC. The risk of increased social injustice and guarding of children's rights is thus a standing challenge.

There are a wide range of studies showing the extensive impact of poverty on all aspects of children's lives but there is no simple explanation for poverty and how it can be addressed due to its multifaceted nature. Notwithstanding, as discussions about increased poverty and widening inequality have re-emerged in the UK, so too has the dominance of an individualised discourse to explain poverty (Dermott and Pomati, 2016). For example, poverty and poor outcomes are related to several factors including parental education, family structure and neighbourhood. As Sheffield Morris et al. (2017, p.389) point out 'economically disadvantaged families experience environments characterised by chaos, lack of control, and high levels of stress'. However, a major barrier to education for poorer children lies in the culture of education itself. Problems are more likely to arise at school for poorer children not because their parents are less likely to be either well off financially or well educated themselves, but because the form of participation that is required of them at school does not closely match the one that is required of them at home and in their immediate surroundings. The promotion of parental involvement in schooling to increase academic success raises issues of equity, since rates of parental involvement are significantly higher among middle-and upper-class parents than in low-income families (de Carvalho, 2001).

Children's less successful progress in education is often blamed on their own and/or their parents' poor aspirations. This discourse is reinforced through the special status attributed to parenting (Dermott, 2013). In June 2010, the then British Prime Minister, David Cameron, commissioned Frank Field MP to conduct an independent review on poverty and life chances. The emphasis in the Frank Field Report (2010) on the early years and the availability of quality services for children and their families was welcomed at the time; with recommendations that concentrated on young children, arguing that the early years are crucial. However, the Report (2010) detracts attention away from income poverty, and away from structural drivers of poverty towards individual failings, notably parents. It explicitly refers to the role of 'good parenting' and notes at the outset that: 'We imperil the country's future if we forget that it is the aspirations and actions of parents which are critical to how well their children prosper' (Field, 2010, p.11). Shortly after, another government commissioned report on developing effective interventions with families at risk of multiple disadvantage stated that 'the right kind of parenting is a bigger influence on their [children's] future than wealth, class, education or any other common social factor' (Allen, 2011, p.xiv). What is clear from these reports is that policy-makers now believe very strongly in what Furedi (2001, p.67) calls 'parent determinism' as they are firmly committed to the idea that there is a direct, causal relationship between what parents do and why things go wrong in society (Lee, 2013).

Neoliberalism and the 'new politics of parenting' discursively positions parents as a reason for, and remedy to, child poverty. This has influenced the diffusion of an approach to child poverty which sees ECEC services move from optional extra to key policy level (Simpson et al., 2015, p.332).

The relationship of child poverty to early childhood education, particularly given the focus of this book (which is about empowering early childhood educators through socially just pedagogies), needs to embrace a vision for a fair allocation of resources such as economic, cultural and social capital. Early childhood education is perceived by many politicians (and some academics) as one of the routes or, sometimes, as the route to solving the challenge of child poverty (Case, 2006). For example, in the UK researchers involved in the longitudinal Effective Settings of Early Childhood Settings Education Study (EPPE/EPPSE) with over 3,000 children found that children's cognitive and behavioural outcomes improved significantly if they attended a high quality early childhood provision, and that the effects were especially significant for children with poor home learning environments (Sylva et al., 2011). Bennett (2008) also recorded the educational benefits of early childhood programmes in Australia, France, Ireland and New Zealand. However, a critical factor often overlooked by policy-makers is that there is often an inverse relationship between quality and accessibility. Furthermore, high quality settings with excellent child / staff ratios and highly trained teachers is not always replicated in every early childhood setting (Falenchuk et al., 2017). Moreover, Moss (2010, p.4) argues that the neoliberal promotion of ECEC across several nation states is 'a story of quality and high return' and is about control and calculation; a regime of truth that exercises power over thoughts and actions while directing or governing action (Simpson et al., 2015). In tackling child poverty, a political and social consensus on core ethical values is needed which view children as a shared responsibility and a social rather than economic investment, based on children's rights to an early childhood education.

The notion of rescuing children can be traced back to McMillan's idea of early intervention (Giardiello, 2014), which to some extent has provided a compensatory model of early childhood education. In trying to eradicate the effects of poverty, and bridge the huge divide between rich and poor, the core values are compromised. For example, when considering the role of early childhood education and care from an anti-poverty perspective, it is vital to consider the purpose of early childhood institutions. Increasingly in England, policy initiatives focus on only one dimension, which is the efficient production of predetermined outcomes. Such an approach misses the opportunity to build on the potential of ECEC provision as a space where active participation, and a reflective culture are woven into complex yet meaningful relationships between children, their peers and adults (MacNaughton, 2005). Consequently, educators have an important role in advocating for children by taking a proactive approach towards recognising the rights of all children, as discussed in Part 2 of this book. The rights-based argument for educators as advocates for children is grounded squarely on the United Nations Convention of the Rights of the Child UNCRC (1989) particularly Articles 12 (children's views) and 13 (freedom of expression). If children have opportunities in their early childhood setting to be valued as social actors, this brings about a totally different climate and environment which requires knowledgeable and critical reflexive educators. In a study carried out by White et al. (2012) on staff awareness and understanding about poverty issues some educators viewed attitudes toward poverty as a systemic problem, taking a 'deficit' approach that focuses too much on what children and their families lack instead of building on their strengths. This links to earlier discussions about parent determinism and viewing poor and socially excluded families as responsible for their own marginalisation. Other educators spoke of the need to raise awareness about poverty-related issues within the school community by providing more opportunities for staff to learn about poverty and to share strategies that they find helpful in supporting children and families dealing with poverty. This requires an ongoing debate to develop a clearer understanding of the variously understood concepts of child poverty and social justice and how to better promote relationships with learners, educators and their communities (Mistry and Sood, 2011).

In order to generate social justice, there is a need to understand connections between child poverty and extreme circumstances, such as the impact of persecution and conflict resulting in refugees, migration and displacement. The following section explores these issues. Currently there is much concern in England, as in other countries in Europe about the impact of changing demographics on the social fabric of the country and, in particular, on public services such as education and health. In addition, attention has been focused especially on patterns of migration. The proportion of children from ethnic minority backgrounds is increasing, as is the proportion speaking English as an Additional Language (Ainscow et al. 2016). In a recent report: *Uprooted: The Growing Crisis for Refugee and Migrant Children* (UNICEF, 2016b) a bleak picture is painted; worldwide, an estimated 50 million children are refugees or migrants, with the number of child migrants having doubled and the number of refugees having increased by 21 per cent in the past ten years (*Lancet* editorial, 2016). It is estimated that 23,000 refugee and migrant children arrived by sea to Greece, Italy and Spain in 2018, the vast majority fleeing conflict, extreme poverty and persecution. Despite this, children make up a smaller share of migrants in Europe than in any other region of the world. The largest number of migrant children in Europe live in the United Kingdom, followed by the Russian Federation, Spain, France and Germany. These five countries host 56 per cent of all migrant children in Europe (UNICEF, 2016b). In England, the percentage of children aged 5–16 in primary and secondary schools who have English as an Additional Language has more than doubled from 7.6 per cent in 1997 to 16.2 per cent in 2013 (Strand et al., 2015). Overcoming language barriers was seen to be critical for migrant children and the UNICEF report said pupils did much better if they were immersed within mainstream lessons, rather than being taught separately with other language learners.

One of the primary sites in which care and support may occur is within early years settings and primary and secondary school environments, where children and young people from either refugee or migrant backgrounds may first develop relationships with both peers and adults in their new country. In considering best-practice for the care of refugee and migrant children, Newbigging and Thomas (2011) outline six elements for organisational delivery of good social care. These are: (1) organisational commitment to promoting well-being, (2) multi-agency partnerships, (3) local strategies developed according to specific needs assessments, (4) engaging with and involving refugees in the development of services, (5) workforce development and (6) monitoring and review. This focus on care in terms of relationships is particularly important for children and young persons with refugee backgrounds, who may bring particular expectations (such as those relating to forms of punishment and control) that may impede relationships if time is not put into getting to know individual children (Due and Riggs, 2016).

An early childhood setting is probably the first environment in which refugee and migrant children can be immersed in different linguistic and cultural contexts (Pascal and Bertram, 2009). For these children, therefore it is the first opportunity to actively participate in the host society, speaking the host language. Early childhood settings and schools should be able to provide both learning and healing opportunities by means of incorporating structure for migrant children who may have experienced chaos. In this way, a sense of belonging and a new way of life is nurtured. Educators can help children integrate with their classmates, who will have had very different life experiences, and can help the migrant children to rebuild their self-esteem, self-worth and develop mutual friendships.

This chapter now moves on to consider wider early childhood issues from a Swedish perspective.

Inclusion and intercultural perspectives on early childhood education in Sweden

Increasing diversification challenges the perception of Swedish society as culturally homogeneous. This has had an impact on social justice and in particular children being valued as equal participants and co-workers in society as reinforced by UNICEF (2016b). In addition, the Education 2030 agenda (UNESCO, 2015b) sheds light on equity in education and access for all children, in particular, gender, wealth, location, ethnicity, language, social economic status and disability (Marope, 2016). Issues of interculturalism, human rights and citizenship are becoming increasingly relevant in Sweden (Nejadmehr, 2012), and also in relation to the early childhood provision.

Through an inclusive educational agenda, Swedish children and parents can be supported in their social participation regardless of cultural background using preschools as an arena for participation and citizenship, so multiethnicity can bring new possibilities (Karlsson Häikiö, 2018a; Lunneblad, 2014)

Intercultural aspects are highlighted in the regulation for the new ECE curriculum in Sweden (SKOLFS, 2018, p.50) as well as aspects that deal with diversity and internationalisation. It notes how early childhood settings should be a 'social and cultural meeting place' where children can develop 'an ability to understand and put themselves in the conditions and values of other people' (SKOLFS, 2018, p.2). It 'should lay the foundation for children's understanding of different languages and cultures, including the languages and cultures of the national minorities' (SKOLFS, 2018, p.2). Lorentz (2016) defines intercultural skills as ability to communicate 'with people of different backgrounds with regard to ethnicity, culture, language, religion, etc.' (p.161). Although intercultural competence is not explicitly mentioned in the regulation, it implicitly describes the importance of the development of the abilities described by Lorentz. At the same time, the emphasis on internationalisation can be interpreted from a position where the understanding of the surrounding world and international relations is emphasised. But still, a broader perspective is avoided such as understanding cultural diversity, pluralism and interculturalism, or an interactive perspective on cultural interaction.

In the context of cultural interaction, Ahmed (2004) makes the point that self-identity is related to 'likeness', for example in relation to gender, class and ethnicity. She argues that we come to understand differences relationally. Central to the production of differences is the production of collective emotions and people's ethical responsibility to care for and support the collective. Developing intercultural education, requires educational contexts where similarities and differences and how common concepts, which uphold normative collective identities, can be discussed.

A conscious creation of an inclusive, equal and democratic pedagogy (Freire, 1972; Giroux, 2011; Gundara and Portera, 2008) often stays on a theoretical level. Through transformative learning (McLeod, 2015; Moss, 2014) preschools and schools can potentially become an arena for participation where the schools' democratic mandate and respect for differences can be the basis for collective change. Such an approach could lead to the development of intercultural perspectives, approaches and methods that takes into greater consideration intercultural aspects of education (Lahdenperä and Lorentz, 2010). Supporting a positive sense of identity as part of an intercultural transformative perspective in early childhood requires an awareness of the power relations between children and adults to achieve children's empowerment (Wall, 2010).

Intercultural creative pedagogies

Reflection on cultural differences and intercultural aspects can be integrated into education and contribute to learning through developing empathy. Elam et al. (2017) define empathy, aesthetics and culture as driving forces to facilitate inclusive working approaches. Intercultural pedagogy encompasses dialogic processes to create empathy and understanding, where art and aesthetic learning processes can contribute to the creation of intercultural skills in different forms. In this way the open and flexible conditions for learning and socialisation are created. Working with art and aesthetics can be useful in dealing with complex issues associated with racism, gender, class or power perspectives. However, Lunneblad (2013) has found that the work of interculturalism often only occurs in relation to work with established national traditions. Work with cultural differences are often based on a normative view of 'Swedishness' that leads to the pursuit of heterogeneity, and where other cultural traditions are seen as deficient in relation to the Nordic preschool context (2013, p.3–4).

> Studies made at preschools and schools in Sweden show that the teachers are looking for what unites and is in common with the children. In heterogeneous children's groups, the communion is created around the Swedish language and the preschool and school's traditions and practices. Teachers avoid talking about the children's experiences and cultural differences are toned down. Occasions when the children's cultural identities are recognized as an asset are usually related to festivities and aesthetic expressions.
>
> *(Lunneblad, 2013, p.2–3).*

Such an attitude towards children and parents does not create good conditions for addressing and treating cultural differences in a respectful manner (Karlsson Häikiö, 2018b).

In Sweden, migrants especially those from non-European countries, face high levels of segregation. Many live in neighbourhoods on the outskirts of cities which can create ghettoes and lead to further segregation (Popul, 2018).

The following three case studies demonstrate ways of working with children in a Swedish preschool that is located in a socially and economically deprived and segregated area.

CASE STUDY 1: WORKING WITH CHILDREN AND FAMILIES IN SEGREGATED AREAS

At a preschool located in a suburb of a larger city in Sweden, educators use a theme-based approach. This is because the children at preschool represent nearly 30 languages, and a majority of the children are multilingual with a different cultural background, as well as the educators, who have different specialisations and different linguistic capabilities. Themes related to diversity, interculturalism and value-based issues are used which consist of conversations around images as a way of creating dialogue with the children and parents, to create reciprocal communication between families and the pre-school (Karlsson Häikiö, 2018b). Identity is related to the mother [native] tongue and is important for all, children, parents and educators. Much of the conversation is about perceptions, language development, and creating nuances in relation to the work with children and parents. The educators use documentation as a reflexive tool which is valued as quality practice (Håkansson, 2014). The educators meet weekly in reflection groups discussing issues surrounding the educational activities, specific problems, planning of the teaching and in-service training. The inspiration for this work is based on a project work model inspired by Bassa Reggiana, an offshoot of the Reggio Emilia Approach. Documentation can be based on the children's own stories about their families, experiences, memories related to their own culture, or be initiated by the educators as more general themes based on the planning of the teaching.

At the early childhood setting the educators have for a long time consciously worked on the theme of identity for both children and parents. Many of the families they encounter come from cultures where Swedish society, with its values, is alien. Examples of themes are work with taboos, the culture of chastity and women's right to their own life. Different methods have been used to find ways of working with the parents. A material used is *Freedom and Control*, a UNESCO material with the UNCRC as a basis. The early childhood setting uses process-oriented value-base dialogue in meetings with parents of the children. The image analysis method is originally from Senegal and is used, *inter alia*, in addition to Senegal and Sweden in Kenya, Tanzania, Liberia, Sierra Leone, the United States and England. Basically, this is a parent support programme that deals with the right of parents to raise their children based on their culture and children's rights, but also to help families with meaningful democratisation processes regarding parenting, human rights, women's rights, children's rights, conflict resolution, sexual relations and cohabitation. Through various dialogical tools, the educators can create an idea of the family's background, cultural background, how they came to Sweden, possible difficult circumstances and other events that relate to their encounter with Swedish culture.

CASE STUDY 2: HEART PROJECT – WORKING WITH CHILDREN TO PROMOTE AGENCY AND PARTICIPATION INSPIRED BY THE REGGIO EMILIA APPROACH

At the same preschool a recent project was initiated by the children, called the Heart Project. The project originated because the preschool had been exposed in various ways to gang-related conflicts that exist in the area. This involved shootings between different gangs nearby encroaching on the preschool outdoor environment. Initially the violence only took place at night, but then the shootings escalated to daytime, and parents became even more afraid and worried. This situation was an indescribable concern for children, parents and educators. Despite wanting to play outdoors, the children were too afraid. As a result, the children started a protest action where they re-claimed their space. The children's fear was allayed by the educators who responded to children's initiative. Together they planned the 'Heart Project'. In this project, the art studio (atelier) was an important space where the children had access to creative materials to produce individual heart shapes. These were displayed outside the preschool building, in the surrounding environment and were also sent to other preschools in the area. Together the children and the adults marched around the area shouting: '*We don't not want to be afraid! We don't want to be dead*!' The children were helped to write an open letter to those who were responsible for the shootings and the letter was displayed around the preschool. The children's activity gained media attention and the children received letters from other preschools that heard about the project. (A film about the project is available in Swedish at the Children's Department (Sw. Barnaministeriet), UR, Vi vill inte bli döda [We don't want to be dead]: https://urskola.se/Produkter/183573-Barnaministeriet-dokumentar-Vi-vill-inte-bli-doda).

The project led to a closer relationship between the educators and the parents. Many of the parents also saw the police from another perspective, in terms of supporting a social system and not just exercising authority as was the experience for many families who come from other countries with different societal circumstances.

The use and trading of drugs as well as increasing criminality in the city was part of the situation. Many of the families have also experienced the trauma of war and corruption. Through the Heart Project, relationships with the parents were improved, and attitudes changed in relation to the police and authorities. More importantly the children were empowered as agents of change.

CASE STUDY 3: USING IMAGES TO PROMOTE A RESPECT FOR EQUALITY AND INTER-CULTURE

Light projections, digital media, interactive smartboards and other audio-visual media are important pedagogical tools, especially with the children for whom Swedish is not their first language. Various types of audio-visual tools such as easy to use mini-projectors, smartboards and laptops are used as part of reflective processes with children so they can engage in conversations about the images. Also paint, clay as well as recycled materials are used. The interests of the children are used as a starting point for working in small groups, which is important for children who are not familiar with the Swedish language.

As well as working with the children, the educator coaches their preschool colleagues to dare to experiment with new materials and equipment, such as multi-modal and audio-visual tools that are more flexible to use with the children. Using these tools can help children develop communicative strategies and acquire skills that enable them to participate in preschool and society in meaningful ways.

The mini-project

A group of 4- and 5-year-olds were interested in different characters, symbols, badges and emblems representing their home countries for example flags and football kits. This interest was used as a provocation for further exploration. The educators put up pictures of famous football teams and players that the children knew and talked about. Pictures of both women and men football players were displayed. Through this work, the educators were able to discuss gender issues with the children. Earlier discussions by the children had focused on what was typical of girls or boys, women or men, in their view. The pictures of the football players were the starting point for discussions on cultural similarities and differences, as well as gender and ethnic issues. As footballers can come from any country but still play in local teams, this led to many discussions between the children about origin, as many of the children were in the same situation as the football players, that is they came from one country, but lived in another, and had friends from different parts of the world. Through this mini-project, which was part of a larger project on countries and continents from a geographical perspective, questions about intercultural relations could be talked about based on their own lived experiences and perceptions of the world.

POINTS FOR REFLECTION

- What factors do you face in supporting young children's health and well-being?
- What are the benefits to children and families in poverty that ECEC can bring?
- How would you go about developing meaningful relationships with migrant children and their families?

As seen in this chapter, children's lived experiences are varied and often complex. In seeking to tackle the wider issues that children may encounter, educators should seek to foster a reflexive, reciprocal and transactional pedagogy to promote learning and meaning making in a global society.

References

Ahmed, S. (2004) 'Collective feelings; Or, the impressions left by others', *Theory, Culture & Society*, April (21), p.25–42.

Ainscow, M., Dyson, A., Hopwood, L. and Thomson, S. (2016) *Primary schools responding to diversity: Barriers and possibilities*, University of York: Cambridge Primary Review Trust.

Allen, G. (2011) *Early intervention: The next steps: An independent report to her majesty's government*, London: Cabinet Office.

Ayre, D. (2016) *Poor mental health: The links between child poverty and mental health problems.* Retrieved 29 January 2019 from: www.childrenssociety.org.uk/sites/default/files/poor_mental_health_report.pdf.

Barrett, R. (2017) *Everything I have ever learned about values*, Barrett Values Centre LLC, Lulu Publishing Services.

Ben Arieh (2008) 'The child indicators movement: Past, present and future', *Child Indicator Research Journal of the International Society for Child Indicators*, 1(1), p.3–16.

Bennett, J. (2008) 'Early childhood services in the OECD countries: Review of the literature and current policy in the early childhood field', Innocenti working paper 2008–2001, Florence: UNICEF Innocenti Research Centre.

Bradshaw, J. (2015) 'Child poverty and child well-being in international perspective', in: Fernandez, E., Zeira, A., Vecchiato, T. and Canali, C. (2015) *Theoretical and empirical insights into child and family poverty: Cross national perspectives*, Cham, Heidelberg, New York, Dordrecht, London: Springer.

Bronfenbrenner, U. (1979) *The ecology of human development*, London: Harvard University Press.

Case, A. (2006) 'The primacy of education', in: A.V. Banerjee, R. Bénabou and D. Mookherjee (Eds.), *Understanding poverty*, New York: Oxford University Press, p.269–284.

Child Poverty Act (2010) Retrieved 30 January 2019 from: www.legislation.gov.uk/ukpga/2010/9/contents.

The Children's Society (2017) *The good childhood report.* Retrieved 14 March 2019 from: www.childrenssociety.org.uk/sites/default/files/the-good-childhood-report-2017_full-report_0.pdf.

de Carvalho, M.E. (2001) *Rethinking family school relations: A critique of parental involvement in schooling*, New York: Teacher's College Press.

De Neve, J.-E., Diener, E., Tay, L. and Xuereb, C. (2013) 'The objective benefits of subjective well-being', in: Helliwell, J., Layard, R. and Sachs, J. (Eds.) *World happiness report 2013*, New York: UN Sustainable Development Solutions Network.

Department for Education (DfE) (2016) *DFE consolidated annual report and accounts 2015 to 2016.* Retrieved 31 January 2019 from: www.gov.uk/government/publications/dfe-consolidated-annual-report-and-accounts-2015-to-2016.

Dermott, E. (2013) 'Poverty versus parenting: An emergent dichotomy', *Studies in the Maternal*, 4(2). Retrieved 30 January 2019 from: www.mamsie.bbk.ac.uk/.

Dermott, E. and Pomati, M. (2016) '"Good" parenting practices: How important are poverty, education and time pressure?' *Sociology*, 50(1), p.125–142.

Due, C. and Riggs, D. (2016) 'Care for children with migrant or refugee backgrounds in the school context', *Children Australia*, 41(3), p.190–200.

Elam, K., Hansson Stenhammar, M.-L., Karlsson Häikiö, T., Kupferberg, F., Nejadmehr, R. and Wallin Wictorin, M. (2017) 'Educating responsible citizens; Intercultural competence and aesthetic education', in: G.-B. von Carlsburg (Ed.) *Learning scenarios for social and cultural change: Building through academic teaching*, Series: Erziehungskonzeptionen und Praxis, Peter Lang Publishing, p.61–81.

Ellyatt, W. (2018) *Understanding the Flourish Model*. Retrieved 31 January 2019 from: www.flourishproject.net/uploads/1/8/4/9/1849450/understanding_the_flourish_model_july_2018.pdf.

European Anti-Poverty Network (2013) 'Poverty: What is it?' Retrieved 30 January 2019 from: www.eapn.eu/en/what-is-poverty/poverty-what-is-it.

Falenchuk, O., Perlman, M., McMullen, E., Fletcher and Shah, P.S. (2017) 'Education of staff in preschool aged classrooms in child care centers and child outcomes: A meta-analysis and systematic review', *PLoS ONE*, 12(8). Available from: doi.org/10.1371/journal.pone.0183673.

Field, F. (2010) *The foundation years: Preventing poor children becoming poor adults*, London: Cabinet Office.

Fraser, N., Gutiérrez, R. and Pena-Casa, R. (2011) 'Introduction', in: N. Fraser, R. Gutiérrez and R. Pena-Casa (Eds.) *Working poverty in Europe*, New York: Palgrave MacMillan, p.1–14.

Freire, P. (1972). *Pedagogik för förtryckta* [*Pedagogia do oprimodo*], Stockholm.

Furedi, F. (2001) *Paranoid parenting. Abandon your anxieties and be a good parent*, London: Allen Lane/Penguin.

Giardiello, P. (2014) *Pioneers in early childhood education; The roots and legacies of Rachel and Margaret McMillan, Maria Montessori and Susan Isaacs*, Abingdon: Routledge.

Global Issues (2013) *Poverty stats and facts*. Retrieved 30 January 2019 from: www.globalissues.org/article/26/poverty-facts-and-stats.

Giroux, H.A. (2011) *Rethinking education as the practice of freedom; Paulo Freire and the promise of critical pedagogy: On critical pedagogy*, New York: Continuum Publishing, p.152–166.

Gundara, J. and Portera, A. (2008) 'Theoretical reflections on intercultural education', *Intercultural Education*, 19(6), p.463–468.

Håkansson, J. (2014) *Systematiskt kvalitetsarbete i förskola, skola och fritidshem* [*Systematic quality work in early childhood provision, compulsory school and leisure time activities center*], Lund: Studentlitteratur.

Heckman, J.J. (2011) 'The economics of inequality: The value of early childhood education', *American Educator*, 35(1), pp. 31–47.

Huppert, F.A. and Johnson, D.M. (2010) 'A controlled trial of mindfulness training in schools: The importance of practice for an impact on well-being', *The Journal of Positive Psychology*, 5, 264–274. DOI: doi:10.1080/17439761003794148.

JRF (2018). *UK Poverty 2018*. Retrieved 1 February 2019 from: www.jrf.org.uk/report/uk-poverty-2018.

Karlsson Häikiö, T. (2018a) 'Barns kulturella deltagande i förskolan och samverkan med föräldrar [Children's cultural participation in early childhood settingsand cooperation with parents]', in: R. Nejadmehr (Ed.) *Interkulturell dialog; teori och praktik* [*Intercultural dialogue; theory and practice*], Forskningsrådet för interkulturell dialog (FID), publication 1. Västra Götalandsregionen: nordienT.

Karlsson Häikiö, T. (2018b) 'Förskolan som visuell kultur [Early childhood settings as visual culture]', in: M. Bendroth Karlsson, T. Karlsson Häikiö and L.O. Magnusson, *Skapande verksamhet i förskolan – kreativt arbete med analoga och digitala redskap* [*Creative activity in early childhood provision: Use of analogue and digital tools*], Lund: Studentlitteratur.

Karila, K. (2012) 'A Nordic perspective on early childhood education and care policy', *European Journal of Education*, 47(4), p.584–595.

Lahdenperä, P. and Lorentz, H. (Eds.) (2010) *Möten i mångfaldens skola; interkulturella arbetsformer och nya pedagogiska utmaningar* [*Meetings in the diversified school: Intercultural forms of work and new educational challenges*], Lund: Studentlitteratur.

Lee, E. (2013) 'A policy driven by prejudice masquerading as research'. Retrieved 30 January 2019 from: https://blogs.kent.ac.uk/parentingculturestudies/files/2011/06/A-Policy-Driven-By-Prejudice-Masquerading-As-Research1.pdf.

Lorentz, H. (2016) 'Interkulturell pedagogisk kompetens; Transformativt akademisk kunskap om integration i dagens skola [Intercultural educational skills: Transformative academic knowledge about integration in today's school]', in: H. Lorentz and B. Bergstedt (Eds.) *Interkulturella perspektiv; Pedagogik i mångkulturella lärmiljöer* [*Intercultural perspectives; Pedagogics in multicultural learning environments*], Lund: Studentlitteratur.

Lunneblad, J. (2014) 'Ett integrationspolitiskt projekt: mottagandet av nyanlända i förskolan [An integration-political project: The reception of newly arrived children in pre-school]', in: O. Sernhede and I. Tallberg Broman (Eds.) *Segregation, utbildning och ovanliga lärprocesser*, Liber: Stockholm.

MacNaughton, G. (2005) *Doing Foucault in early childhood studies: Applying poststructural ideas*, Abingdon: Routledge

McLeod, N. (2015) 'Reflecting on reflection: Improving teachers' readiness to facilitate participatory learning with young children', *Professional Development in Education*, 41(2), p.254–272.

Marmot, M. (2010) 'Fairer society, healthy lives: Strategic review of health inequalities in England post 2010'. Available from: www.marmotreview.org.

Marope, P.T.M. (2016) 'Quality and development-relevant education and learning: Setting the stage for the Education 2030 Agenda', *PROSPECTS Comparative Journal of Curriculum, Learning, and Assessment*, 46(1), p.1–3.

Maslow, A.H. (1962) *Toward a psychology of being*, Princeton, NJ: D. Van Nostrand Company.

Mental Health Foundation (2010) *Mindfulness report*. Retrieved 30 January 2019 from: www.mentalhealth.org.uk/sites/default/files/Mindfulness_report_2010.pdf.

Mistry, M. and Sood, K. (2011) 'Rethinking educational leadership to transform pedagogical practice to help improve the attainment of minority ethnic pupils: The need for leadership dialogue', *Management in Education*, 25(3), p.125–130.

Morris, A.S., Robinson, Hays-Grudo, J., Claussen, A., Hartwig, S. and Treat, A. (2017) 'Targeting parenting in early childhood: A public health approach to improve outcomes for children living in poverty', *Child Development*, 88, p.388–397.

Moss, P. (2014) *Transformative change and real utopias in early childhood education: A story of democracy, experimentation and potentiality*, New York: Routledge.

Moss, P. (2010) *We cannot continue as we are: The educator in an education for survival*. Retrieved 30 January 2019 from: https://journals.sagepub.com/doi/pdf/10.2304/ciec.2010.11.1.8.

Nejadmehr, R. (2012) *Multicultural education in Sweden*, in: J.A. Banks (Ed.) *Encyclopedia of diversity in education*, SAGE Publications.

Newbigging, K. and Thomas, N. (2011) 'Good practice in social care for refugee and asylum-seeking children', *Child Abuse Review*, 20(5), p.374–390.

Nitecki, E. and Wasmuth, H. (2017) 'Global trends in early childhood practice: Working within the limitations of the global education reform movement', *Introduction to Global Education Review: Global Trends in Early Childhood Practice*, 4(3), p.1–13.

Ochsner, K.N., Bunge, S.A., Gross, J. and Gabrieli, H.D. (2002) 'Rethinking feelings: An FMRI study of the cognitive regulation of emotion', *Journal of Cognitive Neuroscience*, 14(8), p.1215–1229.

Ofsted (2019) *Education inspection framework 2019: Inspecting the substance of education*. Retrieved 18 January 2019 from: www.gov.uk/government/news/ofsted-launches-a-consultation-on-proposals-for-changes-to-the-education-inspection-framework.

Pascal, C. and Bertram, T. (2009) 'Listening to young citizens: The struggle to make real a participatory paradigm in research with young children', *European Early Childhood Education Research Journal*, 17(2), p.249–262.

Persson, S. (2014) 'Förskolan och social ojämlikhet [Early childhood education and social unequality]', in: O. Sernhede and I. Tallberg Broman (Eds.) *Segregation, utbildning och ovanliga lärprocesser [Segregation, education and unusual learning processes]*, Liber: Stockholm.

Popul, E.J. (2018) 'Residential segregation of European and non European migrants in Sweden: 1990–2012', *European Journal of Population*, 34(2), p.169–193.

Pulkkinen, L. (2012) 'Ten pillars of a good childhood: A Finnish perspective', *Childhood Education*, 88(5), p.326–330. DOI: doi:10.1080/00094056.2012.718680.

Raphael, D. (2011) 'The political economy of health promotion: Part 2, national settings of the prerequisites of health', *Health Promotion International*, 28(1), p.112–132.

Rasi, H., Kuivila, H., Pölkki, T., Bloigu, R., Rintamäki, H. and Tourula, M. (2017) 'A descriptive quantitative study of 7- and 8-year-old children's outdoor recreation, cold exposure and symptoms in winter in Northern Finland', *International Journal of Circumpolar Health*, 76(1). DOI: doi:10.1080/22423982.2017.1298883.

Reinhart, C. and Rogoff, K. (2011) 'From financial crash to debt crisis', *American Economic Review*. Retrieved 31 January 2019from: www.aeaweb.org/articles.php?doi=10.1257/aer.101.5.1676.

Roberts-Holmes, G. (2015) 'The "datafication" of early years pedagogy: "If the teaching is good, the data should be good and if there's bad teaching, there is bad data"', *Journal of Education Policy*, 30(3), p.302–315. DOI: doi:10.1080/02680939.2014.924561.

Salminen, J. (2017) 'Early childhood education and care system in Finland. [Prace z warsztatu. Nauki o wychowaniu]', *Studia interdyscyplinarne*, 2(5). DOI: doi:10.18778/2450-4491.05.09.

Sernhede, O. and Tallberg Broman, I. (Eds.) (2018) *Segregation, utbildning och ovanliga lärprocesser [Segregation, education and unusual learning processes]*, Liber: Stockholm.

Simpson, D., Lumsden, E. and McDowall Clark, R. (2015) 'Early childhood settings practitioners, child poverty and social justice', *International Journal of Sociology and Social Policy*, 35(5), p.325–339. Available from: https://doi.org/10.1108/IJSSP-10-2013-0101.

Sipilä, J. (1997) 'Introduction', in: J. Sipilä (Ed.) *Social care services: The key to the Scandinavian welfare model*, Avebury: Aldershot.

SKOLFS (2018) *50.Statens skolverks författningssamling [The statal statutory collection]. Förordning om läroplan för förskolan [Regulation on the curriculum for early childhood provision]*, Stockholm: Skolverket [National Agency for Education].

Smith, G., Sylva, K., Smith, T., Sammons, P. and Omonigho, A. (2018) *Stop start: Survival, decline or closure? Children's centres in England, 2018*. Retrieved 28 January 2019 from: www.suttontrust.com/wp-content/uploads/2018/04/StopStart-FINAL.pdf.

Strand, S., Malmberg, L. and Hall, J. (2015) *English as an Additional Language (EAL) and educational achievement in England: An analysis of the National Pupil Database*, London: EEF and the Bell Foundation.

Sylva, K., Melhuish, E., Sammons, P., Siraj-Blatchford, I. and Taggart, B. (2010) *Early childhood matters: Evidence from the effective early childhood settings and primary education project*, London: Routledge.

Tang, Y., Ma, Y., Wang, J., Fan, Y., Feng, S., Lu, Q., *et al.* (2012) 'Improving executive functioning and its neurobiological mechanisms through mindful-based interventions', *Child Development Perspect*, 6361–6366.

Tourula, M., Fukazawa, T. and Isola, A. (2011) 'Evaluation of the thermal insulation of clothing of infants sleeping outdoors in Northern winter', *European Journal of Applied Physiology*, 111, p.633–640.

UNCRC (1989) *Convention on the rights of the child*. Retrieved 30 January 2019 from: downloads.unicef.org.uk/wpcontent/uploads/2010/05/UNCRC_united_nations_convention_on_the_rights_of_the_child.pdf?_ga=2.105161091.1666008301.1548973360-595607080.1548973360.

UNESCO (2015a) *Education for all 2000–2015: Achievements and challenges, Education for all global monitoring report*, Paris: UNESCO.

UNESCO (2015b) *Incheon declaration. Education 2030: Towards inclusive and equitable quality education and lifelong learning for all.* Available from: https://en.unesco.org/world-education-forum-2015/incheon-declaration.

UNICEF (2016a) *The state of the world's children 2016: A fair chance for every child*. Retrieved 9 January 2019 from: www.unicef.org/publications/index_91711.htm.

UNICEF (2016b) *Uprooted: The growing crisis for refugee and migrant children*. Retrieved 9 January 2019 from: www.unicef.org/publications/index_92710.html.

UNICEF (2014) *Is the world a better place for children?* Retrieved 31 January 2019 from: www.unicef.org/crc/files/02_CRC_25_Years_UNICEF.pdf.

UNICEF (2009) *State of the world's children report*, New York: UNICEF Research Centre.

UNICEF (2007) *An overview of child well-being in rich countries*. Retrieved 31 January 2019 from: www.unicef.org/media/files/ChildPovertyReport.pdf.

Wall, J. (2010) *Ethics in the light of childhood*, Washington, DC: Georgetown University Press.

White, M., Hill, I., Kemp, S., MacRae, J. and Young, L. (2012) *Poverty and education: A teacher's perspective— Summary of the findings of the focus group research*. Retrieved 30 January 2019 from: www.bctf.ca/PovertyResearch.aspx.

Whitebread, D. (2017) 'Free play and children's mental health', *The Lancet Child and Adolescent Health*. Retrieved 31 January 2019 from: from: www.thelancet.com/journals/lanchi/issue/vol1no3/PIIS2352-4642(17)X0004–7.

Williams, P., Sheridan, S. and Pramling Samuelsson, I. (2015) 'Gruppstorlekens betydelse för barns möjligheter att lära och utvecklas i förskolan [The importance of group size for children's possibilities to learning and development in pre-school]', in: *Vetenskapsrådets resultatdialog [Dialogue of results, research council], 2015.*

'Wise up: Prioritising wellbeing in schools'. NCB publication. Retrieved 30 January 2019 from: https://youngminds.org.uk/get-involved/campaign-with-us/wise-up/.

10

HOPE FOR THE FUTURE

New possibilities for sustaining a reflexive approach

Naomi McLeod, Tarja Karlsson Häikiö and Pernilla Mårtensson

We started this book by recognising key pressures faced by early childhood education professionals, most prominently through expectations around testing, accountability and competition. This is manifested recently in the Programme for International Student Assessment (PISA) (OECD) and the launch of the controversial International Early Learning and Child Well-being Study (IELS), more commonly referred to as 'Baby PISA' (OECD, 2018), which as noted assesses in a very narrow way (Urban, 2017). The promotion of quality early childhood education based on positive dispositions to learning and imaginative play incorporating participatory approaches has been emphasised throughout this book as being in direct contrast to the focus on standardisation, a narrowing curriculum and test-based accountability for educators. This has resulted in a high stakes testing approach which is deficit in design and deficit in output, reinforced by Global Education Reform Movement (GERM) (Sahlberg, 2010, 2011, 2013). Being aware of and questioning this top-down politically imposed approach in early childhood practice is the first step in being GERM resistant (Alexander, 2014; Moss, 2019) (as discussed in Chapter 1).

As a stimulation for questioning output driven views of ECE, throughout this book we have presented different international pedagogies as provocation with the intent of empowering early childhood educators through challenging and deconstructing ideas and understandings around the purpose of education, so a more participatory and respectful approach to learning can be reconstructed and embedded. At the heart of empowering educators in their pedagogical understanding we have established the need for reflexivity, through internal questioning and wisdom (phronesis), an awareness of power (politics) and a focus on 'what is right?' (ethics). Each chapter has explored the democratic, ethical and socially just nature of early childhood education and the educator's engagement in this entangled, rhizomatic process, as developed by Deleuze (2004), so children's learning and development can be promoted from a rights-based perspective as framed by the UN Convention on the Rights of the Child (1989). Within this shifting paradigm of humanising education, our final chapter offers a methodological sustainable framework for professionalism, grounded on and in ethically responsible educational practice involving open communication with equal rights for all participants and a commitment to self-awareness and consciousness (Vandenbroeck, Urban and Peeters, 2016). This involves a shared power balance that is respectful of educators, children and the environment and takes a 'bottom up' approach (Katz, 2012). As a way of empowering educators rather than relying on training for generating changes in practice and enhancing the quality of practice, Pascal and Bertram (2012, 2018) turn this idea upside down, noting the need to start directly with practice so the complexity of the real world is revealed (Robson, 2011) and training is viewed rather as inquiry as part of everyday practice.

A hope for the future

As a way of authenticating the robustness of reflexivity within the current political climate and the emphasis on data and an outcome-driven model of education (in particular, in England), we concur with Pascal and Bertram (2012, 2018) who emphasise the need for educators to have a more astute awareness about power (politics) alongside a sharpened focus of values (ethics) in all our thinking and actions. At the heart of professional inquiry is the need for reflexivity (phronesis) and action (praxis) (ibid.). This mix of phronesis, praxis, ethics and power is referred to as 'praxeological', which collectively can enable an authentic worldview of modern early childhood. Fundamentally praxeological inquiry is about questioning 'how' and 'why' and is always situated within local contexts about real world situations. This 'bottom-up' approach associated with empowering educators in developing a personal understanding of quality early childhood practice, challenges the top-down approach associated with government policy and training in which educators are powerless and pawns in the promotion of outcomes and standardisation. It is this approach to professionalism (building on social critical theory in Chapter 2) that we take as an effective way forward for supporting the conditions for embedding and sustaining praxeology (Pascal and Bertram, 2012, 2018; Vandenbroeck, Urban and Peeters, 2016). According to McCormack and Boomer (2007), creating appropriate conditions or a supportive environment for questioning by educators requires working respectfully *with* colleagues in local contexts so an empowered ownership of understanding of their own situation and position can be developed. We therefore focus on the importance of working '*with*' participants (educators and children) using participatory and emancipatory action learning / professional development within local ECE projects. Firstly, the significance of facilitating appropriate conditions are discussed (such as a collaborative, open and trusting, safe environment so that uncertainty and willingness to take personal risks can be embraced by both educators and children). Case study examples are also offered to promote discussions. Next, mentoring, coaching and the use of journal-keeping are explored as ways for sustaining professional development. Examples of how educators and students have found journal-keeping to be useful as a tool for sustaining a praxeological approach to professional development are shared. As part of an embedded approach to professionalism we also advocate the use of creative and participatory research methods that give authentic voice to children. Finally, the chapter concludes with a series of reflective questions that relate to current global challenges and debates in ECE.

'Bottom-up' rather than 'top-down'

Working 'with'

McIntosh (2010) as well as McCormack and Boomer (2007) emphasise the essential nature of safe, trusting relationships as part of collaborative inquiry in supporting educators become aware and critical of their own practice and the various political imbalances so they are confident and empowered in confronting society about ethical alternatives (Bath, 2009). The focus for such emancipatory collaborative inquiry is on respectful engagement, authenticity and openness, working '*with*' educators rather than doing '*to*', so each person / participant has a voice. Respecting educators' experience and valuing them as co-researchers as part of a comfortable environment is vital, according to McCormack and Boomer (2007). Working '*with*' means creating an environment so participants feel safe and comfortable to air their views and ask questions about personal uncertainties pertinent to participatory practice. For educators to 'have a go' there is a need to feel safe in the knowledge that making mistakes is okay (McCormack and Boomer, 2007). Often, the temptation can be to just 'copy' different pedagogical approaches as exemplar blue prints (such as Reggio Emilia, Montessori or Te Whāriki), rather than evaluating the contextual needs of an individual setting or a personal pedagogical practice. It is the importance of creating an appropriate environment that we focus on as part of this concluding chapter, for without this, educators may not feel able to take risks and leave the safe harbours of what is familiar.

Facilitating appropriate conditions

Change can be uncomfortable, and challenging or questioning government directives around assessment or outcomes may well produce anxiety, fear, resentment and feelings of being threatened or intimidated, which can act as a barrier to participatory practice and reflexivity (Scharmer, 2009). To illustrate the process of creating appropriate learning conditions, we draw on the work of McCormack and Boomer (2007) and a project involving a group of early childhood professionals who were keen to improve their practice by asking 'How can we, individually and collectively, improve the learning and wellbeing of young children as they progress through children's services?' The project started by creating agreed conditions for a community of practice as part of a workshop session. Each participant was invited to select words that represented their expectations as part of engaging in the project. These words effectively became the conditions necessary for creating a safe space. They included the following features as identified in Table 10.1. The interpretations by the group are their own understandings of what was required to establish a collective safe, respectful and trusting space (Givvin and Santagata, 2011) necessary for identifying shared tensions between birth to three provision and school attainment priorities.

Creating a safe, trusting space was crucial in nurturing a readiness to share their individual interpretations of school readiness (McLeod, 2011, 2015, 2017; Scharmer, 2009). Through open and honest sharing, each participant had a 'voice' that was listened to and appreciated. As they evaluated personal practice in the light of others' insights and critiques, they appreciated new ways of being. Creating a safe trusting environment was the first step in encouraging the participants to be ready to engage in a process of critical reflection. This involved the following features, which were integrated as part of the workshops.

It was important to start with where the participants were in terms of their openness, self-awareness of personal values and experiences in relation to the focus of the project which was 'school readiness' (Loucks-Horsley et al., 2003)

TABLE 10.1 Word interpretations

Word chosen	*Interpretation by the group*
Listen	Acknowledgment of others and feelings
Involvement	With group / contribute / take risks / be sensitive / non-judgemental / respectful
Attitude	Being open to challenges and be challenged
Peace	Resolve / respect / dis-equilibrium / being uncomfortable
Friendship	Communication / honesty / trust / right intention
passion	Motivate each other / justify / for the children
Communicate	reading body language / other stuff in life
Trust	Look after each other / takes time / honesty to be truthful
Joy / Fun	New ideas / banter / learn / new / pride / confirmation
Value	All contributions and ideas / respect / give and allow time to think / reflect / try out new ideas / constructive feedback verbal and non-verbal
confidence	Being willing to have a go / questioning / seeing from children's point of view
Safe	Sense of belonging / knowing each other and life outside work.
Inspire	Be inspired by others in the group and inspire / successes / impact on the children and sharing to inspire others
Impact	On wider teams / continue / embed / be sustainable
Time	Belief / reflective / process / journey
Being aware	Personal and emotional / whole heartedness / all the above

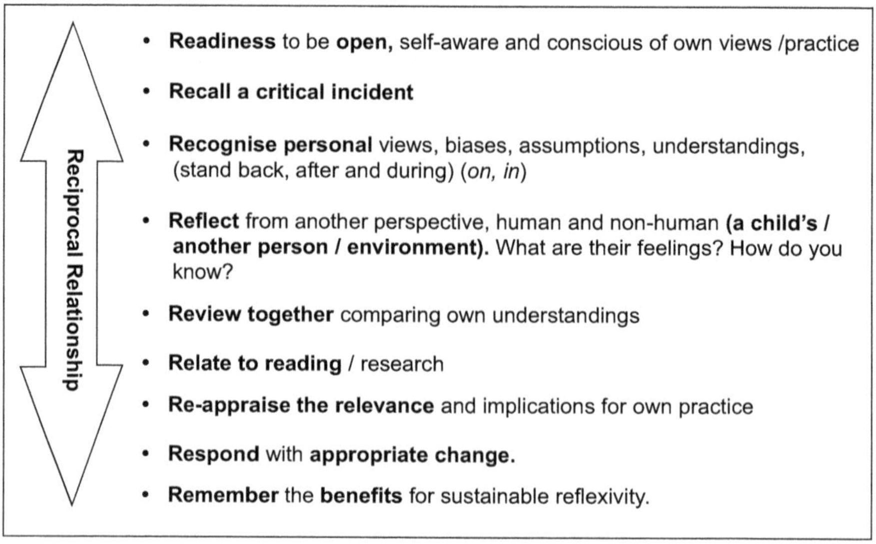

FIGURE 10.1A Reflexivity Framework
(McLeod, 2019)

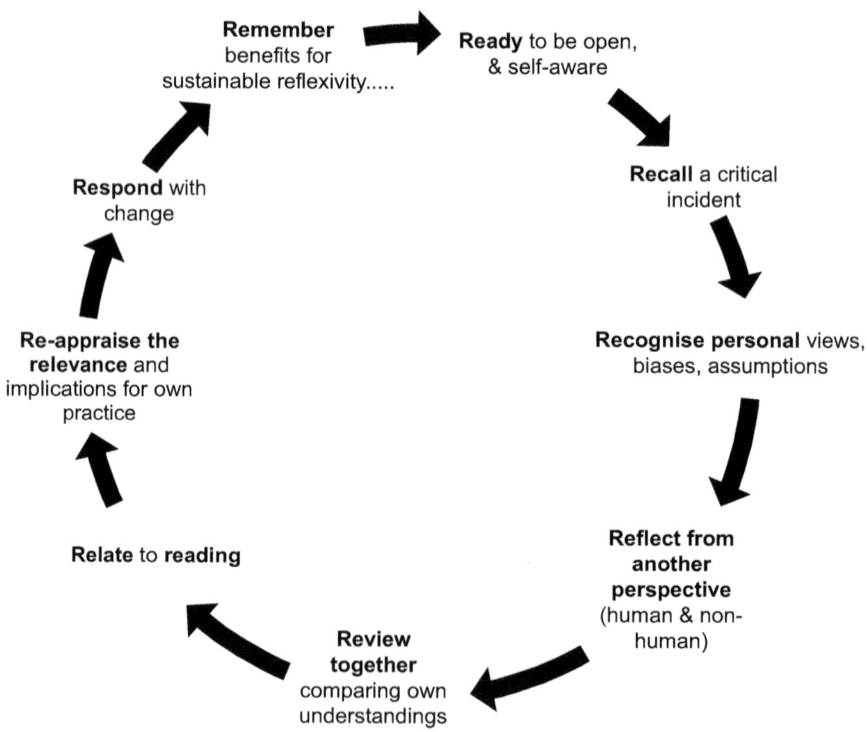

FIGURE 10.1B Reflexivity Framework
(McLeod, 2019)

and their readiness for change because, as Moon (2008) reinforces, a person cannot be made to reflect. The workshops could only happen through appropriate conditions in relation to the habits already formed by the participants. The nucleus of an authentic, open approach as Scharmer (2009) recognises, is an open mind, heart and will and is core in terms of creating the conditions for reflexivity. In relation to this study, the intention was that the participants would begin to see for themselves the influence of their own thinking habits on their practice (Hassan, 2005). In this way, critical reflection / reflexivity was central to each of the workshops. It was essential that the first workshop started by creating an environment in which everyone felt comfortable and valued (McCormack and Boomer, 2007).

Professional development through mentoring and journaling

Rather than using an approach to professional development that trains people to 'fit in' and conform to a dominant system (Whisker et al., 2008), van Nieuwerburgh (2012) and Davey and Ham (2010) talk about the value of mentoring as a conceptual form of professional learning for educators that really makes a difference, and is consistent with democratic respectful relationships and reflexivity. The reason for its effectiveness is put down to the way mentoring addresses authentic participation and engagement so changes to practice are sustainable (ibid.). In this way mentoring enables the mentor to reflect on their personal values, decisions, actions and skill set (Whisker et al., 2008) which promotes engagement 'with' the mentees as part of the mentor's modelling guidance and support. This form of mentoring shares qualities associated with coaching which negates positions of power but rather offers voice. It utilises respectful relationship building, listening and the open questioning skills of the coach to prompt the coachee to identify their goals and strategies (ibid.). For example, the coach might gently guide the coachee to come up with suggestions for actions but will not direct the coachee. Complementary parallels can be made with the approach described by pedagogues in Denmark (in Chapter 8) as part of Case study 2 and the way they work 'with' parents to facilitate new ways for seeing.

> *We co-work with parents in a respectful way. Pedagogues use a coaching approach so rather than telling parents, it's about seeing and appreciating from the child's perspective, so parents answer their own questions.*

Professional development through journaling

As a way of gaining a sense of autonomy and freedom as part of practice, Mason (2002) recommends the use of reflective diaries. Engaging in the process of journaling can reveal to the writer, things about a subject area and about themselves, that was previously unknown to them (Richardson, 2000). In this way reflective journaling can be used for 'recapturing the pleasures in teaching and learning' (Goodley, 2018, p.167). By developing an awareness of ontological views, and disciplined noticing, power imbalances can be addressed. As the author of the diary writes and analyses reflective entries, they become agents of change (Goodley, 2018). Moon (1999, 2004, 2006, 2008) and Scardamalia and Bereiter (1991) note how the process of writing can increase the quality of reflection on practice and illuminate personal thoughts and ideas so new knowledge is created (ibid.; Schön, 1987). This is more meaningful when critical incidents are used within familiar contexts. In this way Moon (2008) explains how reflective learning through writing shifts from a description to a deep reflective account. It progresses from no questions (as a narrative) to the asking of questions and responding to questions; it then advances to a stage where the response to questions is implicit in the writing (Scardamalia and Bereiter, 1991) and is comparable with reflection-in-action (Schön, 1983). As an awareness of personal emotional influences is developed, there is an increasing ability to stand back and question from an alternative perspective (Moon, 2008). Reflective journaling, then, can support self-awareness (phronesis), a consciousness of other perspectives and new insights about power (politics) and what is ethically right as part of early childhood practice. In this context, McLeod's Reflexive Framework (2015) is offered as a tool for structuring the process of journal-keeping. Next we provide examples of how the framework was used by early childhood educators and students to support the process of keeping a journal but ultimately how it revealed new insights.

The following case studies written by master's students are presented as examples of how reflective writing, according to McLeod, can be used as tool in educational studies to enhance professional thinking.

CASE STUDY 1: PROVIDED BY A MASTER'S STUDENT, HELEN LOWRY

'I began my reflective journey with a desire to understand what makes education in different countries "better" than in England and why we are starting to use practice such as Singapore Mathematics and Forest School education as part of teaching. Through discussions with peers, research into past philosophies and journal keeping, I began to look more closely at what I understood about the purpose of education and in turn how I saw children. With the recent birth of my son these reflections became even more important; I needed to explore where my views, attitudes and understanding came from (Davies and Artaraz, 2009 *). I was particularly interested in the choices and decisions children are given and how I listen to children, which I feel are important in early childhood education.*

To keep a reflective journal, I used McLeod *'s framework (*2015*) which has been key in transforming my thoughts and helping me reflect on challenges I faced both as part of keeping a journal, and also as part of my practice and the implications'.*

An extract of one entry is included later on.

Freedom:
Glitter everywhere

Recall: *Children were engaged in creative art work but as the class teacher enters the room and notices the amount of glitter everywhere, she is angry. It made me question why something so enjoyable was seen in such a negative light.*

Recognising my personal view: *First, I had to think about why my response was so different to the other teacher. All the children had chosen to continue with their art work. They were engaged and interested in what they were doing and the mess they had created was easily cleaned up. I knew that resources had been wasted, but the school had plenty of funding for resources. However, attainment in the school was low so Mathematics and English were a key focus involving very structured lessons when perhaps they needed to be more creative. I believe it is due to my love for art and creativity that I found the situation amusing and sad from the children's perspective. As a child I was encouraged to be creative and when a mess was made my mum would not get angry but ensure we just tidied up after wards.*

Reflecting from the adult's perspective: *I realised the class teacher was not happy with the mess and the freedom the children had been given.*

Reflecting from the children's perspective: *I could see it was the first time they'd managed to access the glitter away from the watchful eye of the teacher and were excited. Had it been available as part of an everyday resource, there wouldn't have been such a reactive explosion and mess.*

I spoke to the children when entering the classroom and they were all in good spirits, clearly enjoying the freedom they had been given. To them they had had fun, they were enthusiastic to show me their creations and discuss what they had been doing. Without prompting they all got involved to help clean glitter off the tables and vacuum the carpet.

Relating to reading: *As Waite et al. (2013) note, giving children freedom away from the surveillance of adults is important as they are able to betters self-regulate their emotions and actions.*

The class teacher, however, was not happy that they had seemingly given the cleaners extra work, wasted resources and behaved in such a way. Behaviour was an issue in the school, resulting in the teachers and senior leadership team having strict rules about behaviour and sanctions. The need for control was clear in this school which I now realised was influencing me in terms of believing I had to control the children to be a good teacher!

Relating to reading: *Having reflected on the incident it is clear to me that it is again more about control and how children are viewed. In this situation the children are perceived as naughty, in need of discipline, resulting in a reactive disciplinary policy (Sorin and Cook, 2005).*

Re-appraising the relevance: *For future practice I appreciate the importance of including freedom of choice for engagement, enthusiasm and enjoyment in* *learning. I can see that this will also encourage a sense of responsibility in making personal choices, something that is not always practiced in England due to a fear of risk (Furedi cited in Waite et al., 2013). As Ghaye (2010) says: if you want a positive atmosphere based on trust it has to be embedded.*

This critical incident has made me realise control inhibits listening to children. I will focus on building mutual respect, in the hope of facilitating more participatory learning (Shier, 2001).

Keeping a journal

I am consumed by time constraints inside and outside of school. There is always something more important to do. Trying to negotiate a career and the relationships associated with family life can lead to an overburdened schedule and burnout in one or both areas (Livingston, 2014), not leaving much time for reflection and keeping a journal. With a new born baby, a house to look after and a masters to complete, finding time to keep a journal has been extremely difficult for me.

Being a NQT with limited knowledge of strategies to draw on in relation to critical incidents. I found McLeod 's framework (2015), and Brookfield 's lenses (1995, 2017), particularly useful for enhancing my practice and focusing on wider concerns such as workload, results based culture and thinking about making a difference and what really matters. Given that so many teachers become disheartened, with 31% of teachers that qualified in 2011 leaving the profession within 5 years (Savage, 2017) I can see how useful keeping a reflective journal is in helping me become aware of personal influences and appreciating different lenses.

The final difficulty for me came with the last aspect of reflection; 'Remembering'. Once a reflection has been completed and the situation arises again, it is hard to remember the behaviour you have decided to change whether in or out of the classroom. Behaviour is learnt over time and is shaped by the environment (Shaffer, 2009) and while in a situation it is hard to 'think about doing something while doing it' (Schön, 1983). van Manen (1995) agrees with this, questioning whether reflective practice can ever happen in the moment as teachers must 'constantly act on the spot and cannot step back and postpone acting' in a busy classroom. This is also true outside of the classroom as the skill of stopping and thinking before acting is hard to master and, for me, one of the most emotionally challenging as I tend to be reactive in situations, often not thinking before I speak.

The reflective journey has been difficult and challenging for me, making me realise that perhaps I am not as 'ready' (McLeod, 2015) as I thought. The process of reflection is extremely personal requiring me to look inwards, question why, and is not an easy task (Jelfs, 2011). However, I do believe it is essential in changing patterns of practice, inherited through cultural, societal and institutional influences, that may not be the 'best' practice but rather what has always been done (Hanson, 2011). McLeod 's framework (2015) has been helpful in the structure which has enabled me to take on board personal influences and value different perspectives. The framework prevented my entries from being descriptive shallow accounts (Moon, 2008).

The process has made me realise that my view of children and need for control is prohibiting me from listening to them and allowing them freedom, effecting my relationships with the children and my ability to be what I consider a good teacher. Although changing my view of children as needing protection will be challenging, it will hopefully allow me to listen more and improve important relationships. Whilst reflecting upon my ability to give children freedom of choice it has brought to my attention that I may not have freedom of choice as an educator. Can I be a good teacher and help children in the current climate of neoliberalism if I must teach to a strict curriculum to get 'good outcomes' (Moss, 2017) in turn being graded against a rigid set of standards? The question is deeply troubling to me as I am only just beginning my career as a teacher. I had previously given it little thought, knowing that I was being graded but unaware I had very little freedom over how I behaved and structured learning. Given that home schooling is not as socially damaging for children as I had first thought, would that be a better option for my child and myself?

The reflective journey has left me with more questions regarding my beliefs and values but also my future practice, possibly significant for research:How can I create an environment with mutual respect and a culture of listening?

How can I give children more freedom of choice whilst still being able to follow the curriculum and 'manage behaviour'?

How can I create a more equal balance of power between teacher and student?

*By considering these questions in more detail I hope to improve my practice whilst also creating a better environment***for children to learn in.**

CASE STUDY 2: PROVIDED BY MIKAELA NUGENT-JONES, A MASTER'S STUDENT AND TEACHER WITH 15 YEARS' EXPERIENCE.

'I kept a reflective journal throughout my Masters journey. Using McLeod's *Framework (*2015*), I captured and explored thoughts, observations and conversations at a deeper level. Usually this process took place after the school day when the children had gone home and the school environment was quiet, allowing the time and space for my reflection. I was ready at this time to recall what had happened during the day (McLeod, 2015). My reading and research helped me to relate the significance of the situations and I was able to remember with raised awareness for the future. Through my own critical reflections I was able to reflect both 'on action' and 'in action' (*Dewey, 1933).

On one occasion, I noted an informal conversation with a parent in my Reception class. It illustrates the lack of value for education as a process and the present product driven model as described by Moss (2017). Daily I see the negative impact this has on children'.

Recall: *I've just had a conversation with parent about her child's school report. I didn't want her to be upset that the computer generated report showed in colour (red) that her child was deemed to be 'not on track'. The child's learning and development in language and social skills has been significant since the beginning of the year. However, according to descriptors she is developing at a slower rate to other children in the class.*

Recognising personal views / influences: *I was upset that the report did not show anything positive and was so discouraging, demotivating and upsetting for the child who was just 4 years of age. Her mum hugged me and thanked me for pointing out positive points and achievements and said she would take it 'with a pinch of salt'.*

Reflecting from the parent's perspective: *I could see how the parent valued the happiness of her child over the developmental progress.*

Reviewing together & Relating to Reading: *The conversations with fellow students and reading helped me make connections between theory and practice and the wider socio-cultural and political pressures which enabled me to appreciate the value of democratic learning in my classroom. Allowing myself time to reflect was important and helped me to grow as an educator so I was able to question and see new alternatives. The self-awareness part of my research journey has perhaps been the most challenging but significant aspect for me. Critical reflection / reflexivity is now an embedded part of my every day practice that I make time for now as a matter of course. Allowing time to reflect is something I feel should be fostered in all schools at all levels for deepening a critical understanding and empowering educators about the purpose of education.*

CASE STUDY 3: REFLECTIONS ON JOURNAL-KEEPING

Reflections on journal-keeping

In this example, as part of a research project, an educator (Julie) shares her reflections of using McLeod's Reflexive Framework (2015) as a structure for journal-keeping and for supporting new ways of seeing. Another educator (Emma) is also present, along with the author as the facilitator (Naomi). Different elements of the framework that are evident are included in brackets.

JULIE: *'This involved a planned activity with an opening for the children to join in. I sat on the carpet... and started my literacy input without asking any of the children to sit down so that if they wanted to they could come and join in. I sang a song that was really nice and cheery'.*

(Providing an opening by being flexible)
Julie reads what she has written in her journal...

> *'The children began to come over and asked if they could join in and by the time the tune had finished, most had come over. There were only 3 boys who had decided not to join me on the carpet at that point. They sat in the play dough area and kept looking over to see what was going on, so were interested but decided to stay at the play dough table'.*

(Reflecting on the child's perspective as it happens)
(Reappraising the relevance as it happens)
(Responding by not asking the children to sit on the carpet)

> *'The literacy lesson I'd planned was on alliteration. It included picking out different sounds and then us thinking and writing different sounds together. Then one child said "I've got another way we could do that where you say 'A' out loud in your head" ... and so we did that instead. I had to change my plans'.*

(Valued and respected child's ideas and feelings)
(Recalling the situation and relevance of an opening)
(Reappraising the relevance as it happens)
(Responded by making appropriate changes to plans)

JULIE: *'I wrote in my journal how I was really impressed to see how many children chose to come and join in but I wasn't sure if it because it was the first time I'd really done it so it was quite novel. They probably didn't realise that they had a choice. I've also written 'I enjoyed seeing the value on the children's faces when we changed the game. That was from my perspective and from the children's point of view'.*

(Recognising different perspectives and views herself)
(Evaluating – Reappraising the relevance as part of the risk taken)
(Reviewing together to compare understandings)

EMMA: *'Why do you think the three boys stayed at the table'?*
JULIE: *'Well, I think it was like an agency thing because they could and because I didn't tell them they couldn't'.*
EMMA: *'Because you hadn't said or told them, "Come and sit on the carpet" and they sort of tested that'.*

(Reviewing together)

JULIE: *'Ah but as they sat at the table, they joined in with what we were doing on the carpet. They still put their hands up and came up with suggestions'.*

(Value of reviewing together)

NAOMI: *'And normally, sitting on the carpet would they have participated'?*
EMMA: *'They're just quite active'.*

(Reviewing/comparing views together)

JULIE: *'They were more effectively engaged than if I'd asked them to sit on the carpet. And do you know, having the play dough to play with helped. It was something else that enabled them to engage'.*

(Recognising different perspectives and views herself)

> *'I wrote that "I could tell that they enjoyed the activity and were interested by the way they came over out of choice and stayed"'.*

(Reflected on child's interests and holistic ways of communicating interests)

JULIE: *'Yes and I've written about Treseder in my links to reading and how if we include the children's interests it will boost their self-esteem. After the lesson the child who had come up with the idea for the alliteration game, gave me a hug and said that she loved the way I loved all of her ideas'.*

(Valuing views and feelings of children)
(Valuing links to relevant reading)
(Demonstrated by responding)

JULIE: *'Ah, it was great and we had a little chat about how I do love their ideas and how it is lovely that we all get to share in deciding different things together... and I've written about the "100 languages" and the children's smiling, laughing and visual body language as evidence for participation and enjoyment'.*

(Really valuing children's ideas)
(Recognising the benefits through a variety of convergence of meaning with the children)
(Relating to reading)

'I was worried that they weren't going to come over, but that's why I did the tune and a new book, because I thought they might think "Ooh what's this?" and they did. I was worried because they're not strong on alliteration either and it's on the Early Learning Goals so it's something they really need to know'.

This demonstrates the challenging situation for Julie: the dilemma of feeling pressured to teach towards goals whilst also valuing the benefits of participatory teaching.

(Being open and Remembering the benefits)

'Had they been part of the whole group, I don't think they would have engaged and learnt as much as they did as being at the dough table. So as part of my journal/response for future practice, I've put that I think I would do this more but I'm unsure in terms of whether it would be as successful. Do you know as they become more used to not having to join in if they don't want to so I just have to make sure that I respond and include their interests'.

(Reappraising the relevance and the personal commitment)
(Recognising the dilemma involved)
(Remembering)
(Being open)

'They were involved and chose to join me'.

(Sharing of responsibility and power – Reappraising the relevance)

'They knew they were listened to'.

(Reappraising the relevance)
(Remembering the benefits)
(Clear transformations in openness and the impact on participatory practice – Reciprocal nature of the framework)
(The need to remember)

Julie's view of the children as capable learners enabled her to be more open, step back and facilitate their agency. Valuing the benefits of participation was key in terms of sustaining participatory practice, whilst contending with the pressure of meeting targets (Dimova and Loughran, 2009; Wilkins, 2011). McLeod's Framework as a supportive tool in facilitating participation, potentially offered a way forward of embedding participation as sustainable.

As Julie noted:

'I think that until you go through the process of journal keeping and reflection as part of everyday practice, you don't realise how important it is. I am keen for

continued inspirational reading to back up my understanding. For me it will be sustainable … I think it would really benefit everybody but only if they are ready to let go and allow themselves to see other views. I couldn't go back now because I'd feel like I would just be totally devaluing the children. There's no going back'.

A collective summary of the features essential for sustainable professional development as identified by teachers and students who engaged in using reflective journaling using McLeod's Framework (2015) are listed as follows:

- A genuine personal interest and desire
- A respect for children
- Remembering the benefits for the children and teachers
- Commitment and enthusiasm
- Seeing participation as sharing responsibility with children as part of their learning
- Creating the right conditions including time to establish an open and trusting, safe, relational space
- Being open and willing to develop self-awareness
- Exploring emotions to understand identity
- Letting go and willingly embracing participatory practice
- A desire to share the value of participation with other colleagues
- Allowing time to embed critical reflection / reflexivity as a meaningful, integrated part of practice

An example of professionalisation from Sweden

Next, we share an example of professionalisation involving preschool teachers / *pedagogista* in Sweden using reflective logs as a way of enhancing in-depth understanding and reflexivity.

In Sweden, the professionalism of early childhood educators has a close relationship with the way the child is viewed, so listening to the child is promoted and learning is valued as a co-construction based on children's interests and curiosity. As an optional, free professional development course at a university in Sweden, preschool teachers have the opportunity to engage in furthering their knowledge and conceptual understanding of preschool pedagogy through studying reciprocal mentor tutoring and coaching in a co-constructive way. The course is inspired by the professional role of being a pedagogical facilitator or a *pedagogista*, as in some of the preschool districts in the north of Italy in the Emilia Romagna region, where the professional role began in the 1970s (Alnervik and Kennedy, 2010; Häikiö, 2007).

The preschool teachers study the potential role as *pedagogista*, aiming at developing the everyday practice that also includes coordinating the pedagogical work in preschools. This involves collaboration using a mentoring approach about the didactic work with children and how to document and analyse project work reflexively. Hirsh and Bergmo-Prvulovic (2018) refer to this middle-manager role as pedagogical supervisor, tutor, process leader or *pedagogista* (Sw. *mellanledare*). It is a role that is used for teachers who have a recognised position to lead developmental processes at their local units. This role can be combined with responsibility as an educator in preschools, or other pedagogical units, such as schools, and has come to be regarded as a way of raising the profile of quality within teaching. The university course in this example is valued as a professional development education that has a strong impact in this field nationally, not least because it contains studies on cultural and aesthetic aspects in relation to small children's learning processes that more recently has decreasing amounts of scheduled time and more often is an optional aspect in the preschool teacher programs in Sweden (Ehrlin and Wallerstedt, 2014). As part of the professionalisation course, as a way of enabling professionals to demonstrate their lived experiences and be open to in depth reflections in relation to early childhood education, artistic presentation is used. In doing so feelings of doubt and resistance about the learning process are shared along with the student's confusion and going outside their comfort zone. While they talk about feelings of doubt and resistance as part of their studies, at the same time they also refer to the joy of gaining new understanding as part of the content in their reflective log during the course. The reflective log can be analogue or digital, but should document the learning process of the student (rather than just focusing on the output). In this way, the aim is to enhance professional identity and self-awareness throughout the course. The reflective log shares many similarities with McLeod's Reflexive Framework (2015) and is written using different lenses as suggested in the following:

- Entrance log where the student recalls and describes their expectations of the course in relation to where they are in their professional role at the start of the course.
- A reading log is kept as a tool to record what happens in the reader's mind when reading provokes new thoughts or perspectives that the student would like to discuss.
- University teaching / Process log recalling reflections, feelings and thoughts about study group sessions.
- Workplace log recall own professional experiences / role (during the course) so can challenge.
- Self-assessment log to capture new insights and re appraise new personal professional developments from a metacognitive perspective.
- Response to feedback notes to fellow students and each other's process logs.

(Mårtensson, 2008).

At the end of the course the professionals give an artistic presentation using a variety of ways, such as multi-modally and live performances, to illustrate how the creative processes they have engaged in as part of the course, have supported their new learning rather than more traditional ways (Jewitt, 2011; Kress, 2011). For example, one group called their presentation 'Revolution – Reflection as Culture', which was about their journeys to and from the course, as they travelled together several times a month to attend the evening classes. During train or car journeys to the course, the professionals discussed and processed the course content and came to value the conversations as contributing to their learning process and understanding different readings. Their presentation consisted of a multimodal design, where their reflections about their learning process during the course were presented as an act of performance poetry, while at the same time, in the background, a video showed a film of a rollercoaster-ride taken from the internet.

The idea was for the simulation to become a metaphor for the inner journey of self-awareness experienced by the pedagogues during the course. It provided insight into the students' experience of doubt, uncertainty and resistance about participating in the learning process, as illustrated by 'deep valleys and dark tunnels' in the film. Speed and movement symbolised the turmoil of emotions when the students perceived that they did not keep up with the flow in the learning process, and the breath-taking feeling when the rollercoaster was on top to continue down a steep hill. This epitomised the feeling of confusion when going beyond the comfort zone, as well as experiencing the joy of gaining new insights. The video as visual expression, and the physical movements and gestures of the students, are examples of intra-action (Barad, 2003), that weaved together and constituted each other in the performative act mirroring the learning process. The students wanted to illustrate the complexity of learning, look at it from different perspectives, and explain the challenges faced as part of engaging in the course. The presentation also reflected the conceptual learning acquired by the students, such as entangled rhizomatic learning (Deleuze and Guattari, 1988; Lenz Taguchi, 2012), intra-action (Barad, 2003) and their embodied change as educators. As Barad (2003) notes:

> A performative understanding of discursive practices challenges the representationalist belief in the power of words to represent pre-existing things. Performativity, properly construed, is not an invitation to turn everything (including material bodies) into words; on the contrary, performativity is precisely a contestation of the excessive power granted to language to determine what is real. . . . performativity is actually a contestation of the unexamined habits of mind that grant language and other forms of representation more power in determining our ontologies than they deserve.
>
> *(2003, p.802).*

The pedagogue's evaluation of the course revealed a new appreciation for children's questions as a starting point for learning and using readings to support knowledge perspectives. Pedagogues developed a problematising attitude which involved looking at things form different perspectives, rethinking, and having the courage to question and unpick personal values and assumptions. They valued the possibility of multiple answers and different interpretations of situations. They also appreciated how interpretation of reading is dependent on personal perception and knowledge, as well as the ability to be open to new and unexpected combinations and dimensions in learning. Here assemblage theory is useful as a bottom-up framework for analysing social complexity by emphasising fluidity, entanglements, exchangeability, multiple functionalities and different configurations. Assemblage theory as an ontological framework was developed by Deleuze and Guattari (1988), and notes that, within a body, the relationships of component parts are not fixed; rather, they can be displaced, replaced and reconfigured within and among other external bodies.

In relation to the previously discussed professional learning experience, Deleuze and Guattari's (1988) post-humanist theories reinforce how our thinking is guided by personal beliefs that frame and limit freedom of thought through what they term as 'truth regimes'. In other words, our thinking tends to reflect what is already known or approved so thinking 'outside the box' or new knowledge creation beyond the norm is limited (Deleuze, 2004) (cited in Atkinson, 2015). Instead Atkinson (2015) urges us to be open to the not-yet-known, or what has not yet taken shape in the learning process, colouring the learning in a continuous process of change. Professionalism of the early childhood educator and an appreciation of democratic practice and agency for young children involves an entangled relationship with the way a child is viewed. At the heart of this, being open to questioning 'truth regimes' and valuing different perspectives are essential.

As we have seen throughout this book, children's agency, in different contexts, is dependent on being listened to, having voice and addressing power imbalances. Given we have established the need for a bottom-up approach to professionalism, associated with empowering educators, there needs also to be a review of action learning / research and associated research methods that empower children as part of early childhood educational daily practice and the production of knowledge.

Participatory research methods / research '*with*' children

One such example of a participatory action learning research method, is the Mosaic Approach, developed by Alison Clark (2017), which starts from the viewpoint of respecting young children as competent meaning-makers and explorers of their environment. It acknowledges children's right to be listened to and for their views and experiences to be taken seriously. In doing so it demonstrates the difference listening can make to understanding children's priorities, interests, concerns and how children feel about themselves. The Mosaic Approach brings together a range of methods that position children as experts and the researcher as the 'inexpert', which is important so the adult listens to learn from the child (Kellett, 2011). A variety of different tools including familiar methods, such as observations as part of natural play-based environments and informal child group conversations, can be used so children feel comfortable and the findings are authentic. Additionally, young children can take photographs of things that are important to them. They can then be invited to talk about what they have photographed and why. Alternatively, children can be invited to take the adult on a tour of their setting so they can describe what is important to them. In pulling all the pieces of the mosaic together, a richly informed, child's-eye view of what is important to the child is captured.

Critical reflection is an essential element of the Mosaic Approach, for both the adults and children involved, and is sometimes known as the 'magic carpet' which unearths personal views, values, feelings and assumptions through questioning. It is essential that throughout the process of the Mosaic Approach adults remain impartial and do not influence the children's views or opinions. Such reflexive visual research methods (Alpers, 2007; Fors and Bäckström, 2015) are crucial in the current climate of an increasing multicultural and global society as they can be used to make visible the non-verbal aspects of learning, so children can participate in personal reflections and generate meaning (Karlsson Häikiö, 2018).

Sustaining reflexive professional development

Reflexive professional development has the potential to be sustainable and offer hope for the future of early childhood education. However, it requires appropriate conditions and depends on the strength of participants' convictions in their ownership of knowledge. This is more effective when it is part of a whole school or setting approach so participants / educators can be empowered collectively. As part of this professional journey of exploration, McLeod's Framework can be a useful tool in provoking self-awareness and in sustaining reflexivity as an ongoing process.

POINTS FOR REFLECTION

- What is important to you about early childhood education and why?
- What 'political' questions might you ask about early childhood education?
- What have you taken / learnt from this chapter that could inform your understanding and practice?
- How might you address unequal power imbalances in future as part of your practice?

References

Alexander, R. (2014) 'The best that has been thought and said', *Forum*, 56(1), p.157–169.

Alnervik, K. and Kennedy, B. (2010) 'Pedagogista', in: M.-A. Colliander and C. Wehner-Godée (Eds.) *Om värden och omvärlden; Pedagogik i praktik och teori med inspiration från Reggio Emilia* [*On values and world: Pedagogics in theory and practice with inspiration from Reggio Emilia*], Liber: Stockholm.

Alpers, P. (2007) *Etnografiska metoder; Att förstå och förklara samtiden* [*Ethnographic methods: To understand and explain contemporary times*], Malmö: Liber.

Atkinson, D. (2015) 'The adventure of pedagogy, learning and the not-known', *Subjectivity*, 8(1), p.43–56.

Barad, K. (2003) 'Posthuman performativity: Towards an understanding of how matter comes to matter', *Signs*, Spring, p.801–831.

Bath, C. (2009) *Learning to belong: Exploring young children's participation at the start of school*, London: Routledge.

Brookfield, S.D. (2017) *Becoming a critically reflective teacher*, (2nd edn.) San Francisco, CA: Jossey-Bass A Wiley Company.

Brookfield, S.D. (1995) *Becoming a critically reflective teacher*, San Francisco, CA: Jossey-Bass A Wiley Company.

Clark, A. (2017) *Listening to young children, expanded: A guide to understanding and using the Mosaic Approach* (3rd edn.), London: Kingsley Publishers.

Davey, R. and Ham, V. (2010) 'It's all about paying attention! . . . but to what? The 6 M's of mentoring the professional learning of teacher educators', *Professional Development in Education*, 36(1–2), p.229–244. DOI: doi:10.1080/19415250903457158.

Davies, S. and Artaraz, K. (2009) 'Towards an understanding of factors influencing early years professionals' practice of consultation with young people', *Children and Society*, 23(1), p.57–69. DOI: doi:10.1111/j.1099-0860.2008.00142.x.

Deleuze, G. (2004). *The logic of sense*, London: Continuum.

Deleuze, G. and Guattari, F. (1988) *A thousand plateaus: Capitalism and schizophrenia*, London: Athlone Press.

Dimova, Y. and Loughran, J. (2009) 'Developing a big picture understanding of reflection in pedagogical practice', *Reflective Practice*, 10(2), p.205–217. DOI: doi:10.1080/14623940902786214.

Ehrlin, A. and Wallerstedt, C. (2014) 'Preschool teachers' skills in teaching music: Two steps forward one step back', *Early Child Development and Care*, 184(12), p.1800–1811.

Fors, V. and Bäckström, Å. (2015) *Visuella metoder* [*Visual methods*], Lund: Studentlitteratur.

Ghaye, T. (2010) 'In what ways can reflective practices enhance human flourishing?' *Reflective Practice*, 11(1), p.1–7. DOI: doi:10.1080/14623940903525132.

Givvin, K.B. and Santagata, R. (2011) 'Towards a common language for discussing the features of effective professional development: The case of a US mathematics program', *Professional Development in Education*, 39(3), p.439–451. DOI: doi:10.1080/19415257.2010.527711.

Goodley, C. (2018) 'Reflecting on being an effective teacher in an age of measurement', *Reflective Practice*, 19(2), p.167–178. DOI: doi:10.1080/14623943.2018.1437401.

Häikiö, T. (2007) *Barns estetiska lärprocessser; Atelierista i förskola och skola* [*Children's aesthetical learning processes: Atelierista in pre-school and school*]. Dissertation. Gothenburg Studies in Art and Architecture, nr 24. Acta Universitatis Gothoburgensis. Göteborgs Universitet.

Hanson, K. (2011) '"Reflect": Is this too much to ask?', *Reflective Practice*, 12(3), p.293–304. DOI: doi:10.1080/14623943.2011.571862.

Hassan, Z. (2005) *Connecting to source*. Retrieved 24 July 2010 from: www.worldchanging.com/.

Hirsh, Å. and Bergmo-Prvulovic, I. (2018) 'Teachers leading teachers: Understanding middle-leaders role and thoughts about career in the context of a changed division of labor', *School Leadership & Management*. DOI: doi:10.1080/13632434.2018.1536977.

Jelfs, H. (2011) 'Through the U: A transformational research journey retold', *Reflective Practice: International and Multidisciplinary Perspectives*, 12(3), p.401–413.

Jewitt, C. (2011) *The Routledge handbook of multimodal analysis*, Routledge: London/New York.

Karlsson Häikiö, T. (2018) 'Förskolan som visuell kultur [Preschool as visual culture]', in: M. Bendroth Karlsson, T. Karlsson Häikiö and L.O. Magnusson. *Skapande verksamhet i förskolan; Kreativt arbete med analoga och digitala redskap* [*Creative activity in preschool through use of analogue and digital tools*], Lund: Studentlitteratur.

Katz, L. (2012) 'Multiple perspectives on the quality of early childhood programs', *ERIC Digest*. ERIC clearinghouse on assessment and evaluation. Available from: http://ericae.net/edo/ed355041.htm.

Kellett, M. (2011) 'Engaging with children and young people', *Centre for Children and Young People: Background Briefing Series*, 3. Lismore, NSW, Australia: Centre for Children and Young People, Southern Cross University.

Kress, G. (2011) 'What is mode?' in: Jewitt, C. (Ed.) *The Routledge handbook of multimodal analysis*, London/New York:Routledge.

Lenz Taguchi, H. (2012) *Pedagogisk dokumentation som aktiv agent; Introduktion till intra-aktiv pedagogik* [*Pedagogical documentation as active agent: Introduction to intra-active pedagogics*], Malmö: Gleerups.

Livingston, B. (2014) 'Bargaining behind the scenes: Spousal negotiation, labor, and work–family burnout', *Journal of Management* [online], 40(4), p.949–977. Available from: journals.sagepub.com/doi/pdf/10.1177/0149206311428355.

Loucks-Horsley, S., Love, N., Stiles, K.E., Mundry, S. and Hewson, P.W. (2003). *Designing professional development for teachers of science and mathematics*, (2nd edn.) Thousand Oaks, CA: Corwin Press.

Mårtensson, P. (2008) Seminar on pedagogical documentation and project work, 2008-10-11. Academy of Music and Drama, University of Göteborg.

Mason, J. (2002) *Researching your own practice: The discipline of noticing*, Falmer: Routledge.

McCormack, B. and Boomer, C. (2007) *Creating the conditions for growth. Report on the Belfast City Hospital and The Royal Hospitals collaborative practice development programme*, Belfast, NI: Belfast Health and Social Care Trust.

McIntosh, P. (2010) *Action research and reflective practice: Creative and visual methods to facilitate reflection and learning*, London: Routledge.

McLeod, N. (2015) 'Reflecting on reflection: Improving teacher's readiness to facilitate participatory learning with young children', *Professional Development in Education*, 41(2), p.254–272.

McLeod, N. (2011) *Critical reflection as a tool for developing pedagogical participation with young children*. Doctoral thesis. University of Sheffield.

McLeod, N., Wright, D., McCall, K. and Fuji, M. (2017) 'Visual rhythms: Facilitating young children's engagement at Tate Liverpool', *European Early Childhood Educational Research Journal*, 26(1), p.1–15. DOI: doi:10.1080/1350293X.2017.1380888.

Moon, J. (2008) *Critical thinking: An exploration of theory and practice*, Oxford: Routledge.

Moon, J. (2006) *Learning journals: A handbook for reflective practice and professional development*, London: Routledge.

Moon, J. (2004) *A handbook of reflective and experiential learning*, London: Routledge Falmer.

Moon, J. (1999) *Reflection in learning and professional development*, London: Routledge Falmer.

Moss, P. (2019) *Alternative narratives in early childhood: An introduction for students and practitioners*, London: Routledge.

Moss, P. (2017) 'Power and resistance in early childhood education: From dominant discourse to democratic experimentalism', *Journal of Pedagogy*, 8(1), p.11–32. DOI: doi:10.1515/jped-2017–0001.

OECD (2018) *International early learning and child well-being study (IELS)*. Retrieved 14 March 2019 from: www.oecd.org/education/school/international-early-learning-and-child-well-being-study.htm.

Pascal, C. and Bertram, T. (2018) 'Effective early learning: A praxeological and participatory approach to evaluating and improving quality in early childhood education', *Revista da FAEEBA – Educação e Contemporaneide, Salvador*, 27(51), p.105–120. DOI: doi:10.21879/faeeba2358–0194.2018.v27.n51.p105–120.

Pascal, C. and Bertram, T. (2012) 'Praxis, ethics and power: Developing praxeology as a participatory paradigm for early childhood research', *European Early Childhood Education Research Journal*, 20(4), p.477–492. DOI: doi:10.1080/1350293X.2012.737236.

Richardson, L. (2000) 'Writing: A method of inquiry', in: N.K. Denzin and Y.S. Lincoln (Eds.) *Handbook of qualitative research*, Thousand Oaks, CA: SAGE, p.923–948.

Robson, C. (2011) *Real world research*, (3rd edn.) London: John Wiley and Son.

Sahlberg, P. (2013) 'The most wanted teacher and teacher education in Finland', in: Darling-Hammond, L. and Lieberman, A. (Eds.) *Teacher education around the world: Changing policies and practices*, Oxon: Routledge, p.1–20.

Sahlberg, P. (2011) *Finnish lessons: What can the world learn from educational change in Finland*, New York: Teachers College, Columbia University.

Sahlberg, P. (2010) 'Rethinking accountability in a knowledge society', *Journal of Educational Change*, 11(1), p.45–61.

Savage, M. (2017) 'Almost a quarter of teachers who have qualified since 2011 have left profession', *The Guardian* [online], 8 July 2017. Available from: www.theguardian.com/education/.

Scardamalia, M. and Bereiter, C. (1991) 'Literature expertise', in: K.A. Ericson and J. Smith (Eds.) *Toward a general theory of expertise: prospects and limits*, Cambridge: Cambridge University Press, p.172–194.

Scharmer, C.O. (2009) *Theory U: Leading from the future as it emerges*, San Francisco, CA: Berrett-Koehler Publishers.

Schön, D.A. (1987) *Educating the reflective practitioner toward a new design for teaching*, San Francisco, CA: Jossey-Bass.

Schön, D.A. (1983) *The reflective practitioner: How professionals think in action*, New York: Basic Books.

Shier, H. (2001) 'Pathways to participation: Openings, opportunities and obligations', *Children and Society*, 15(2), p.107–117. DOI: doi:10.1002/CHI.617.

Sorin, R. and Cook, J. (2005) 'Changing images of childhood – Reconceptualising Early Childhood Practice', *International Journal of Transitions in Childhood*, 1(12), p.12–21.

Urban, M. (2017) 'We need meaningful, systematic evaluation, not a preschool PISA', *Global Education Review*, 4(2), p.18–24.

van Manen, M. (1995) 'On the epistemology of the reflective practice', *Teachers and Teaching: Theory and Practice*, 1(1), p.33–50.

van Nieuwerburgh, C. (2012) *Coaching in education*, London: Routledge.

Vandenbroeck, M., Urban, M. and Peeters, J. (2016) *Pathways to professionalism in early childhood education and care*, Oxon: Routledge.

Waite, S., Rogers, S. and Evans, J. (2013) 'Freedom, flow and fairness: Exploring how children develop socially at school through outdoor play', *Journal of Adventure Education and Outdoor Learning* [online], 13(3), p.255–276. Available from: https://doi.org/10.1080/14729679.2013.798590.

Whisker, G., Exley, K., Antoniou, M. and Ridley, P. (2008) *Working one-to-one with students: Supervising, coaching, mentoring and personal tutoring*, Oxon, England: Routledge.

Wilkins, C. (2011) 'Professionalism and the post-performative teacher: New teachers reflect on autonomy and accountability in the English school system', *Professional Development in Education*, 37(3), p.389–409. DOI: doi:10:1080/19415257.2010.514204.

AFTERWORD

A meeting place

Naomi McLeod and Patricia Giardiello

Our final thoughts consider a meeting place for valuing an ethical and participatory pedagogical approach to early childhood education both in the current climate and the future.

While approaches to ECE in Sweden, Finland, Denmark, New Zealand, Te Whāriki pedagogy and Denmark are considered internationally to be of high quality and in UNICEF's report (2009) are listed among the 11 best countries in the world, to some extent it is unfair to make direct comparisons with England. The top-down approach to ECE in England fuelled by political pressures involving data collection, testing, accountability and measuring outcomes (Murris, 2013; Urban, 2017) makes it difficult to step back and question in comparison to the more democratic approaches to learning associated with the Nordic countries, where there is not a culture of testing and an obsession with outcomes. Here the paradigm of children as agents in their own lives renders an unfair comparison. To some extent, it is like comparing apples with pears. Rather as Jane Williams-Siegfredsen (2017) says,

> *You can't compare one with the other. It's important to have realistic expectations and take small steps to appreciating and using nature(pedagogy). Educators need to feel comfortable and good about what they are doing with an understanding of why – so they are able to take the next small step. They need to feel secure and safe in their own context . . .and know what is right for them. It's good to highlight and help educators see what they've achieved. Memory is an emotional thing and will impact on making it sustainable. It's small steps.*

We have already seen with the case studies provided as part of this book how educators in Nordic countries are beginning to feel pressure to get children ready for formal schooling and the recently revised early childhood education curricula's in Denmark, Finland, Sweden and Aotearoa / New Zealand that include a more visible focus on outcomes. One wonders what the reality would be if outcomes were measured and how participatory practice would be. As the conversation with one educator from Finland showed, 'If testing came to Finland, . . . practice would change!'

While presenting international early childhood pedagogies as provocation has been a key part of this book, our central message is that empowerment comes (for educators and children) through engaging in critical self-awareness. As we have seen, this begins with a 'readiness' as a first step and being open to new (ethical) ways of seeing and being. Engaging in a process of personal questioning and self-awareness / reflexivity (phronesis) so that it is embedded at the heart of professional activity, provokes the purpose of education to be questioned. This in turn can enable children to be valued as active creative participants and agents of change, rather than passive partakers in high stakes testing. Ultimately, a heightened awareness about power (politics) and a new appreciation of participatory practice (praxis) as a pedagogy of hope that is just and right (ethical) can offer empowerment for early childhood educators in the current education 'crisis' (Moss, 2010, 2017).

If early childhood educators are empowered through critical self-awareness, a strong participatory change in practice, from a technical approach to one of ethics of care is possible. Through appropriate conditions that enable a professional culture of collaboration and learning, and joining the growing resistance movement (that Moss talks about in the Foreword of this book), it is possible to challenge top-down models of education that prioritise an obsession with data, a narrowing of the curriculum, high stakes testing and accountability, thereby creating a pedagogy of hope and early childhood education pioneers for the future.

It is our wish that this book inspires early childhood educators to be activists in this endeavour.

References

Moss, P. (2017) 'Power and resistance in early childhood education: From dominant discourse to democratic experimentalism', *Journal of Pedagogy*, 8(1), p.11–32. DOI: doi:10.1515/jped-2017–0001.

Moss, P. (2010) 'We cannot continue as we are: The educator in an education for survival', *Contemporary Issues in Early Childhood*, 11(1), p.8–19.

Murris, K. (2013) 'The epistemic challenge of hearing a child's voice', *Studies in the Philosophy of Education*, 32, p.245–259.

UNICEF (2009) *State of the world's children report*, New York: UNICEF Research Centre.

Urban, M. (2017) 'We need meaningful, systematic evaluation, not a preschool PISA', *Global Education Review*, 4(2), p.18–24.

Williams-Siegfredsen, J. (2017) *Understanding the Danish Forest School Approach early years education in practice*, Oxon: Routledge.

INDEX

Note: bold page numbers indicate tables; italic page numbers indicate figures; page numbers containing n refer to chapter endnotes.

For Product Safety Concerns and Information please contact our EU representative GPSR@taylorandfrancis.com
Taylor & Francis Verlag GmbH, Kaufingerstraße 24, 80331 München, Germany

www.ingramcontent.com/pod-product-compliance
Ingram Content Group UK Ltd.
Pitfield, Milton Keynes, MK11 3LW, UK
UKHW022221071025
463689UK00009B/41
9781138309678